WITHDRAWN
No longer the property of the
Boston Public Library.
Sale of this material benefits the Library

BY EDMUND MORRIS

The Rise of Theodore Roosevelt

Dutch: A Memoir of Ronald Reagan

Theodore Rex

Beethoven: The Universal Composer

Colonel Roosevelt

THIS LIVING HAND

THIS
LIVING
HAND

And Other Essays

EDMUND
MORRIS

RANDOM HOUSE

NEW YORK

Copyright © 2012 by Edmund Morris

All rights reserved.

Published in the United States by Random House,
an imprint of The Random House Publishing Group,
a division of Random House, Inc., New York.

RANDOM HOUSE and colophon are registered
trademarks of Random House, Inc.

Most of the essays that appear in this book have been previously published,
a number in different form, in various publications including: *Air & Space,
American Heritage, The American Spectator, Forbes FYI, Harper's, Litchfield
Magazine, National Review, The New York Times, The New York Times Book
Review, The New York Times Magazine, The New Yorker, Newsweek, Quest81,
Smithsonian, The Wall Street Journal, The Washington Post, The Washington Post
Book World*, and *Wilson Quarterly*.

Permission credits are located on page 477.

ISBN 978-0-8129-9312-7
eISBN 978-0-679-64466-8

Printed in the United States of America on acid-free paper

www.atrandom.com

9 8 7 6 5 4 3 2 1

FIRST EDITION

Book design by Barbara M. Bachman

Except I be by Silvia in the night,
There is no music in the nightingale;
Unless I look on Silvia in the day,
There is no day for me to look upon:
She is my essence; and I leave to be,
If I be not by her fair influence
Foster'd, illumined, cherish'd, kept alive.

—SHAKESPEARE, *Two Gentlemen of Verona*, III.i.

"I just like writing," said Ludovic. "In different ways about different things. Nothing wrong with that, I suppose?"

—EVELYN WAUGH, *The End of the Battle*

CONTENTS

PREFACE

A FREELANCE WRITER'S CAREER OBLIGES HIM TO ACCEPT (OR MORE often, solicit) assignments from as wide a range of periodicals as will help him pay his rent. This calls for a commensurate charivari of styles, column inches, and heights or depths of brow. One winter might find him reviewing an anthology of humorous prose for *The New Yorker*, subjecting his nether parts to the scrutiny of a Savile Row tailor at the whim of *Forbes FYI*, publishing an op-ed in *The Washington Post* in defense of a fellow scribe's libel case before the Supreme Court, and addressing a literary symposium at the Library of Congress. If the proceeds of all these (in the last case, a free lunch only) are measured against the current cost of living index, you can be sure that the same writer had to hack other work—advertising copy, appliance manuals, travel brochures—that he is now loath to remember, let alone reprint.

Nevertheless, he cannot help feeling, as he flips through forty years' worth of copy, that everything he wrote in the past sharpened his pen and amplified what Evelyn Waugh called "a writer's capital"—the raw material from which any mature style must derive. If he is lucky, as I was in my midthirties, he will have ended up in a genre conducive to book contracts. Thanks to the biographical appeal of Theodore Roosevelt, Ronald Reagan, Ludwig van Beethoven, and my present subject, Thomas Edison, I no longer have to depend on the kindness of strange editors.

I don't apologize for the variety of *disjecta membra* collected here. None were written merely for money, and all were as good as I could make them. I have always believed that a professional writer should be able to produce on demand poems, pamphlets, screenplays, reviews, translations, monographs, bawdy lyrics, and whatever other commissions may challenge him. He must labor as hard on a sympathy letter as on an op-ed article, or the opening page of a novel.

It is common for collections to be arranged thematically— sometimes with a concluding miscellany, like the one in my old Collins Keats anthology, charmingly entitled "Reflective, Occasional, and Humorous." I have chosen a chronological sequence, in what amounts to a scrapbook of one man's literary life. If sequitur-minded browsers are disconcerted to find an interview with Nadine Gordimer followed by a profile of an obscure American painter, or an essay on punctuation sandwiched between a tribute to Ronald Reagan and a literary portrait of my wife, I hope that other readers may find the clash of subject matter agreeable—and possibly stimulating, should the roving eye encourage excursions back and forth.

The initial essay, from 1972, is the first piece I hoped to see in print— a desire ungratified till now. The three that follow were written at various times, but are grouped together for autobiographical background. All the rest, beginning with "A Ghostly Tour With TR," appear in order of composition. Four did not run for sundry reasons. The other fifty-one have been published, or, in the case of lectures and broadcasts, given some sort of airing.

Outside of literature in general and biography in particular, my non-book work has consisted mainly of commentary on the presidency and writings about classical music. The latter subject attracts me not simply because I find regular absorption of intellectually ordered sounds as necessary as breathing, but because I enjoy the difficulty of trying to construe a superior language. A writer's duty is surely to reach, after Goethe, for *das Unbeschreibliche*, the abstract that resists verbal articulation—if only to strain one's abilities to the limit. Out of strain comes strength to handle the task words are best suited for: truth-telling, whether the factualness of nonfiction or the higher truths of poetry and novels.

There is also, in these pages, much of what I consider to be humor. All experience hath shewn that what cracks this immigrant up does not necessarily amuse his compatriots. Most Americans, alas, suffer from a severe irony deficiency. Hence their neglect of Ambrose Bierce, this nation's supreme cynic, and their hunger for political pieties. I suppose it's a consequence of the New World spirit of optimism, the "willingness of the heart" that F. Scott Fitzgerald rightly praised. The Old World's tendency to mock and disbelieve is not defensible. But I am afraid that having to listen to the King's speech every Christmas when I was a boy infused me with a satiric sense that I cannot shake.

Mindful of the Hon. Ernest Woolley's caution about not being "young enough to know everything," I have tried to resist the temptation of a graybeard writer to edit his old prose. Only when a favorite quotation, such as Coriolanus's "There is a world elsewhere" recurred too often, or where two pieces featured the same anecdote, did I hit the delete button.

That last phrase was not part of the vernacular when I first began to turn out manuscripts. And they really were *manuscripts*, which is to say, things handwritten with pen and ink before being laboriously typed. Several of the essays in this book lament the electronification of prose (although I must say that Ctrl + F, and citations that renumber themselves automatically, are God's gifts to a biographer). What's gone now is the physical pleasure scribes used to take in directing the flow of cursive words across the page. I never was a fan of the typewriter (see page 64), but can understand the need thwackers still feel for the impact of metal on layers of paper, carbon, and hard rubber. While such a dependency was never as fundamental as that which links a visual artist with his material (see page 370), it was, nevertheless, intimate. Parker man or Remington man, one felt a closeness to the finished product that the glass screen of computer display now coldly precludes.

I remember my first sight of a "word processor" at the Woodrow Wilson International Center for Scholars in the fall of 1983. It was a fat humming machine called the Lexitron, and words tapped into it (by a staff operator only: amateurs were not allowed to profane the keyboard) materialized like greenglowing tadpoles in a black aquarium. They arranged themselves in perfect rows that mocked the disorder of a cut-and-paste manuscript, and every row looked as good as the next—even when it wasn't. You could feed in a paragraph by Pearl S. Buck, and the Lexitron made it look as stylish as the work of P. G. Wodehouse.

When the time approached for me to deliver a "colloquium" at the

Center, in return for my stipend, I presented the operator seventy-five densely scribbled sheets on the subject of "Theodore Roosevelt the Writer." A few days later she brought me a beautiful printout, along with a sort of flexible tile, five and a quarter inches square. "There's room on that floppy," she mysteriously remarked, "for hundreds more pages."

Perhaps so, but I'm glad I kept the printout (page 95), because whatever tadpoles thrived in the Lexitron's tank are as extinct now as those of DOS, not to mention DisplayWrite, the IBM software that "preserves" for posterity the communications of Ronald Reagan's White House.

This book has a few other features not normally seen in a collection of essays. One is the use of illustrations. Generally, when I write, I'm haunted by a visual image of some kind. Explanatory footnotes are attached to obsolete references, such as to aspects of pre-apartheid South Africa. But I've not attempted to rewrite passages that may read strangely to anyone not born in a colony. To paraphrase another émigré, V. S. Naipaul, one is what one is. Or rather, was.

A final word on the word *essay* itself. Since it connotes literary effort (as a verb in both French and English), I've let it apply to a few lectures that were painstakingly scripted. In one case, "The Portraitist's Shadow" (page 150), I've made a single essay out of two addresses on the art of biography. In another, I've amplified an op-ed I wrote about the First Amendment case mentioned above with some paragraphs from an *amicus curiae* brief filed at the same time. The last essay in the book is an expanded conflation of three seminars I taught in 2003 as writer in residence at the University of Chicago. Elsewhere I've restored sentences that, in the unforgettable words of an editor at *The New York Times Book Review*, "might upset Mrs. Sulzberger." I also made a punitive expedition in search of youthful semicolons. It yielded several bulging netfuls, the disposal of which required a special permit at the dump in

KENT, CONNECTICUT

MARCH 2012

THIS LIVING HAND

THE BUMSTITCH

Lament for a Forgotten Fruit

NO ONE I KNOW HAS EVER HEARD OF THE BUMSTITCH, MUCH LESS tasted it. No encyclopedia mentions this rarest of fruits. Its name, which for me has such mystic overtones, provokes laughter and ridicule wherever I go.

At times I wonder, sadly, if my disbelievers are right. Am I indeed prey to some ancient delusion? Yet always, in such moments of self-doubt, that ambrosial flavor fills my mouth, and suddenly I am nine again, and in Kenya, and munching Bumstitches.

In those days, Kenya was still a quiet outpost of the British Empire: two hundred thousand square miles of grasslands, volcanic mountains, and flamingo-pink lakes, settled by fewer whites than would fill Wembley Stadium, and ruled by a fat Governor in a feathered helmet. His Excellency spent most of the year on safari, ostensibly in pursuit of elephant poachers. Every June, he would return to Nairobi (always with plenty of confiscated ivory) and hold a garden party in honor of King George VI's

Unpublished, 1972.
Drawing by the author.

birthday. My school abutted on the grounds of Government House, and if we behaved ourselves, we were allowed to sit around the great lawn and watch the festivities.

Open-mouthed, we admired a rich pageant of colonial society. Here were coffee farmers perspiring in cutaway coats and striped trousers; muscular missionary ladies in mail-order frocks; malaria-yellow Indian Army colonels (ret'd.); and occasionally, if we were lucky, a genuine Bishop in gaiters.

On one such King's Day, I sat next to a pudgy classmate named Georgie Blowers, who had once hijacked a tractor and was confirmedly the Naughtiest Boy in the School. He was bored with the garden party, and proposed a visit to the Governor's wattle plantation, on the far side of the lawn.

"But it's out of bounds," I said nervously. "We'll get six of the best!"

"Who cares?" snorted Georgie Blowers, a veteran of many canings. "Come on, I'll show you the Bumstitch Bush!"

I was strangely excited. "The what?"

Georgie Blowers made no reply. He jumped to his feet and dashed toward the wattle plantation, straight through the legs of the crowd. Women screamed. Champagne spilled. I shut my eyes in horror. When I opened them again, the garden party had regained its equilibrium. I went home convinced that Georgie Blowers had been seized by the Governor's *askaris* and thrown into juvenile prison.

But next day at school, when the eight o'clock bell rang for arithmetic, he arrived in triumph, a bulging satchel on his back. He took his place in the extreme rear of the classroom, and as soon as the teacher turned to the blackboard, threw a pellet of paper at me.

I unscrewed it.

"HAVE 54 BUMSTITCHES," it read. "WILL SWAP ONE FOR A GLASSY."

Fascinated, I tossed over a marble. In exchange, I received a hard, leathery-skinned berry that looked like a desiccated walnut.

I suspected that I was a victim of a con job, and semaphored my disappointment.

"*Watch me!*" mouthed Georgie Blowers, extracting another Bumstitch from the satchel. He gripped its stalk between his teeth and twirled it until it broke free. Then he inserted the point of a drawing compass under the thick skin, pried off a strip, and began to chew it. I did likewise.

At first the skin seemed tough and tasteless, but soon it began to soften, and my mouth was filled with an indescribably delicious flavor, something like vintage apricot jam laced with Château d'Yquem. I masticated blissfully for several minutes, swallowed, and glanced over for further instructions.

Georgie Blowers peeled the rest of his Bumstitch, storing the strips of skin in a pocket for future reference. I followed suit, and laid bare a cluster of kerneled quarters, like the inside of a petrified kumquat. These fell apart easily under the sharp edge of my ruler: they were brown and hard, glazed with a sticky juice. I sucked one. It was, if anything, even more delicious than the skin, and to this day I am unable to remember the 7-times multiplication table, which we were being taught at the moment.

I became hooked on Bumstitches—if I may use so gross an expression for so exquisite an attachment—for the rest of the term. I squandered my entire marble collection before Georgie Blowers, relenting, led me to the Bumstitch Bush and told me to help myself. It stood about the height of a small apple tree, dropping its knobbly riches in the hot dust. Experiment proved that Bumstitches baked in this dust for a few days were tastier, though tougher, than fresh ones. We hoarded them jealously, Georgie Blowers and I. Life was sweeter for us than for other boys.

Eventually the term ended and the long holidays began. Bumstitches were forgotten in the excitement of flying bamboo kites, bicycling up the Ngong Hills, and swimming in tepid water holes. The seasonless sun blazed on, week after week. Then suddenly, climactically, the rains came, and it was time to go back to school.

At the first opportunity I returned to the Bumstitch Bush. Rain pounded down as I ran across the Governor's lawn. The wattle plantation was bedraggled, and the Bush stood in a sea of mud. Not a fruit was to be seen on its gnarled branches. I knew there would be no more of its delights that year.

The vintage of '50 was smaller than that of '49, but equally good; '51 was a bumper crop, although variable in quality. Then, on 3 October 1952, the world changed. Another of my classmates, Fatty Wright, went home and found his mother chopped into pieces. Within a week, Mau Mau terrorism engulfed Kenya. Policemen built a great wall around our school, erected a searchlight tower on the Governor's lawn, and cut down the wattle plantation. There were no more garden parties. And no more Bumstitches.

Georgie Blowers and I grew up (he to six feet four), and went our separate ways. Many years ago, I heard that he had prospered briefly as a farmer in the White Highlands. Shortly after decolonization, however, he had thrown the new minister of agriculture into a sheep-dip and been deported. When last seen, informed sources said, Georgie Blowers was heading for Australia.

I wonder if he remembers the times we went Bumstitching together. It seems that he and I are the only people in the world who have eaten of that mysterious fruit. Perhaps we owe to it our knowledge of good and evil.

HOW I ESCAPED DEATH BY SNAKEBITE

And Lived to Write About Beethoven

WHEN I WAS A FOURTEEN-YEAR-OLD BOY LIVING IN KENYA, my father asked me one night after dinner if I would like to hear a new recording of Beethoven's Eighth Symphony. I eagerly said yes, since I was already a lover of music and felt starved for it. Kenya in those days had no television and just one radio station, which devoted most of its time to news of steamship arrivals in Mombasa and coffee-crop quotas "upcountry." Its rare broadcasts of classical music were relayed from overseas via BBC shortwave, and tended to fade in and out of audibility, according to the number of vultures roosting on the transmission mast a few miles from my school.

Anyway, Dad put this shiny flexible LP on his turntable, threw a few more logs on the fire (at six thousand feet, Nairobi nights are crisp), switched off the standard lamp, and I heard for the first time the joyous opening bars of the Eighth. We listened in darkness right through to the end of the record. By that time the fire had burned low, and Africa's myr-

Press release for *Beethoven: The Universal Composer*, February 2005.
Drawing by the author.

iad nocturnal noises, temporarily drowned by Beethoven's finale, resumed their cacophony outside.

The question now was, which of us was going to get up and turn the
lamp back on? I was too poleaxed by the music to move, so Dad did. This
was fortunate, because the light disclosed a six-foot cobra that had
somehow snuck in and coiled up on the warm parquet in front of the
fire. Had I been the one to go to the lamp, I would have trodden barefoot
on the cobra, and it would have made its displeasure known.

So I guess I owe my survival to Beethoven, the most life-affirming of
composers. To write *his* life now, and communicate something of the
hypnotic power of his music, is both the least and most I can do, in gratitude.

THE CCURFEW TTOLLS THE KNELL
OF PPPARTING DAY

Remembering Mr. Atkinson

IT IS THE FATE—SOME WOULD SAY, THE BLESSING—OF COLONIES that they perpetuate certain eccentric institutions of the old country, long after the originals have been modernized. Thus it was that the Prince of Wales School, Nairobi, Kenya, resembled in the early 1950s nothing so much as a British private school of the period preceding World War I. Equatorial heat notwithstanding, we wore flannels, ties, and navy-style blazers that glittered at breast and wrist with the insignia of discipline and sportsmanship. (My own was conspicuously drab.) We studied the speckled, damp-smelling texts of ancient publishers: Hillard and Botting's *Shorter Latin Primer*, Bagehot on the British Constitution, Spenser's *Faerie Queene* with the naughty stanzas asterisked. There was Chapel every morning, and Flag Parade every Saturday. Once a year we were bused through the bush to the Kenya Girls' High, where exquisite

Originally published in *The Washington Post*, 8 November 1982.

The Prince of Wales School, Nairobi, 1953. Photograph by Ron Bullock.

creatures in white blouses and gray skirts faced us in debate. When dreams of them tormented us afterward, the squeaky-voiced school chaplain, who believe it or not was named Father Capon, prescribed cold showers.

Our "masters" were generally Oxbridge types seeking refuge from Clem Attlee's welfare state—boozy bachelors with malodorous pipes, talking endlessly about rugby. I, in turn, sought refuge from them in novels which I wrote, under cover of my atlas, at the rearmost possible desk of every class. Then, one new term, Mr. E. G. A. Atkinson walked through the door, and the world opened like a flower.

He merely nodded and smiled—a portly, silver-fringed, sixtyish man—yet the sight of him was cathartic. I became intensely aware of texture, of sounds: the wooden desktop grainy beneath my fingers, the *shamba* boy outside swishing his scythe through the kikuyu grass.

Mr. Atkinson's mild blue eyes swept the room. His lower lip shot out, and his throat worked convulsively. "Ggggggood morning," he said.

There was an explosion of giggles, and for the first time in my life I felt uncontrollable anger. "Shut up!" I screamed. "You *bastards!*" But Mr. Atkinson seemed merely amused.

"Your lllanguage, young man, lleaves much to be dddddddddd—"

"Desired, sir?"

"If you *ever* interrupt me again," said Mr. Atkinson, suddenly articulate, "I'll knock your block off."

A flash of ice in the blue gaze chilled us to respect. Humor and authority had been established in a matter of seconds. There was a moment of utter silence, broken only by the click-*swish*—click-*swish* of the scythe outside. Mr. Atkinson, catching it, beat time to the rhythm. His large hand moved hypnotically through the air. "How vvvvery convenient! I was planning to teach you boys the Augustan cccouplet today!"

Eyes closed, he began to recite Gray's "Elegy Written in a Country Churchyard," the syllables coinciding with the swing of the steel. I had not heard it before, much less seen an English landscape. Many of the words (*glebe?*) were as foreign as those in Hillard and Botting. But never in thirty years since has poetry sounded so beautiful. Mr. Atkinson's stammer, far from distorting the meter, enhanced it with *tempo rubato*, and added subtle onomatopoeic effects:

The ccurfew ttolls the knell of pppparting day,
The lllowing herd wwind slowly o'er the llea,
The pploughman homeward plods his wweary way,
And lllleaves the wworld to darkness and to mmme.

In the weeks and months that followed, Mr. Atkinson imbued us with the literature, art, and manners of England in the eighteenth century. No other place, no other period was worthy of consideration. "Balance! That's what they had in the Augustan era, bbbalance!" The finely turned wit of Johnson, the symmetries of Chippendale and Sheraton, Handel's *da capo* arias, the formal landscapes of Gainsborough ("Don't anybody mention Constable, the man was a pppppp—" "Peasant, sir? Ouch, sir! Sorry, sir!")—all these represented, for him, civilization at its brief apogee. "With the exxxxxxception of Jane Austen, nobody created anything worth a dddamn after the Regent took over." Frowning and beating time, he rumbled the matchless invective of Shelley:

An old, mad, blind, dddespised, and dying King,
Pprinces, the dregs of their ddull race, who fflow
Through ppublic scorn,—mud from a mmuddy spring. . . .

Although my worship of Mr. Atkinson must have been obvious, he never paid me much attention. He was too aristocratic to be familiar. Indeed, had he ever winked, or addressed me by anything other than my surname, I would have recoiled in disillusion. I loved his remote, otherwordly air, the way his eyes, half-closed, seemed to contemplate vanished horizons. He aroused in me a strange nostalgia for lands I had not seen, times I (and for that matter he) could never have known. Only twice, as I recall, did he venture an opinion of me. There was an epigram on my report card, so graceful I did not know whether to laugh or cry: *Despite his natural levity, he habitually gravitates to the bottom.* The other comment, scrawled in red ink on the last essay I handed him, *did* make me cry. "You," wrote old E.G.A.A., "have the most precious gift of all—originality."

Mr. Atkinson taught us only two terms, then for some reason went "Home" on leave and never came back. For a while I was inconsolable, but the memories of boys are short. Only gradually, as I grew older, did I realize how much he had done to unlock my eyes and ears and mind, and stimulate the vague yearning that drives the writer's pen. "*Full many a fflower,*" he used to remind us, "*is bborn to bblush unseen.*" For what petals I have been able to grow and sell, I give him all thanks.

THE LAST SNOWS OF KILIMANJARO

A Lament

D URING MY BOYHOOD IN KENYA, THE ICY EMINENCE OF MOUNT Kilimanjaro, across the border in Tanzania, was a constant on my horizon. Wherever one went on the plains south of Nairobi, there floated in the dusty distance that miraculous cone of snow, seemingly detached from the earth at times when the blue of its foothills merged into the blue of the sky. *Kibo,* the Masai called it, *Kibo* the white crest of *Kilimanjaro,* "the gleaming mountain."

I hitchhiked there as a teenager, with a school friend, and climbed all 19,341 feet up to Kaiser-Wilhelm-Spitze (I bet *that* name's been changed!). It tipped the crest, rising out of the first snowfield I had ever seen. We

National Public Radio commentary, 10 December 2003.
Sunrise, Kilimanjaro. Oil painting by Eric Morris, 1957.

raced the last few powdery yards, sobbing for oxygen, and one of us—who shall be nameless—was first to become the highest man in Africa.

Except for my father, perhaps. Dad was chief pilot of East African Airways, and he flew weekly over Kilimanjaro on his regular run to Dar-es-Salaam. He used to come home marveling that the ice cap never looked the same, since it acted as a mirror to the clouds, and shimmered differently according to the hour of the day.

He was also an artist, and once saw such a unique refraction coming off Kibo that he gunned both engines of his DC-3 and got back to Nairobi ahead of schedule, in order to paint what he had seen. The resulting canvas, showing a bar of light that seems to slice right through the snow cap, hangs in my study—so "the gleaming mountain" is still part of my horizon, and will loom there, I guess, until I die.

Sadly, Kibo itself may die first. The snows of Kilimanjaro, celebrated by Ernest Hemingway, are in retreat. Already that white cone is little more than a fragile circlet. According to some scientific estimates, the mountain's last glacier will melt away in about twenty years. Deforestation of the lower slopes is apparently the cause. It used to be the transpiration of millions of trees that caused moisture to flow up the slopes, over the saddle between Kibo and Mawenzi, and freeze around the steepness of the crater.

One scientist has seriously proposed enshrouding the peak—capping the cap—with an immense pall of canvas, in order to insulate it while efforts are made to persuade the Chagga tribe to reforest Kilimanjaro's piedmont.

It is a measure of the gravity of the situation that so grotesque a proposal is being seriously considered. Tanzanians might well ask if we, in turn, would kindly build a greenhouse across the forty-eight contiguous states, in order to contain the gases we at present release into the winds of the world.

The double probability, of course, is that we will continue to pollute, and Kibo will continue to melt. If so, twenty years from now, I will have nothing but my father's picture to remind me of what was once the most beautiful sight in Africa. That, and the sad lines of A. E. Housman:

Into my heart an air that kills
From yon far country blows:
What are those blue remembered hills,
What spires, what farms are those?
It is the land of lost content,
I see it shining plain,
The happy highways where I trod,
And shall not go again.

A GHOSTLY TOUR WITH TR

The Badlands of North Dakota

THE BADLANDS OF NORTH DAKOTA IS A REGION OF GHOSTS, ES-
pecially when clothed in the spectral whiteness of winter. Ghosts of
long-vanished rivers flow through a dry maze of buttes and gorges.
Ghosts of petrified trees jut from the bare clay slopes. Abandoned log
cabins sit in the cottonwood bottoms, and the wind groans through
their chinks. On clear nights the *aurora polaris* hangs in the sky, like an
enormous, frozen wraith. In all this weird landscape the only movement
seems to be that of the sluggish Little Missouri, and by December even it
is in its death throes, choked with thickening ice.

Originally published in *The New York Times*, 26 January 1975.
Cartoon by Jay N. "Ding" Darling, 1919.

Consequently I was not surprised, on a recent solitary hike through Theodore Roosevelt National Park, to see a flash of teeth and spectacles, and hear the high-pitched croak of Old Four Eyes himself. "This," he said, waving a translucent buckskin sleeve, "is where the romance of my life began."

"It doesn't look particularly romantic this morning, Mr. President," I said respectfully. We were standing at Badlands Overlook, with its horizon-filling panorama of thousands of buttes. Their white caps broke level: stony flotsam on a tossing sea of clay. A cold rush of air was on its way down from Canada, and the sky had that furry look that foretells more snow.

TR chuckled. "You know what old General Sully called it. 'Hell with the fires out.' It's not the kind of country everybody likes. No pretty colors, no cozy little nooks. But for me it has a curious, fantastic beauty of its own. I fell in love with it the moment I stepped out of that train in eighty-three. It was still the Wild West in those days, of course."

"*A land of vast silent spaces,*" I murmured, "*of lonely rivers, and of plains where the wild game stared at the passing horseman.*"

"Exactly!" said TR, impressed. "Who wrote that?"

"You did, Mr. President. In your autobiography."

"Thought it sounded familiar," said Old Four Eyes. "Come! I'll show you what brought me here."

We walked for a mile or so along the Scenic Loop Drive, a thirty-eight-mile circuit of the park's fifty-thousand-acre South Unit. The asphalt was a smooth, virgin white, the park empty and still. Since early morning I had seen not a single visitor's car, nor any sign of life save an occasional swooping magpie. But now TR, putting his finger to his lips, led me down into a narrow valley, and I saw, silhouetted against a white background of snow, the most majestic animals in North America. Their blunt dark heads, shaggy shoulders, and elegantly tapering hindquarters stood out with the ageless impact of prehistoric cave paintings.

"There are about three hundred bison wandering around in the Badlands today," said TR, "and they multiply so fast the rangers have to thin the herd once a year—which makes for plenty of buffalo steaks down there in Medora. And very good they are too!"

"How big was the herd when you first came here?"

"I doubt that there were ten bison between here and Montana. It took me almost two weeks to get within shooting distance of one. Up every morning at four, crawling all day through greasy creeks, splattered to my eyes in gumbo. By Godfrey, it was fun!"

"Judging by what I've seen above the fireplace at Sagamore Hill," I said, "you finally got your buffalo."

"I don't much like your tone, young man, but—yes, I did, over there in the neck of Little Cannonball Creek. I never was so proud of anything in my life. If it hadn't been for that buffalo I never would have settled here, and if it hadn't been for my years in North Dakota I would not have become President of the United States." At which Old Four Eyes, looking rather peeved, galloped silently away.

I SPENT THE REST OF the day wandering alone through the park, enjoying that rare reward of the winter traveler, Having The Whole Place To Oneself. Even in summer, when temperatures climb into the hundreds, and the Badlands bake under lazy veils of blue dust, Theodore Roosevelt is a lightly visited National Park. From fall through spring it remains pretty nearly deserted, especially the remote North Unit, which is separated from the South by forty miles of National Grassland. Only once in the afternoon did I see another human being, in the form of an unshaven gentleman in a bright orange jacket. Strapped to the roof of his station wagon were five whitetail deer. Ribbons of blood flowed down the sides of the car as he sped triumphantly by.

About an hour before sunset the furry clouds blew away toward the Rockies, and the whole expanse of the park burst into brightness. I understood what Western writers mean by the "luminous light" of the prairies. The enormous sky burned so blue that its few wisps of cirrus cloud seemed almost incandescent. Beneath, the monochromatic Badlands dissolved into a Turneresque orgy of color: violet canyons, orange cliffs, pink and cream buttes, sheets of golden grass. Even the snowdrifts—thinning now—glowed with reflected tints, and twinkled as they thawed.

What had seemed, earlier that day, to be a landscape of death now began to vibrate with life. Prairie dogs emerged from their underground cities to sunbathe. Deer picked their way delicately through the cotton-woods. A small herd of wild horses drummed down into Paddock Creek. I several times heard, but never saw, a coyote. Judging by the anxious yipping of the prairie dogs, he must have been pretty near.

BUFFALO STEAKS, TO MY CHAGRIN, were not to be found that evening in Medora, the historic village (pop: 129) which serves as the southern gateway to the park. I was told that they are indeed a specialty at the Rough Riders Hotel, a splendidly creaky establishment where TR himself used to stay, but it was closed for the season. The Little Missouri Saloon on the village square consoled me with some superlative short-cut beef, and a carafe of Eleven Cellars Californian Burgundy—at $1.50 a bargain all over North Dakota. I emerged into the frosty night exhaling grateful clouds of *bonhomie.*

The little town lay spaced out and shining under its soft yellow lamps. There was not a soul about. For a while I stood hypnotized by the silence of the place. It was such that I could hear the dull jostle of ice floes in the nearby river. I walked out along the right bank, away from the illuminated streets, and became aware of a sky almost white with stars. The dark water at my feet struggled tiredly northward, freezing as it flowed. A few more weeks and it would be solid. I recalled TR's unforgettable description of the Little Missouri in midwinter: *The river lay in its bed fixed and immovable as a bar of bent steel. . . . At night wolves and lynxes traveled up and down it as if it had been a highway.*

The moon was just rising behind the buttes, which loom like cliffs on both sides of the river flats, and it sent a horizontal beam over the roofs of Medora to spotlight an immense and solitary chimney, incongruously surrounded with grass. This brick landmark, which most visitors pass by in puzzlement, stands as an ironic monument to one of the strangest figures in American frontier history.

Antoine-Amédée-Marie-Vincent-Amat Manca de Vallombrosa, Marquis de Morès, was a wealthy French aristocrat who arrived in the Badlands in March 1883, a few months before Theodore Roosevelt. He had heard that this desolate landscape, recently cleared of its buffalo, was the cattle country of the future, with limitless grazing on the surrounding prairie, and millions of ready-carved winter shelters among the buttes.

The Marquis was an impulsive man, and after one look at the Badlands he decided to establish a cow town here, to be named after his beautiful wife, the New York heiress Medora von Hoffman. He would build a giant abattoir, slaughter steers direct from the range, and ship the dressed beef east in refrigerated railroad cars. If necessary, said de Morès, he would invest millions in this surefire scheme, and with the resultant billions he would finance his blood-claim to the vacant throne of France.

Within a month, construction of Medora had begun—the first brick was laid, ominously, on April Fool's Day—and by the time a bespectacled young assemblyman from New York arrived in September, the abattoir's chimney was already discharging noisome fumes into the clear Dakota sky.

Roosevelt had come West to hunt, but he, too, soon caught "cowboy fever." In the spring of 1884 he returned to the Badlands to settle, and to recover from the stunning, simultaneous deaths of his mother and young wife. Medora was already booming, with three hotels, a church, several stores, and numberless saloons. Conscious of their dignity as the two local bluebloods, TR and the Marquis kept aloof from the town and each other, the former retiring to his Maltese Cross ranch, seven miles upriver, and the latter to a magnificent thirty-room "château" overlooking the whole Little Missouri Valley.

Both these buildings are preserved, and are open to visitors all year round. The Maltese Cross has been moved to the Medora entrance of the park, where it stands dwarfed by the great bare buttes behind it. It is nothing more than a little oblong log cabin with a pitched shingle roof. Half of it is a living room, furnished with the writing desk and rocking chair that are a feature of all Rooseveltian interiors. Here TR would sit talking about cattle and politics to his men, who, once they had gotten used to his pince-nez (regarded out West as a sign of defective moral character) loved him as a brother. "You're a plumb good sort," allowed tough Joe Ferris, after the asthmatic dude had driven him to the point of total exhaustion during a buffalo hunt. TR never allowed this affection to erode his stature as "boss." Every night, at a given signal, the men would mount a ladder into the attic, while he bedded down warmly in the small alcove by the kitchen.

The Château de Morés, maintained by the State Historical Society of North Dakota, is an almost comical contrast to the rough simplicity of Roosevelt's cabin. Huge, rambling, and drafty, it is a treasure-house of High Victorian camp. Bear rugs cover the floor of the cream-and-gold living room, Wagner's *Siegfried* lies open on the dropsical piano. English Minton china gleams all round the dining room, part of a set that could have served the entire population of Medora. Antlers, guns, and suits of armor festoon the corridors. Hundreds of distinguished bottles lie empty in what was one of the best wine cellars in America. Empty, too, is the exquisitely enameled safe in the Marquis's study, from which he drew so often, and so recklessly.

Medora boomed for three short years on the de Morès millions, but by 1886 it was apparent that the Badlands cattle empire was doomed. Consumers in the East simply preferred corn-fed beef to range meat, and there was nothing any Western cattleman could do about it. Roosevelt himself, having invested $80,000 here, found it impossible to make money and hurried back to New York to resume his political career. The Marquis, too, shut up house and left. That winter, Nature, seemingly exasperated by the attempts of man to tame the Badlands, overwhelmed Dakota Territory with a blizzard of inconceivable fury. An old cowboy ballad, still to be heard in and around Medora, goes:

I may not see a hundred
Before I see the Styx,
But coal or ember, I'll remember
Eighteen-eighty-six.
The stiff heaps in the coulee,
The dead eyes in the camps,
And the wind about, blowin' fortunes out,
As a woman blows out lamps.

The blizzard raged, almost nonstop, for four months. When warmth returned the following spring, every draw and ravine was choked with dead cattle, and Medora became, to all intents and purposes, a ghost town.

BEFORE LEAVING THE BADLANDS I decided to make a pilgrimage to the site of TR's second ranch, the Elkhorn, which he built some forty miles downriver in 1884. My local map indicated that it lay about halfway between the North and South Units of the park, and there was an inset reading "Persons Wishing To Visit This Site Should Obtain Full Information At Park Headquarters Before Attempting Trip." The Medora ranger was not encouraging. "It's a nice dusty road in summer, sir, but at this time of year. . . . " He gestured outside at the brilliant early morning sunlight. "Sun thaws out the ice slicks. Next thing you know, you're up to your axles in clay."

Having stayed up late reading TR's inspirational prose (*a man becomes fearless by sheer dint of practicing fearlessness*) I took a last wistful look at civilization and spurred my Pinto north into hilly grasslands. The road seemed firm enough, save for isolated slopes that caught the full glare of the sun, and by keeping up a steady momentum of 30 mph, I managed to plow through the gumbo. The craggy, fantastic cliffs of the Badlands drifted by on my right, and once or twice I saw deer etched against the skyline. On my left gold meadows sloped down toward the bottoms of the Little Missouri, hidden in its perpetual thicket of cottonwood trees.

After a couple of hours I came to the deserted schoolhouse where a sign directed me west toward Elkhorn, along an even more primitive road. Fortunately most of it was still frozen stiff, and I approached the right bank of the river without mishap. Here the road petered out, and, donning rubbers, I trudged down to the water's edge.

Immediately opposite, across thirty yards of shining ice floes, was a scene familiar to me from photographs taken by TR in 1885. The stately row of cottonwood trees, the grassy bottom, the bluffs behind, rolling away to the west. . . . Only the long low ranch house, with its frieze of interlocking elkhorns, was gone. *Gone to the isle of ghosts and strange dead memories,* I murmured to myself.

"Who wrote that?" said a voice at my elbow.

"You did, Mr. President," I said, pleased to have company in this lonely spot. "I have your autobiography right here. Would you like to hear some more?"

There was a flattered silence. I pulled the book from my pocket and read: *In the long summer afternoons we would sometimes sit on the piazza, when there was no work to be done, for an hour or two at a time, watching the cattle on the sand-bars, and the sharply channeled and strangely carved amphitheater of cliffs across the bottom opposite; while the vultures wheeled overhead, their black shadows gliding across the glaring white of the river-bed. Sometimes from the ranch we saw deer, and once, when we needed meat I shot one across the river as I stood on the piazza.*

Roosevelt laughed with delight. "I did, too! Got him right where you're standing now. Ah, it was still the Wild West in those days."

I gazed all around me, at the tremendous emptiness of the landscape, the clean blue of the sky. "Has it really changed all that much?"

"Well, here in the Badlands, hardly at all I guess. That's why," said Old Four Eyes cheerfully, "I like to haunt the place."

DOCUMENTING THE INTANGIBLE

The New York Public Library's Dance Collection

DANCE, THE OLDEST AND MOST UNIVERSAL OF THE ARTS, IS BY its nature the most difficult to preserve. The strokes of Giotto's brush, the jabs of Beethoven's pen, the blows of Rodin's chisel, are tangible evidences of genius for future generations. But what of the flutter of Camargo's arms, the spin of Taglioni's body, the thrust of Nijinsky's legs? Those arcs in space, which for a second or two could ravish the hearts of thousands, dissolved even as they came into being, like ripples in water.

From the earliest days of cave-painting, men have attempted to record the ephemeral beauty of the dance. Choreography was formally committed to paper as long ago as the Renaissance, and countless prints

Originally published in *The New York Times*, 10 August 1975.

Ballets Russe poster, 1928.

and photographs make it possible to reconstruct, albeit jerkily, the flow of Romantic ballet. In this century, of course, we have been fortunate in that the invention of the movie camera, not to mention videotape, has made it possible to capture at least a trillionth of the mimetic movements into which the human body is constantly breaking.

But even as recently as 1948, when a young music major named Genevieve Oswald took over the New York Public Library's Dance Collection, the technology of preserving dance on film was in its infancy. Thanks to her passionate encouragement of that technology, Miss Oswald has built up the world's greatest archive of what she still insists is "an intangible art." Her collection—few would dispute the possessive pronoun—is now well on its way to amassing its two millionth foot of film, and a glance through its ten-volume catalog gives an idea of the staggering wealth of materials that crowd its vaults: 120,000 manuscripts; 6,000 prints, lithographs, and engravings; 3,000 libretti; 200,000 photographs; 470 stage and costume designs; 4,500 playbills and posters; 70,000 programs; 200,000 clippings; and 1,000 taped oral history interviews.

Despite its titular affiliation with New York, the Dance Collection is a truly international resource. Ten-page queries from Moscow are answered as conscientiously as telephone calls from Harlem. Venezuelans write for information about Merce Cunningham. Upstaters seek re-creations of eighteenth-century French *contredanses*. British ballerinas stop by to view movies of the Kirov School curriculum. Choreographers in Australia wire for pictures of Hopi Indian rites. The Collection's quiet, carpeted reading room at Lincoln Center is something of a club for the dance fraternity. On any given day, one may see Natalia Makarova researching the footwork of a predecessor, or Frederick Ashton thumbing through a few of his old programs, or Alvin Ailey refreshing his memory of an Alvin Ailey ballet.

I arrived at the Collection recently, knowing as much about dance history as the average crayfish salesman. The sheer diversity of its holdings, which range from the world's first ballet program to Isadora Duncan's traveling trunk, bewildered me. An hour's conversation with Miss Oswald, who is a lady of restless intellect and little patience with writers unable to spell the name of Guglielmo Ebreo (a famous Italian dance master from the fifteenth century), left me, on the whole, no wiser than before. I was on the point of giving up my assignment when an exhibit in memory of Charles Weidman, who died earlier this year,* caught my eye. I decided to take this choreographer, of whom I'd never heard, and see how much I could find out about him in a single afternoon, using the Collection's varied facilities.

The afternoon, it turned out, was not long enough to look at all the material on file. I doubt if a skilled researcher could plow through it in half a year. Entries under "WEIDMAN" in the Dance Collection Catalog occupy nine triple-column pages of dense print. Selecting completely at random, I asked for a souvenir program, a photograph, an article, a scrapbook, a tape, a costume design, a letter, a playbill, a sketch, and a movie. Deferential young assistants brought me boxes and folders, and set up an array of audio and video machines. During the next few hours I learned a surprising amount about Charles Weidman.

The souvenir program told me he was born in the Midwest in 1901, and that upon leaving school, his soul had yearned more for the dance studios of New York than the law offices of Nebraska. The photograph showed me a slender young man with high cheekbones and a pointed, humorous profile. The article discussed his studies with Ruth St. Denis and Ted Shawn, and his participation in their famous Oriental tour of 1925–1926. Browsing through his scrapbook of the next decade, I found that he had discovered a soul mate at Denishawn in the person of Doris Humphrey, and that after returning from the Far East they had split off to form their own company, devoted to "a new American dance technique." Perfectly matched both as dancing partners and choreographers (she provided the ice, he the heat) they were, by the mid-1930s, admired as innovators of the first rank.

Through earphones, I heard a former pupil nostalgically recall her first glimpse of Charles Weidman at a rehearsal of *With My Red Fires* in 1936: "moving backwards slowly, leaning on the air . . . devious, beautiful, promising, vibrant." A costume design of seven years later showed me Weidman decked up for a Rainbow Room engagement at Rockefeller Center in a green bandana, tight blue jacket, and pink trousers revealing

* On 15 July 1975.

lots of green-striped sock. In contrast to the jauntiness of this pose, a sketch made in 1944 showed him rumple-haired, tired-eyed, and trying to smile. The caption, partially erased, read "Charles after five drinks."

A letter to Doris Humphrey, postmarked 28 July of the same year, hinted that maybe he needed those drinks: "I have been working like hell on *Sally* and it's sort of a thankless task, because the music and lyrics are so dull—it's so hard to get any idea out of them."

A playbill, also dated 1944, indicated that by that fall, at least, Weidman had broken his creative block. It announced the opening of *Sing Out, Sweet Land!* at the Colonial Theatre in Boston, starring Alfred Drake and Burl Ives "and a brilliant cast of seventy singers and dancers," choreographed by Weidman and Humphrey.

My last, and certainly most vivid, encounter with Charles Weidman was an amateur movie filmed in 1925, during Denishawn's tour of Asia. There, on the flickering screen, a group of Ceylonese dancers leap and twirl to the beat of an inaudible drum. Behind them, against a background of palm trees, stand the pale figures of Ted Shawn and Charles Weidman, the whiteness of their limbs accentuated by the blackness of their leotards. At first they look on as politely as any ordinary spectators: then, gradually, the rhythm of the dancing begins to seep into their bones, and their arms undulate. Their feet shift. After a while they can stand it no longer: they join in to gyrate with the Ceylonese, Shawn terse and muscular, Weidman gracefully angular, white men and brown men caught up in the universal ecstasy of the dance.

On my way out of the Dance Collection, I took respectful leave of Miss Oswald. "Look at this!" she said, flourishing the transcript of an urgent phone call. "We get these requests all the time." I glanced at the message. It was from the executor of an estate who asked to be relieved of an unsorted "carload" of dance documents. The name of the deceased was Charles Weidman.

HEARD MELODIES ARE SWEET,
BUT THOSE UNHEARD ARE SWEETER

A Low-Calorie Diet for the Musically Obese

THE NEWS THAT WNCN, "NEW YORK'S 24-HOUR STEREO CONCERT Hall," has returned to our airwaves makes this music-lover, at least, heave an ungracious sigh. As a station, it is undeniably superior to, say, WFUV, whose classical-music programs seem to be broadcast out of some painful sense of religious duty, or WBAI, whose Monteverdi seeps out of the speakers furtively flavored with marijuana, or WQXR, whose hearty announcers all sound as if they wear orange socks and eat too much cheese. Indeed, if the FCC ever ruled that we were allowed only one classical-music station per city, I would lobby for WNCN. But even so, isn't twenty-four hours of the stuff, seven days a week, rather too much of a good thing?

Originally published in *The New York Times*, 9 November 1975.
"An Oompah," from Hoffnung's Acoustics *by Gerard Hoffnung* (London, 1959).

What we need, I submit, is not more music but less. The latest issue of *FM Guide* contains the alarming information that during this month our antennas will be bombarded with no fewer than six *Eroicas*, four Tchaikovsky B-flat minors, and three complete *Traviatas*. It is a truism that truly great art will bear any amount of exposure, but I defy anybody to listen to Beethoven's Third Symphony six times in thirty days and not find it wearing a bit thin. Of course, no sane person would do such a thing, but the mere fact that such sublime music is pumped into the air so often, so casually, like air freshener, is saddening. It seems to cheapen it, somehow.

Even more alarming is the assembly-line productivity of today's record industry. Take the works cited above. Schwann's *Record and Tape Catalog* currently lists fourteen versions of the symphony, eight of the opera, and no fewer than twenty-nine of the concerto. No wonder you keep reading, in reviews, such dismissive phrases as "a bargain *Emperor*," or "ideal Brahms."

Bulk packaging is another ominous trend. Music is being marketed in bigger and bigger boxes, presumably for commercial reasons. It is now possible to take your shopping cart to Sam Goody and load up Haydn's 103 symphonies, the complete works of Chopin, and every single song that Schubert ever wrote, including dozens he was rightly ashamed of. If you're lazy, just call Time/Life Records and they will send you *all* of Beethoven through the mail.

A similar elephantiasis seems to be afflicting the concert world. Last season the harpsichordist Fernando Valenti programmed a hundred Scarlatti sonatas in five consecutive concerts, to the applause of large audiences. One wonders whether they were congratulating themselves, or him. I doubt they paid sustained interest to the Neapolitan master's sonatas. Those miraculous miniatures, arranged in groups of four or six, sparkle like diamonds; *en masse,* they degenerate into tinsel. The day is surely not far off when some contrabassist hires Carnegie Hall to play the complete concertos of Bottesini.

THE CUMULATIVE EFFECT of all this *embarras de richesses* is that we grow fat on music, like those Strasbourg geese who are force-fed with grain until they choke on their own livers. Our sensibilities coarsen. We gobble up symphonies nine at a time, swallow opera cycles whole, feeling only the gross pleasure of consumption. As gluttons constantly yearn for more spice, we seek out new quirks of interpretation to stimulate our appetite—an exaggerated *pianissimo* here, a surprise blare of trumpets there—anything that adds zest to the overfamiliar.

It seems to me that the true music-lover should discipline his listening, just as the true gourmet eats sparingly, with more attention to variety than volume. Abstinence restores to even the most hackneyed masterpiece its power to chasten and subdue. Of course that power was always there, in the music: the restorative process takes place within ourselves.

Anybody who plays an instrument knows the joy of returning to it after a period of separation: how rich it sounds, how naturally melodies take shape and float out of it! Can this be the same instrument that produced such lifeless notes only a short time ago?

The same applies to listening. Some time ago I indulged in a Wagnerian orgy that left me so musically surfeited I felt the need for a vacation in the Midwest. For a while I actually enjoyed the refreshing jangle of country and western tunes pouring out of my car radio. After a few days, of course, the racket became intolerable, and I turned the set off. Toward the end of the trip, somewhere in the Badlands of North Dakota, I switched it on again, and the slow movement of Schubert's Third Symphony (beamed from Canada) wafted out of the dashboard with such intoxicating sweetness that I nearly went off the road. I had shed my musical calories, and was hungry for beauty again.

For some time after that I toyed with the idea of publishing a book called *Here's Fat in Your Ear: A 12-Month Diet Revolution for the Musically Obese.* I devised a severe regimen of obscure quartets and *singspiels*, sweetened only occasionally with a voluptuous slice of Rachmaninoff. But the impossibility of embracing all tastes—the only universally effective thing I could think of was an all-Mahler diet, which is enough to make anyone crave real music—forced me to abandon this project. Let every connoisseur devise his or her own fast.

AT THE RISK OF SOUNDING like a masochist, I would also suggest to those so fortunate as *never* to have heard any particular masterpiece that they continue to avoid it as long as possible. Those of us who were born in the sticks can remember the rapture of first hearings rather better, perhaps, than city kids, who are exposed to the whole spectrum of classical music before puberty.

The Australian music writer Ernest Hutcheson once touchingly recalled his own first exposure to the Schumann Quintet as a student in Leipzig in the 1880s. "Have you *never* heard the Schumann Quintet?" his teacher asked incredulously. When the fifteen-year-old shook his head, the teacher looked at him long and kindly. "I envy you," he said.

Like Hutcheson, I was a colonial boy who took what music he could get growing up, and had to imagine the rest by reading scores. (Classical gramophone records were almost unobtainable, since the only music store in Nairobi catered mainly to Ismaili Muslims.) To hear Beethoven's Fifth Symphony, I had to wait for a rare BBC Overseas Service broadcast. I monitored it guiltily beneath boarding-school bedclothes. Shortwave transmission caused all sorts of *crescendi* and *decrescendi* not written into the score, and the crackling of my crystal set added the occasional unexpected *sforzando*, but the music that surged through those earphones was so overwhelming that to this day I have declined to listen to it more than once a year. Consequently the Fifth still retains its cataclysmic force, and I can understand Goethe's remark after his own first hearing: "This is very great; quite wild; it makes me fear that the house might fall down."

Be warned that dodging masterpieces is no easy task. Already, at thirty-five, I've been pursued, tackled, and brought to ground by practically every heavyweight in the repertory. For years I managed to outrun the giant tread of Bach's Mass in B minor, but only the other day the Kyrie waylaid me while I was hanging wallpaper, and had me paralyzed while the glue dried on the roller. Now I'm in mortal dread that *Parsifal* will sneak up on me unawares. How much chance does a man have of keeping such music at bay until he's old enough to deserve it?

About as much chance, I suppose, as Francis Thompson had of escaping the Hound of Heaven.

THEODORE ROOSEVELT THE POLYGON

Address at the National Portrait Gallery

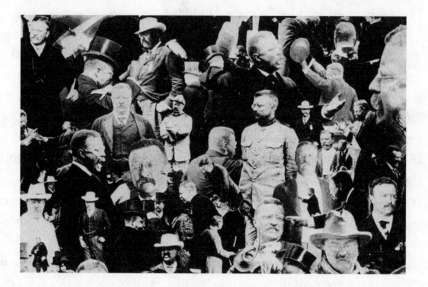

LET US DISPOSE, IN SHORT ORDER, WITH THEODORE ROOSEVELT'S
faults. He *was* an incorrigible preacher of platitudes. Or to use Elting E.
Morison's delicious phrase, he had "a recognition, too frequently and
precisely stated, of the less recondite facts of life." He *did* significantly
reduce the wildlife population of two continents. He *did* (let us not deny
it) pile his dessert plate with so many peaches that the cream spilled over
the sides. And it's true that on at least one drive through Washington in
his presidential carriage, he was seen making rude faces at small boys in
a passing streetcar.

Lecture delivered on 30 October 1980. An abridged version published in *American Heritage,* June/
July 1981.

Photo collage of TR in action, 1907.

Perhaps those last two delinquencies are forgivable if we heed Cecil Spring-Rice's warning, "You must always remember the President is about six." TR's preachiness may be excused by the fact that the American electorate dearly loves a public moralist. As to his most regrettable failing—a bloodlust that compelled him to bring down large fauna, whether they be rhinoceri or members of the United States Senate—it is paradoxically so much a part of his virtues, both as a man and a politician, I will leave it for discussion in a larger context.

ONE OF THE MINOR irritations I have to contend with as a biographer is that whenever I go to the library to look for books about "Roosevelt, Theodore," they are invariably mixed up with books about "Roosevelt, Franklin." I guess FDR scholars have the same problem in reverse. Time was when the single word *Roosevelt* meant only Theodore. Even after Franklin became president, he had frequently to insist that he was not TR's son. He was merely a fifth cousin, and what was even more distant, a Democrat. In time, of course, Franklin succeeded in preempting the family name, to the point that TR's public image, which once loomed as large as Washington's and Lincoln's, began to fade like a Cheshire cat from popular memory. By the time of FDR's own death in 1945, little was left but the ghost of a toothy grin.

Only a few veterans of the earlier Roosevelt Era survived to testify that if Franklin was the greater politician, it was only by a hairsbreadth, and as far as sheer personality was concerned, Theodore's superiority could be measured in spades. They pointed out that FDR himself declared, late in life, that his "cousin Ted" was the greatest man he ever knew. Presently the veterans too died. The academics continued their work of building and rebuilding sand statues of the Great Presidents and solemnly measuring their relative heights. (The latest news from the beachfront, courtesy of the United States Historical Society, is that Lincoln and Washington still tower above the others, followed by FDR as No. 3 and TR as No. 4.)*

Meanwhile that ghostly grin continued to float in the national con-

---

* A variety of polls since this one in 1977 have consistently ranked TR among the top five greatest presidents. In 2009 a C-SPAN survey put him at No. 4, after Lincoln, Washington, and Franklin D. Roosevelt. In 2010 the Siena College Research Institute

sciousness, as if to indicate that its owner was meditating a reappearance. I first became aware of the power behind the grin in Washington, in February 1976. The National Theatre was then trying out an ill-fated musical by Alan Jay Lerner and Leonard Bernstein, *1600 Pennsylvania Avenue*. For two and a half hours Ken Howard and Sada Thompson worked their way through a chronological series of impersonations of historic First Couples. The audience sat on its hands, stiff with boredom, until the very end, when Howard clamped on a pair of pince-nez and a false mustache, and bared all his teeth in a grin—to an instant joyous ovation.

What intrigued me was the fact that few of those people could have known much about TR beyond the ancient clichés of San Juan Hill and the Big Stick. Yet somehow, subconsciously, they realized that here—for once—was a *positive* president, warm and tough and authoritative and funny, who believed in America and who, to quote Owen Wister, "grasped his optimism tight lest it escaped him." And there came into my mind a nostalgic passage by H. G. Wells, describing an interview with TR in the White House garden on 6 May, 1906:

> He hadn't, he said, an effectual disproof of a pessimistic interpretation of the future. If one chose to say America must presently lose the impetus of her ascent, that she and all mankind must culminate and pass, he could not deny that possibility. Only he chose to live as if this were not so. He mentioned my *Time Machine*. . . . He became gesticulatory, and his straining voice a note higher in denying the pessimism of that book as a credible interpretation of destiny. With one of those sudden movements of his he knelt forward in a garden-chair . . . and addressed me very earnestly over the back . . . thrusting out his familiar gesture, a hand first partly open and then closed.
>
> "Suppose, after all," he said slowly, "that you're right, that our civilization will end in your butterflies and morlocks. *That doesn't matter now*. The effort's real. . . . It's worth it. It's worth it—even so."
>
> I can see him now and hear his unmusical voice saying, "The

---

poll of presidential scholars for the first time put TR at No. 2, ahead of Lincoln and Washington, with only his cousin ahead of him.

effort—the effort's worth it," and see the gesture of his clenched hand and the—how can I describe it?—the friendly peering snarl of his face, like a man with the sun in his eyes.

"He sticks in my mind," Wells concludes, "as a very symbol of the creative will in man . . . amidst perplexities and confusions. I know of no other a tithe so representative of the constructive purpose, the goodwill in humanity as he."

So much for nostalgia. But in the last year or so Theodore Roosevelt—who by the way, greatly disliked being called "Teddy"—has made his long-promised comeback, coinciding with that of the Ayatollah Khomeini in Iran. He has been the subject of a *Newsweek* cover story on American heroes. Russell Baker has called him a cert to carry all fifty states if he were running for the White House today. There was a joke going around town last summer about the ghost of the Rough Rider listening aghast to a briefing from President Carter on American foreign policy initiatives—our fearless withdrawal of athletes from Rome in protest against the Soviet invasion of Afghanistan, our advocacy of prayer as a solution for Africa's ills, our deployment of a few malfunctioning helicopters to rescue our hostages in Tehran, and all the sorry rest of it. "I suppose the next thing you're going to do," TR snapped, "is give away the Panama Canal." He's now starring on Broadway in *Tintypes*, on television in *Bully*, and we'll soon see him on the big screen in *Ragtime*. Historiographically speaking, this may be an appropriate moment to study that giant personality in color and fine detail.

I DO NOT USE the word *giant* loosely. "Every inch of him," said William Allen White, "was over-engined." Lyman Gage likened him, mentally and physically, to two strong men combined; Gifford Pinchot said that his normal appetite was enough for four people; Charles J. Bonaparte estimated that his mind moved ten times faster than average; and TR himself, not wanting to get into double figures, modestly remarked, "I have enjoyed as much of life as any nine men I know." John Morley made a famous comparison in 1904 between the President and Niagara Falls, "both great wonders of nature."

John Burroughs wrote that TR's mere proximity made him nervous. "There was always something imminent about him, like an avalanche that the sound of your voice might loosen." Ida Tarbell, sitting next to him at a musicale, had a sudden hallucination that Roosevelt was about to burst. "I felt his clothes might not contain him, he was so steamed up, so ready to go, to attack anything, anywhere." Richard Washburn Child found him so explosive as to tax not only his clothes, but the walls of any room that held him too long. "Whether you like Roosevelt or whether you don't," Mark Sullivan commented, "the bigness of his personality is the one undisputed thing. That immense and varied Titan could not be compressed into the small smooth mold of any epigram."

Reading all these remarks it comes as a surprise to discover that TR's chest measured a normal forty-two inches, and that he stood only five feet nine in his size seven shoes. Yet unquestionably his initial impact was physical, and it was overwhelming. Over the years I have collected the many metaphors that contemporaries used to describe this Rooseveltian "presence." Here's a random selection. Edith Wharton and Lincoln Lang both called him radioactive; Archie Butt and others used phrases to do with electricity, high-voltage wires, generators, and dynamos; Lawrence Abbott compared him to an electromagnetic nimbus; John Burroughs to "a kind of electric bombshell, if there can be such a thing"; Congressman James E. Watson was reminded of TNT; and Senator Joseph Foraker used the improbable image of "a steam-engine in trousers." There are countless other steam-engine comparisons, from Henry Adams's "swift and awful Chicago express" to Henry James's "verily, a wonderful little machine: destined to be overstrained, perhaps, but not as yet, truly, betraying the least creak." Extraterrestrially, we have Owen Wister and William Bayard Hale comparing TR to a solar conflagration that cast no shadow, only radiance.

These metaphors sound exaggerated, but they refer to TR's physical effect, which was felt with equal power by friends and enemies. People tingled in his company. There was something sensually stimulating about it: they came out of the presidential office flushed, short-breathed, energized as if they had snorted cocaine. He had, as Oscar Straus once said, "the quality of vitalizing things." His youthfulness (he was not yet forty-three at the beginning of his first term, and only fifty at the end of his second), his air of glossy good health, his powerful handshake—all these things combined to give an impression of irresistible force and personal impetus. "Theodore Roosevelt is a strong, tough man," remarked his White House boxing instructor, "hard to hurt and harder to stop."

But TR was not just a physical phenomenon. In many ways the quality of his personality was more remarkable than its quantity. Here again in my research, I noticed recurrences of the same words in contemporary descriptions. One of the most frequent images is that of sweetness. "He was as sweet a man," wrote Henry Watterson, "as ever scuttled a ship or cut a throat." Most comments are kinder than that. "There is a sweetness about him that is very compelling," Woodrow Wilson sighed. "You can't resist the man." A veteran journalist wrote after TR's death: "He had the double gifts of a sweet nature that came out in every hand-touch and tone . . . in itself a conquering force—and a sincerely powerful personality that left the ineffaceable impression that whatever he said was right. Such a combination was simply irresistible." Those are the words of Robert Livingstone, who spent a lifetime watching politicians come and go. His final verdict was that "Theodore Roosevelt had unquestionably the greatest gift of personal magnetism ever possessed by an American."

That may or may not be true, but there are few recorded examples of anybody, even TR's bitterest political critics, being able to resist him in person. Brand Whitlock, Mark Twain, John Jay Chapman, William Jennings Bryan, and Henry James were all seduced by his charm—if only temporarily. Peevish little Henry Adams spent much of the period 1901–1909 living on the opposite side of Lafayette Square, and penning a series of insults to the President's reputation. (My favorite is "The twelfth century still rages wildly here in the shape of the fiend with tusks and eyeglasses across the way.") But this did not prevent Adams from accepting frequent invitations to dine at the White House and basking gloomily in TR's effulgence. By the time the Roosevelt era came to an end, he was inconsolable. He walked over on the last day and took TR by the hand. "I shall miss you," he said. Privately, Adams confessed to stronger emotion. "My last vision of fun and gaiety will vanish when my Theodore goes. . . . Never can we replace him."

It's a pity that the two men never had a face-to-face dispute, because when it came to personal invective TR could give as good as he got. There was the Supreme Court justice he called "an amiable old fuzzy-wuzzy with sweetbread brains." President Castro of Venezuela was an "unspeakably villainous little monkey," Postmaster General John Wanamaker was "an ill-constitutioned creature, oily, with bristles sticking up through the oil." Woodrow Wilson was "a Byzantine logothete." (Even Wilson had to go to the dictionary for that one.) TR did not cuss—the nearest to it I've found is his description of Charles Evans Hughes as "a psalm-singing son of a bitch." Moreover, he usually took the sting out of such insults by collapsing into laughter as he uttered them.

Humor was Theodore Roosevelt's saving grace. A *New York Times* reporter who spent a week with him in the White House calculated that he laughed, on average, a hundred times a day. "He laughs like an irresponsible schoolboy on a lark, his face flushing ruddy, his eyes nearly closed, his utterance choked with merriment, his speech abandoned for a weird falsetto. . . . The President is a joker, and (what many jokers are not), a humorist as well."

TR was also a spellbinding raconteur. Secretary of State John Hay, no mean storyteller himself, was aware early on that if someone didn't do something to transcribe the President's after-dinner stories about his experiences out West and his days as a Rough Rider, posterity would be the poorer. After one such Rooseveltian monologue in the spring of 1903, Hay was so enchanted that he begged TR to write it down. He was rewarded with a nine-thousand-word letter which is one of the comic classics of American literature. Hay bound it in leather for his children, saying, "It will not lack companionship in a case which holds Lincoln's Second Inaugural and the Gettysburg Address."*

Now if there were nothing more to Theodore Roosevelt's personality than physical exuberance, humor, and charm, he would indeed have been what he is sometimes misperceived to be: a simpleminded amiable bully. Actually he was an exceedingly complex man, a polygon (to use Brander Matthews's word) of so many political, intellectual, and social facets that the closer one gets to him, the less one is able

---

*Published in *Cowboys and Kings: Three Great Letters by Theodore Roosevelt*, Elting E. Morison, ed. (Cambridge, Mass. 1951).

to see him in the round. Consider this random list of attributes and achievements:

He graduated *magna cum laude* from Harvard University. He was the author of two ornithological papers, a four-volume history, *The Winning of the West*, considered definitive in his lifetime, and another history, *The Naval War of 1812*, that remains definitive to this day. He also wrote biographies of Thomas Hart Benton, Gouverneur Morris, and Oliver Cromwell, a military memoir and an autobiography, and more than thirty other volumes of history, natural history, criticism, political analysis, and travel literature—not to mention uncounted hundreds of periodical articles and 150,000 letters.* In youth he spent nearly three years of his life in Europe and the Levant, and before he was forty had built up a wide circle of intellectual acquaintance on both sides of the Atlantic. He habitually read one to three books a day, on subjects ranging from architecture to zoology, averaging two or three pages a minute and effortlessly memorizing the paragraphs that interested him. He could recite poetry by the hour in English, German, and French. He married two women and fathered six children. He was a boxing championship finalist; a Fifth Avenue socialite; a New York State assemblyman; a Dakota cowboy; a deputy sheriff; a president of the Little Missouri Stockmen's Association; United States civil service commissioner; police commissioner of New York City; assistant secretary of the Navy; colonel of the Rough Riders; governor of New York; vice president and finally President of the United States. At various times he was a founding member of the National Institute of Arts and Letters and president of the American Historical Association, and a skilled taxidermist, ornithologist, paleontologist, and zoologist widely recognized as a world authority on the big-game mammals of North America.† After quitting the White House at the early age of fifty, he became a professional journalist, big-game collector for museums, leader of a new political party, and explorer, putting on the map the Rio Roosevelt in Brazil, a river longer than the Rhine.

If it were possible to take a cross-section of TR's personality, as geologists, say, ponder a chunk of continent, you would be presented with a

---

* See page 95.
† As President, TR was sometimes asked to help identify faunal specimens that confused experts at the Smithsonian.

picture of seismic richness and confusion. The most order I have been able to make of it is to isolate four major character seams. They may be traced back to childhood. Each seam stood out bright and clear in youth and early middle age. Then they began to merge, and the white heat of the presidency fused them into solid metal. So long as they were distinct, they may be identified as aggression, righteousness, pride, and militarism. I'd like to explain how they originated.

THE MOST FUNDAMENTAL characteristic of Theodore Roosevelt was his aggression—conquest being, to him, synonymous with growth. From the moment he first dragged breath into his asthmatic lungs, the sickly little boy fought for a larger share of the world. He could never get enough air. Disease had to be destroyed. He had to fight his way through big heavy books to gain a man's knowledge. Just as the struggle for breath made him stretch his chest, so did the difficulty of relating to abnormally contrasting parents extend his imagination. Theodore Senior was the epitome of hard, thrusting Northern manhood; Mittie Roosevelt was the quintessence of soft, yielding Southern femininity. The Civil War—the first political phenomenon little "Teedie" was ever aware of—symbolically opposed the one to the other. There was no question as to which side, and which parent, the child preferred. He naughtily asked God, in Mittie's presence, to "grind the Southern troops to powder," and the victory of Union arms reinforced his belief in the superiority of Strength over Weakness, Right over Wrong, Realism over Romance.

Teedie's youthful observations in natural history gave him further proof of the laws of natural selection, long before he fully understood Darwin and Herbert Spencer. For weeks he watched in fascination while a tiny shrew successively devoured a mass of beetles, then a mouse twice her size, then a snake so large it whipped her from side to side of the cage at the same time as she was gnawing through its neck. The rule of tooth and claw, aided by superior intelligence, became a persistent theme in Theodore Roosevelt's writings. Blood sports enabled him to feel the "strong eager pleasure" of the shrew in vanquishing ever larger foes. His exuberant dancing and whooping after killing a particularly dangerous animal struck more than one observer as macabre. From among his own kind, at college, he selected the fairest and most unobtainable mate, Alice Hathaway Lee of Boston—"See that girl? I'm going to marry her. She won't have me, but I am going to have *her*!"—and ferociously hunted her down.

During his first years in politics, in the New York State Assembly, he won power through constant attack. Alice's death, coming as it did just after the birth of his first child,* only intensified his will to fight. He hurried West, to where the battle for life was fiercest. The West did not welcome him. It had to be won, like everything else he lusted for. Win it he did, by dint of the greatest physical and mental stretchings-out he had yet made. In doing so he built up the burly body that later became an inspiration to the American people (one frail boy who vowed to follow the President's example was the future world heavyweight champion Gene Tunney). By living on equal terms with the likes of Hashknife Simpson, Bat Masterson, Modesty Carter, Bronco Charlie Miller, and Hell-Roaring Bill Jones, he added another mental frontier to those he had already acquired by birth and inheritance. Theodore Roosevelt, Eastern son of a Northern father and a Southern mother, could now call himself a Westerner as well.

TR's second governing impulse was his personal righteousness. As one reviewer of his books remarked, "He seems to have been born with his mind made up." No violent shocks disturbed his tranquil, prosperous childhood in New York City. Privately educated, he suffered none of the traumas of school. Thanks to the security of his home, the strong leadership of his father, and the adoration of his brother and sisters, Teedie entered adolescence with no sexual or psychological doubts whatsoever. Or if he had any, he simply reasoned them out, according to the Judeo-Christian principles Theodore Senior taught him, reached the proper moral decision, and that was that. "Thank heaven!" he wrote in his diary after falling in love with Alice Lee, "I am perfectly pure." His three youthful bereavements (the death of his father in 1878, and the almost simultaneous deaths of his mother and wife in the same house and on the same night in 1884) came too late in his development to do him any

---

* Alice Lee Roosevelt Longworth (1884–1980), the famous "Princess Alice" and doyenne of Washington Society for seventy years.

permanent emotional damage. They served only to convince him more that he must be strong, honest, clean-living, and industrious. "At least I can live," he wrote, "so as not to dishonor the memory of the dead whom I so loved."

Experiment after experiment proved the correctness of his instincts—in graduating *magna cum laude* from Harvard, defying the doctors who ordered him to live a sedentary life, remarrying successfully, and winning international acclaim as a writer and politician long before he was thirty. In wild Dakota Territory, TR proceeded to knock out insolent cowboys, establish the foundations of a local government, pursue boat thieves in the name of the law, and preach the gospel of responsible citizenship. One of the first things he did after Benjamin Harrison appointed him civil service commissioner was to call for the prosecution of a postmaster who just happened to be the President's best friend. "That young man," Harrison growled, "wants to put the whole world right between sunrise and sunset."

TR's egotistic moralizing as the reform police commissioner of New York City was so insufferable that the *Herald* published a transcript of one of his speeches with the personal pronoun "I" emphasized in heavy type. The effect, in a column of gray newsprint, was of buckshot at close range. This did not stop TR using the personal pronoun thirteen times in the first four sentences of his account of the Spanish-American War. A story went around that halfway through the typesetting Scribner's had to send to the foundry for an extra supply of capital *Is*. When the book came out in 1900, Finley Peter Dunne wrote a famously funny review suggesting that it be retitled *Alone in Cuba*.

To TR's credit, he was as amused by this review as everyone else. As President, he once recited it from memory at a White House champagne supper. In the audience, slowly turning purple, was Finley Peter Dunne himself. "I never knew a man with a keener humor," Dunne said afterward, "or one who could take a joke on himself with better grace."

The third characteristic of Theodore Roosevelt's personality was his sense of pride, both as an aristocrat and an American. From his birth on, servants and tradespeople deferred to him. Men and women of high quality came to visit his parents and treated him as one of their number. He accepted his status without question, as he did the charitable responsibilities it entailed. At a very early age he was required to accompany his father on Sunday excursions to a lodging house for Irish newsboys and a night school for "Little Italians." It cannot have escaped his attention that certain immigrant groups were more debased than others. Extended tours of Europe and the Levant as a child, teenager, and young man taught him that this was not due to ethnic inferiority so much as to centuries of economic and political deprivation. Prosperous, independent countries like England and Germany were relatively free of slums and disease. But in Italy women and children scrabbled like chickens for scraps of food, and in Ireland people lay down in the road from sheer hunger. From what he read, things were no better in the Slavic countries. Only in America, with its limitless economic opportunities and freedom from political bondage, might these peasants begin to improve their stock. And only in the American melting pot could they revitalize their racial characteristics.

TR's own extremely mixed ancestry suggested to him that two or three generations of life in the New World were enough to blend all kinds of inherited foreignness into a new, dynamic Western breed. (As President, he had a habit when shaking hands in ethnic neighborhoods of saying, "Congratulations, I'm German too!" and "Dee-lighted! I'm also Scotch-Irish!" Newspapermen dubbed him as "Old Fifty-Seven Varieties.")

TR realized that the gap between himself and Joe Murray, the Irish ward heeler who got him into the New York State Assembly, was unbridgeable outside of politics. But in America a low-born man had the opportunity—the *duty*—to fight his way up from the gutter, as Joe had done. He might then merit an invitation to lunch at Sagamore Hill, or at least tea, assuming he wore a clean shirt and observed decent proprieties. I should emphasize that TR was not a snob in the trivial sense. He had nothing but contempt for the Newport set, and the more languid members of the Four Hundred. When he said, at twenty-one, that he wanted to be a member of "the governing class," he was aware that it was socially beneath his own. At Albany, and in the Badlands, and as Colonel of the Rough Riders, he preferred to work with men who were coarse but efficient, rather than those who were polished and weak. He believed, he said, in "the aristocracy of worth," and cherished the Revolution that had allowed such an elite to rise to the top in government.

On the other hand (to use his favorite phrase) TR rarely appointed impoverished or unlettered men to responsible positions. He made great political capital, as President, out of the fact that his sons attended the village school at Oyster Bay with the sons of his servants—of whom at least one was black. However, as soon as the boys reached puberty, he whisked them off to Groton. Roosevelt was a patrician to the tips of his tapering fingers, yet he maintained till death what one correspondent called an "almost unnatural" identity with the masses. "I don't see how you understand the common people so well, Theodore," complained Henry Cabot Lodge. "No, Cabot, you never will," said TR, "because I am one of them, and you are not."

Here he deluded himself. His plebeian strength was due, as Lodge surmised, to understanding rather than empathy. "Whenever I see in an audience," the President told John Hay, "a grim-featured old fellow with a hickory shirt and no collar or cravat and only one gallus to keep up his trousers . . . there is a man to whom if I am only to strike the right note, I can surely appeal in the name of something loftier and better than his mere material well-being or advantage." One notes the rather patronizing tone of those words. Perhaps TR best defined his righteous appeal when he said that in addressing crowds he "tried to express the thoughts which they had in their hearts and minds, and felt but could not say."

The fourth and final major trait of Theodore Roosevelt's character was his militarism. I will not deal with it in much detail because it is a familiar aspect of him, and in any case did not manifest itself much during his presidency. There is no doubt that in youth and again in old age, he was in love with war, but oddly enough of all our great presidents to date, he was the most pacific (indeed, he won the Nobel Peace Prize in 1906) and the only one not thought of as a wartime leader.* He did not lack for military influences as a child. Four of his Georgian ancestors had been military men, and stories of their exploits were told him by his mother. Two of his uncles served with distinction in the Confederate Navy—a fact that he proudly boasts in his *Autobiography*, while making no reference to his father's civilian status.

---

* The Philippine War, which TR inherited from President McKinley, greatly vexed him, and he brought it to a somewhat contrived end in 1904.

When TR learned to read he reveled in stories "about the soldiers of Valley Forge, and Morgan's riflemen," and confessed, "I had a great desire to be like them." In his senior year at Harvard, he developed an interest in strategy and tactics, and began to write *The Naval War of 1812*. Within eighteen months he was the world expert on that subject. As soon as he left college he joined the National Guard in New York, and quickly became a captain. This stood him in good stead when he was called upon to lead a cavalry regiment in 1898. Throughout his literary years he made a study of historic campaigns, both classical and modern, and would wage imaginary battles with knives and forks and spoons on his tablecloth. No doubt much of this fascination with things military related to his natural aggression, but there was an intellectual attraction too: he read abstract tomes on armaments, navigation, ballistics, and line administration as greedily as swashbuckling memoirs. Nothing is more remarkable about *The Naval War of 1812* than its cold impartiality, its use of figures and diagrams to destroy patriotic myths. Roosevelt understood that major victories are won by thinking men, that mental courage is superior to mere physical bravado. Nobody thrilled to the tramp of marching boots more than he, but he believed that men should march only for "moral" reasons, in obedience to the written orders of a democratically elected Commander-in-Chief. In that respect, at least, the pen was mightier than the sword.

TO WHAT EXTENT DID these character traits—aggression, righteousness, pride, and militarism—affect TR's performance as President? The answer is, strongly, since he was a strong character and a strong Chief Executive. The way he arrived at the "personal equation" (his own phrase) of all four qualities is interesting, because he was in a weak position at the beginning of his first administration. When TR took the oath of office on 14 September 1901, he was the youngest man ever to do so (still only forty-two)—a vice president elevated by assassination, confronting a nervous Cabinet and a hostile Senate. Yet from the moment he raised his hand in Ansley Wilcox's little parlor in Buffalo, it was apparent that he intended to translate his personal power into presidential power. That hand did not stop at the shoulder. He raised it high above his head, and held it "steady as if carved out of marble." His right foot pawed the floor. *Aggression.* He repeated the words of the oath confidently, adding an extra phrase, not called for in the Constitution, at the end: "And so I swear." *Righteousness.*

His two senior Cabinet officers, John Hay and Lyman Gage, were not present at the ceremony. TR announced that they had telegraphed promises of loyalty to him. Actually they had not—they were thinking of resigning—but TR knew any such resignations would be construed as votes of no confidence in him, and he was determined to forestall them. By announcing that Hay and Gage would stay, out of loyalty to the memory of the dead President McKinley, he made it morally impossible for either man to quit. *Pride.* As for *militarism,* TR was seen much in the company of the New York State Adjutant General the next few days, and an armed escort of cavalrymen accompanied him wherever he went. This was perhaps understandable, in view of the fact that three presidents had been assassinated in the last thirty-five years, but it is a matter of record that more and more uniforms were seen glittering around TR as the months and years went on. Toward the end of his second administration *Harper's Weekly* complained (in an article entitled "Monarchical Manners in the White House"), "there has been witnessed under President Roosevelt an exclusiveness, a rigor of etiquette, and a display of swords and gold braid such as none of his predecessors ever dreamed of."

Reporters noticed TR's theatrical behavior at his inauguration, and I hereby confirm that he was one of the most flagrant showmen ever to tread the White House boards. He had a genius for dramatic entrances— and always made sure the spotlight was trained his way before he did so. The first thing he asked at Buffalo, for example, was "Where are all the newspapermen?" Only three reporters were present. His secretary explained that there wasn't room for more than three. "I think there is," TR said, and sent our for the rest of the press corps. Two dozen scribes joyfully crowded in, and the subsequent proceedings were reported to the nation with a wealth of detail unmatched in the history of earlier inaugurations.

Here again one sees a pattern of presidential performance developing. The exaggerated concern for reporters, the carefully staged gestures—it was as if he sensed at once that a tame press, and an infatuated public, would guarantee his political security. To win election in his own right in 1904 (TR's overriding ambition for the next three years), he would have to enlist their aid in moral warfare against his political opponents—notably, Senator Mark Hanna. (Hanna was chairman of the Republican National Committee, and the obvious choice to take over McKinley's government after "that damned cowboy," as he called Roosevelt, had filled in as interim caretaker.)

Except for reactionary resistance at both extremes of the political spectrum—the corporate-conservative and the left-wing populist—both press and public instantly fell in love with TR. Neither cared much that administratively and legislatively, he accomplished little in his first year in office. As David S. Barry of the New York *Sun* wrote, "Roosevelt's personality was so fascinating, so appealing to the popular fancy, so overpowering, so alive, and altogether so unique . . . it overshadowed his public acts; that is, the public was more interested in him, and the way he did things . . . than they were about what he did."

This does not mean that TR tried to please all the people all the time. He was quite ready to antagonize a large minority in order to win the approval of a small majority. The sods had hardly stopped rattling on McKinley's coffin when the White House issued the following statement:

> Mr. Booker T. Washington of Tuskegee, Alabama, dined with
> the President last evening.

This press release, the shortest and most explosive Washington had seen since the Civil War, has always been regarded as reluctant confirmation of the discovery of a reporter combing TR's guest book. Actually the President himself issued it at two o'clock in the morning, i.e., just in time for maximum exposure in the first edition of the newspapers. By breakfast time white supremacists all over the South were gagging over their grits at such headlines as ROOSEVELT DINES A NIGGER, and PRESIDENT PROPOSES TO CODDLE THE SONS OF HAM. Never before had a president entertained a black man in the first house of the land. The public outcry was deafening—horror in the South, acclamation in the North—but overnight nine million Negroes, hitherto loyal to Senator Hanna, trooped into the Rooseveltian camp.

Although I have no doubt TR had the redistribution of Southern patronage in mind when he sent his invitation to Booker T., another motive
was surely to stamp a bright, clear, first impression of himself upon the
public imagination. "I," he seemed to be saying, "am a man *aggressive*
enough to challenge a hundred-year prejudice, *righteous* enough to do
so for moral reasons, and *proud* enough to advertise the fact."

Again and again during the next seven years, he reinforced these perceptions of his personality. He aggressively prosecuted J. P. Morgan, Edward H. Harriman, and John D. Rockefeller—the holy trinity of American
capitalism—in the Northern Securities antitrust case; threw the Monroe Doctrine at Kaiser Wilhelm's feet like a token of war in the Carib-
bean; rooted out corruption in his own administration; and crushed
Hanna's presidential challenge by publicly humiliating the Senator at
an opportune moment in 1903. He righteously took the side of the
American worker and the American consumer against big business in
the great anthracite strike (as the first president ever to intervene in a
labor dispute); proclaimed the vanity of muckraking journalists; forced
higher ethical standards upon the food and drug industry; ordered the
dishonorable discharge of 160 Negro soldiers after the Brownsville
affair—on his own willful reading of the evidence, or lack thereof—and,
to quote Mark Twain, "dug so many tunnels under the Constitution that
the transportation facilities enjoyed by that document are rivaled only
by the City of New York."

The anthracite strike furnished a case in Twain's point. TR's obvious
sympathy for the miners that freezing fall of 1902, and for the millions of
Americans who could not afford a rise in fuel prices, began to worry conservative members of Congress. One day Representative James E. Watson was horrified to hear that the President had decided to send Federal
troops in to reopen the Pennsylvania mines on grounds of general hardship. Watson rushed round to the White House. "What about the Constitution of the United States?" he pleaded. "What about seizing private
property for public purposes without due processes of law?" TR wheeled,
shook Watson by the shoulder, and roared, "*To hell with the Constitution
when the people want coal!*"

It was remarks like that which caused Speaker Joe Cannon to sigh,

"Roosevelt's got no more respect for the Constitution than a tomcat has for a marriage license."

TR's *pride*, both in himself and his office, was particularly noticeable in his second term, the so-called imperial years when Henry James complained, "Theodore Rex is distinctly tending—or trying to make a court." This was an overstatement. Although the Roosevelts entertained much more elaborately than any of their predecessors, they confined their pomp and protocol to occasions of state. At times, indeed, they were remarkable for the all-American variety of their guests. On any given day a Rough Rider, a poet, a British viscount, a wolf hunter, and a Roman Catholic cardinal might be found at the White House table, each treated with the gentlemanly naturalness that was one of TR's most disarming traits. His pride manifested itself more noticeably in things like his refusal to address foreign monarchs as "Your Majesty" (he used the simple second person, counting them as equals), and in his offer to mediate the Russo-Japanese War (no previous American president had such global presumptions). When he won the Nobel Peace Prize for bringing that war to a conclusion, he declined to accept the $40,000 prize money personally. This was not an easy decision, because TR could have used the funds. He spent all of his presidential salary on official functions, and was not a particularly wealthy man. He confessed he would have liked to put the Nobel money into a trust fund for his children, but decided that it belonged to the United States.

Pride and patriotism were inseparable in Theodore Roosevelt's character. Indeed, if we accept Lord Morley's axiom that he "was" America, they may be considered complementary characteristics. And neither of them was false. Just as he was always willing to lose a political battle in order to win a political war, so in diplomatic negotiations he would sedulously allow his opponents the chance to save face, as long as the essential victory was his.

TR's *militarism* did not figure as largely in his presidential years as it did before and after. Under him, the organizational structure of the U.S. Army was revamped to strengthen the powers of the Commander-in-Chief, but Secretary of War Elihu Root was responsible for that. TR took deserved credit for expanding the American Navy from fifth to second place in the world during his seven and a half years of power—in keeping with his policy, inherited from George Washington, that "to be prepared for war is the most effectual means to promote peace." The gunboat TR sent to aid the Panama Revolution of 1903 is the only example of him shaking a naked mailed fist in the face of a weaker power. For the rest of the time he kept that fist sheathed in a velvet glove. The metaphor of velvet on iron, incidentally, was TR's own. It makes a refreshing change from the Big Stick, and it has inspired the title of a new study of TR's foreign policy by Frederick Marks.* I recommend the book to anyone interested in the record of one of the master diplomatists of the twentieth century.

If I may be permitted a final metaphor of my own, I would like to quote one from *The Rise of Theodore Roosevelt,* in an attempt to explain why, on the whole, TR's character shows to better advantage as President than in his years out of power.

> The man's personality was cyclonic, in that he tended to become unstable in times of low pressure. The slightest rise in the barometer outside, and his turbulence smoothed into a whir of coordinated activity, while a core of stillness developed within. Under maximum pressure Roosevelt was sunny, calm, and unnaturally clear.

This may explain why the first Roosevelt Era was a period of fair historical weather. Power became Theodore Roosevelt, and absolute power became him best of all. He loved being President, and was so good at his job that the American people loved him for loving it. He dreaded having to leave the White House, and let us remember that a third term was his for the asking in 1908. But his knowledge that power corrupts even the man who most deserves it, and his reverence for the Washingtonian principle that power must punctually revert to those whose gift it is, persuaded him to make this supreme sacrifice in his prime. For that, if for nothing else, let us remember old Fifty-Seven Varieties with admiration.

---

* Frederick W. Marks III, *Velvet on Iron: The Diplomacy of Theodore Roosevelt* (Lincoln, Nebraska, 1979).

THE LINE OF CONCERN

An Interview with Nadine Gordimer

AHOT SUNDAY AFTERNOON IN JOHANNESBURG. I WALK SILENTLY, on fallen jacaranda blossoms, through the wealthy part of town. Nannies snooze in the shade, their bare toes poked through the wheels of shiny perambulators. Doves croup in the mimosa trees. Lawn sprinklers hiss. I am tempted to rip off a granadilla, knowing that one mouthful of its pulp will evoke floods of *temps perdu,* but I also know that granadillas tend to squish in all directions, and Nadine Gordimer (judging from the coolness of her telephone voice) is not likely to be receptive to a sticky handshake.

Originally published in *The New York Times Book Review,* 7 June 1981.

Photograph of Nadine Gordimer by David Goldblatt, 1982.

It is not just the memory of the voice that makes me pause outside the large white walled-off house. From my first exposure to her work, I have been aware of her merciless eye—it was a Gordimer story, for example, that first alerted me to the ugliness of miniature trees—and her lack of humor daunts the would-be interviewer. Yet I can no longer deny myself the privilege of meeting South Africa's most formidable creative intelligence. I am already thirty-five seconds late for our appointment. I search for the bell.

No bell. The wall is high, the gate has no handle. I skulk round to the kitchen entrance. Black hands point me toward the rear garden. A gentleman rises in alarm from his newspaper; a mastiff roars for my blood; I take refuge in the house; and there, small and smiling in her caftan, is Nadine Gordimer.

We sit in a cool study, its window screened against the sunshine. From time to time she turns her face to this window, and the light sculpts her profile, of which, one suspects, she is rather proud. Elegant wings of gray hair flow off her brow. Her nose has a haughty arch to it. Her tapered hands gesture gracefully. She should be sketched in silverpoint.

"I've hurt my foot. You don't mind if I rest it here, do you?" She lifts it carefully, deposits it with a sigh. I remember the hurt foot in *Burger's Daughter:* "From under an eyelid of skin red pain runnelled. . . . " That is how her writing lingers in the mind: microscopic observation, language so sharp it stings.

"Miss Gordimer, your primary subject is this country, but unlike other South African writers you seem equally at home on the French Riviera, or the American motel circuit. Did you travel much as a child?"

"No, I never left Africa until I was thirty. Twenty-six years ago," she adds with a touch of feminine wistfulness. "Of course I'd preconceived the outside world through reading. When I stood in London for the first time it seemed familiar. But I saw it through Virginia Woolf's eyes, rather than my own. I have traveled a lot since then—all over Africa too, you know—and I do absorb what I experience. I suppose that explains—"

"Absorption, yes," I say. "You seem to have total recall. How do you achieve such density of description? Do you take thousands of notes?"

She is put out by the interruption. I sense that she cares about the shape of her spoken sentences, as if they are being written, so I let her continue at her own pace. The voice is quiet and measured, distinctly South African with its long *a*'s, pinched *i*'s, and singsong intonation.

"No, I have a purely subconscious recall. I don't feel I'm noticing much at the time, but it comes out afterwards in the flow of the writing. I remember sitting as a child in the back of my parents' car and somehow learning the landscape around us. I could reproduce every detail of it now. I listen too—I've always been a great eavesdropper in restaurants and buses. I'm fascinated by observed moments of tension between people: my mind immediately invents causes for this tension. I like"—she ponders the phrase—"to compose alternate lives."

"You must also do a certain amount of library research."

"Oh yes, I never write about anything I don't fully understand. *A Guest of Honor*, for example, required all sorts of knowledge about trade unions. But no amount of research can compensate for lack of personal experience. The only novel I couldn't finish dealt with the youthful experiences of a black African prime minister. It began well—a do-good Englishwoman abducts this unschooled, deprived child from Soweto, takes him to Botswana with her, educates him, and his potential explodes into politics. But just at this point of explosion, in his late teens, my inspiration failed me. I just couldn't follow him any further. He was moving into areas beyond the scope of my own adolescent experience. So the novel had to be set aside."

I stare at her, puzzled. "But it sounds familiar."

"Well I included it, you see, as one of my selected stories. I forget the title now. . . ." Again the profile turned to the window, her eyebrows raised in thought. "Ah, yes, 'Not for Publication.' "

The eyebrows, resettling, remind me of something else. "You wrote in your last novel of a 'vertical line of concern' between Lionel Burger's eyes. Your own line of concern—your political awareness—seems to have deepened over the years. Aren't you afraid it might become a deformity, distracting attention from your more artistic features?"

"Such as what?"

"Well, lyricism, drama—"

"Oh,"—she waves the first aside—"my lyrical powers don't seem important anymore. When one has seen so much of the world, one begins to be interested in fundamentals. Here we live in a society which is fundamentally out of joint. One cannot but be politically concerned. But I don't see myself, as an artist, becoming politically obsessed to the point that I start writing tracts. I don't understand politics except in terms of what politics does to influence lives. What interests me is the infinite variety of effects apartheid has on men and women."

"What effect has it had on you personally?"

"Well, rereading my stories—which I began writing when I was twenty—I am amazed at how I've changed in my attitude to blacks. The 'line of concern' was always there, of course, but I didn't quite understand *what* concerned me. For example, I wrote a story called 'Is There Nowhere Else Where We Can Meet?' about a young white woman who is confronted by a black tramp in wild country. She tries to toss her handbag at him, hoping the money will keep him from raping her. That gesture, that buying off—I was struck by the sheer fear of it. I couldn't write that way now."

"Now, on the contrary, you seem to seek out black contacts. Your new novel, *July's People*, has a white protagonist, yet takes place entirely in a *kraal*."

"That's where the virility is these days—in areas where white and black cultures clash." She is elegantly excited. The hurt foot comes down, and she leans forward, wincing. "I can't believe there's anybody born here, with a writer's sensitivity, who can't feel the potential. Our fathers' culture—white culture imported from Europe—never had a chance in the South African context. It wasn't indigenous: it wouldn't blend. All it did was to harm black culture. In missionary days, blacks had their own rich oral tradition—*we* superimposed literary forms upon it. In the process we suffered more than they. At least, today, blacks are expressing themselves in those forms. We, however, never appropriated anything from them. We've woken up to it rather late—can we now strike roots in what has been debased by us?"

"Can *you*?"

Miss Gordimer sits back, looking suddenly small and tired. "In a country like this," she sighs, "it's become the fashion to say that whites can't write about blacks, and vice versa. To you or me a white character in a black novel might seem like a caricature, or simply crude and inaccurate. Nevertheless *that's how they see us.* We must try to see them with equal clarity. If there is to be a true South African culture . . . " She pauses for a long time. Outside the house, crickets are beginning to sing; the quick African night descends. " . . . there should have been an inter-mingling of black and white."

I note the shift of tense from future conditional to past regretful. "You sound"—I suppress the word *pessimistic*—"a little unsure that it can ever happen."

"Who can be sure of anything in politics? In life?" She is smiling now, mocking her own presumptions. "I'm only trying to find out what it all means, and still haven't, quite."

A STRANGENESS IN THE SIGHT

The Shadow World of Tom Bostelle

Here, late one fall afternoon, is the Brandywine River, sliding south under the bridge at Lenape, Pennsylvania. Pause as you cross. Lean on the parapet, look down at your face trembling in the clear water below. A chain of bubbles drifts through your eye socket; pale fronds of algae veil your temples. You stretch out your hand, and the sun spills through your fingers, setting them coldly on fire.

To your right, on the east bank, stands a silent, shut-down amusement park. Carousel horses rest paralyzed in midplunge, impaled on their own poles. Torn posters hang in the motionless air. A barker's box

Originally published in *Quest81*, June 1981.

The Pink Perambulator. *Oil painting by Tom Bostelle, 1960.*

lies suffused in shadow—is that the deeper shadow of a man inside it, or merely a hole in the shape of a bowler hat?

To your left, on rickety piles along the stream, sprawls an ancient dance hall. It appears from this angle to be ruined, but as the roar of a northbound car dies away (you did not see the car—only a speeding shadow as it passed), you can hear Bach cello music floating out from under the eaves. You step off the bridge, follow a sign marked AEOLIAN PALACE GALLERY, and descend a path to step onto a long, creaky porch. The music grows louder as you approach a half-open door. You are entering the world of Tom Bostelle.

At first sight it seems to be a world of no color. To eyes still full of outside glare, the cavernous space is a bewildering *chiaroscuro* of half-lit objects. Huge frames soar toward the rafters, their contents screened by dozens of smaller frames, awkwardly stacked. An upended canoe and an armchair piled with boxes deny access to a triptych that has fragments of other paintings pinned to it. Cobwebs becloud an assortment of glassed-in sketches. A carved wooden eagle, its head knocked off, lies in an old basketwork perambulator. All these things are bathed in the eerie light effects of a riverside room: dapples through the doorway, blades of sunshine slicing between planks.

Only gradually, as your eyes adjust, do you realize that the Aeolian Palace is full of exquisite art—art made out of shadows rather than substance, planes instead of rounds, surfaces seen through other surfaces with no apparent mass in between. Here again, subtly distorted, are the floating faces and the ambiguous silhouettes of the Brandywine Valley. Some of those light effects, it turns out, are not real but contrived. The pale refractions on a female nude do not slip off when you lift the picture up. The shadow cast across a bluegreen perspective is not your own but that of the artist, who "left" it behind when he walked away from the easel. Judging from his painted profile, he seems to be a hulking man with an outthrust jaw and heavy, dangerous shoulders.

Bostelle himself is nowhere to be seen, but the cello music, coming from a separate studio at the end of the building, indicates where he can be found. You knock on the door with some trepidation. Such personal descriptions as you may have gathered on your journey up the Brandywine are not likely to put you at ease. "This is Wyeth country, you know—he's always resented that. There's a lot of rage in Tom, although he tries to be polite." Or, "Just don't get him on a bad day, that's all. He's temperamental as hell."

Today must be a good one, for Bostelle seems to welcome the intrusion. He switches off the radio. "That's okay, come on in. I'm not working this afternoon. But I *am* trying to prepare a lecture for tonight, so don't stay *too* long, if you don't mind." His handshake warns you that for years he had to work steel to keep from starving, yet his body is neither as big nor as threatening as his self-portraits suggest.

Tom Bostelle is a tough, medium-sized man of fifty-nine whose unkempt hair and stubbly cheeks do not obscure the fact that he is handsome. He looks well washed and well laundered, yet his clothing is shabby even by the infamous standards of his profession. It consists of a bulbous sweater, vibrating here and there with loose knots of wool, a thrift-shop shirt, jeans stiff with paint, and unzipped boots. In one hand he carries a bottle of beer from which he never sips. He holds it at an angle precisely calculated at the point of spilling: its lack of head suggests it has been opened for an hour or more.

He is alert, as artists always are, to the movements of his visitor's eyes. "That's a portrait of my old army sergeant in Guadalcanal, in 1944. Literature buff. Loved to talk books with me, but when I switched the subject to painting he began to look lost, like that. . . . Not bad for a kid! Of course my style was realistic then." The sergeant gazes wistfully down, a half-read book in his hand. Thirty-six years, and untold refinements of style, separate this portrait and the unfinished nude on Bostelle's easel. The latter is little more than a pale wash suggestive of opening thighs and arms, but a woman's face, heavy with desire, is already painted in. Her supplicatory attitude is, oddly, not unlike that of the scholarly soldier.

Both paintings, in short, suggest the presence off-canvas of a man aloof, and Bostelle, for all his boyish friendliness, is clearly that person. He is eager for intelligent response to his work, but as soon as comments degenerate into mere praise his smile hardens and he looks away impatiently. Even now, as he conducts a courteous tour of the studio, his voice frequently tails off as he contemplates this work and that, repainting it in his head. He whips out a piece of sandpaper and scratches at a landscape with it. "Hard edge here, soft edge there. You see how it makes the planes tilt? And *look* what's coming out here. Lovely, lovely!" Ghostly remnants of some earlier version surface as the new paint sands away. Image collides with image, a sudden chasm seems to yawn between hills half an inch apart. Bostelle backs off, chuckling with glee. He starts when reminded he is not alone.

"Ah, yes, *The Pink Perambulator.* One of my arrivals."

Arrivals? "I call a painting that when it somehow *arrives* at the point I'm driving at. I step back and shout, '*That's it!*' "

The terrifying shadow careering downstairs and backward tugs, like many Bostelle "arrivals," at something recently seen. Of course! An old perambulator near the door. But this vehicle carries, instead of a headless eagle, a child—or an old woman?—screaming, perhaps with an eagle's voice. Above and beyond the blood-colored silhouette, a series of lightly sketched heads, wearing such hats as were fashionable in the Aeolian Palace's heyday, stare sightlessly out of frame. Older mental images stir: the Odessa Steps sequence in *Battleship Potemkin,* the second chapter of Graham Greene's autobiography. Bostelle is willing to entertain such references (he is a compulsive reader and moviegoer), but he will not be pinned down to specific comment. "My theme was simply indifference," he says, shrugging. "You can see what you like in it."

The studio tour begins to accelerate in the direction of the door. Bostelle pauses briefly by two epic works in progress. One, eleven feet high by fifteen, looks finished but is unsigned. It represents seven months of knee-crippling ladder work, and (the artist admits proudly) forty years of thought. Despite its huge size, the composition seems to breathe air and light. A dozen or so translucent figures mix and merge in a silvery nimbus of white and blue, tinged here and there with terra-cotta. Something about the curve of a hat brim here, the thrust of a pike there, evokes vague memories of—what? "Rembrandt's *Night Watch,*" Bostelle confirms. "Actually this is a study in *pentimento.* There are at least five celebrations of Rembrandt buried underneath—you can see bits of them showing through."

Celebrations? "Oh yes, all my paintings celebrate something. Art should be joyous."

The other canvas, which Bostelle calls *Local Journey,* is patently autobiographical in that it fuses segments of his earlier work, bodily cut from old paintings, with the images that have preoccupied him in recent years: Christlike children on carousel horses, shadowy men in hoods, naked women glimpsed through screens or floating "panes" that gracefully distort their bodies.

More tugs at the memory. Was it not Robert Frost who wrote of the hypnotic effect of gazing at reality through prisms?

> *I am drowsing off.*
> *I cannot rub the strangeness from my sight*
> *I got from looking through a pane of glass*
> *I skimmed this morning from the drinking trough*
> *And held against the world of hoary grass . . .*

Bostelle scowls at the mention of Frost's name. "He came here once, shaking hands at some reception, and said to me, 'Do you also paint like Wyeth?' I said, 'No, I paint like *Bostelle*' and turned my back on him."

He slides the door open, evidently eager for solitude. Then, to soften the sense of dismissal, he asks, "Why don't you come to my lecture tonight? It'll mark the opening of my new show at the Chester County Art Association."

CIRCULATING IN THE CROWD at an opening-night exhibition is a good way of picking up biographical information, along with stray glimpses of art. Bostelle, apparently, has been the *enfant terrible* of this wealthy and conservative corner of Pennsylvania since his days as a truant West Chester schoolboy. Solitary, fatherless, and fiercely devoted to his mother, he would do nothing in class but paint. At thirteen his talent was so precocious that a committee of local patrons took him to a school for gifted children in Philadelphia. Young Tom was back home, painting, before the committee returned.

Quitting school at the earliest opportunity, he enrolled briefly at the Pennsylvania Academy of the Fine Arts, and, to pay his way, took the first of a twenty-year series of laboring jobs. His academic training was

soon abandoned for obsessive private study of the old masters, and cultivation of whichever living painters, musicians, and writers he could
meet. Horace Pippin, the great black primitive artist, submitted patiently
to Bostelle's youthful idolatry, and sat for a portrait that ended up in the
National Portrait Gallery. The artist gave a one-man show at seventeen,
won his first major award shortly afterward, and married just before the
army claimed him in 1943. Serving as an engineer in the Pacific and
Japan, he received a series of jolts to his artistic consciousness, including
a vision of crowds as dark waves of threat or suffering, moved by inscrutable forces.

His paintings grew increasingly somber after the war, as child followed child and poverty weighed upon him. Exhibits as far afield as Paris
won him prestige but no money. Bostelle was forced to spend more and
more time away from art: at one New York show he was billed as "a steelworker."

Revolutionary ideas have a way of germinating in the midst of despair, and Bostelle was possessed, one Jamesian afternoon in 1947, with
a concept of painting based on two dimensional shadow rather than
three-dimensional reality. His first triumph in this genre was *Severance of
Communication* (1951), which so impressed Lincoln Kirstein that New
York's Hewitt Gallery ordered a roomful of Bostelles for sale. But the pictures were too subtle, and the artist too uncompromising, for its fashionable clientele. Another New York show found only one buyer: Gloria
Vanderbilt.

A measure of security entered his life in 1961, when the Franz Bader
Gallery in Washington, D.C., began to sell his work at prices that esca-
lated steadily for a decade. Meanwhile word got around that the unshaven "steelworker" was capable of amazingly elegant portraits, and
a series of other Vanderbilts, du Ponts, and Philadelphia Main Liners
clamored to sit for him. Bostelle was forced to announce that he would
paint only those people who interested him.

With success came growing intractability, reclusiveness, and stylistic
experimentation. Bostelle became more and more his own man, to the
point that he gave up all big-city connections. With the help of his fellow
artist and business manager, Tania Boucher, he opened a gallery at the

Aeolian Palace in 1969 and began to sell directly to the public. Since then he has become something of a cult figure, collected by a small but widening circle of connoisseurs.

Why, then, is Bostelle's lecture, "The Figure in Art," so sparsely attended? Anybody surnamed Wyeth could pack not only the auditorium, but an overflow marquee as well. Part of the reason, one suspects, lies in the artist's eccentricity. Garrulous, rumpled, and grinning, he paces like a cougar in front of a row of nervous matrons, sucking noisily at a cola, and smacking at the projector screen with his pointer. "You see how that line flows and repeats here! There! Here! *Hah!*" Calm and articulate in private, he is not a good public speaker. At times his passion for art makes his words (enunciated with bizarre Harvard and London overtones) pour out in an incoherent flood. At others he practically chokes with the effort to translate sight into sound, and sympathetic listeners volunteer the word he is gasping for.

Eventually the rhythmic succession of slides on the screen calms him, and he becomes persuasive, even moving, as he demonstrates the art behind the art of his beloved masters—the cave painters of Lascaux, "dear, dear Rembrandt," Cézanne, and Balthus. (He caresses the last's *Golden Days* with the tenderness of a priest fingering an icon.) But as before in the studio, his voice tails off too often for total communication. Surrounded by ears that cannot hear, Bostelle is a man talking mainly to himself.

So too with his art. Perhaps those hauntingly poignant refractions of inner emotion will always remain a minority taste in a world where the majority prefers the recognizable banalities of an Andrew Wyeth. ("There are guys around here who make a living painting the other side of barns painted by Andy," Bostelle says, smiling wickedly.) Perhaps he should not have quit the big-city circuit when he did. There are signs now and then of resurgent ambitions that must burst the narrow confines of the Brandywine Valley. His latest works are too overwhelming for anything except a big museum.

Yet the images that linger when you leave the world of Bostelle are not his epic achievements so much as the elusive inspirations that make his "arrivals" unique. The spectral hands of shadow passengers in a car that seems to be soaring toward the sun; the profile of a beautiful woman split into shards; those sleepy-eyed children riding carousel horses into space; such things do not fade, nor do the unpainted Bostelles that you will see for weeks afterward in odd window reflections, darkened doorways, or the ghosts of an unfocused television screen.

Once you have gazed through Bostelle's painted panes, you will never quite rub the strangeness from your sight.*

* Tom Bostelle died in 2005. Some of his art may be seen at tombostelle.net.

THE PEN IS MIGHTIER THAN
THE SMITH CORONA

Typing and the Murder of Style

W HEN ROBERT LOUIS STEVENSON WAS A CHILD, HE DREAMED of thousands of pens scratching across paper. The fact that he found the sound sensuously satisfying was prophetic of his future career. As a mature writer he wielded his pen happily, until "a wilful convulsion of brute nature" stilled it in midsentence, leaving unfinished *Weir of Hermiston*, the most magnificent stretch of narrative in nineteenth-century English fiction.

Today's would-be Stevensons dream, presumably, not of scratching pens, but of the buzz, rattle, and smack of typewriters (interrupted periodically by a bell, and that sickening *swishhhh-thunkk* of carriage return). But if a modern author dies in midsentence, I suspect that the element of grace will be lacking in his last words. The typewriter, as Finley Peter Dunne remarked, is "the murderer of style."

Originally published in *Quest81*, September 1981.
Original article illustration by Gary Allen, 1981.

Consider its mechanics. It is designed, along with such other lethal instruments as the guillotine and the torpedo, to move as fast as possible in one direction. Getting it to reverse tracks to alter something is a major operation. Depending on your model, you either have to drag the carriage sideways by main force or else prod a key that makes it shudder hideously in reverse, like an armadillo trying to back up a washing board.

When you finally get to the phrase that needs improving, you have to rotate the platen downward in order to squeeze fresh words above it. You mustn't rotate *too* far, however, otherwise your insert will collide with the preceding line. So you search out that button that frees the platen, find a midway level, and tap the new characters out. Then you press the button again, rotate to an approximation of the old level, and zip forward to where you left off. But damn! Just when the machine is rattling back into action, you notice out of the corner of your eye that you forgot to xxxxxxx out the original offending phrase. . . .

Because of this awkwardness, the tendency of the typer, as opposed to the writer (in Truman Capote's famous distinction), is to move ever forward, ever faster. Why waste thirty seconds revising an obscure clause, when you can tack on an explanatory sentence in five? Hence paragraphs come out longer than they should be, and an accretion of verbal debris weighs the typescript down. Such debris, of course, can be cleared away in revision. But the tolerance that permitted it in the first place tends to lower critical standards the second time around.

The pen, on the other hand, is an instrument of thrilling mobility. Its ink flows as readily as the writer's imagination. Its nib flickers back and forth with the speed of a snake's tongue, deleting a cliché here, an adjective there, then rearing up suddenly into white space and emitting a spray of new words.

Just as important is the pen's ability to dawdle in midstroke, fattening the curve of a *y*, for example, while pondering whether to follow up with a comma or not. The pen is patient, as instruments of art must be. Unlike the electric typewriter, it does not buzz irritatedly when motionless, as if to say, *Hurry up, I'm overheating.* It sits quietly in the hand, comforting the fingers with acquired warmth, assuring you that the sentence you are searching for lies somewhere in its liquid reservoir. There is no keener pleasure, for a blocked writer, than to see those longed-for words uncurl from the nib, and dry into permanence on the page.

This physical delight in handwriting is something foreign to today's keyboard-bashers. But no one examining the manuscripts of some of the great writers of the past, such as Dickens, Keats, and Stephen Crane, can fail to sense the joy they felt when words and ink were flowing well. William Dean Howells and Henry James are classic examples of stylists "murdered" by the typewriter. James did not actually type himself, but he dictated his last novels directly to a stenographer, and the clacking of her keys stimulated him to regrettable orotundities. One rereads *Washington Square* and sighs for the lost delicacy of his handwritten style.

It is not necessary, of course, to be an elegant penman to be an elegant phrasemaker. Some of literature's shapeliest scribes—Thomas Hardy, Arnold Bennett, William Faulkner—wrote their fair share of clunking prose. The reverse is also true. A Tolstoy holograph looks like a cross-section of one of his own haystacks at Yasnaya Polyana, yet we all know what pure perfume breathes from those tangled stalks.

Today, alas, the tyranny of the keyboard seems virtually complete. It is no longer possible for one writer to recognize another by the telltale lump of callous on the first knuckle of the second finger. The author whose security (and delicious freedom) is a pen in his pocket is looked on as an eccentric. I once traveled abroad with an American journalist and saw him reduced to wordlessness because he had forgotten to pack an adapter for his Smith Corona. But he waved aside my spare Montblanc with loathing. "Maybe I can rent a cassette recorder."

It may be significant that the few good stylists we have left tend to be pen-and-ink men. Shelby Foote's calligraphy makes his three volumes on the Civil War works of art as well as literature. William Styron, Gore Vidal, and the highly regarded short-story writer Mark Helprin all write in longhand. With the price of electric current rising hourly, aspirant authors should practice this sweet discipline. Simply follow the instructions of one of the finest wordsmiths of them all:

> *Take a pot of ink and a pen—either a goose or turkey quill or, failing them, a wooden penholder with a metal nib. Hold it so that your fingers are at least ¾ inch from the point. Dip the point ¼ inch in the ink. If*

you keep the point downwards there is no possibility of the ink flowing up to the fingers. Do not wipe the nib in your hair or on your face. Do not suck it. You will find that you remain perfectly clean.

Evelyn Waugh added a useful footnote: *If you balance a basket of eggs on your head while writing, it will help cure curvature of your spine.*

MUSIC V. MUSICOLOGY

Sir Donald Francis Tovey, Counsel for the Defense

MUSICAL ANALYSIS, TRADITIONALLY ONE OF THE DRIEST OF prose forms, has reached new extremes of desiccation since Sir Donald Francis Tovey died in 1940. One wonders what that cantankerous pedagogue, whose passion for melody was such he once started from a dinner table, crying, at the sound of a distant music box, would think of the work of, say, the cryptographer Eric Sams, who seems to want to prove that Schumann wrote propositional calculus. Tovey could be as cerebral as the next man, as his bar-by-bar *Companion to Beethoven's Piano Sonatas* proves, yet he felt a lifelong, almost religious reverence for the sound that gives delight, and hurts not.

Originally published in *Harper's Magazine*, December 1981.

Portrait of Tovey, ca. 1936, by Sir William Rothenstein.

This reverence was backed by a learning so profound as to intimidate all who came into his presence. Even old Joseph Joachim, an intimate of Brahms and the preeminent violinist of the nineteenth century, conceded that Tovey, at twenty-two, knew more about music than anybody alive. He was also—unusually for a musician—erudite in other intellectual fields. In 1898 he graduated from Oxford with classical honors in philosophy and literature, and the resultant cross-fertilization gave a richness to his critical writing surpassing that of George Bernard Shaw. Who among today's theory-obsessed musicologists could draw such graceful parallels between Berlioz and Cyrano de Bergerac, or liken a peculiar coupling of bassoons and fourth-string violins in Haydn's *Creation* to Tennyson's "moan of doves in immemorial elms"?

MY OWN DISCOVERY of Tovey's classic *Essays in Musical Analysis* (7 vols., Oxford, 1935–1944) in the library of the Prince of Wales School, Nairobi, Kenya, was roughly coincident with my discovery of music itself. Indeed the latter commodity was in such short supply (the local airwaves were dominated by the stride recordings of Charlie Kunz, and marches played by the King's African Rifles) that my first "hearings" of most of the masterpieces of the repertoire were not through my own ears, but by proxy through Tovey's. Fortunately he had an uncanny gift for describing the indescribable:

> The tonic is restored with a sudden plunge into extreme darkness. Out of subdued mutterings the first theme again arises and hovers, while the air seems full of whisperings and the beating of mighty wings.

That was the coda of the first movement of Brahms's B-flat major Piano Concerto. How I thrilled to its extraordinary sound when, years later, I first got hold of the Wilhelm Backhaus recording! To this day I cannot hear those bass trills without sensing, somewhere overhead, "the beating of mighty wings."

I fell further under the influence of Tovey when, at the age of fourteen, I wrote to the Associated Board of the Royal Schools of Music for his edition of the Beethoven piano sonatas. The dark red volumes arrived several months later, somewhat the worse for Mombasa mildew, but with all the music and Tovey's thirty-two commentaries intact. So closely did I pore over his every word, in relation to every note, that as I struggled to play the sonatas in turn, I began to hallucinate Sir Donald bending over me.

"A hail-storm," he would murmur, after too many octaves *martellato,* "is more sublime than a coal-shoot." Thanks to his preternatural aural sensitivity, I came to appreciate subtleties such as the staccato bass in the slow movement of Op. 2, No. 2, which reinforces the handheld harmony above through sympathetic vibration of open strings, "like a very ethereal pedal." When I quailed before the icy abstractions of the late sonatas, Tovey encouraged me to persevere. "It is no use deferring the study of such music until you feel ripe for it," he would say. "Remember that experience cannot come except by experience."

I SUSPECT THAT Tovey's own understanding of Beethoven came not from experience, but from that mysterious spring in which the musically gifted bathe as infants. Born the son of an Eton schoolmaster, on 17 July 1875, he soon emerged as a child prodigy, and was composing at the age of eight. A formidable female pianist, Sophie Weisse, undertook to train him for the concert platform, and she became his mother-substitute, educating him at her private school for girls. The psychic scars this may have caused can only be guessed at. It is a matter of record that Tovey's first marriage was desperately unhappy, and that his mature compositions (which include an opera, a piano concerto, and much chamber music) suffered from a lack of emotional fullness.

Whether or not his larger gifts were thus cramped, young Tovey flourished around the turn of the century as pianist, composer, and concertmaster. He was already drawn to the art of musical analysis. Some of the collected *Essays* date back as far as 1900. These early pieces, which were written to accompany his own concerts, are by no means inferior to the products of his old age. Indeed the most masterly item in the whole canon, "The Classical Concerto," was published in 1908, when Tovey was twenty-eight.

London concert audiences, used to pretty little Victorian program leaflets, with a paragraph or two vaguely descriptive of musical sense, were intimidated by his gigantic analyses—that of Bach's *Goldberg Variations*, for example, extending to twenty-four thousand words, or forty-eight pages of print, densely packed with musical examples. Conscientious listeners who tried to read them on the spot were frustrated when a symphony came to an end while they were still pondering Tovey's explanation of the *adagio* introduction. What was more, his frequent wisecracks at the expense of popular idols (such as a remark, apropos of *Childe Harold's Pilgrimage* and *Harold in Italy*, that "no definite elements of Byron's poem have penetrated the impregnable fortress of Berlioz's encyclopaedic inattention") had about them an air of intellectual arrogance. It was generally agreed that Tovey was "too clever by half" and the public began to boycott his concerts.

His career languished, although he continued to appear as pianist with the Joachim Quartet until 1914. Then, in his fortieth year, he was appointed Reid Professor of Music at Edinburgh University, and found the niche he was to occupy in tranquillity the rest of his life. "The Athens of the North" perfectly suited him, and he became famous as a teacher. Swarms of bright young people clustered in his piano studio to hear him play, and be borne away like dragonflies on the stream of his conversation—brilliant, humorous, and free-flowing, liable at any moment to burst the bounds of subject and spill over the whole field of human knowledge. The word *genius* appears too often in the published reminiscences of these students, many of whom became distinguished musicians, for us to doubt its validity. "It has never been my good fortune to meet anybody," writes the composer W. B. Wordsworth, "whose mind and soul seemed so to dwarf all other views of music as did his."

Professor Tovey founded the Reid Orchestra (1917) and organized the Reid concerts, which still dignify Edinburgh's musical life. At the urging of his students he resumed his youthful practice of writing analyses to accompany every program. Despite his repeated pleas that he was an apologist, rather than a musicologist ("The duty of the 'writer of programme notes' is that of counsel for the defence"), these witty and scholarly leaflets were circulated to connoisseurs all over the world, and pressure grew for their publication in book form. In 1935, he grumblingly consented to edit them. The first three volumes of *Essays in Musical Analysis*, covering symphonies from Haydn through Holst, and concertos from Mozart through Walton, were published that year by Oxford University Press. Vols. 4 and 5 (illustrative and vocal music) appeared in 1937, and Vol. 6 (a series of miscellaneous essays, plus glossary and index) in 1939. Four years after his death on 10 July 1940, a final "Supplementary Volume" made available his unpublished writings on chamber music. These seven books, covering more than 250 works, have never been out of print, and comprise the most distinguished body of music criticism in the language.

Rereading them, I am struck by their cumulative impression of youthful ardor. Whether an essay dates from his twenties or his sixties, the freshness of Tovey's feelings (so reminiscent of Robert Schumann's) is the same. Age cannot weary his love of music, nor custom stale his response to compositions he must have heard and taught thousands of times. The "counsel for the defence" is always there, arguing with flushed face and wig askew on behalf of his clients. He conscientiously addresses us, the open-minded jury, rather than the judge who understands nothing but academic rules and regulations.

Tovey's list of clients is a restricted one, consisting mainly of Germanic composers of the eighteenth and nineteenth centuries. Chopin receives scant attention, as do Tchaikovsky, Dvořák, Debussy, and, oddly enough, Handel. Purcell and Monteverdi are barely mentioned, Stravinsky and Bartók ignored altogether. What twentieth-century names do appear on the list are (except for Sibelius) clearly included out of a sense of duty rather than pleasure. Tovey tries hard to be open-minded, but his impatience shows. Richard Strauss is accused of "frequent bursts of prettiness." There are several respectful essays on Sir Edward Elgar, yet they are rendered dubious by Tovey's naughty retitling of *The Dream of Gerontius* as "Gerry's Nightmare"—a name that still sticks in some British circles.

Most of the essays therefore concern themselves with Bach and the Viennese classics: Haydn, Mozart, Beethoven, Schubert, Schumann, and Brahms. This does not mean that Tovey is incapable of recognizing and promoting obscure talent. Indeed his eloquent piece on Joachim's "Hungarian" Concerto persuades us that it is one of the most important documents in Romantic music. Nor does Tovey reject all composers alien to him—his essays on Berlioz, for example, are among his freshest and funniest. (At one point he disarmingly confesses that although Berlioz's music tempts him to irreverence, he feels "fierce resentment against anyone who dares to say a word against it.") The pure musician in Tovey cannot help but respond to originality, however much it offends his taste. He reserves his contempt for meretricious composers, as when he remarks of Meyerbeer studying with the tubercular Weber, "It is a pity [they] did not exchange their physical constitutions."

ALLOWING FOR TOVEY'S essential conservatism, well-tempered music lovers may still browse these volumes with delight, and educate themselves besides. He takes for granted only a rudimentary knowledge of musical notation and terminology, and even the latter is further elucidated by an excellent glossary in Vol. 6. Do not make the mistake of reading the *Essays* chronologically. As the author reminds us, they were produced at various times and under many circumstances, so repetitions and inconsistencies abound. The best way to read them is to remember that they were written either in anticipation of a musical performance, or in the dreamy mood after one, well described by Shelley: "Music, when soft voices die, / Vibrates in the memory."

Individual essays vary greatly in length as well as depth. You may be disappointed that Schubert's big C major Symphony rates only six pages (an indication, not of Tovey's disrespect, but of the limits of his original program booklet). On the other hand, you will find that Beethoven's Ninth gets two definitive treatments: a bar-by-bar *précis* in Vol. 1, and a forty-five-page prose analysis in Vol. 2. Pretty well all the staple works of the concert repertory are covered.

Tovey's major musical arguments stand out self-evidently. The introduction to Vol. 1 propounds his essential creed, "that no piece of music can be understood from *a priori* generalizations as to form. . . . All music must be followed phrase by phrase as a process in time." In other words, the shape of a symphony is never perceived whole, as is the silhouette of a cathedral, or the composition of a painting. Instead, it continuously reveals new aspects of itself, so its form is not apparent until it is over.

And *then*, of course, it has no form at all. Tovey goes on to blast "theories of absolute music which apply equally well to absolute nonsense." He has no patience with the kind of analysis that seeks to visit the laws of geometry on something essentially plastic. His essays show that all works of genius, however "perfect" their proportions may seem, are subtly irregular.

"The Classical Concerto," introducing Vol. 3, is a revelatory demonstration of the fact that this most instrumental of forms is actually vocal in origin. Indeed it derives even farther afield than in music itself:

> Nothing in human life and history is much more thrilling or of more ancient and universal experience than the antithesis of the individual and the crowd; an antithesis which is familiar in every degree, from flat opposition to harmonious reconciliation, and with every contrast and blending of emotion, and which has been of no less universal prominence in works of art than in life. Now the concerto forms express this antithesis with all possible force and delicacy. . . . The classical composers, to whom music was music no matter how profoundly it affected humanity, adapted their art-forms to this condition of the antithesis between one and many, or between greater and less.

This whole essay is a *locus classicus* of the art of communicating musical intangibles in tangible prose. It is full of characteristic imagery, such as his explanation that Bach's vast forms change, with new instrumentation, "no more . . . than the forms of mountains change as the light falls at morning and evening." And I cannot resisting quoting Tovey's *mot*, "A bad cadenza is the very appendicitis of music."

Vol. 4 features a double analysis of Beethoven's *Leonora* Overtures No. 2 and 3, full of acute insight into the thought processes of that tortured genius. Vol. 5 contains six splendid essays on Bach's choral music, notably the B minor Mass, and Vol. 6 includes a famous diatribe, "Wagner in the Concert Room." The Supplementary Volume, arguably the most valuable of the seven, has Tovey's magisterial analysis of the *Goldberg Variations*, plus another of *Die Kunst der Fugue*. The latter essay was written to accompany a complete recording of 1936, in which Tovey himself worked out the last, unfinished fugue on the piano. He was prouder of this achievement than of anything else he ever did.

The old professor's final words are contained in a charmingly garrulous "Retrospective and Corrigenda," appended to Vol. 6. In this essay Tovey looks back over his lifelong love affair with music and cheerfully admits that sometimes, in his passion, he has slipped up over minor pedantic points. A typical slip that New Musicologists chortle over is his defense as "subtle" a note in Bach's F-sharp minor Prelude (Book Two of the "Forty Eight") which does not appear on the original manuscript.

Tovey was inspired, apparently, by a printer's error. But he is serenely unrepentant. The Adornists and Schenkerians may make what they like of him. "Peace be to their waste-paper baskets and to mine."

LAND OF LOST CONTENT

South Africa Revisited in the Last Days of Apartheid

THERE IS A BIRD IN SOUTH AFRICA CALLED THE HONEY BIRD. IT *likes to gorge itself on beehives, but dislikes being stung in the process. So it calls out to man with a compelling note, and flies from tree to tree leading him toward a hive. When man has chased the bees away and taken all the comb he wants, the Honey Bird swoops down and feasts on the remainder.*

As a dropout from Rhodes University in the early 1960s, I followed a Honey Bird of sorts to Natal, and the Transvaal, and Southern Rhodesia, but none of the musky repositories it sought had any appeal for me. I craved more sophisticated sweets, available only in the northern hemisphere at gourmet stores that also, no doubt, purveyed the milk of Paradise. The desperate Bird

Copyright © 1982 by *National Review*, Inc. Reprinted by permission.
Table Mountain seen from Bloubergstrand, South Africa. Photograph by David Goldblatt, 1986.

was forced to flap farther and farther afield—across the Equator, through Europe, west over the Atlantic. It was 1968 before we finally reached Manhattan, and thirteen years more before we could afford to splurge at Zabar's delicatessen on the Upper West Side. Now, satiated, my tired Bird wishes to go home. I visit the South African Airways counter at JFK and buy two tickets to Johannesburg—one single, one return. Within twenty-four hours the Honey Bird has been set free. As his happy squawks fade away, I find myself standing alone in the city of my earliest memories.

Johannesburg looks smaller and shabbier than when I last knew it. I stare in amazement at the sheer, jostling number of black people on the sidewalks, and realize that as a white African I never really "saw" them before. They were an unnoticed part of the cityscape, a benign, if fecund, species of local fauna. I stroll along Commissioner Street and take a quick color survey of passers-by. It works out to five blacks to every white, precisely the national average. In this inexorable ratio lies the dread of the ruling minority, both Afrikaans- and English-speaking. There is little feeling of threat in the air, although two *tsotsis* do stare thoughtfully at my wallet pocket.

Can this little skyscraper be Eskom House? I remember ascending it as a boy, convinced that its twenty-fourth-floor observation window was the world's supreme elevation. Peering up now, I am overwhelmed with the desire to make a private pilgrimage to the poorer part of town.

Rosettenville, on the edge of the mine dumps, is where my mother was born and raised. She returned there temporarily from Kenya when I was three, while my father did a spell of RAF duty in Egypt. We stayed in my grandmother's flat, and I went to an infants' school nearby.

I find the neighborhood subtly transformed. The ugly little brick houses have been decorated with grapevines and pink and blue shutters. A fishmonger advertises fresh *bacalhau,* and the cinema where I saw *Pinocchio* is now showing something called *A Ilha dos Amores.* Rosettenville has evidently "gone Portuguese" since the fall of Mozambique. I am afraid that Victoria Court will be transformed too, but the squat apartment block is much the same, and its privet hedge gives off an achingly familiar fragrance. Walking down Daisy Street, I come upon Mrs. Lucas's schoolyard. After thirty-five years the plumbago bushes are still profuse with sticky blue flowers, and apricots are ripening in the trees that shaded us during out-of-door lessons. Under those branches, in 1943, I winced at the squeaking of Mrs. Lucas's chalk, and learned the mysterious incantation *affa apple, biffa bat, ciffa cat. . . .*

The afternoon sun grows hot, and jet lag beclouds my brain. I cross to the park opposite, and flop down in a jacaranda grove. Here, lulled by the sound of Portuguese children at play, Mrs. Lucas's erstwhile pupil drowses off.

I WAKE UP MUCH LATER, in the shocked realization that I am late for tea with one of my aunts. I call to apologize. "No hurry, dear. But I'm glad you rang, because I've located that revolutionary friend of yours."

"Mike Kirkwood?" I am overjoyed. "Fantastic, Aunt Peg! How? Where?"

"Right here in Joburg. I mentioned his name to Aunt Pat, and she mentioned it to Aunt Sheila, and *she* said she knew Mike's aunt—" Her voice undulates on, while I think of P. G. Wodehouse's line about aunt calling aunt like mastodons across some primeval swamp.

Time was when Mike and I were beach bums together. We enrolled as students at Natal University, Durban, but we spent our days bodysurfing, and our nights writing reams of poetry. His effusions were generally to do with the liberation of the blacks. Mine were about a girl with hair like maize silk. We lived for months on mashed bananas. When the banana season came to an end, Kirkwood and I went our separate ways—he into underground political activity, I to foreign fields. The last I heard of Mike was that he was in jail, writing Marxist tracts with burnt matches. . . .

Aunt Peg's voice reclaims my attention: "So I rang him in his office and told him you were here. He sounded delighted."

"Mike in an office? Don't tell me he's stooped to capitalist employment!"

"Well, I'm not sure what *kind* of office." She gives me the address. "He says he'll be there till six."

I REACH MY DESTINATION, a nondescript building near the university, with ten minutes to spare, and walk through doors marked RAVAN

PRESS—BOOKS FOR AFRICA. A huge Geronimo-like figure, all forelock and cheekbones, unfolds from behind a desk.

"I'd forgotten how tall you were," I say. "I always think of you as sort of horizontal—you know, sticking out of a wave and shouting at me to get out of the way."

We reminisce about our beachcombing days, eyeing each other nervously. I am intrigued by Kirkwood's respectable white shirt and tie, and the profusion of glossy publications laid out for my inspection. He is plainly anxious to talk about his work, but I force him into a review of the years lost to me. Imprisonment in 1964 for alleged political activities prejudicial to the stability of the Republic; early liberation, thanks to a quirk in the banning laws; a lectureship in English at the University of Natal; adulation by dozens of female students, one of whom he married; birth of three sons; two years in England, writing a book on the literature of colonialism; poverty; odd jobs with buckets and betting boards; a hasty return to South Africa in 1973, when the black trade unions began to rise ("I felt I was needed"); further lecturing; a cycle of poems published.

"Then in seventy-seven I got a call from this publishing house. It was going downhill, would I like to take over? I was so bored with academe, I thought, *Why not!* And you know, the moment I got here . . ."

He turns shy, and lights a cigarette. I pick up the Ravan catalog. It is elegantly printed on heavy stock, and runs to twenty-eight pages. "For a house that was going downhill, Mike, you're sure putting out plenty of new titles."

The cover display is a silhouette that used to fascinate me as a child. I remember pondering its savage and stubby shape, its sense of impenetrable blackness. It was the geographical outline of Africa. This rendering is tonally varied, and the variations (as I stare at them) blend into a montage of Hamitic faces—coal-black and finely chiseled in Nigeria, aquiline in Ethiopia and Somalia, fuller of feature below Zimbabwe. I notice that the faces to the north, west, and east are open-eyed, whereas the profile filling out South Africa is that of a sleeping giant.

I browse through the catalog's list of books, some of which bear the proud superscription BANNED IN SOUTH AFRICA. Ravan publishes only in English, yet its authors—novelists, poets, playwrights, economists—have such names as Mtutuzeli Matsh Attih-Kubi and Zakes Mda. Moved, I say, "Mike, if ever you were made for anything, it was to be editor in chief of a black publishing house."

His face glows with pride. "Well, not just black. Look, this guy"—he picks up a slim volume by Ahmed Essop, entitled *The Hajji and Other Stories*—"is an Indian, and he's marvelous. Just won the Olive Schreiner Award.* J. M. Coetzee, here"—tossing me a novel called *In the Heart of the Country*—"is as white as you or me.† Next year we're putting out the first big book ever to come out of the Cape Malay community."

I ask if he knows Nadine Gordimer.

"Nadine? Sure. We're co-publishing *July's People*."

THAT EVENING I SIT talking to Marilyn Kirkwood in an expensive restaurant in the northern suburbs. She is a tiredly pretty, thirtyish woman. When she leans forward in the candlelight I notice years of worry finely etched in her skin.

"Do you know, I can't remember when Mike and I last ate out."

Her husband has been absent for some time—he is a man given to sudden, unexplained disappearances—but the spell of her voice is such that I do not miss him.

"We've never had much money, of course. We practically starved in England, and even now Ravan pays very little. Mike's sure the press will run at a profit next year, but with three kids—"

It is much the same speech as one might hear from some young mother in Connecticut or California, except that American women of her type—intellectual, liberal, politically active—do not live with the fear of being woken at night by men in uniforms. Should Mike ever publish a book the government considers inflammatory . . .

Kirkwood materializes out of the shadows and falls joyfully upon the menu. I suggest he order some mashed bananas, and he laughs in the old way, with sniffs and shaking shoulders. Emboldened, I ask, "Mike, do you still expect a bloodbath here?"

* South Africa's top literary prize.
† Coetzee won the Nobel Prize for Literature in 2003. See page 473.

He looks hurt, and I recall that despite his terrifying demeanor in the surf, Kirkwood is a famously gentle person.

"I've never expected that—at least, not on a countrywide scale. But I do see creeping warfare on the border, and more and more terrorism in the cities, until the blacks get what they want. Complete and radical change."

"Is that what *you* want?"

"Of course. But my help must be as practical as possible. To defuse the threat of too much violence too soon."

"You're not as angry as you used to be," I tease.

"Well," he says slowly, "one can't stay angry forever."

I am not entirely convinced by his passive pose. But the night is warm, the wine is smooth, and I ask no further questions.

AT NOON THE NEXT DAY I fulfill a childhood ambition by checking into a sleeper on the Blue Train, the world's last luxury long-distance special, and a major symbol of South African prestige. Every gleaming inch of its ten-car length is locally designed and manufactured.

My valet, a gravely polite Cape Colored, comes in to introduce himself. Only when he goes, clicking the door behind him, do I realize we have left the station. The Blue Train whispers south through the city, riding as smoothly as a needle on mercury. I am struck by the mellow beauty of the light that pours into my compartment. A little blue booklet tells me that it is caused by "an extremely thin layer of gold diffused onto the face of the glass in order to deflect heat and glare."

The great mines of the Witwatersrand drift into view, their bright yellow dumps crenellated by erosion. They look like heaps of abstract jewelry. I sit bathed in a golden glow, gazing at gold through gold. This is a country unimaginably richer than the one I quit sixteen years ago.

Braamfontein, Roodepoort, Westonaria . . . The mining towns slip by at increasing speed. I am riding, like Alice, through a checkerboard landscape: squares of white bungalows alternating with black blocks where migrant workers sweat in celibacy. Elsewhere in South Africa the races may live at greater extremes of wealth and deprivation, yet nowhere is the harsh geometry of apartheid more visible than here, at the heart of the national economy.

Bricks give way to blue gums wavering in long rows above new-plowed fields. The last smudge of industrial smoke vanishes behind us, and the train begins to rock slightly. We are speeding westward across the *platteland* of the Transvaal. Gongs sound for lunch.

THE *KINGKLIP,* SOUTH AFRICA's finest fish, is tender in its shell of batter, and the Nederburg Riesling crisp and chill. I eat and drink under the placid gaze of Mrs. McDonald, my eighty-eight-year-old table companion. (She has sent her Karoo lamb back for more cooking—"*Very* well done, if you please.") She leans plumply against the window, pearls trembling on her bosom. Her hair is so blue it seems to blend into the sky. The illusion that I am riding through Looking-Glass Land persists. Like the White Queen, Mrs. McDonald talks half to herself, in a soothing stream of consciousness that requires no assistance from me, beyond occasional diversion into fresh channels. Were we in Britain, her phraseology would identify her as lower middle class. Here it proclaims a genteel dowager of independent means.

"If that fish isn't sufficient, young man, you just tell 'em. They'll fetch more! No, no, steward, that's still not done. Almost *shriveled,* please. And another serving for the gentleman. I suppose you're going to write something pessimistic about the future of South Africa. Well, I always say, 'Today is the tomorrow you worried about yesterday.' Why doesn't the world leave us alone? All this foreign propaganda has ruined the Afs, you know. They just won't work, anymore. You should see 'em sleeping all day in Joubert Park. *Swarms,* facedown in the sun! Cheeky devils."

The carcinogenic remains of her lamb arrive, and the old lady tucks in with relish, sipping at intervals from a glass of pink gin. "My, this is good! Steward! More vegetables." The peas are pale, the carrots thickly glazed with syrup, Afrikaans style. I order a third filet of *kingklip* and drink more wine.

Ceiling speakers announce that we are passing through Potchefstroom. The train slows almost to a halt. Some black schoolchildren scamper beside the dining car, waving and laughing. "Pity it's climate-controlled," says Mrs. McDonald. "We could of tossed some pennies to those *picanins.*" A memory stabs me, and I alarm her by groaning aloud.

I am eighteen, en route to Grahamstown in a second-class carriage. My fellow traveler is a squat, cheerful Afrikaner, who periodically slides down the window and spits into the veld. We are drawing out of some such dorp *as this. Half a dozen black boys are running alongside, hoping for coins. The Afrikaner leans out, brandishing a bright half crown. Their eyes widen with joy, and they scamper closer to the wheels, arms outstretched. The train accelerates, and he shouts, "C'mon, kaffirs, move!" Their bare feet fly over the trackside stones. Several of them stumble and fall. One boy outstrips the others, and manages to keep pace. The half crown glitters within inches of his hands. But then it is whipped away, the window shoots up, and the Afrikaner repockets the coin, roaring with laughter. My last view is of a receding black face, distorted with pain and anger. . . .*

"What's wrong, dear, lost your appetite? Time for pudding. Steward! Two vanilla ice creams, and a bottle of Worcester sauce."

"Worcester sauce, madam?"

"You heard me. Makes it taste just like caramel, dear. You just pull out the wafer and pour the sauce into the hole—"

I excuse myself and return to my compartment.

AS I SINK BACK on the cushions a little depot speeds toward me, signposted CONTENT. It flashes by and is gone. I sit staring at my *Doppelgänger* in the golden glass. How briefly his content at being back in South Africa has lasted! The poignance of nostalgia, the joy of meeting an old friend, are swept away by a sense of hopeless political imbalance, and of the terror that lies behind racial hatred. Why am I so depressed? Because I did not pull up that remembered window, and fling out a half crown of my own? Because sixteen years ago I sought to flee, not the injustices of South African society, but only its cultural poverty?

Thinking still of the boy's distorted face, I flick through a copy of *Staffrider*, Mike Kirkwood's new radical monthly. He boasts that it sells in phenomenal quantities. I am not tempted to subscribe. It is concerned almost exclusively with the literature of the upraised black fist—a boring genre, however impassioned. I search in vain through forty-eight pages of poems, short stories, playlets, and interviews for just one authentic African image. There are endless references to chains, sweat, blood, vomit, and castration, but these clichés are available to me in New York, in any issue of *Amsterdam News.* Where is the black equivalent of Camões's Adamastor, looming "with divine menace" over the Cape of Storms, or Roy Campbell's unforgettable zebras, drawing the dawn across the plains, their flanks "zithered" with fire?

I find what I am looking for—the soul, the voice of South Africa—unexpectedly in Ahmed Essop's little volume of stories.

A foreword explains that his fiction "centers on the vivid aromatic world of Johannesburg's Indian community in Fordsburg." I have not been there, but I am familiar with equally "aromatic" parts of Durban (a hot reek of turmeric on the breeze, singsong street cries, gutters running pink, on rainy days, with expectorated betel nut). I feel a surge of interest and turn to the first story.

> When the telephone rang several times one evening and his wife did not attend to it as she usually did, Hajji Hassen, seated on a settee in the lounge, cross-legged and sipping tea, shouted, "Salima, are you deaf!"

Delighted, I read on. Essop's prose moves with the nervous liquidity of Indian music. At times it surges into arabesques of humor and caprice, at others it drops to depths of gloom. Yet it never settles at any fixed pitch, no mood lasts long enough to cloy. I sway in the speeding train like a hypnotized cobra. Outside the Transvaal is merging into the Cape Province, but I am a hundred miles away, in Fordsburg, in a Little World more exotic than that of Guareschi's Don Camillo.

Here are almond-eyed youths slouching in cafés that smell of sweetmeats and subtropical fruit; pale, guilty Jews wallowing in racial profligacy with Muslims; dark, dangerous Xhosas, befuddled with *dagga* and lusting after half-caste girls ("black-haired and blue-eyed, with complexions like the white flower of the gardenia"); gangsters with names such as Akbar and Gool, meditating extortion over the click of billiard balls; kinky-haired retail millionaires courting girls by proxy; and a glossy little waiter who strolls in the streets late at night, "with the houses looming above him, and the coolness of tears on his cheeks."

When I come to the end of the last story I find that five hours have gone by. The sun is setting. A windmill spins slowly on the horizon, its vanes throwing off sparks like a Roman candle. I am filled with the sleepy calm—Content!—that good writing evokes. Only an African, in particular a South African, could have written these stories, yet according to the ludicrous classifications of apartheid, Ahmed Essop is an "Indian." I think it likely that he has not ventured further across the Indian Ocean than the few yards necessary to surf back to his native shore. Fordsburg is not really an "Indian" community. It is as African as the lush northern suburbs of Johannesburg, the thatched villages of Zululand, the bleak Dutch towns of the Orange Free State.

This country, I conclude, is no more the black man's birthright than it is the exclusive *Vaderland* of the Afrikaner. It belongs to a polyglot population of Greeks, Gujaratis, Zulus, Chinese, Scotsmen, Malays, Xhosas, Boers, Mauritians, Hindus, Cape Coloreds, Jews, Bushmen, Portuguese, Englishmen, and other tribes too numerous to list. Such mutually attractive, mutually repellent ingredients cannot be prevented from loosely combining. Nor can they be squeezed into a homogeneous block. South African culture must grow, as natural cultures do, out of the osmosis of permeating solutes, the harmonious flow of nutrients and wastes. In time, surely (and time is what such complex chemistry needs), the acids of racial hatred will be neutralized by the alkali of racial understanding.

I TURN OUT THE LIGHTS and get into bed. Outside, a full moon is etching the Karoo plateau into a pattern of black anthills and silver grass, like a giant printer's block. Four or five white cranes, disturbed by the rush of the locomotive, rise from a lake and flap alongside in spectral convoy. The rhythm of their wings, beating in the moonlight, combines hypnotically with the rock of the train.

I wake to a changed landscape of crumbling hills, valleys full of fruit trees and vines. The hills are flat-topped, each with its dolerite *koppie*, level fragments of the plateau we have left behind. Only the valleys deepen as we descend toward the sea. Far ahead, in the haze where two oceans meet, the largest residual remnant looms: Adamastor at last!

I am that vast cape locked in secrecy
That Cape of Hurricanes your people call . . .
I round out Africa's extremity
In my hid headland, where the shore lines fall. *

My parents welcome me at Cape Town in brilliant noon sunshine. The sea air is so ambrosial I suggest we lunch out of doors. "Nothing but the best today, Dad. Let's try the Mount Nelson."

He looks pleased. "Just what I was going to say."

The hotel is a short drive through the city, on an estate overlooking the Houses of Parliament. I have not visited it before, yet on getting out of the car I am overwhelmed by a sense of *déjà vu.* Surely I have stood here, shaded by these "deferential palms," looking up at this "large, proud, rosecolored hotel"?

My mother listens patiently as I stumble over the quotation. "You always were one for poetry, dear."

"Not poetry. It's the opening of *Tender Is the Night.*"

And upon inquiry I discover that the Mount Nelson is indeed modeled on Fitzgerald's favorite hotel at Cap d'Antibes.

The feeling that I am back in the Twenties persists as we wander through the gardens. Ancient military types slouch in deck chairs. Their wives wave wet cigarette holders. The talk is of cricket, sun blisters, wogs, and royalty.

Lunch, served by a courteous Malay in *kanzu* and *kaffiyeh,* follows the Edwardian sequence extinct elsewhere in the world, yet still standard in South Africa: soup, fish (fresh or pickled), entrée with four vegetables, cold cuts, salad, pudding, cheese, cream crackers, and "coffee in the lounge." With two bottles of the best Cape wine, the bill comes to $47.50 for three.

Later we take the cable car to the top of Table Mountain. Usually this great bare eminence is windy, but today the air is so still we can hear the surf pounding in Camps Bay, three thousand feet below. The only movement is the nervous vibration of hummingbirds among the proteas. Here, at our feet, the Dutch East India Company built Cape Town, about

---

* Luís de Camões, *The Lusiads,* Canto IV, translated by Leonard Bacon (New York, 1950).

the same time that the Dutch West India Company built New Amsterdam on Manhattan, half a world away. So civilizations germinate, blossom, and spread.

THE NEXT WEEK is a mélange of family reunions and excursions through the lovely Cape wine lands. There are breakfasts under a plum tree so fecund the sun-warmed fruit falls right into my cereal, lunches of pearly crayfish and Grunberger *blanc de blancs* on seaside patios, brandy-and-soda "sundowners" with members of Somerset West's Kenyan community, candlelight dinners where my father, staring into his wine, talks of the fortune Grandfather made and lost, and of how Great-Grandfather used to run ox wagons up to Kuruman. Inevitably, this evokes his favorite yarn, about the time the latter spent the night in a deserted farmhouse, woke to a vision of a white ghostly hand at the end of the bed, and shot his big toe off.

"Dad, I rather suspect you stole that story from Herman Charles Bosman."*

"*Ag,* no, the old man used to tell it to us when we were children, and when he came to the end he would take off his shoe and sock so we could *see.*"

We drive into town to observe the weekend influx of Cape Coloreds (shrill, gap-toothed, and jolly in the early morning, dangerous when the sun climbs high and bottles of methylated spirit pass from mouth to mouth). We visit Cape Town's Nico Malan Opera House for a multiracial performance of *Carmen,* superior to any I have seen in New York or London. I surf many times in the tingling sea, wishing Mike were with me. Dad buys fresh fish on the Strand—*snoek, kabalyo,* and yellowtail, still sparkling with salt. We *braai* them over coals in the garden.

One night I browse the old books I used to read, guiltily, with a flashlight under the blankets in bed: *Gone with the Wind, The Adventures of Tom Sawyer,* Emil Ludwig's *Napoleon,* Helen Gardner's *Art Through the*

---

* Bosman (1905–1951), was a gifted comic novelist and short-story writer, still revered in South Africa. His subject matter—the lore of that country's white rural minority in the mid-twentieth century—is unfortunately too parochial for foreign readers to understand.

Ages. Each of these volumes did its bit to pervert an African boy into one who identified with "a world elsewhere." The white columns and social equipoise of the Old South aroused indescribable longings, as did the splendors of the French Empire and the majesty of the Mississippi. And the superabundance of world culture, as detailed by Miss Gardner, flowered everywhere, it seemed, except on this barren continent.

MY FATHER HAS always identified with the Cape, although he grew up in Vryburg, an Afrikaans cattle town on the dry flats we used to call Bechuanaland. Similarly my mother, with painful childhood memories of Johannesburg, has a strong attachment to the eastern province of Natal, where her own mother was raised, and where my brother and sister still live. For her and their sakes, as well as my own love of the port city of Durban, I persuade Dad to drive us there by car. It is a journey of more than a thousand miles.

We set off along a highway linking the old Dutch *dorps* of the interior: Touws Rivier, Beaufort-Wes, Graaff-Reinet, Indwe. Sprawling, dusty, tree-shaded towns, each with its colored slum, its whitewashed hotel smelling of urine and sour beer, its gabled housefronts and prosperous *kerk* (whence floats, every Sunday, the most lugubrious psalmody in Christendom). Here "natives" still step aside, twenty or thirty at a time, while an Afrikaans girl strolls barefoot in her loose print dress, blind to the crowd that opens before her, and closes behind.

These little towns are painfully familiar to me. I have hitchhiked through them many times, penniless in my university blazer. (For reasons unclear to me now, it was a point of honor never to carry money, only a pocketful of beef *biltong* shavings.) I have slept under these dry bridges, and awakened covered with blown sheep droppings. These dour, guttural people have lavished hospitality upon me, although I never learned more than forty words of their language. They are the true *verkramptes,* rigid, God-fearing farmers whose votes (weighted to overbalance those of *verligte* city dwellers) perpetuate the Nationalist Party in power. Deep inside them, they carry the memory of Dingaan butchering their ancestors; deeper still the knowledge that these Coloreds—so ominously numerous, wherever one goes in the Cape Province—are their racial cousins. Try as they might, they cannot escape the consequences of past miscegenation. Kinky-haired "throwbacks" are still being born in the blondest of families. How at college we used to torment poor "Midnight" Kruger! "Hey, Midnight, where's your passbook?"

After two days driving across the Karoo we begin to ascend the piedmont of the Drakensberg range. A sign warns: YOU ARE NOW ENTERING THE TRANSKEI. I hitched past it so often in youth I do not at first notice that the word REPUBLIC has been appended. But I soon see that this fertile region is not governed by the same hands that prevailed twenty years ago. It is now officially a *Bantustan,* free to set—or not set—its own environmental standards. Once-green hills are scarcely stippled with tufts. The soil shows through in spots of reddish brown, or, where the tufts have loosened and blown away, in patches that corrugate into long channels of erosion. The channels will link up when it rains, and spill more and more red alluvium into the rivers. This is a landscape bleeding to death. Its murderers are not the skeletal cattle and goats tearing at the remaining tufts, but natives who have reverted to their traditional habits of agriculture: straight plowing regardless of topography, underfertilizing, and overstocking. If, as the old proverb says, it takes a thousand years to unmake a peasant, a hundred should be enough to turn the Transkei into another Kalahari.

My father nudges his straining car over Naude's Nek, at three thousand meters the highest pass in South Africa (sheets of silvery grass changing color in the wind like stroked velvet, thousands of arum lilies, Christmas beetles whistling in the poplars). We drop back down into the Transkei, and judder for hours along a road that threatens to dislodge our fillings. We slow to dead speed whenever we see a wandering cow. "Run over one of their animals," Dad says, "and there's no knowing what they'll do to you."

Another sign instructs us to stop and present our passports at a roadside depot.

"Passports?" I boggle as my parents produce theirs.

"Yes, this is an independent country now, remember."

"Will they accept my South African visa?"

It occurs to me, with horror, that as a U.S. citizen I might need special documentation to pass through a *Bantustan.* Suddenly the guard at the gate, scratching himself with his bayonet, seems full of menace. I notice two police Land Rovers parked beside the depot, and my mouth goes dry. Slouching deep in the back seat, I pretend to be asleep.

"You're lucky," my father murmurs, "they've waved us on."

"Lucky is right," says a South African immigration officer when we finally quit the Transkei. "Those kaffirs can get nasty. You could of lost a few teeth and ended up in *klep.*"

WE RIDE SMOOTHLY into Natal, greenest and most "English" of the provinces, despite its huge Zulu population. I roll down the window and inhale a remembered fragrance of roast maize, thatch, sugarcane, trodden earth, and sea. *"There is a lovely road that runs from Ixopo into the hills,"* I recite. It is one of my mother's favorite texts.

"The hills are grass-covered and rolling," she continues, *"and they are lovely beyond any singing of it."**

She sighs. This farmland is where she spent the happiest days of her youth, on a rich cousin's estate. There was thick fresh *maas* every morning for breakfast, spooned right out of the gourd onto her *matabela* porridge. Black servants ironed her dresses and taught her their click-tongued songs. It took all day to go into town by ox-wagon. Every Saturday night, after polo, she would write names like Cockburn and Shepherd-Smith on a little dance card with a silver pencil.

"What happened to Taffy's farm?" I ask her.

"Divided up. All the horses sold. There's a rumor this whole area will be declared black soon."

Mists fill the valleys as we descend toward Durban.

STOP! YOU'RE WALKING PAST
WOOLFSON'S MENSWEAR!
HAVE A LOOK AT OUR DISPLAY!

*From Alan Paton, *Cry, the Beloved Country,* chapter I.

I do not have to be told where I am, nor what's for sale inside. Here, in this grubby blue-tiled building, I began my professional career, writing retail advertising copy for translation into the Zulu: "SOKKIS.* Were R 3.50, now R 2.00. This Weekend Only." After a couple of years of creative frustration, my break came when I was asked to design a flyer for Father's Day. I drew a melancholy fish and hand-lettered the headline, *Science Informs Us the Male Cod Fertilizes 256,000 Eggs in a Single Ejaculation, Then Swims Off to Oblivion and Dies.* On the inner page, in smaller letters, I wrote, *Don't Let Your Man Feel Lost and Forgotten on Father's Day. Shop at Woolfson's!*

Mr. Woolfson, who sixty years before had begun his career selling shirts out of a barrow on West Street, stared at this layout in silence. Then he called for his secretary. "To whom it may concern," he dictated. "It is with great regret that Mr. Morris leaves us of his own accord, and we wish him every success in doing so."

WHEN I LEAVE DURBAN this time, it is without regret—although I am frustrated by too brief a reunion with my brother and sister. They are both married now, and settled in pleasant apartments by the sea. Being young and good-looking and white, they will doubtless prosper in South Africa's continuing economic boom—"until the revolution." The phrase is no longer whispered, or even uttered in jest. Since Rhodesia became Zimbabwe, a sense of doom has settled upon English-speaking South Africans. Unlike the Afrikaners, who have nowhere to go, they are prepared to decamp in droves. Many have secretly acquired foreign passports.

A little girl, blond and delicate as a prawn, sits next to me on my connecting flight to Johannesburg. Her parents are across the aisle, with a baby. "We're going to visit my uncle," she tells me.

"In the Transvaal?"

"No, in Australia."

"You'll have a lot to tell your friends when you come back."

"We're not coming back. We're *emigrating*," she says, with a resentful glance at her father.

* Socks.

He is staring out of the window, down at the receding hills of Natal. Something about the back of his head indicates that he is crying.

A SURPRISE LUNCH invitation saves me from the ennui of waiting six hours between planes at Jan Smuts International Airport. It comes from Ahmed Essop, whom I telephone to pay my respects (since finishing *The Hajji*, I have read his new novel, *The Visitation*, with even greater delight).

"Just enough time for you to hire a car and drive here," he says.

"How do I get to Fordsburg?" I say.

"Ah, but Fordsburg is no more. We've been moved to Lenasia."

He gives me directions. I bypass Johannesburg and speed into the rolling country that hides its nonwhite suburbs. Lenasia looms up, a clinically clean "new town" of large and small houses, shopping centers, and parks full of brown children. The skyline is dominated by a mosque.

Essop comes out into his garden to greet me. He is a slight, dark, fortyish figure in white shirt and cravat, smiling furrow-eyed in the sun. "Come in and meet my wife."

Farida Essop is exquisitely shy, retreating with rustling sari back into the kitchen.

"And this is my daughter." Liquid black eyes, lustrous black hair, arms silhouetted against white dress. She looks like a negative image of my blond companion on the plane.

We sit in a little room glittering with Islamic filigree. Essop tells me that he used to teach English at Indian schools, before his outspoken political views began to annoy the government. "They didn't dismiss me. Just kept transferring me to schools further and further from home. I sued the Bureau of Indian Affairs, a futile procedure. While the case dragged on, I wrote *The Hajji*."

"And discovered you were a writer."

"Well, at least that I had an authentic South African voice—had something original to say. I also found that I had a ready-made audience, starved for literature about itself. Do you know what authors the Bureau forces our children to read? Jane Austen! Conrad! The Romantic poets! What have they to do with boys and girls brought up here?" He gestures out of the window, at the mosque and blue gum trees.

"You wouldn't want to eliminate Keats entirely, would you?"

"Of course not, although"—he begins to laugh—"I have seen one of my colleagues flapping her arms and making bird noises, trying to make her class understand 'Ode to a Nightingale.' But this neglect of native writers is deliberate, and universal. It stretches from black schools to white universities. The government seems to fear that people who know the truth about themselves will be more difficult to govern. As a result, it's impoverishing our intellects, emotions, imaginations—our humanity."

Farida summons us to lunch. She serves bowls of chicken curry, steaming rice, *sambals,* a sauce of fresh coriander and curdled milk. The talk ranges over wide fields of politics and literature, from Ronald Reagan to V. S. Naipaul, from typesetting to yoga. I sit thinking, *These people cannot vote, they have to live where they are sent.*

"All of us in this country have so much to discover about each other," Essop sighs. "But apartheid has made such a rift, such a great human rift. You know those words of Olive Schreiner? 'The line at which light race meets dark is the line at which human sociability is found at the lowest ebb. . . . There are found the darkest shadows which we have cast by our injustice and egoism across the earth.' "

I DRIVE BACK to the airport past the yellow mine dumps, almost incandescent now in the setting sun. As a child I used to think these hills were real gold, awaiting compression into ingots. What fantasies, I wonder, does Ahmed Essop's daughter have of her environment? Does she, too, imagine herself to be living in a land of treasure, or has her father taught her that for an "Indian," all is slag?

Then I think of some naked black youths we saw on our trip through the Transkei, their faces ghastly with circumcision paint, their eyes dull with centuries of ignorance. If Essop deserves a vote, do they, by virtue of their shared swarthiness, deserve it also? Manifestly not. A sophisticated modern society, however undemocratic, cannot be given over to a plurality of peasants without disaster.

The only conceivable sharing of power here, I conclude, must be among those of any color who are educationally qualified for it—and by that standard, many semibarbarous rural Afrikaners will learn what it is to be governed by superiors of another race. South Africa's thundering economy already requires more skilled jobs than the white sector can provide. To survive, the government must mortgage itself to the principle of universal, free, and equal education. Those Transkei youths, when their foreskins heal, will shortly be fathering children. God help this lovely country if another generation of blacks is denied its birthright. And God help us Americans if we desert the whites in the fraught interim.

Yet here am I, *hypocrite auteur,* doing just that. Night comes as my plane takes off. Johannesburg's myriad lights stream away in the blackness, like sparks shed from the wing. Simultaneously, it seems, the last vestiges of Africa in me fall away too. I feel calm and purged.

"Dinner, sir?"

"No thanks. I'll wait till I get home."

Pleasantly suspended between old and new loyalties, between hemispheres as separate yet interdependent as Yin and Yang, the returning traveler sleeps.

THEODORE ROOSEVELT THE WRITER

*Colloquium at the Woodrow Wilson
Center for Scholars*

"THIS IS NOT WRITTEN VERY CLEARLY: MY TEMPERATURE IS 105 degrees," Theodore Roosevelt scrawled on the top of a manuscript submitted to *Scribner's Magazine* in April 1914. He might have mentioned, in further excuse, that he had thick gloves on, and that a cowl of mosquito netting was obscuring the vision of his one good eye, for he was writing in the depths of the Brazilian jungle, and was surrounded by a miasma of bloodsucking insects.

The editor of *Scribner's*, Robert Bridges, was not surprised by the superscript. He had been publishing Roosevelt's work for many years, and knew that no matter where his peripatetic contributor might be—on the banks of the Amazon, or the Mississippi, or the Nile—and regardless of how sick or exhausted or busy he was, TR always delivered. Moreover, he delivered in duplicate, to insure against mail loss. He wrote with indeli-

Paper presented on 17 May 1983. Abridged version originally appeared in *Smithsonian*, November 1983.

Memorial Edition of The Works of Theodore Roosevelt. *Photograph by Benjamin M. Rosen, 2012.*

ble pencil on specially made blocks of varicolored carbonated paper, which he kept in a watertight, ant-proof metal case. One copy of every manuscript remained with the author. The other two went off by different routes. His book on his African safari, for example, was dispatched chapter by chapter from the heart of the Dark Continent, some runners heading east toward Nairobi, others north to Gondokoro and Khartoum. "The blue canvas envelopes often arrived much battered and stained," Bridges recalled, "but never did a single chapter miss."

Roosevelt could not afford to have them miss. He had lost half of his patrimony in youth, in the Dakotas, and had spent all his salary as President on entertaining. He had even given away his $45,000 Nobel Peace Prize (1906), saying that he felt that the money belonged to the nation, not to himself. He wrote, therefore, out of necessity. All the same, there is something abnormal about a man who writes with gloves on while running a temperature fit to kill. Why couldn't he wait until his fever went down in the morning? Why this obsessive desire to record experience in the midst of experience? The answer is plain. Theodore Roosevelt wrote because he could not help it. He began writing as a child, and was correcting the proofs of a magazine article on the day of his death.

The results of this half century of literary labor are staggering in quantity and diversity. The "Memorial Edition" of *The Works of Theodore Roosevelt* (New York, 1926) comprises twenty-four volumes. That set does not include thirteen further volumes that he either wrote or contributed to extensively. In addition to that we have the great eight-volume Harvard edition of *The Letters of Theodore Roosevelt* (Elting E. Morison and John M. Blum, eds., Cambridge, Mass., 1951–1954). These eight volumes each average nine hundred pages of close text. They reprint only some of the letters previously published in *Selections from the Correspondence of Theodore Roosevelt and Henry Cabot Lodge* (Lodge, ed., 2 vols., New York, 1925) and the bestselling *Theodore Roosevelt's Letters to His Children* (Joseph B. Bishop, ed., New York, 1919). Professor Morison tells us that for every one of the 15,000 letters included in the Harvard edition, ten were discarded. In other words, TR's total known correspondence amounts to some 150,000 items. He also wrote several volumes of diaries—see, for example, his *Diaries of Boyhood and Youth* (New York, 1928). I will not even attempt to estimate the size of his journalistic output, except to quote Edward Wagenknecht's plaint, "TR's articles . . . are like the sands of the sea in number." Indeed it is hardly possible to calculate his total production of words. Lawrence Abbott tried to once, and reckoned it at 18 million, equal to about thirty years in the life of a full-time professional writer. But Abbott, again, took no account of magazine and newspaper pieces. R. W. G. Vail began a complete Roosevelt bibliography in the 1920s, and gave up when his collection of 5 x 8 cards reached five thousand, with no end in sight.

WHAT OF THE DIVERSITY of Theodore Roosevelt, as reflected in these writings? We have here works of history, natural history, naval history, military history, literary criticism, hunting lore, exploration reports, political commentary, social rhetoric, biography, and autobiography. The quality of the books varies greatly, and understandably, in view of the fact that while writing them the author was at various times preoccupied with two wives, six children, and a series of careers culminating in the presidency. Much of what Roosevelt wrote is unreadable today, either because it is dated, or was dull to begin with. TR made a distinction between literature and polemics, investing quality time in the former and churning out the latter as so much everyday fodder for the masses. He never intended this fodder to be preserved. Nevertheless, it has been— sack after sack after sack full of dry grain, with not a green shoot anywhere. To read Roosevelt's campaign speeches, or his World War I preparedness rhetoric, is to wonder how so many millions of Americans could have cherished so much banality. But when we reopen the few volumes into which he poured the best of himself, we find them full of freshness and vigor:

> It was still the Wild West in those days. . . . In that land we led a free and hardy life, with horse and with rifle. We worked under the scorching midsummer sun, when the wide plains shimmered and wavered in the heat, and we knew the freezing misery of riding night guard around the cattle in the late fall round-up. In the soft springtime the stars were glorious in our eyes each night before we fell asleep; and in the winter we rode through blinding

blizzards, when the driven snow-dust burnt our faces. . . . We knew toil and hardship and hunger and thirst, and we saw men die violent deaths as they worked among the horses and cattle, or fought in evil feuds with one another; but we felt the beat of hardy life in our veins, and ours was the glory of work and the joy of living.*

In addition to freshness and vigor, we find a large measure of scholarship. Theodore Roosevelt, was, after all, a president of the American Historical Association as well as President of the United States. After leaving the White House he lectured learnedly at the Sorbonne, the University of Berlin, and Oxford. He twice contemplated careers in academe, first as a natural scientist and later as a professor of history.

While still a Harvard undergraduate, he began a statistical and tactical history, *The Naval War of 1812* (New York, 1882), remarkable for its scientific precision and objectivity. His self-described "magnum opus," *The Winning of the West* (4 vols., New York 1889–1896) has fared less well historiographically, in that it belongs to the old-fashioned narrative school of Prescott and Parkman. But it was regarded as a work of major originality in its time, not least because of its exhaustive research in frontier archives, and can still be read with pleasure. William H. Harbaugh has subjected the book to modern analysis in his *Power and Responsibility: The Life and Times of Theodore Roosevelt* (New York, 1961). On the strength of this analysis he calls TR "a historian of brilliant, though uneven, literary power; of broad, and often acute, comprehension; and of extraordinary narrative force."

Roosevelt was scholarly, too, in other fields—so many, indeed, that it is as difficult to divide his entire oeuvre thematically as it is to view all sides of a polygon at once. I will attempt instead to list his published titles *seriatim*, discussing the important ones as they arise in the context of his life. His first printed pieces, written when he was still a teenager, were two ornithological treatises, *The Summer Birds of the Adirondacks in Franklin County, N.Y.* (with H. D. Minot, New York, 1877) and *Notes on Some of the Birds of Oyster Bay* (New York, 1879). Although little more

* From "In Cowboy Land," chapter 4 of TR's *Autobiography* (1913).

than leaflets, they were of scientific value at the time, and received respectful reviews from the zoologist C. Hart Merriam, who became TR's lifelong friend. Today these rare leaflets are the items most sought after by collectors of Rooseveltiana.

TR began *The Naval War of 1812* at Harvard in 1879, partly to work off the frustration of a difficult love affair, partly because he was irritated by the inaccuracies of the then-standard history of the war, which he found in the Porcellian Library, and partly to save himself the chore of having to write an honors thesis. By then he had given up for good his dream of becoming a professional natural historian, having decided that biology, as currently practiced, was too much science of the laboratory and the cloister. He saw himself destined for work in the field, if not in science, than in the rougher, tougher world of politics. From about this time dates TR's obsessive contempt of those "bitter, sour, ineffective men who [indulge] scholarship of a wholly unproductive type." He nevertheless plunged into deep research for *Naval War,* even mastering the abstract disciplines of ballistics and logistics. But by the time he graduated *magna cum laude* and a member of Phi Beta Kappa on 30 June 1880, he was more convinced than ever that his future lay elsewhere than in academe. Perhaps he paid heed to the alarming advice of the commencement speaker that day, Oliver Wendell Holmes, Jr.: "Remember . . . that the duty of the scholar in this country is to make poverty respectable."

Poverty was no problem of TR's during the next year and a half, which saw him living lavishly just off Fifth Avenue in New York City, attending numerous socialite balls, and preparing himself for a political career. In between times he continued to work on *Naval War* at the Astor Library, consulting American, British, and French sources, and sending off to Washington for trunksful of official captains' letters, logbooks, and shipyard contracts previously untouched by any scholar. He even carried the manuscript around Europe during his delayed honeymoon in the summer of 1881, determined to let nothing, even pretty Alice Hathaway Lee, get in between himself and his muse.

The critical acclaim that greeted *Naval War* when it was published in 1882 was enough to turn the head of any scholar, except that Roosevelt by then was a New York State assemblyman, and absorbed in a new career. His book was recognized on both sides of the Atlantic as a naval classic, remarkable for almost inhuman objectivity. Eleven years later, when William Laird Clowes was editing the official history of the British Navy, he paid TR the unprecedented compliment of asking him to contribute the installment of that work dealing with the War of 1812.

Its merits, as I pointed out in *The Rise of Theodore Roosevelt* (New York, 1979), "are as simple as those of any serious piece of academic writing: clarity, accuracy, and completeness, backed by massive documentation." The density of research is such that TR often quotes a different authority for every sentence. However, it must be admitted that *Naval War* appeals today only to the most abstract specialist. Roosevelt himself joked that the book was "so dry as to make a dictionary seem light reading by comparison." A few sentences will give something of its flavor:

> The *Constitution* only carried 32-pound carronades, and once 54 and once 52 guns. . . . Her broadside force consisted of fifteen long 24s on the main-deck, and on the spar-deck one long 24, and in one case 10, in the other eleven 32-pound carronades— a broadside of 704 and 736 pounds (nominally: in reality about 7 percent less on account of the short weight in metal).

SOME OF TR'S MOST engaging characteristics as a writer—lucidity, lyricism, natural observation, and that indefinable quality which his contemporaries could describe only as "sweetness"—are present in his next book, *Hunting Trips of a Ranchman* (New York 1885). Just as it is hard to believe that *Naval War* was written by a young man ecstatically in love and newly wed, so does the imagination boggle to learn that this paean to the beauties of nature was written two years later by a widower of twenty-six. *Hunting Trips of a Ranchman* and its sequels, *Ranch Life and the Hunting Trail* (New York, 1888) and *The Wilderness Hunter* (New York, 1893) are among the best of Roosevelt's books. Paul Russell Cutright calls them "a natural history trilogy of the West." They have never been out of print, since their various chapters are consistently anthologized. For example, *Northwest Orient*, April 1983, contains a long photo essay based on *Ranch Life*, and *American Bears* (Colorado Associated University Press, 1983) is drawn largely from TR's Western trilogy.

The editor of the latter volume is Dr. Paul Schullery, a historian of the American conservation movement and a trained field naturalist. Dr. Schullery addresses himself in his introduction to the vexed subject of "Roosevelt's Hunting as Historical Scandal," and does so to good effect, criticizing me, among other biographers, as a presentist layman unable to understand the ethics of nineteenth-century sportsmanship. His arguments are convincing, but they lie beyond the scope of this paper, which deals only with literary matters. I mention the controversy simply because TR's threefold repetition of the word *hunting* in the titles under discussion might give modern readers the off-putting impression that his trilogy will be full of blood and guts. Actually Roosevelt writes very little about the killing of animals. He is more interested in their life habits, which he observes with an accuracy of eye and ear, and an understanding of the three-way relationship between flora and fauna and man, that is more than scientific—almost poetic. Just as Shakespeare senses the hurt of a snail "whose tender horns being hit, shrinks back in her shelly cave with pain," so TR feels (and communicates) the numb stiffness of an antelope in a prairie hailstorm, the bighorn's delight in its sinewy nimbleness, the relief of a horse when the hot saddle comes off and cool air plays on its back. He describes the structure of a prairie wildflower as microscopically as he communicates the texture of a pronghorn's skin:

> The hair is . . . very long, coarse, and brittle; in the spring it comes off in handfuls. In strong contrast to the reddish yellow of the other parts of the body, the rump is pure white, and when alarmed or irritated every hair in the white patch bristles up on end, greatly increasing the apparent area of the color.

Details like this are tossed off in passing, for Roosevelt is always in a hurry to get on with his story. The reader is hardly aware that valuable scientific information is being imparted—for in the 1880s much of what Roosevelt had to say about Western animal and plant life was quite new to biologists. His chapter on the bighorn in *Ranch Life* was considered authoritative for decades, while his many writings on the bear comprise, in the words of Dr. Schullery, "the finest contribution by a single author to our knowledge of bear habits and hunting prior to the work of William Wright." Professor Merriam (whom, by the way, TR once bested in a zoological argument to do with the differentiation of species) confirmed that on the basis of this trilogy Roosevelt was "the world's authority on the big game mammals of America. His writings are fuller and his observations more complete than those of any other man."

Zoology aside, the reader revels in these books for their sheer literary charm. TR was neither a polished, nor a facile stylist. "Writing," he confessed, "is horribly hard work to me. My style is rough, and I do not like a certain lack of sequitur that I do not seem able to get rid of." He tended to be repetitious, and lacked the fine instinct of where to begin and where to end. Metaphor for the sake of metaphor interested him hardly at all, although occasionally he was capable of some original imagery, as in this extract from the magnificent chapter named "Winter Weather," in *Ranch Life:*

When the days have dwindled to their shortest, and the nights seem never-ending, then all the great northern plains are changed into an abode of iron desolation. Sometimes furious gales blow down from the north, driving before them the clouds of blinding snow-dust, wrapping the mantle of death round every unsheltered being that faces their unshackled anger. They roar in a thunderous bass as they sweep across the prairie or whirl through the naked canyons; they shiver the great brittle cottonwoods, and beneath their rough touch the icy limbs of the pines that cluster in the gorges sing like the chords of an aeolian harp. Again, in the coldest midwinter weather, not a breath of wind may stir; and then the still, merciless, terrible cold that broods over the earth like the shadow of silent death seems even more dreadful in its gloomy rigor than is the lawless madness of the storms. All the land is like granite; the great rivers stand still in their beds, as if turned to frosted steel. In the long nights there is no sound to break the lifeless silence. Under the ceaseless, shifting play of the Northern Lights, or lighted only by the wintry brilliance of the stars, the snow-clad plains stretch out into dead and endless wastes of glimmering white.

Like Dickens and Oscar Wilde before him, Roosevelt was never one to waste a good simile. He used that line about rivers standing in their beds "as if turned to frosted steel" at least three times in subsequent books. Elsewhere in his writings we will occasionally come across such images as "drink the wine of life with brandy in it," or encounter Assistant Secretary of State Josiah Quincy "hunting through the Departments for patronage as a pig hunts truffles," or see the Oyster Bay fishmonger arriving at Sagamore Hill to present his bill, "looking like a queer sea-growth from among his own clams." In the *Rough Riders* we read about cavalry trumpets that "tore the tropic dawn," and there's a description somewhere in his letters of his six-year-old son surrounded by gap-toothed schoolmates: they looked "like a class of ruminants, varied by an occasional narwhal." Best of all is a line he wrote late in life: "Wings of myriads of sea-fowl make a kind of shifting cuneiform script in the air." Yet a consistent fecundity of metaphor, such as distinguishes all great writers from good, is not to be found in the works of Theodore Roosevelt.

WHAT THEN ARE his literary virtues, as apparent in the Western trilogy? First, I would cite the transparency of his language. Rooseveltian sentences read beautifully aloud—always a good test of pared-down prose. Even when skimmed with the eye, they never have to be reread. This is due in part to the clarity of TR's mind, yet it is in larger part due to a natural feeling for rhythm (he loved strongly metric ballads, and was a good rider and dancer), and to deliberate use of such style-enhancing techniques as alliteration and onomatopoeia.

For example: "Suddenly a small animal swam across the little pool at my feet. It was less in size than a mouse, and as it paddled rapidly underneath the water its body seemed flattened like a disk, and was spangled with tiny bubbles, like specks of silver." Reading, one is not conscious of all those *s*'s, as one might be in poetry; yet they make the picture extraordinarily vivid. Again, "The little ducks went along like bullets, their wings working so fast that they whistled; flop, flop, came the great eagle after them, with labored-looking flight."

Roosevelt's mastery of onomatopoeia relates to the second unique feature of his writing—his phenomenal auditory imagination. This joy in things heard dates back to his first thirteen years, when he was so myopic as to be half-blind, and before getting spectacles had to rely on his ears to make sense of the blur in his eyes. (His juvenile notebooks almost always identify birds by their calls, rather than their plumage.) *Hunting Trips of a Ranchman* is as full of sound effects as a radio script. I once tried to tabulate them, and found they averaged five per page. In the fall, he hears "the clanging cries" of waterfowl speeding southward. In winter, the wheels of the ranch wagon "creak and sing" as they "grind through the powdery snow," while "trees crack and jar from the strain of the biting frost." In spring comes "the hollow booming" of prairie fowl cocks, and then he writes this unforgettable description of a summer night ride across the prairie:

> For nine hours we rode steadily, generally at a quick lope, across the moonlit prairie. The hoofbeats of our horses rang out in steady rhythm through the silence of the night, otherwise unbroken save now and then by the wailing cry of a coyote. The rolling plains stretched out on all sides of us, shimmering in the clear moonlight; and occasionally a band of spectral-looking antelope swept silently away from before our path. Once we went by a drove of Texan cattle, who stared wildly at the intruders; as we passed they charged down by us, the ground rumbling beneath their tread, while their long horns knocked against each other with a sound like the clattering of a multitude of castanets.

When, in 1902, Owen Wister dedicated *The Virginian*, generally considered the first great Western novel, to Theodore Roosevelt, he was acknowledging his debt to the President as a pioneer of Western writing. TR's three so-called hunting books contain many of the stock scenes that later became the clichés of Hollywood. But when he first wrote them they were both fresh and true, and rooted in his own experience. Here is the dude from New York, otherwise known as "Four Eyes," walking into a saloon for dinner, and being accosted by a drunken bully, whom he proceeds to knock cold with a well-aimed right to the point of the jaw. Here again is our hero, riding off alone onto the prairie to recover from the death of his girl, carrying no props but his gun, his sleeping blanket, some matches, and some salt. A few pages later, he draws a bead on a dangerous-looking Sioux who protests, "How! Me good Injun." (TR goes on, "I told him with sincerity that I was glad that he was a good Indian, but that he must not come any closer.") The nineteen-page boat-chase sequence in *Ranch Life* ranks as one of the best narratives in frontier literature.

Roosevelt being Roosevelt, he not only wore his deputy sheriff's star throughout this expedition, but took along a notebook and camera, and, by way of light entertainment, Matthew Arnold's *Discourses in America* and Tolstoy's new novel, *Anna Karenina*.

AT INTERVALS BETWEEN his Western books, TR produced two biographies, *Thomas Hart Benton* and *Gouverneur Morris* (Boston, 1887 and 1888); *Essays in Practical Politics* (New York, 1888), recounting his experiences in the New York State Legislature; the first two volumes of *The Winning of the West* (New York, 1889); and a *History of the City of New York* (London, 1891). The two biographies no longer merit serious attention, although *Benton* was his third book in a row to achieve standard status in its day, and the French scenes in *Gouverneur Morris* can still be enjoyed for their Gallic *éclat*. It is amusing, in view of the scholarship Roosevelt lavished upon *The Naval War of 1812* and *The Winning of the West*, to read a letter he wrote to Henry Cabot Lodge, while working on *Benton* in North Dakota in the spring of 1886:

> I wonder if your friendship will stand a very serious strain. I have pretty nearly finished *Benton,* mainly evolving him from my inner consciousness; but when he leaves the Senate in 1850 I have nothing whatever to go by; and being by nature a timid and, on occasions, by choice a truthful man, I would prefer to have some foundation of fact, no matter how slender, on which to build the airy and arabesque superstructure of my fancy—especially as I am writing a history. Now I hesitate to give him a wholly fictitious date of death and to invent all the work of his later years. Would

it be too infernal a nuisance to hire someone to look up, in a bio-graphical directory or elsewhere, his life after he left the Senate in 1850?

Essays on Practical Politics is dated now, of interest only to scholars of New York State parochial affairs in the early 1880s. This is a pity, be-cause some pages, to do with the rather snobbish young Roosevelt's ex-periences with working-class Irish politicians, are very funny:

There were two [state] senators, both Celtic gentlemen, who were rivals for the leadership of the minority; one of them a stout, red-faced little man, who went by the name of "Commodore," owing to his having seen service in the navy; while the other was a dapper, voluble fellow, who had at one time been on a civic com-mission and was always called the "Counselor." A mild-mannered countryman* was opposing the [Catholic Protectory] Bill on the ground (perfectly just, by the way) that it was unconstitutional, and he dwelt upon this objection at some length. The Counselor, who knew nothing of the Constitution, except that it was con-tinually being quoted against all of his favorite projects, fidgeted about for some time, and at last jumped up to know if he might ask the gentleman a question. The latter said, "Yes," and the Counselor went on, "I'd like to know if the gintleman has ever personally seen the Catholic Protectoree?" "No, I haven't," re-plied the astonished countryman. "Then phwat do you mane by talking about its being unconstitootional, I'd like to know? It's no more unconstitootional than you are! Not one bit! I know it, for I've been and seen it, and that's more than you've done." Then, turning to the house, with slow and withering sarcasm, he added, "The throuble wid the gintleman is that he okkipies what lawyers would call a kind of *quasi-position* upon this bill," and sat down amid the applause of his followers.

His rival, the Commodore, felt he had gained altogether too much glory from the encounter, and after the nonplussed coun-

* Assemblyman Roosevelt.

tryman had taken his seat, he stalked solemnly over to the desk of the elated Counselor, looked at him majestically for a moment, and said, "You'll excuse my mentioning, sorr, [Mr. Roosevelt] knows more law in a wake than you do in a month; and more than that, Counselor Shaunessy, phwat do you mane by quotin' Latin on the flure of this house, when you don't know the alpha and omayga of the language!"

WHICH BRINGS ME to that gigantic fragment, *The Winning of the West.* (It's a fragment in the sense that TR intended to follow the first four volumes with another four, covering two full centuries of American history, but was distracted by war and politics from completing his grand design.) As it stands, the book tells the story of the spread of the United States across the American continent, from the day Daniel Boone first crossed the Alleghenies in 1774 to the day Davy Crockett dies at the Alamo in 1836.

When Roosevelt began it, he was nearly thirty years old, and convinced that he had no future in politics. His catastrophic stock losses in the North Dakota blizzards of 1886–1887 had so reduced his fortune that he could not even survive by living off his farm at Sagamore Hill, Oyster Bay. With a new, growing family to support, and much frustrated ambition to satisfy, he decided to devote himself full-time to a literary career. "I should like to write some book that would really take rank in the very first class," he confessed to a friend, "but I suppose this is a mere dream."

A dream it was to remain. Even so, *The Winning of the West* was a major achievement. Writing it, Theodore Roosevelt drew upon the most fundamental elements of his character and experience. If I may again quote from the first volume of my biography:

Among them were his years in the West, living with the sons and grandsons of pioneers; his belief, inherited from Thomas Hart Benton, that America's Manifest Destiny was to sweep Westward at the expense of weaker nations; his fascination with the racial variety of the West, and its forging of a characteristic frontier "type," never seen in the Old World; his wide readings in Western history; his efforts, through [his own] Boone and Crockett Club, to save Western wildlife and promote Western exploration; all these combined into one mighty concept which (the more he pondered it) he saw he might handle more authoritatively than anyone else.

The resultant book, dedicated to Francis Parkman, was based on massive research in primary sources in Tennessee, Kentucky, Virginia, Georgia, Wisconsin, California, Canada, and Washington, D.C.—thousands of letters, diaries, frontier memoirs, Revolutionary folios, and Spanish government dispatches, most of them untouched by previous scholars. Roosevelt indeed did so much work that, like many another young historian proud of his energy, he splattered the first two volumes with an excess of footnotes and citations.

Since these volumes came out only a year after signing his contract, he was asking for critical trouble—all his life, TR suffered from the inability of ordinary men to appreciate how fast, yet how thoroughly he worked—and sure enough it came, in the shape of a pseudonymous notice in the New York *Sun.* He was accused of plagiarism and fraud, on the grounds that "it would have been simply impossible for him to do what he claims to have done in the time that was at his disposal."

TR annihilated this reviewer—James R. Gilmore, a historian whose own works had been rendered obsolete by *The Winning of the West*—in an open letter too long for me to quote (unfortunately, because it is a classic example of that perilous literary genre, the Author's Reply). It ends:

I hereby offer a thousand dollars . . . to anyone who can show that ten lines of [*The Winning of the West*], notes or text, were written by anyone but myself. The original manuscript of the book is still in the hands of the publishers, the Messrs. Putnams, 27 West 23rd Street, New York; a glance at it will be sufficient to show that from the first chapter to the last the text and notes are by the same hand and written at the same time.

Mr. Gilmore did not take up the challenge, but I did, ninety years later. The manuscript of *The Winning of the West* has long been considered lost, but since I had the same publishers, I thought there was a chance I might find it buried in the corporate vaults. No such luck.

One day, quite by chance, I came across a misfiled card in the manuscript department of the New York Public Library. And there, perfectly preserved but for a few missing pages, was the handwritten holograph of TR's great work. Text and notes were indeed "by the same hand."

It is instructive to see what agonies that manuscript cost him. Paragraph after paragraph is scarred and blotted and scrawled over. Interlineations crowd claustrophobically between the scratched-out sentences. Balloons full of new words soar to the top of the page, like blimps over burned-out forest. Writing was indeed "horribly hard work" to Theodore Roosevelt, and one cannot begrudge him the scholarly praise he earned for *The Winning of the West.* Notwithstanding Gilmore's diatribe, the book was a bestseller (the first edition disappeared in little more than a month) and a critical success on both sides of the Atlantic. In Britain, Roosevelt was hailed as a historian of model impartiality (as he had been after publishing *The Naval War of 1812*). *The Athenaeum* went as far as to call him Bancroft's successor. In the United States he earned the praise of none other than Frederick Jackson Turner, who called *The Winning of the West* "a wonderful story, most entertainingly told." Turner further said that its author demonstrated "breadth of view, capacity for studying local history in the light of world history, and knowledge of the critical use of material."

Since Turner wrote these words in 1889, and did not expound his famous Frontier Thesis until 1893, the interesting question arises as to what extent he was inspired to it by *The Winning of the West.* Turner's thesis—"that the existence of an area of free land, its continuous recession, and the advancement of American settlement westward explain American development"—is identical with Roosevelt's, although TR of course states it much more loosely, in the form of a historical allegory. We know that Turner, in his personal copy of Vol. 1, marked a passage describing the "true significance" of "the vast movement by which this continent was conquered and peopled." Wilbur R. Jacobs, in *The Histori-*

cal World of Frederick Jackson Turner (New Haven, Conn., 1968) says that Turner wrote an unpublished essay, "The Hunter Type," in 1890, "based almost entirely upon the early volumes of *The Winning of the West.*" Roosevelt had little to do with the massive research that went into Turner's paper, but it may well be, as Jacobs suggests, that he "provided the inspiration for it." Significantly, TR was one of the few American historians who took any notice of the Frontier Thesis when it was first published early in 1894. He wrote Turner an encouraging letter of praise, and quoted the thesis in his third volume. A lifelong friendship resulted.

ROOSEVELT'S FINANCIAL PROBLEMS worsened in the early 1890s, as did the nation's, to such an extent that he accepted more and more literary assignments, with less and less time to spare for them. His *History of the City of New York,* written for a British publisher, is mere hasty hackwork, and can be passed over, except for a passage where he describes policemen attacking the Draft Rioters "with the most wholesome intent to do them physical harm." Thirty rioters were killed—"an admirable object lesson to the remainder." This hint of physical cruelty, of bottled-up resentment seeking surcease, brings us to a rather less attractive aspect of Theodore Roosevelt the writer than any we have discussed so far. It is increasingly noticeable in the decade preceding the Spanish-American War, a period that saw TR holding three appointive jobs in succession, each of which lacked the absolute power he craved. The civil service commissionership (1889–1895) allowed him to identify federal spoilsmen, but not to prosecute them. As police commissioner of New York City (1895–1897) he was outwitted to the point of nervous collapse by a Machiavellian colleague, and as assistant secretary of the Navy (1897–1898) he found his sedentary superior maddeningly deaf to his pleas for more battleships, more guns, more coaling stations—anything that would hasten the war he felt this soft-fibered nation needed. Such frustrations, aggravated by financial worry and a secret scandal in his own immediate family, brought out the worst in Theodore Roosevelt, in such forms as chauvinism, jingoism, snobbery, reverse snobbery, bellicosity, vituperation, and what a contemporary critic called "muscular Christianity minus the Christian part."

An example of Rooseveltian chauvinism is his attitude to the expatriate writers and artists who chose to make Europe their domicile during this period. It manifests itself first in a two-fisted article, "Reply to Some Recent Criticism of America," published in the British *Murray's Magazine*, September 1888. The piece (which was the talk of London the month it came out) begins splendidly with a refutation of some recent Civil War criticism by Lord Wolseley, "that flatulent conqueror of half-armed savages," then moves on to attack the Matthew Arnold *Discourses* mentioned above. Roosevelt admits Arnold is right in saying that Americans lack literary sophistication. "Unquestionably—and very naturally—we have not produced writers that stand as relatively high as our statesmen and soldiers," he blusters. "We have *done* a good deal more than we have *written*. . . . After all, taming a continent is nobler work than studying *belles lettres*."

This from an intellectual who read, on average, a book a day, and whose idea of an idyllic afternoon was to sit in the woods with his wife and read Swinburne by the hour! It perhaps illustrates the old paradox that what we most deprecate in others is what we won't admit to in ourselves. But the thirty-year-old TR has more to say, in answer to Arnold's comment that Americans of creative genius have no choice but to seek fulfillment in the Old World:

> Those who do . . . are men too weak to make their way at home; they belong to some such class as that of our so-called "realistic" novelists . . . men who apparently seek to supplement French realism, which consists in depicting the unspeakably nasty, by a realism of their own, the portrayal of the unutterably trivial. It is distinctly to our discredit as a nation that we have produced these men; but then it is much to our credit that, when produced, they are driven to live somewhere else. The Americans who do good work are invariably those whose Americanism is most pronounced, and who are themselves American in heart and spirit, in marrow and fiber. The acquisition of a species of flaccid cosmopolitanism is one of the surest signs of a feeble nature.

Even this is mild compared to the invective he lavished upon his *bête noire*, Henry James, who at various times is "a little emasculated mass of inanity," a "miserable little snob," and an "undersized man of letters, who flees his country because he, with his delicate, effeminate sensitiveness, finds the conditions of life on this side of the water crude and raw . . . because he finds that he cannot play a man's part among men." George Kennan* heard TR holding forth on Henry James one day—the Master was by then "a malignant pustule"—and said to himself, "If this young civil service commissioner fully develops his capacity for hatred and his natural gift for denunciation, he will be, in the maturity of his powers, an unpleasant man to encounter."

Note TR's tendency to castrate his less robust compatriots—"beings whose cult is nonvirility," "sublimated sweetbreads," "a small body of shrill eunuchs," and so on. Nor did this invective apply only to the cosmopolitans. He wrote with equal contempt of mugwumps, pacifists, anti-imperialists, and of course those most epicene of perverts, Democrats.

In fairness, it must be said that the majority of his brutal remarks were made in private. But whenever he touched on such subjects as expatriate authors or labor unrest or the declining birthrate—"race suicide," he called it—rampant heterosexuality tended to unbalance his pen. The most ball-breaking invective of Theodore Roosevelt's final years, expressing his frustration over America's slowness to enter the great war in Europe, was reserved for the man who seemed to him "the arch-typical [*sic*] neutral of all time," Woodrow Wilson.

IT SHOULD BE POINTED OUT in his defense that whatever TR did, whether it be to denounce or praise, to attack or embrace, he always did to excess. Finley Peter Dunne was appalled by the energy with which he performed that most routine of political acts, baby kissing. A whole generation, Dunne predicted, would grow up scarred like German university students. John Burroughs noted that "he killed mosquitoes like lions, and lions like mosquitoes." Roosevelt's physical exuberance was so great, his passions so strong, his sense of self-righteousness so unwavering, that it is no wonder Henry Adams likened him to the Chicago ex-

---

* Biographer, journalist (1845–1924).

press. When he scrutinized a magazine, he literally tore his way through it, ripping out each page as he read and crumpling it on the floor, while the contents registered in his Lexitron-like memory.* When he borrowed Cahun's *L'Histoire de l'Asie* in 1905, the lender, French ambassador Jules Jusserand, was surprised to get the book back in a new binding. Roosevelt confessed that by the time he had finished with it, the original cover was dangling on strings.

Booth Tarkington, one of his countless literary protégés, went so far as to say that Roosevelt indulged in invective for the sheer joy of it. He liked to think up epigrammatic insults, and "one often heard the undertone of Homeric chuckling," when he delivered himself of them, "as if, after all, he loved the fun of hating what he hated."

The ones I have quoted above are but a small, deliberately negative selection. Most of his brickbats are both original and funny. People who opposed hunting were "logical vegetarians of the flabbiest Hindoo type." English oysters tasted like "corroded halfpence," and the knights in Tennyson's *Idylls of the King* were nothing but "blameless curates, clad in tin-mail." He immortalized the leader of the Populist movement as "a well-meaning, pin-headed, anarchistic crank, of hirsute and slabsided aspect." Later on, he dismissed the president of Venezuela in one word as "a Pithecanthropoid." George Bernard Shaw was "a blue-rumped ape," and Sir Mortimer Durand, Ambassador to the United States from the Court of St. James's, had "a mind that functions at six guinea-pig power."

All of the above-quoted insults were written, but TR was equally fecund in coining others *viva voce*. He was a superb, if rather overbearing, conversationalist. The Western novelist Hamlin Garland heard him in full swing at a literary luncheon at Columbia University in 1897, and was enchanted by his humor and brilliance—as was William Dean Howells, who also attended. Roosevelt's anecdotes about his experiences as police commissioner on the Lower East Side were, according to Garland, "art of high quality . . . literature hot off the griddle." All present begged him to write them down, but he never did.

* See page xix.

AS THE NINETEENTH CENTURY moved to its close, and public distractions crowded in, TR turned more and more to the typewriter, that
"murderer of true style" (Finley Peter Dunne's phrase), and to the undis-
criminating secretary who sat before it. In other words, he stopped writing and began dictating, and the books he produced in those years show
a commensurate decline in quality. *Hero Tales from American History*
(New York, 1895), coauthored by Henry Cabot Lodge, is a collection of
schoolboy stories of the cherry-tree variety; *American Ideals and Other
Essays* (New York, 1897) is full of prewar jingoism, and was deliciously
panned by Henry James, as follows:

> Mr. Theodore Roosevelt [proposes] to tighten the screws of the
> national consciousness as they have never been tightened be-
> fore. . . . It is "purely as an American," he constantly reminds us,
> that each of us must live and breathe. Breathing, indeed, is a tri-
> fle; it is purely as Americans that we must think, and all that is
> wanting to the author's demonstration is that he shall give us a
> receipt for the process. . . . These pages give us an impression of
> high competence. . . . But his value is impaired for intelligible per-
> cept by the puerility of his simplifications.

Roosevelt's next work was his famous volume of war reminiscences,
The Rough Riders (New York, 1899). This, too, was dictated, and despite
passages of considerable power, it is marred by excessive use of the personal pronoun—twelve times, for example, on the first page of the typescript. We may be grateful for this stylistic tic, however, for it stimulated
"Mr. Dooley," alias Finley Peter Dunne, always TR's most trenchant
tease, to compose a devastating parody. It is entitled simply, "A Book Review." This is but a short extract:

> "Well sir," said Mr. Dooley, "I jus' got hold iv a book, Hinnissy, a
> gran' book, th' grandest iver seen. I tell ye 'tis fine."
> "What is it?" Mr. Hennessy asked languidly.
> " 'Tis Th' Biography iv a Hero by Wan who Knows.' 'Tis 'Th'

Darin' Exploits iv a Brave Man by an Actual Eye Witness.' 'Tis 'Th' Account iv th' Desthruction iv Spanish Power in th' Ant Hills,' as it fell fr'm th' lips iv Tiddy Rosenfelt an' was took down by his own hands. I will lave the janial author to tell the story in his own words.

" 'The sicrity of war had offered me,' he says, 'the command of a rig'ment,' he says, 'but we had no sooner landed in Cubia than it become nicessry fir me to take command iv th' ar-rmy which I did at wanst. I discovered that the inimy was heavily in-threnched on th' top iv San Joon Hill immejiately in front iv me. But it soon became apparent that I was handicapped by the prisence iv th' ar-rmy,' he says, 'so I sent 'em all home and attacked San Joon Hill meself. Ar-rmed only with a small thirty-two I climbed that precipitous ascent in th' face iv th' most gallin' fire I iver knew. I dashed madly on cheerin' as I wint. Th' Spanish throops was dhrawn up in a long line in th' formation known among military men as a long line. I fired at th' man nearest to me an' I knew be th' expression iv his face that th' trusty bullet wint home. It passed through his frame, he fell, an' wan little Spanish family was made happy by th' thought that their riprisintative had been kilt be th' future Governor of Noo York State. Th' bullet sped on its mad flight and passed through th' intire line, fin'lly imbeddin' itself in th' abdomen iv th' Ar-rchbishop iv Santiago eight miles away. This ended th' war.

" 'They has been some discossion' he says, 'as to who was th' first man to r-reach th' summit iv San Joon Hill. . . . I will state fir th' binifit iv Posterity that I was th' only man I see. An' I had a tillyscope.' "

"Well," said Mr. Hennessy. "I think Tiddy Rosenfelt is all r-right an' if he wants to blow his hor-rn lave him do it."

"Thrue fir ye," said Mr. Dooley, "But if I was him, I'd call th' book 'Alone in Cubia.' "

The Rough Riders was followed by a volume of imperialistic, breast-thumping essays, *The Strenuous Life* (New York, 1900). Shortly after its publication Roosevelt, exhausted by a hard legislative season in Albany, came home to Sagamore Hill for a month's vacation. "I don't mean to do one single thing [this] month," he told his sister, "except write a life of Oliver Cromwell." He indeed managed to dictate some sixty-three thousand words between 1 July and 2 August, only occasionally referring to his notes, pouring out names and dates as copiously as an Oxford don. The resultant biography was remarkable for clarity and concision, if not for psychological insight. It had nothing to add to any of the standard lives of Cromwell, and soon went out of print. Perhaps the best that could be said of it was Arthur Lee's crack, "the book is a fine imaginative study of Cromwell's qualifications for the Governorship of New York."

ROOSEVELT'S ACCESSION to the Presidency in September 1901 caused a seven-year hiatus in his writing career. Despite the distractions of office, however, he did manage to assemble the manuscript of another hunting book, *Outdoor Pastimes of an American Hunter* (New York, 1905). It was largely a patchwork of earlier articles, with only one new and charming chapter, "At Home," which itself was reworked later into the best chapter of his autobiography. As President, and an enthusiastic patron of struggling American authors, he also wrote many introductions and forewords and prefaces to works that would not have sold without his blessing. (The largely untold story of Theodore Roosevelt as patron of the arts—"I'd like to be remembered that way," he said—is too substantial to be summarized here).

As "a bully pulpit," the White House stimulated TR's gift for coining terms and phrases that buried themselves in the national subconscious. In 1906 a political commentator noted: "Roosevelt is the undisputed phrasemaker to the nation. He is the first of our presidents . . . to have brief passages from his writings during his own term framed and sold in the shops like mottoes." Many of his original contributions to the vernacular have become hackneyed—"the Big Stick," "the Square Deal," "malefactors of great wealth," "the Strenuous Life," and later on "the Bull Moose," "hyphenated Americans," and "the Great Adventure." Other Rooseveltian coinages have become popular, but we forget it was he who minted them—"clean as a hound's tooth," "weasel words," "we've beaten them to a frazzle," "undesirable citizens," "pussyfooting," "the right stuff," "Mr. Two-Face," "mollycoddles," the verb "to falsify," the challenge "my hat is in the ring," and that marvelous phrase "the lunatic fringe," as in his letter to Amos Pinchot, "Dear Sir, when I spoke of the Progressive Party as having a lunatic fringe, I had specifically you in mind." The term *Armageddon,* so trendy these days, was introduced by TR as a deliberately recondite reference, as was Bunyan's "Man with the Muckrake." Still others of his coinage are less familiar, yet they remain vital and unique—"torrential journalism," "just legally honest," "rubber-stamp Congress," "rosewater reformers," "outpatients of Bedlam," and my own favorite, "If you go in close enough, your sword will be long enough."

At times in the period 1901–1909, TR turned to the occasional article as relief from the rigors of office, such as "The Ancient Irish Sagas," written at the height of the Brownsville crisis, and a piece on the Louisiana canebrakes that coincided with the financial panic of 1907. He also wrote an introduction to a book of poems by Edwin Arlington Robinson, and appointed the starving author to a federal post on the understanding that he would spend all his time writing poetry. Robinson went on to win three Pulitzer Prizes. "I don't know where I would be without your astonishing father," he wrote Kermit Roosevelt. "He fished me out of hell by the hair of the head."

But the President's principal literary production during these years was, inevitably, correspondence. Nothing in his formal published output shows the breadth of his mind, the depth of his knowledge, the variety and extent of his intellectual friendships as impressively as the thousands and thousands of letters he addressed to paleontologists, cowboys, statesmen, sculptors, wolf trappers, archaeologists, convicts, cartoonists, scientists, editors, ornithologists, historians, philosophers, and poets. Merely to glance at the subject index to the collected edition is to be staggered by TR's productivity. There was, as Edward Wagenknecht has remarked, "so much of him."

We have Secretary of State John Hay to be thanked for one of the longest and finest of these letters, which TR dictated on 9 August 1903 in response to another request that he preserve some of his dinner-table conversation for posterity. This delightful account of his cross-country tour in the spring of that year captures, I think, the charm of Roosevelt's personality more than anything else he ever wrote—although two other gigantic letters describing his grand tour of Europe in 1910 are even funnier. Thirty years ago, Elting Morison published all three in a little volume entitled *Cowboys and Kings: Three Great Letters by Theodore Roosevelt* (Cambridge, Mass., 1954). It should be kept permanently in print.

Historically speaking, some of the presidential correspondence is of extraordinary value, because it was Roosevelt's habit to write what his family teasingly called "posterity letters" after all the major events of his two terms in office. By the same token, these letters must be treated with caution. TR was a truthful man, but his zeal for the truth did not impel him to record it when it did not redound to his own advantage. Much more rewarding, from the biographical point of view, are those letters he addressed to his intellectual correspondents, many of whom, interestingly enough, were English. (He soon outgrew the anglophobia of his youth.) George Otto Trevelyan, the distinguished historian and biographer of Lord Macaulay; John St. Loe Strachey, editor of the London *Spectator;* James Bryce, Regius Professor of Law at Oxford and author of the classic *The American Commonwealth;* and John Morley, biographer, editor of *Fortnightly Review,* and secretary to India, were the most active of these transatlantic correspondents, along with Sir Cecil Spring Rice, Viscount Lee of Fareham, Lord Edward Grey, Rudyard Kipling, and others. TR also kept in epistolary touch with such farther-flung luminaries as Baron d'Estournelles de Constant of France, Count Albert Apponyi of Hungary, Guglielmo Ferrero of Italy, and Kentaro Kaneko of Japan.

He was, in other words, a cosmopolitan intellectual long before he entered the White House, thoroughly at home in the best parlors on both sides of the Atlantic. During his second European honeymoon, for example, we find him being put up at the Athenaeum, lunching with the Duke of Westminster, weekending with Lord North, and visiting with all the reigning *literati* of London, including the inevitable tea with Robert Browning. His lifelong intimacy with Trevelyan and Morley and Bryce dates back to this time. Trevelyan was the one to whom he poured out most of his soul, and the older man was equally ardent in return. In the words of David H. Burton, they "spoke of Thackeray or Dickens, of Hawthorne or Poe . . . of James II, of Philip of Spain, or Jefferson Davis. . . . They mourned together the death of John Hay, refought the battles of the American Revolution and the Spanish-American War. And they compared political systems."

Twenty years Roosevelt's senior, Sir George confessed once that TR was "the best and closest friend I have made in the evening of my life, when a man is very seldom fortunate enough to make such a friend." There hovered over their relationship the august ghost of an Englishman Roosevelt never met, but who influenced his intellectual and political development as much as any of his American, or for that matter Roman and Greek mentors—Trevelyan's uncle Thomas Babington Macaulay. TR began reading the latter's famous *Essays* and *Histories* in youth, and ignored the decline in their reputation around the turn of the century. A volume of Macaulay, along with a volume of Plutarch, was a staple in his saddlebag wherever he went. "Upon my word," he wrote Trevelyan, "the more I read him . . . the greater my admiration becomes." And again, long after leaving the presidency: "I am rather a fanatic about Macaulay. . . . In all the essentials he seems to me more and more as I grow older a *very* great political philosopher and statesman, no less than one of the two or three very greatest historians. Of course I am undoubtedly partly influenced by the fact that he typifies common sense mixed with high idealism, but also the sane and tempered radicalism which seems to me to make for true progress."

Finding parallels is one of the most facile of historical tricks, but even so the portrait that arises in Keith Hope's paper "Moderation and Merit in Macaulay's '*Lays of Ancient Rome*' "* is so Rooseveltian that I cannot resist listing some of its features. The extremely close family background, leading to adult perception of the domestic hearth as the focus of all bliss; the naïve mannerisms; the cheerful equivocality on the subject of religion; the overwhelming loquacity masking personal privacy; the "terrifying sense of personal rightness"; the "encyclopaedic knowledge . . . constantly marred by crudity of interpretation"; the lifelong pull between literature and politics; the "insatiable appetite for bad novels" and belief in the poetic superiority of ballads and myths; the Anglo-Saxon imperialism; the aristocracy of outlook, tempered by invocation of "a national elite drawn mainly from the pivotal middle orders";

---

* A colloquium delivered at the Wilson Center a few weeks before this one.

the constant search for "distant contemporaries" (Frederick M. Turner's phrase); the belief in a meritorious bureaucracy; the "extraordinary inability to question anything"—all these attributes of Macaulay were in turn attributes of TR—and the list could be extended indefinitely. Trevelyan himself remarked that TR's memory reminded him of nothing so much as the legendary mechanism of Macaulay. More to the point is the conscious influence of Macaulay upon Roosevelt as historian and writer. I like to think that the clarity of TR's best prose is due to it, although he never approached the elegance of that great stylist.

ROOSEVELT'S TWO FINAL testaments as a historian were lectures he gave after leaving the White House—at Oxford University in the spring of 1910, and at Boston, as president of the American Historical Association, in December 1912. The first of these, "Biological Analogies in History" (published under the same title in London, 1910), was an overambitious attempt to integrate his two great intellectual passions, rather along the lines of the man in *Pickwick Papers* who wrote a paper on Chinese Metaphysics after looking up "China" in the encyclopedia, then "Metaphysics," and combining his information. The lecture was also, at least in its first draft, extremely controversial. TR showed it to his friend Henry Fairfield Osborn of the American Museum of Natural History, who recalled:

> The manuscript . . . was full of analogies between the extinct animal and the kingdoms and principalities in the human world, in which he compared one moribund government in Europe to the *megatherium*, and another that ceased to progress about three centuries ago to the *glyptodon*. I drew heavy pencil lines across these pages with the word "omit" in the margin and wrote: "I have left out certain passages that are likely to bring on war between the United States and the governments referred to."

Roosevelt willingly accepted these deletions: in that respect he was an editor's dream. "I always regard with stoical calm the mutilation of my bantlings," he told Richard Watson Gilder of *The Century Magazine.* "Biological Analogies in History" was thus rendered rather bland by the time TR presented it as the Romanes Lecture on 7 June 1910. "In the way of grading which we have at Oxford," the Archbishop of York said afterward, "we agreed to mark the lecture 'Beta Minus,' but the lecturer 'Alpha Plus.' While we felt that the lecture was not a very great contribution to science, we felt sure that the lecturer was a very great man."

TR's subsequent address to the American Historical Association, published under the title *History as Literature* (New York, 1913) is, in contrast, one of his most valuable pronouncements. It is a passionate plea for imagination in the writing of history—even then the shades of "scientific" methodology were darkening the halls of academe. But Roosevelt is at pains to emphasize that by imagination he does not mean fiction:

> History can never be truthfully presented . . . unless profound research, patient, laborious, painstaking, has preceded the presentation. No amount of self-communing and pondering on the soul of mankind, no gorgeousness of literary imagery, can take the place of cool, serious, widely extended study. The vision of the great historian must be both wide and lofty. But it must be sane, clear, and based on full knowledge of the facts and of their interrelations.

Having said this, Roosevelt makes a declaration that should be engraved in marble on the façade of every history department in the country:

> [The historian] must ever remember, that while the worst offense of which he can be guilty is to write vividly and inaccurately, yet that unless he writes vividly he cannot write truthfully; for no amount of dull, painstaking detail will sum up the whole truth unless genius is there to paint the truth.

And then, in peroration:

The true historian will bring the past before our eyes as if it were the present. He will make us see as living men the hard-faced archers of Agincourt, and the war-worn spearmen who followed Alexander down beyond the rim of the known world. We shall hear grate on the coast of Britain the keels of the Low Dutch sea-thieves whose children's children were to inherit unknown continents. We shall thrill to the triumphs of Hannibal. Gorgeous in our sight will rise the splendor of dead cities, and the might of older empires. . . . We shall see the dancing girls of Memphis. The scent of the flowers in the Hanging Gardens of Babylon will be heavy to our senses. We shall sit at feast with the Kings of Nineveh when they drink from ivory and gold. With Queen Meave in her sunparlor we shall watch the rearing chariots of the champions. For us the war-horns of King Olaf shall wail across the flood, and the harps sound high at festivals in forgotten halls.

Some day the historians will tell us of these things.

In the two and a half years separating his two historical lectures, Roosevelt published no fewer than eight books, but most of these were progressive tracts, from which the dancing girls of Memphis were conspicuously absent. However, *African Game Trails* (New York, 1910) is a splendid, if straightforward, account of the great safari TR undertook on behalf of the Smithsonian in 1909–1910. The book sold prodigiously, and, along with two lucrative contributing editorships at *The Outlook* (1909–1914) and *Metropolitan Magazine* (1914–1918), helped make his last years relatively affluent. *Game Trails* remains one of the classics of Africana, as full of documentary observations as TR's youthful Western trilogy.

The most one can say about *Theodore Roosevelt, an Autobiography* (New York, 1913) is that it was a masterpiece of the art of selective amnesia. TR was an angry man when he wrote it, having been rejected in his bid for a third term in the White House, and betrayed, as he thought, by many of his friends. You would not guess, from its pages, that his father ever bought a substitute soldier in the Civil War, that TR ever had a wife called Alice Hathaway Lee, that he was blind in one eye as President, that he appointed Oliver Wendell Holmes to the Supreme Court, or that anything called the Brownsville Affair ever occurred on his watch. Three of the chapters, to do with Roosevelt's boyhood, cowboy years, and home life, are pleasant, but the others are preachy and dull.

Through the Brazilian Wilderness (New York, 1914), is another superb travelogue. Grimmer and terser than *African Game Trails*, it tells the story of TR's exploration of the River of Doubt, a thousand-mile tributary of the Amazon (subsequently renamed "Rio Roosevelt" in his honor). As we have seen, the trip nearly killed him, and he wrote little of literary consequence during the last four years of his life. This does not mean to say he did not write much. On the contrary, he produced another nine books, whose titles tell all that we want to know about their contents: *Why America Should Join the Allies* (London, 1915); *Fear God and Take Your Own Part* (New York, 1916); *Americanism and Preparedness* (New York, 1917); *The Foes of Our Own Household* (New York, 1917), and so on.

Exception can at least be made to *Life-Histories of African Game Animals* (with Edward Heller, New York, 1914), Roosevelt's last important contribution to zoology, and to *A Book-Lover's Holidays in the Open* (New York, 1916), whose charmingly clumsy title is again self-referential. Roosevelt was also still capable of producing excellent letters and the occasional first-class magazine piece. But more and more he allowed himself to become the preacher militant. Finley Peter Dunne, his colleague at the *Metropolitan,* tried to coax him away from the typewriter, back to the pen:

> It annoyed me to hear him bawling out his articles to his secretary. . . . I told him so, but he laughed.
>
> "They read all right to me," he said. "But you're no judge," I said. "You are damaging your reputation as a writer. Look at those wonderful things you did about your experiences in South America."
>
> "Oh, well," he laughed, "you must suit your implement to your subject. A pen is all right for a naturalist with a poetic strain in him—"
>
> "A what?"
>
> "A poetic strain," he said. "You didn't know I had it, but I have and I can use it at times. But when you are dealing with politics

you feel that you have your enemy in front of you and you must shake your fist and roar the Gospel of Righteousness in his deaf ear."

And he resumed his march up and down the room, striking his palm with a clenched fist and shouting an article that no one but himself ever read.

Twice more, at least, Theodore Roosevelt was both listened to and widely read. On 3 November 1916, the eve of Woodrow Wilson's reelection to the White House, he delivered himself of the magnificent excoriation referred to above. It was inspired as much by Wilson's pacifist foreign policy as by the fact that the President was staying at Shadow Lawn, New Jersey:

There should be shadows now at Shadow Lawn; the shadows of the men, women and children who have risen from the ooze of the ocean bottom and from graves in foreign lands; the shadows of the helpless whom Mr. Wilson did not dare protect lest he might have to face danger. . . . Those are the shadows proper for Shadow Lawn; the shadows of deeds that were never done; the shadows of lofty words that were followed by no action; the shadows of the tortured dead.

Two years later, after America had entered the war, after Wilson had wisely denied the aging TR's request to lead a volunteer regiment into battle, and after the death in an aerial dogfight of Quentin, his youngest, brightest, and most dearly loved son, the old warrior composed his last prose poem, an editorial in *The Kansas City Star.* This time Americans read him with tears in their eyes:

Only those are fit to live who do not fear to die; and none are fit to die who have shrunk from the joy of life and the duty of life. Both life and death are parts of the same Great Adventure. . . . Never yet was a country worth dying for unless its sons and daughters thought of life not as something concerned only with the selfish evanescence of the individual, but as a link in the great chain of creation and causation. . . . Unless men are willing to fight and die for great ideals, including love of country, ideals will vanish, and the world will become one huge sty of materialism. And unless the women of ideals bring forth the men who are ready thus to live and die, the world of the future will be filled by the spawn of the unfit.

And so, having contributed that final phrase, "The Great Adventure," to the many with which he has enriched our language, Theodore Roosevelt fell silent. He told Robert Bridges in the waning days of 1918 that he had used up the last of the multicolored carbonated manuscript blocks he took to Africa. With nothing further to write, he died at sixty years of age on 6 January 1919.

TELLING LIVES

A *Biographer's Quest for* Temps Perdu

I GUESS I SHOULD HAVE KNOWN I WOULD ONE DAY WRITE BIOG-
raphy when, at age eight or so, I discovered that the heroes I most craved
to meet—Alexander the Great, Tom Sawyer, Sir Winston Churchill, and
Chuck Yeager, the American test pilot—were not taxpaying residents of
Nairobi, Kenya. They all lived in another hemisphere, and seemed unlikely to visit mine, except perhaps on safari. Denied their company, I was
forced to improvise novels in which begoggled aviators fought confusedly
with prime ministers wearing Macedonian plumes. I made no distinc-

Originally published in *The Wilson Quarterly*, Summer 1983.
Daguerrotype of Frédéric Chopin by Louis Auguste Bisson, 1849.

tion between the true and imaginary characters. Their common remoteness made them equally real.

Later, I developed an adolescent passion for Brigitte Bardot. But that divine *vision pneumatique* never swam further south than Saint-Tropez, let alone the equator. Lacking her flesh—and what flesh!—I began to write erotic fantasies with lines such as "The ripe mulberries rise in Brigitte's breasts."

Thus diverted, I paid little attention to the face of Theodore Roosevelt, which grinned at me one day from the pages of a civic history entitled *Nairobi: The First Fifty Years.* The caption identified him as a former U.S. president who had made an expedition to British East Africa in 1910, and decimated most of the local wildlife. I stared briefly into his kindly, bespectacled eyes, and forgot about him for the next quarter of a century.

My first serious interest in biography came when I decided to be a famous pianist, and checked Dent's *Master Musicians* series out of the school library. Those excellent short biographies introduced me to men who still loom large in my life: Beethoven, Schubert, Schumann, Chopin, Liszt, and Brahms. I memorized every detail that would enable me to see, hear, feel, and even smell them (that regrettable chamber pot beneath Beethoven's Broadwood piano, those Lisztian cigar stumps moldering on the bosoms of adoring matrons).

Desperate for even closer acquaintance, I combed the iconographical resources of Nairobi's McMillan Memorial Library, i.e., an illustrated encyclopedia. I flicked impatiently past reproductions of painted and drawn portraits. It was the reality of photographs I craved. Curiously enough, only the oldest and blurriest of these excited me: a haunting daguerreotype of the seated, tubercular Chopin, hawk-nosed with a furrow of pain between his eyes. It was taken in 1849; he had but ten months to live. For some reason, the picture overpowered me with a sense of loss, of regret that Chopin's vanished, soft-hued Paris would be forever denied me. Here was I, a hundred years later, imprisoned under the harsh African sky.

MY QUEST FOR *temps perdu* did not, however, become active until I was thirty years old and living in New York as a freelance advertising copywriter. To while away the time between assignments, I began to research the life of Josef Lhévinne (1876–1944), an obscure Russian pianist whose few recordings are among the glories of the RCA archives. I discovered that his ninety-two-year-old widow, Rosina, was still alive and teaching at the Juilliard School of Music.

On impulse, I went to interview Madame Lhévinne. She began to reminisce about Josef's private recitals in Chekov's apartment, of Moscow nights with Rachmaninoff and Scriabin, and of weekends "at Yasnaya Polyana with the Tolstoys."

I listened, enraptured, and came away from her studio determined to create a biography of Lhévinne in sound. For six months, I tape-recorded interviews with his surviving friends and pupils, compiled a chronology and discography, studied microfilms of his press clips, and pored over photographs until I could envision him shambling onstage, with his sleepy eyes and loose red wig. The resultant three-and-a-half hour *Josef Lhévinne: A Radio Portrait* was broadcast by WNCN New York in December 1971, and elicited the biggest listener response in the station's history.

Even then I never assumed that I could make a living doing this sort of thing. As a college dropout, I felt unqualified for scholarly research. Was that not the province of PhDs? I should have been encouraged by Harry Graham, who wrote in *Misrepresentative Men:*

All great biographers possess
Besides a thirst for information
That talent which commands success,
I mean of course Imagination;
Combining with excessive Tact
A total disregard for Fact.

Instead, I tried to become successively a travel writer, a journalist, and a screenwriter. Then, in 1974, President Nixon resigned and made his tearful farewell to White House staffers. Like millions of other Americans watching on television, I was mystified to hear him read a nineteenth-century eulogy, written in a moment of high emotion by one of his predecessors: "She was beautiful in face and form . . . as a flower she lived, and as a fair young flower she died."

"Well," said Nixon after a pause, "that was TR."

At this, a forgotten, bespectacled face floated up from the depths of memory, and I was consumed with curiosity about what tragedy had impelled Theodore Roosevelt to write those words. I dug out Noel Busch's *T.R.*, found the facts to be very moving, then searched and found much more in Carleton Putnam's masterly *Theodore Roosevelt: The Formative Years*. It occurred to me that this period of TR's life, beginning with the death of his first wife in 1884 and ending with his marriage in 1886 to his childhood sweetheart, would make an excellent screenplay— comprising also his cowboy years out West, his conquest of melancholy and ill health, and his discovery that he was destined for the Presidency.

I wrote the screenplay (still unproduced, alas), doing massive research because I wanted to make it as authentic as possible. It was entitled *The Dude from New York*.* Then my agent made a fateful remark, "Since you've done so much work, why don't you write a short, popular biography?" In 1979, the first volume of this "short" work appeared—886 pages of it. By an odd coincidence, I counted 886 gray hairs in my beard on the day of publication. I am now writing a second volume covering TR's Presidency (1901–1909), and will have to write a third before I am through — by which time, no doubt, my beard will be snowy.[†]

I SHOULD BE GRATEFUL to Nixon, because like a foregoing traveler who treads an acorn into the ground, he has afforded years of shade and comfort to someone lost by the wayside. My Rooseveltian oak is sturdy now (although I wish to God it didn't grow so slowly), and may possibly survive me. I count myself lucky to have become a biographer at a time when biography is once again becoming a serious art form, as it was in the late eighteenth and mid-nineteenth centuries.

The gentleman biographer, so elegantly personified by James Boswell and John Lockhart, is reappearing at the toniest dinner parties, although often as not "he" is now a woman. Indeed, one of New York's *plus chic* hostesses, Arianna Stassinopoulos, is the biographer of Maria Callas.

---

* In 2011, HBO acquired *The Rise of Theodore Roosevelt* for development as a miniseries.
[†] This prediction came true.

Barbara Tuchman (*Stillwell*) sits high at any table, and Antonia Fraser (*Mary Queen of Scots*) is no stranger to caviar.

Women, come to think of it, are naturally suited to biography, with their intuition, willingness to ask personal questions, and love of reading other people's mail. When femininity is allied with literary talent, as in the case of Judith Thurman (*Isak Dinesen*), Jean Strouse (*Alice James*), or Cecil Woodham-Smith, whose *Florence Nightingale* is one of the best biographies ever written, the combination is hard to beat.

Which is not to say that the hairy hand may not occasionally wield a competitive pen. Boswell's *Life of Johnson* has yet to be surpassed for depth of sympathy, wealth of detail (those mysterious bits of orange peel!), and tragicomic power. Lytton Strachey's *Queen Victoria* ends with the most poignant flashback in nonfiction, and Richard Holmes's *Shelley* begins as lyrically as any novel I recall.

WHAT ARE THE REASONS for the newfound popularity of biography, apparent on both sides of the Atlantic? One seems to be that a good biographer courageously tackles what Thomas Beer called "that most dangerous of materials, ourselves." Modern novelists largely lack this courage. (Has any contemporary libertine ever yielded a gift more erotic than Frau Chauchat in Mann's *Magic Mountain*, presenting Hans Castorp with an X-ray of her torso?) They also, to my mind, lack the energy to write sustained narrative—the literary equivalent of running a marathon. Biographers *have* to be storytellers, in that their subject is the organic growth of character perceived in action. When the story is well told, and the character original enough to engage our sympathy, we can still feel the sense of final-page regret that used to be the sign of great fiction.

I confess that Boswell remains the master against whom I measure my own efforts. I shamelessly imitate him, particularly in the dramatization of dialogue, a legitimate device (if the words are on record) that for some reason has seldom been used by other biographers:

ROOSEVELT I appointed him because he was the best man, regardless of race, color, or creed. Isn't that so, Mr. Schiff?

JACOB SCHIFF (*rather deaf*). Dot's right, Mr. President, you
came to me and said, "Chake, who is der best Choo I can put in my
Cabinet?"

It is just as legitimate, in my opinion, for a biographer to use the narrative techniques perfected by Tolstoy and Dickens (and in our own century, movie directors), such as rhythmic cross-cutting, dramatic exit and
entry, symbols, clue planting, and cliffhangers. There is no reason either
why the modern biographer should not deploy imagery as calculatedly
as the novelist or poet. For example, I used a subtextual metaphor of
climbing throughout *The Rise of Theodore Roosevelt* (having noticed that
TR could never resist scaling any mountain in his vicinity, even when he
was ravaged by asthma attacks). Chapter after chapter, as he rises
through life, finds him cresting this or that cliff or mountain, descending
occasionally into valleys, yet always reaching higher plateaus, searching out purer air and wider vistas.

On the last page, he is Vice President of the United States, picnicking
atop Mount Marcy, the loftiest point in New York State, at the very moment President McKinley begins to die of an assassin's bullet. He sees a
ranger running up the slopes of the mountain, clutching the yellow slip
of a telegram. "Instinctively," the last sentence reads, "he knew what
message the man was bringing."

Now that sentence, I submit, is as dramatic as any a novelist might
write. I get letters from readers who say it makes their skin prickle. Yet I
don't take credit for it, because it's a matter of fact: Theodore Roosevelt's
own testimony, twice repeated. All I did was recognize a moment of supreme drama for what it was worth. Even if it "sentenced" me to another
two volumes.

THE IDEA OF NORTH
Glenn Gould's Search for Solitude

Aᴆᴛᴇʀ ᴄʟᴏꜱɪɴɢ *GLENN GOULD VARIATIONS*, ᴀ ᴘᴏɪɢɴᴀɴᴛ *FEST-schrift* edited by John McGreevy, one is haunted by "the idea of north"— Gould's own phrase. Chilly images, both literary and photographic, possess the mind. A schoolboy of Chopinesque profile walks off into the Canadian wind, his arms flailing to the beat of an orchestra in his head— "*pa-puh, pa-puh, duh-pa.*" A lonely man guns his Cadillac across frozen wastes, wrapped in a cocoon of rock music. Other layers of insulation— tweed and worsted and leather and knit—swathe him as he poses beside an Arctic-bound train.

Now that Glenn Gould has gone to the northernmost retreat of all (he died of a stroke last year, aged fifty), we may ponder the polar obsession that pulled him, during his lifetime, farther and farther from the

Originally published in *The Washington Post Book World*, 20 November 1983.

Still from The Idea of North, *CBC documentary by Judith Pearlman, 1970.*

warmth of the world. Himself the most articulate of talkers (as he was the most articulate of pianists), Gould explained that his "idea of north" was metaphorical rather than geographical, "a foil for other ideas and values that seemed to me depressingly urban-oriented and spiritually limited thereby." Like Wallich in Mark Helprin's story "The Schreuderspitze," Gould sought out the regions of ice imaginatively, without quitting his own hotel room. Here, simply by locking the door, blinding the windows, and sending out for food, he was transported to a place not so much cold as pure, where there were no bright colors, no unnatural sounds, to distract him from contemplation of God—or of Glenn Gould. The two were interchangeable, as far as his friends were concerned.

In contemplating himself, Gould passed beyond mere vanity into the humble self-understanding of genius. Indeed it seems he never was vain, despite the showy mannerisms that made him so notorious on the concert stage. Richard Kostelanetz explains in these pages that Gould's eccentricities were rational. Thus, his simian crouch low over the keyboard was caused partly by very long arms, and partly because his teacher used to lean down on him as he played. The glass of Poland water beside top C was precautionary, in that the tensions of public performance often made him gag. And his atonal humming (which he tried hard to suppress, to the extent of screening himself with a baffle during recording sessions) was caused by frustration with imperfect pianos. When the keyboard suited him, he kept quiet.

No explanation is given of why he once found it necessary to read a magazine during the nonpianistic parts of a concerto, yet one assumes that he did not think this strange, and that he was as absorbed in music as he was in the article. "Sometimes," John Lee Roberts writes, "he had two or three levels of thought . . . and would have a stream of music progressing at the same time in his mind." Indeed, after retiring from the concert stage Gould produced some amazing radio documentaries that blended separate strands of consciousness into an artistic whole. *The Idea of North*, for example, consisted of five interview tracks, spliced and edited to sound like a conversation, although the "conversants" never met. Above this mix Gould added a music track, and below it a *basso os-*

tinato of running train wheels. The result delighted him, if not his CBC audience, and he claimed to have invented a new aural form.*

Gould himself was so contrapuntal a character that it's tempting to describe his life as a fully worked-out fugue. Like one of Bach's subjects, he emerges from nothing—a plain Protestant home in Toronto, the son of a furrier—and defines himself at once in strong, single tones, full of potential. "He seemed to know, from birth, almost everything about everything." As he develops, under the guidance of his teacher Alberto Guerrero, various counterstrands of personality come into play, some major, some minor: humor, hypochondria, iconoclasm, business instinct, and ruthless ego. At nineteen, the exposition is complete; there is nothing more he can learn. Guerrero drops from the fugue like a spent motif. Gould moves into the first major episode of his career, recognized in his early twenties as one of the greatest pianists of the twentieth century. But the *accelerandi* and *stretti* of public performances drive him toward discord. At times he sounds quite mad, then suddenly there is a harsh interrupted cadence. Silence intervenes. The concert hall, Gould announces, is dead. He will devote the rest of his career to new recording technologies, in the intimacy of the studio. He is just thirty-two.

Quietly, a second major episode begins. Gould plays, writes, lectures for television, produces documentaries. The harmonies of his life grow more refined as he confines himself to close friends, spends more and more time alone or on the telephone (an instrument on which he is also a virtuoso). There is a feeling of broadening out, of growing richness and inevitability, as the double-bar line of his fiftieth birthday approaches. When it is reached, he says, he will stop playing forever: "That will be enough of Gould." In recapitulation, he rerecords the work that made him famous in youth: Bach's *Goldberg Variations.* And as its last suspension resolves, he dies.

The rest, fortunately, is not silence, for Gould left a vast discography (printed by McGreevy as an appendix), as well as scores of articles, interviews, and films. One hopes that his writings will be published in collected form, since the samples reprinted here whet the appetite for more. Gould was an excellent essayist—erudite, lucid, and often amusing. His

* See also page 239.

profile of Leopold Stokowski is a model of the genre, and a piece entitled "Art of the Fugue" is explication at its finest. (I particularly liked the line about a Bach coda "renouncing all foreign entanglements.")

As for personal details, this book is generous yet tantalizing. We want to know much more. One cannot complain about its reticence on sexual matters: Gould seems to have believed, with Bernard Shaw, that the greatest orgasm is that of creativity. But a broader, more detailed biography is required. Painful themes are touched on—his cruel rejection of Guerrero, compulsive pill popping and self-doubt (his favorite Shakespeare character was Richard II)—but they are not explored. There are many excellent photographs, whose cumulative impression is of acute melancholy. Whom did Gould love, if not himself? Was it the north in his soul that led to the gradual whitening of his piano tonality? Did he die alone, or was there at the last some final warmth to comfort him?* One cannot but hope so, and meanwhile await the definitive story of his life.

---

* In 2007 it was reported that Gould (like Beethoven before him) claimed to have been in love with "a certain beautiful girl" who had declined his offer of marriage. This *Unsterbliche Geliebte* was probably the painter Cornelia Foss, who has admitted to an affair with him from 1967 to 1972. She elected to return to her husband, and Gould carried a torch for her the rest of his life. Their love is documented in a recent film by Michèle Hozer and Peter Raymont, *Genius Within: The Inner Life of Glenn Gould.*

A HUNDRED AND FORTY-FOUR MERLINS

Britain's Imperial War Museum

THE MAJESTIC BUILDING THAT HOUSES BRITAIN'S IMPERIAL WAR Museum was once known as "Bedlam," or Bethlem Royal Hospital for the Insane. That old nickname might seem appropriate to its present function as a showcase for instruments of destruction. Yet oddly enough the museum is a peaceful, even nostalgic place to visit. Somehow it manages to recollect in tranquillity insanities greater, and din more deafening, than anything lunatics of past centuries could imagine.

Thus, as you walk up the garden path toward the portico, into the aim of two 100-ton cannons, you hear nothing but the cheep of starlings, and breathe an incongruous perfume of roses. It was Robert Schumann who first thought to combine guns and flowers, in a metaphor describing the music of Frédéric Chopin: here the combination serves as effectively to remind us that man's power to destroy has never been as great as nature's power to recover. Poppies sprouted in the mud of war-ravaged Flanders, and birds sang over Hiroshima after being temporarily shocked into silence.

Originally appeared in *Air & Space/Smithsonian Magazine*, April/May 1986.
Spitfire display, Imperial War Museum, London.

The Imperial War Museum chronicles the story of twentieth-century conflict in the air and on sea and land, with emphasis on Britain's role in the two world wars. Whenever I go there I tell myself I will concentrate, for a change, on the Army and Navy exhibits, but the aviation halls always seduce me. My childhood as the son of a Royal Air Force pilot was dominated by the high-flying exploits of Squadron Leader James Bigglesworth, Captain Albert Ball, and Wing Commander Douglas Bader. I should explain that Bigglesworth was the fictional air ace created by W. E. Johns (*The Camels Are Coming; Biggles in the Blue; Biggles—Air Commodore*), and to this day he is as real to me as the other two. I cannot set eyes on the museum's Sopwith Camel, forever airborne in Gallery 13, without seeing Biggles's goggled face craning out of the cockpit, looking for Huns in the sun.

Actually, this Camel, which has a Zeppelin to its credit, is not one he would have flown. It is a 2F1, the marine version developed for the Royal Naval Air Service in 1917. A muscular, turn-on-a-shilling, stubby little killer, it was almost all engine and propeller, gnawing at the breeze with such eager ferocity that it could jump off a barge towed by a destroyer. In flight, the torque of its huge rotary Le Rhône engine was enough to flip it out of the control of inexperienced hands, but its maneuverability, with an Al Ball at the joystick, could be murderous. Getting the 2F1 down again after a sortie was not so easy. Lacking a landing platform, pilots simply ditched as near the home ship as possible. "The planes," the museum states, "were considered expendable." How many Camels do the dark unfathom'd caves of ocean bear?

I was disappointed during my last visit not to find a cherished Bristol Fighter hanging behind the 2F1. (Exhibits in the galleries change from time to time, and some prize aircraft are transferred to the Imperial War Museum annex at Duxford.) The Fighter has been replaced, intriguingly enough, by a bulky sailplane that seems to have been made out of bed boards and blue-checked sheets. Investigation discloses that the impression is correct. It's a replica of the "Colditz Glider," surely the most original escape machine devised during World War II.

Security at Colditz, the German prison for habitual truants, was supposed to be unbreakable, thanks to its fortifications. Yet the castle's hilltop site was an inspiration to six aeronautically trained British inmates.

Plans for a glider that would waft a pair of them to freedom were drawn up on purloined watercolor paper. These scale drawings, irresistible to anyone who has ever cut and glued balsa airframes, are displayed in a glass case, with a curatorial note explaining that they have been "nibbled at the edges by a resident mouse"—whether ancient or contemporary, the label does not say.

The projected glider was a 240-pound monoplane 20 feet long, with a 33-foot wingspan. Presumably its size was mandated by the heaviness of its longerons and spars, which were ripped at dead of night from wooden beds and the theater floor. But where to construct such a monster? The team found a long attic over the castle chapel where, behind a false partition, fuselage and wings could be built side by side. After both units had been covered with German mattress fabric, and water-tautened, the attic would be broken open, exposing a section of adjoining roof ideal for launching. "Both units would then be assembled on a trolley attached via a system of pulleys to a tub of concrete," the museum explains. "When the concrete was dropped 60 feet through holes made in the castle floors . . ."

Well, you and Rube Goldberg can imagine the rest. Personally, I would have volunteered my seat to anyone else wanting a ride. The glider looks about as airworthy as a Steinway grand. Though fully constructed, it never flew. The war came to an end just in time.

NEXT DOOR, IN GALLERY 14, is an aircraft equally clumsy looking, the Fairey Swordfish of Fleet Air Arm fame, vintage 1936. The biplane squats on the floor, wings folded back, like an immense, corpulent gnat. Here, however, appearances are deceptive. The "Stringbag," as it was affectionately known, had such lift it could take off in a sneeze, and drop down again on a rolling, pitching deck with dandelion grace.

Yet it arouses no emotions in my breast as does the sight of a DH 98 Mosquito T Mark III suspended nearby. Why is it that some old planes evoke such lurchings of the heart, while others, equally romantic, leave one cold? It's the same difference that accounts for Cupid's unpredictability, I suppose. Every person falls in love for inscrutable reasons. The "Mozzy" is, with one exception, the plane I most hope to find on active duty in Heaven when I die. (On earth, it was decommissioned in the mid-1950s.) God probably disapproves of bombers as a genre, but He must make allowances for this masterpiece of aeronautical engineering.

It was not a plane you would have wanted to see homing in on you in '43, if you were aboard a *Kriegsmarine* U-Boat in the Bay of Biscay. Its mere shape is terrifying. With its two big Rolls-Royce Merlins reaching as far forward as its nose, it looks less like a mosquito than three sharks in convoy. Sky-blue below, camouflaged on top, it merged with the elements, attacking so fast that it needed no guns to defend itself. Nothing Germany built could match its 384-mph speed and amazing ceiling of 37,500 feet. The RAF soon discovered that it was equally effective as a fighter, night fighter, fighter-bomber, minelayer, anti-shipping striker, photo reconnaissance craft, and transport, making it one of the most versatile warplanes in history.

Floating high over the Mosquito, a leprous gray Focke-Wulf 190, and the cockpit section of a Hawker Typhoon, is the craft more beautiful to me—and to countless other plane lovers—than anything else in aerial memory. Strictly speaking, the Spitfire's design is not as perfect as its 1931 Schneider Cup sport-racing progenitor, the Supermarine S-6B. Its fin and tailplane seem too small, but nothing can surpass the elegance of its engine nacelle and curving wings. One of the few genuinely ecstatic moments of my life was standing in our garden near Moffit Field in Rhodesia in 1944 and watching my father wheel his Spitfire low overhead. How the engine roared! How those exquisite ailerons swept the sky—trailing sunlight like fire! My father! Dad . . . dropping leaflets!

GALLERY 19'S AIRSPACE is shared by Germany's late-war Heinkel He 162A2 "Volksjäger" jet fighter, a most repulsive airplane, humping its axial-flow engine like some sort of inverted marsupial. It never saw mass production. That well-known aesthete Adolf Hitler preferred to invest in weapons that looked more menacing, such as the V-1 and V-2 rockets. Two specimens are on display here, cut away to expose their workings.

Sinister as these two rockets were in deployment—the one announcing itself in advance, with a death-rattle engine note, the other arriving silently, long before its sound—they caused only localized destruction. It was heavy bombing over wide areas that determined the course of the air war, and Britain's best practitioner of that technique was the Avro Lancaster. The museum, alas, shows only a chunk of Lancaster fuselage, but even this fragment conveys something of the plane's brute power. It represents the forward section, complete with gun turret. The profile of the "Lanc," from the cockpit on down, always reminds me of Desperate Dan, an old British comic-book character: glaring Plexiglas eyes, jutting, gun-bristled chin.

You can gaze through the scratched and bubbled panes into the empty cabin, at the instrument panel with its inert needles, the joystick wrapped around with sweaty cord, the navigator's yellow map under a long-dead lamp, back toward the bomb bay, back into the past. It does not take a viewing of *The Best Years of Our Lives* to see the needles tremble again, and hear, in the silence of Gallery 19, the deep thunder of vanished engines. Was there ever a noise so awesome as the combined roar of a squadron of Lancasters shaking the air and the very ground?

Talking about decibels, the Imperial War Museum is not quiet everywhere. Some halls have piped-in loudspeaker effects, and since the floors are open-plan, sounds often drift from gallery to gallery with weird results. For example, when you stand beneath the Mosquito you may be startled to hear over your shoulder a unique nasal whine: "When I arrived in the desert in *Awgust* 1942 to take *commahnd* of the Eighth *Ahmy* . . ." It's Monty himself (Field Marshal Bernard Law Montgomery) giving a tape-recorded tour of his North African equipage a few yards away. Sometimes such juxtapositions of sight and sound can be moving, as when I strolled through a documentary photographic show entitled "Bomber" and heard, as if from an immense distance, the poignant harmony of French Revolutionary choruses. It came from a neighboring exhibit on Alsace-Lorraine, and irrelevant or not, aroused a strange feeling of nostalgia . . . for what? Another time of horror and devastation, even though one may not have experienced it personally?

I can only hazard the theory that those who fight in war understand, as we in luxurious peace cannot, the absolute values of life, love, and death. This must be why the faces of war-doomed youth, preserved in military museums around the world, look so much purer than ours. We do not envy their fate, but we yearn for the sharpness of their experience. Consider the haunting face of Wing Commander Leonard Cheshire, displayed in the museum's room dedicated to winners of the Victoria Cross. These monklike eyes saw the fireball rise over Nagasaki.

There is, it must be admitted, an awful beauty to engines of war, especially those that fly. "Bomber" is less a history of strategic bombing than a series of magical images. Here is an enormous silver salamander, the *Graf Zeppelin*, floating over a field of tiny, worshipful figures. (So much for the originality of Steven Spielberg's vision in *Close Encounters of the Third Kind.*) Here are balloons trailing a delicate curtain of wires above London in 1917: they look like bluebottles riding on water, waiting to sting the first German glider that swims into their fronds. Here are black B-17s sitting solid against a black sky, while invisible fighters weave arabesques of bright vapor. And here is a box of World War I "flechettes"— pretty little finned steel darts designed to be dropped in showers, some no bigger than a pencil, yet each capable of drilling its victim to the ground. One of them, upturned and accurately enlarged, could be today's Saturn rocket.

I WAS AMUSED, on leaving the museum, to hear a Cockney guard whistling the French Revolutionary tunes with enjoyment. By just such a process of unconscious adaptation did the tune for the French war song "Malbrouck s'en va-t'en guerre" become the song "For He's a Jolly Good Fellow," and the British drinking song "To Anacreon in Heaven" turn into "The Star Spangled Banner." So in music, memory, war, and peace, we are all ultimately cousins.

WE CAME TO AMERICA

The Irrevocable Act of Emigration

OﾍﾄOﾍﾅ OF THE MINOR REWARDS OF LIVING IN THIS COUNTRY IS that the "Weddings and Betrothals" pages of the newspapers are so much more fun to read here than anywhere else. Consider the fecund variety of this list of names, culled at random from *The New York Times:*

> *Sara Lincoln Fish Is Married to Geoffrey Herr Longenecker; Paula Pisani, Immaculata Alumna, Is Betrothed; Zsa Zsa Hui Wed to John W. Wu; Larry S. Snowhite Will Marry Deidre Zeitz, Teacher; Richard Holbrooke Weds Blythe Babyak; J. W. Connelly to Marry Miss Gloria Grimditch.*

Since the *Times* does not celebrate the nuptials of deadbeats, we can infer that the above young people are beneficiaries of the freest, most

First published in the *Newsweek* Special Issue, Summer 1986.

Photograph of Mount Vernon by Nitsa Malik.

rewarding social system on earth. What kind of reception, I wonder, would Miss Babyak have gotten, if her forebears had remained in Bulgaria?* Speaking as an immigrant myself, I am always amazed at how quickly the descendants of immigrants forget the privations—economic, spiritual, cultural—that led to their fortunate birth in the United States. To take America for granted is to deny its history. To parade the flags of lesser nations up Fifth Avenue, and curtsy before visiting princelings, is to forfeit the dignity of free citizenship.

Immigrants who have made it—which is to say, at least built a better life here than elsewhere—wince at such derelictions because of the one characteristic that unites us: pride. Whether we are rich or poor, we have risked what the historian Oscar Handlin has called "the immigrant adventure." We cannot afford to fail. Nothing is more painful than poverty in an alien society, unless it be an abject return home. To come here is to seek more abundant life; to go back is something like death.

For emigration is an irreversible act. It is a spitting out of mother's milk, a slamming shut of schoolbooks, a tearing off of too-small clothes. The positive force of these gestures accelerates the dynamo of American life. Every new immigrant brings his or her extra pulsation of energy. Consider the exuberance of Joseph Pulitzer's journalism, the speed of Balanchine's choreography, Willem de Kooning's volcanic spurts of paint, I. M. Pei's delighted juggling of concrete and air. Immigrants gave us the gravity-defying leaps of the Brooklyn Bridge and the Saturn rocket.

In return, America stimulates miracles of self-transformation, impossible in countries where politics or prejudice inhibit free growth. Jews otherwise destined for the bitter ovens of Treblinka flowered on Broadway and Tin Pan Alley, sweetening the whole world with their song. Only in America, as the cliché goes, could a two-cent Scots bobbin boy named Andrew Carnegie make and redistribute more than $330 million. Where else could the French aristocrat Sanche de Gramont anagrammatize himself as "Ted Morgan" and become a commercially successful biographer? Recently, ve haf even had an immigrant secretary of state.

---

* Only when resurrecting this article did the author notice that Miss Babyak's bridegroom subsequently became famous.

Indeed, were it not for the Constitution's bias against the foreign-born (most unconstitutional, in my opinion), we might soon elect a president named Nguyen or Kim.* Some time ago I was at an educational-awards banquet and met an enchanting young Vietnamese girl who had just been named the valedictorian of her school in Texas. In the course of conversation she told me that just two years before she had been a "boat person," so unable to communicate with Americans that she felt she was deaf and dumb. Her teachers had to start educating her in sign language.

I could not help wondering, as she walked away in her graduation gown, how backward she might be, had those teachers subjected her to the anesthesia of bilingual education. Anything that deadens the first painful shock of American life deadens the necessary reflex, that vital urge to fight back and survive. In 1954, Frances Cavanah edited an instructive anthology called *We Came to America*, consisting of the first-hand accounts of twenty-five ordinary immigrants from twenty-five countries.[†] Most of the narratives speak of early terror and depression. Few describe any rise to wealth or fame, but all vibrate with a sense of pride and catharsis. Here is an old Chinese cutting off his pigtail, vowing never again to wear any badge of caste. Here is an eighteen-year-old French seamstress, wandering tearful and bewildered through New York City. A speeding cab nearly kills her; the driver's curse acts as an emotional catalyst. "I woke up with every sense tingling . . . there was a wonderful roar all around. . . . 'This is life!' I said out loud. 'This is for me!' "

THE AGGRESSIVE STIMULUS of the United States also helps unlock dormant creative ability. Nowadays the Norwegian-American novelist Ole Edvart Rölvaag (1876–1931) is forgotten, but his *Giants in the Earth* (1927) is one of the staples of pioneer literature. As a fisherboy growing up on the edge of the Arctic Circle, Rölvaag seemed unschoolable, destined to a life with the nets. Vague longings for "the unknown and the

---

* Although the Constitution remains unamended in this respect, it has permitted the election of a man surnamed Obama.
† See also the essay on page 210, "Undistinguished Americans."

untried" tortured him. At sixteen, he sailed for America with only one shirt, hoping to find work in South Dakota. He got off the train at a prairie stop and experienced the immigrant's worst nightmare: solitude on a sterile plain, with no map to guide him, nothing to eat or drink.

You'll have to read Rölvaag's book to learn how he survived and became a writer. But here is his description of the moment, in 1906, when he realized he was no longer Norwegian:

> I found myself on a streetcar somewhere in Brooklyn. A huge furniture van had got stuck in front of the car; the horses were balky and refused to move. [Our motorman] turned on the power, brought his car up behind the van, and began to shove. By George, those horses had to move! He shoved them for nearly two blocks, van and all, while the crowd cheered and the bell clanged. . . .
>
> I sat there in the car thrilled to the core of my being. Something had come over me like a wave . . . such a thing as that would never have been done by a European motorman, and I liked it, I liked it. Tears came to my eyes. This was America, my country. I had come home.

ALL HAPPY IMMIGRANTS can cite their own inspiring moments of assimilation. Mine came one summer evening twelve years ago. A group of us were sitting on a Manhattan terrace with a portable television set, watching the final stages of the House Judiciary Committee's move to impeach Richard Nixon. The group (citizens all) consisted of a German born in Manchuria, a Jewish woman who had fled Hungary during the revolt of 1956, a Czech with an Auschwitz tattoo, and my wife and I, from England and Africa respectively. Nobody remarked on our variety. It was not unusual for New York, and besides, we were all riveted by the events on the screen. At length the Jewish woman spoke.

"My friends, do you realize what is happening here?"

She gestured at the image of Representative Peter Rodino, the Judiciary Committee chairman, who had just made his great cry, *So speaks our Constitution.* "We are seeing thirty-eight ordinary men and women bring down the most powerful man on earth! Without a shot being fired!" Her eyes brimmed. "This is incredible."

We agreed that only those born and bred in more authoritarian societies could fully appreciate this drama of democracy. The little set pouring out its uncensored light, the free dialogue, the polyglot viewers, and, all around us, in panorama, the glittering towers of capitalism—it was a show that could play nowhere else in the world.

Perhaps our mood was touched with complacency. While poor Nixon suffered, we were enjoying various degrees of success. Might we have felt equal reverence for the Constitution if we had been tuned in on the Harlem side of Central Park? Well, I for one have been near to starving a couple of times since, yet the reverence endures. I was down to my last (borrowed) buck in 1979, when a naturalization examiner asked me, "Do you believe in the Constitution of the United States?"

Words failed me. All I could manage was a gargling noise, and he doubtless marked me down as "mentally defective." Only once, in church, have I been asked anything as solemn.

OF COURSE, SOMETHING has to die in the process of being reborn as an American. Much as this generous nation may compensate, even overcompensate, for bereavement of birthright, there's always a feeling of scar tissue somewhere, and it aches at unexpected moments. As I write, I am listening to one of the most nostalgic musical performances ever committed to tape: a collaboration between Mstislav Rostropovich and Vladimir Horowitz in the slow movement of Rachmaninoff's Cello Sonata, recorded live at Carnegie Hall in 1976. Both pianist and cellist are ardent Americans (and in proof, have respectively arranged earsplitting versions of "The Stars and Stripes Forever"). But this once-in-a-lifetime rendition of a piece that is the very voice of Old Russia—baritone surges over a steppelike plateau of monotones—evokes from Rostropovich and Horowitz a passionate remembrance of things past. No one can listen to it and imagine that immigrants are ever capable of total identification with the United States.

By the same token, disillusioned immigrants serve as salutary oracles, reminders that this country falls short of perfection. Deep in the woods of Vermont there lives that great, gloomy *éminence grise* of the gulag, Aleksandr Solzhenitsyn. He rarely emerges from his *dacha*, and what he sees of America through the chinks of his fence persuades him he is not missing much. Once, in 1978, Harvard University managed to lure him to Cambridge for its commencement address. The resultant blast against this country's "fragility and friability," "decline in courage," and "hastiness and superficiality," not to mention our "TV stupor and . . . intolerable music" was icy enough to frost-kill all the ivy in Harvard Yard.

About the same time, President Jimmy Carter tried to indulge in a few similar home truths, but Americans do not like breast-beating in the Bully Pulpit. Solzhenitsyn's words, however, were heard with embarrassment and shame. Some of this nation's current moral reawakening can be traced to that admonitory, heavily accented voice from the woods.

Less famous immigrants also perform critical functions. We deplore America's commercial crassness, its disrespect for privacy, its lack of manners, its omnipresent obesity, its brass-band vulgarity, its contempt for nuance, its sick worship of guns. We feel we are entitled (as new citizens) to point out these things, in an effort to improve the society that has improved us. Thus Korean immigrants are civilizing New York City's retail-fruit industry, Nigerian taxi drivers rebuffing the rudeness of Washington congressmen, Italians teaching Chicago what to eat and how to dress, and Japanese coaxing Californians not to let it *all* hang out.

How do Americans take these strictures? With more grace than any most nationals, my experience suggests. (Try telling an Englishman his land laws are feudal!) But Oscar Handlin, himself the son of immigrants and author of the classic study *The Uprooted*, began to worry, several years before Solzhenitsyn's speech, that the Me Generation was listening too little and forgetting too much. Obsession with self, with present pleasure and future fashion, had dulled young people's awareness of the immigrant experience. Contemporary narcissism, Handlin wrote, was a perversion of the individualism that our ancestors rejoiced in, "the glory and the grief of being free." Since narcissism itself perverts into loneliness and paranoia, the danger was that young Americans would end up hating their friends and ultimately their government and their country. "The 1970s," he wrote, "can hardly fail to be a decade of reckoning. It will reveal how many Americans still find the immigrant story valid."

Well, that decade was my first here, and the country sure felt sick for most of it. But America is a basically healthy organism: its antibodies develop spontaneously. It began to purge itself with Watergate, and by 1981, after a final shudder of nausea over Tehran, the process of healing was complete. Once again the nation is a voice of positivism and liberty.

I THINK I SPEAK for all pieces of refuse from teeming shores when I say that we love the United States for its tolerance, its welcome even of misfits. Immigrants are by definition abnormal, but we feel more normal here than anywhere else. Instead of a dull homogeneity, America encourages a profligate exchange of genes, the more motley the better. (Theodore Roosevelt, campaigning, boasted so many ethnic strains in common with voters that he was dubbed "Old Fifty-Seven Varieties.") My closest school friend in Kenya was the son of a hot-blooded Greek father and a cool, upper-class Englishwoman. He grew up crooked, a tree fertilized by two root systems, yearning on the one hand to blossom out as an artist, twisted on the other into the stiff shape of a London barrister. He drank himself to death at the age of forty. If he had immigrated here with me, he would have settled over a taverna in Astoria, Queens, and opened a gallery in Greenwich Village, and I wouldn't be mourning him now.

Mentioning John Manussis reminds me that as boys we vowed to become famous automobile manufacturers. He said he would call his car the *Cyclopedia.* "What about yours?" "The *America,*" I said. "I'll build it in Detroit."

Even at the age of eight, it seems, I was preparing to emigrate. The barbershop in Nairobi where my mother used to take me for haircuts was furnished with ancient copies of *The Saturday Evening Post,* and I remember drooling over full-color advertisements for Betty Crocker pies. But the image that thrilled me most was a photograph (somewhat diffused by fallen hair clippings) of a tall, white-columned Southern mansion. It may or may not have been Mount Vernon. I remember that it evoked agonies of love and longing for a civilization where life was spacious and ordered and cultured, in contrast to the smelly congeries of Jeevanjee Street, just outside the door.

Needless to say, that American dream has proved illusory. But I thought of it again last summer. My wife and I attended a Fourth of July lunch at a house just opposite Mount Vernon, on the left bank of the Potomac. We sat on a patio overlooking the fields of National Colonial Farm (golden corn shucks, wooden wagons, horses inert in the heat), our eyes irresistibly focused on the white house across the water—my barbershop vision at last! After coffee our host asked Supreme Court Justice Byron White to read the Declaration of Independence. The big jurist stood in swimming trunks and began to intone those skin-creeping words, *"When in the Course of human events . . ."*

"Wait a minute!" somebody said. "We forgot Lily." Out came the maid from Guyana, all cheekbones and jet-black eyes. The reading continued as geese honked peacefully overhead and pleasure boats—pursuing happiness?—cruised up and down the river. I rather dreaded the line about merciless Indian savages, but Lily, who had just become a citizen, didn't blink. When Justice White concluded, she joined in the applause. "Is my birthday, too," she said, grinning.

So it is, Lily, yours and mine and all America's. May your swarthy descendants benefit from your labor, and may one of them marry the grandchild of Geoffrey Herr Longenecker and Sara Lincoln Fish.

THE PORTRAITIST'S SHADOW

Biography as an Art

I STAND BEFORE YOU THE REPRESENTATIVE OF AN ABUSED, IF FECUND breed. We biographers are perceived by poets and novelists and playwrights as gossips or drones. We may rate the occasional pub party in Lower Manhattan—we may even be invited uptown to lecture at the New-York Historical Society—but we are unlikely to rub shoulders with the "literary" elite at clambakes in the Hamptons.

All we're good for, it seems, is telling the world more than it wants to know about dead American presidents, or about the mating habits of rock stars and British royalty. Small in our self-estimation, we vicariously relive the lives of large men or, in the field of operatic biography, large women. We are processors of fact, not sharers of sensibility. We reduce the sweet disorder of life to a dry sequence of index cards. What

Address to the New-York Historical Society, 22 October 1986. Some portions previously published in *Biography and Books* (Washington, D.C., 1986).

"Boswell and Johnson in Edinburgh." Cartoon by Samuel Collings, 1786.

do we know of art, of poetic rapture? The only things we roll in a fine frenzy are microfilm machines!

However, it's a fact that you don't see many browsers in the fiction stacks of bookstores these days. Increasingly, readers are turning to biography as their preferred form of literature. I do not want to speculate on why this is so, except to note that contemporary fiction tends to sharpen, rather than satisfy, our natural human hunger for a story about believable characters doing interesting things. Narrative and personality are the warp and woof of biography, and their correct interweaving calls for craftsmanship. I propose to discuss some aspects of this craft, to show how it can be made beautiful and moving, and even elevated into art.

THE BEST OF BIOGRAPHERS, in the opinion of the best of biographers, was Samuel Johnson. But rereading *Lives of the Poets* now, one has to disagree with Boswell. Johnson's essays tell us more about himself than about his subjects. The great man can no more avoid making comments than he can write without ink, and authorial opinion decisively expressed is the bane of biography. For example, he remarks of Swift: "The greatest difficulty that occurs, in analyzing his character, is to discover by what depravity of intellect he took delight in revolving ideas, from which almost every other mind shrinks with disgust."

After that there's really not much that poor Swift can do to regain our sympathy. Johnson does, half-apologetically, conclude his essay, "I have here given the character of Swift as he exhibits himself to my perception; but now let another be heard who knew him better." Thereupon follows a weak encomium by somebody called Dr. Delaney, but the net effect, at the end, is that of a portrait obscured by the monstrous shadow of the artist.

Boswell, when he composed his own portrait of Johnson, slyly inserted himself into the picture, like Velázquez in *Las Meninas*. Doubtless there was some vanity involved, but the technical tricks he proceeded to bring off are the envy of biographers to this day. He invented, for example, the device of transcribed conversation, presented as dialogue:

BOSWELL If, Sir, you were shut up in a castle, and a newborn child with you, what would you do?

JOHNSON Why, Sir, I should not much like my company.

Boswell knew that Johnson without an interlocutor was as a cello with no strings. Those magnificent conversations, if you analyze them carefully, are written (not recorded) with a playwright's skill. Playwrights understand that nothing is less coherent than ordinary speech, accurately transcribed. Even if it is extraordinary, as Johnson's doubtless was, it will be full of longueurs, discursions, and inconsistencies. In committing itself to paper, it will lose the inflections and gestures of real life. At least the playwright can be confident that these losses will be restored in performance. But Boswell was faced with the problem of making Johnson *read* the way he used to *sound*. Accordingly, when the old man was in full flood, Boswell dashed down stenographic notes, and reconstructed the conversations later on. In doing so, he compressed for the sake of lucidity, and edited for the sake of consistency. This required art of a high order, for what resulted was artificial in the extreme. That's why the dialogues in the *Life of Johnson* seem so natural and inevitable.

If any pedants say that by doing these things, Bozzie stepped out of his bounds as a biographer, and perverted the truth (rather than make it more clear), they do not understand the art of biography, which is to extract the essential from the unessential, so that truth shines forth. What is art, but a refinement of the ore of life?

After Boswell's retreat from foreground to middleground, the nineteenth-century biographer stepped even more discreetly aside. However, some degree of personal intimacy between author and subject was still preferred. Lockhart and Forster, being respectively Scott's son-in-law and Dickens's close friend, got more critical respect than Carlyle, who could not presume to have known Frederick the Great. Intimacy perverted into reverence during the High Victorian era, when Murray burned Byron's randy journals and hagiographers tried to hide the fact that David Livingstone converted only one black man in all his years as a missionary.

IT TOOK LYTTON STRACHEY, at the dawn of a more scientific, skeptical century, to topple these two-volume tombstones. Before Freud's dread influence cramped narrative biography, the form enjoyed a brief golden age. Honesty of method combined, in skilled hands, with beauty of style and virtuosity of technique. Strachey, for example, used literary flashback to exquisite effect in the death scene at the end of *Queen Victoria*. One by one, seminal events and impressions that occurred in chronological order during the course of the biography are recapitulated in reverse—anti-chronologically—until the cycle is closed, and we are back where we began:

> She herself, as she lay blind and silent, seemed to those who watched her to be divested of all thinking—to have glided already, unaware, into oblivion. Yet, perhaps, in the secret chambers of consciousness, she had her thoughts, too. Perhaps her fading mind called up once more the shadows of the past to float before it, and retraced, for the last time, the vanished visions of that long history—passing back and back, through the cloud of years, to older and ever older memories—to the spring woods at Osborne, so full of primroses for Lord Beaconsfield—to Lord Palmerston's queer clothes and high demeanour, and Albert's face under the green lamp, and Albert's first stag at Balmoral, and Albert in his blue and silver uniform, and the Baron coming in through a doorway, and Lord M. dreaming at Windsor with the rooks cawing in the elm trees, and the Archbishop of Canterbury on his knees in the dawn, and the old King's turkey-cock ejaculations, and Uncle Leopold's soft voice at Claremont, and Lehzen with the globes, and her mother's feathers sweeping down toward her, and a great old repeater-watch of her father's in its tortoise-shell case, and a yellow rug, and some friendly flounces of sprigged muslin, and the trees and the grass at Kensington.

Evelyn Waugh experimented with tragic parody in his biography of Edmund Campion, telling the story of the saint's martyrdom as if retelling the story of the *Via Crucis*. Thomas Beer, one of the most radical experimenters in American biography, mixed sound effects, pointillism, journalism, and rhetoric into a new, terse style of extraordinary vividness and poignancy. He ends his life of Mark Hanna with a description of the late afternoon of 15 February 1904 that is spliced together like fragments of documentary film, shot from multiple angles:

> A blankness hung in Washington. . . . Monday was gray. The Senate idled. Lads ran in to mutter in some ear that it had not come yet. Senators walked out in the midst of speeches and found a telephone. Many dinners were canceled and a ball postponed before dusk, and at six o'clock watchers spread below the Arlington. The big young marine stood with his hands in his pockets close to Juliet Balch and may have seen that she was pale and weeping.
>
> "Know him?"
>
> "Yes. Are you a messenger from the White House?"
>
> "No," he said. "Mamma wired me to be here. He was good to my folks out home."
>
> Minutes marched. A new lad would come on his clicking bicycle, and a new cigar would glow among the reporters. Everything waited for the news. Carriages stopped and drivers bent down to ask if it was done. To his last he commanded a world's attention. People must wait and wait. It was half past six. It was twenty minutes to seven. A figure came through the brilliant doors and raised a hand. The young marine took off his cap and turned away. These living bodies separated and disappeared into the night.

IT WAS VIRGINIA WOOLF who first used the phrase *the art of biography*, in an essay written in 1939. She admitted to being drawn to this art—for creative rather than scholarly reasons. *Orlando* is actually subtitled *A Biography*, although it is a novel about an androgynous youth who lives for hundreds of years. The author began it in February 1927, when she was badly blocked. By chance she doodled that subtitle, and, to use her own words, "No sooner had I done this than my body was flooded with rapture and my brain with ideas, and I wrote rapidly till 12. But listen; suppose Orlando turns out to be Vita. . . ."

Of course (and she admitted it) Orlando was Vita Sackville-West, her sometime lover. Much of the book's ravishing imagery is directly related to the facts of Vita's life—for example, the scene where Orlando makes love meltingly to his maid on the ice. It is an artistic consummation of Vita's first meeting with Violet Trefusis, which also took place on ice, that was duly recorded in Virginia's diary.

She went on to write a conventional life of Roger Fry, which is, in the opinion of Leon Edel, "one of the most beautiful biographical portraits of our time." But her conclusion, alas, was that biography was not an art; it represented "life lived at a lower degree of tension" than fiction or poetry. In a discouraging passage she wrote:

> The artist's imagination at its most intense fires out what is perishable in fact; he builds with what is durable; but the biographer must accept the perishable, build with it, instill it in the very fabric of his work. Much will perish; little will live. And thus we come to the conclusion that he *is* a craftsman, not an artist; and his work is not a work of art, but something betwixt and between.

She said that despite Boswell and Lockhart, there are no "immortal" biographies. Mr. Micawber would survive Lytton Strachey's Queen Victoria.

This may be true, although there is at least as much of Dickens's father in Mr. Micawber as there is of the real Queen in Strachey's book. We cannot deny, however, that Dickens had the luxury of combining his original with other originals, real or imaginary, in proportions known only to himself. This freedom to invent is the essential difference between fiction and nonfiction. Indeed, were we biographers given such pure oxygen to breathe, we would become heady. Let us grant that the greatest triumphs of the creative imagination will always outsoar our own more shackled art. But we might also insist that the finest biographies outsoar ninety-nine percent of the rest of literature. Is not Shakespeare's

Henry V vastly more interesting than many of his purely imaginary characters? Scott is almost impossible to read these days, but Lockhart is still inexhaustibly interesting. Painter's *Proust* is to some tastes better than Proust's Proust.

IN CLAIMING THAT biography may improve itself by absorbing the finest elements of the imaginative arts (always remaining within the membrane of scholarship), I don't suggest that a reverse osmosis can be to the benefit of fiction. "Faction," to use the current buzzword, combines the worst elements of each—biography's lack of invention, fiction's lack of responsibility. If we wish to know all about Gary Gilmore—although I can't think why—do we really want him novelized by Norman Mailer for easier consumption?

By the same token, in my opinion, biographers should stay away from Freud. Let such novelists as D. M. Thomas discover, to general delight, that the good doctor has more to offer their art than ours. Here I begin to tread on difficult ground, for our ranks abound with psycho-biographers, some of whom (Leon Edel comes to mind) are distinguished authors of distinguished books. Yet I cannot rid myself of Scott Fitzgerald's notion that "action is character," even more so in biography than in fiction. If action is presented characteristically enough, no intrusive analyzing on the part of the narrator is necessary. The ideal biographer should be godlike in the Flaubertian sense—apparent everywhere, visible nowhere.

When the modern biographer disobeys this elementary rule of good composition—which is to say, good narrative—the results are almost always unfortunate, particularly in the field of historical biography. History is a memory, a dream. Any harsh voice from the present jerks us awake, to our discomfort. The voice of Philip Ziegler, a recent biographer of Lord Melbourne, is more mellifluous than harsh, yet it intrudes all the same, destroying the spell that Lord David Cecil cast so magically in *Melbourne* (1939, 1954). In a gracious foreword, Mr. Ziegler explains why he has presumed to rewrite "one of the most delightful biographies of our age." Much new material has come to light—many thousands of letters, and a large fragment of Melbourne's own autobiography. Mr. Ziegler also confesses he could never understand why Lord David's Melbourne, "a man so insouciant, detached, and free from ambition," could have prevailed so in politics. *His* vision, then, is much more bourgeois and grainy—authentically 1970ish. "Every biographer perhaps to some extent," he hazards, "is a victim of his generation and of his prejudices. If so, Lord David has enjoyed incomparably the happier lot. But, almost regretfully, I fear that I am right."

His portrait of Lady Caroline Lamb also suffers from this kind of presentism. It is relentlessly editorial, despite the author's caveat: "To be eschewed, however, is the temptation to apply modern psycho-analytic techniques to the scraps of information which survive about her and thus to arrive at some glib formula which would 'explain' her as a textbook of the latest fashionable neurosis." Lord David, one feels, would have eschewed both the psychoanalysis and the conversational aside. Of the forty-four descriptive sentences Mr. Ziegler proceeds to give Lady Caroline, seventeen contain subjective inflections and mood-shattering remarks. His portrait is not without charm—"her eyes perpetually smudged as if she had just been crying or intended soon to do so"—but let's check Lord David's. It has not one voiced opinion in twenty-five sentences. It is, surprisingly, less romantic than Mr. Ziegler's, and more psychologically penetrating (instead of giving us inferences, he quotes observers). It is also, because the earlier writer does not step with tweeds and a pipe into Lady Caroline's satin drawing room, more elegant and more vivid. These adjectives apply throughout to his portrait of Lord Melbourne. ("Smiling, indolent and inscrutable he lay, a pawn in the hands of fortune.")

IF, AS SOME CRITICS SAY, we are entering another golden age of biography, we must consider how to advance its hopeful progress toward art. What allowances must biographers make for other mushrooming disciplines, such as data processing and chemistry? It's hardly possible to note, these days, that Hemingway took a train somewhere without interviewing the conductor's granddaughter, measuring the track with a folding rule, and sending off the ticket stub for analysis. Perhaps the imaginative leaps of Boswell and Beer are no longer permissible.

I see no reason, however, why we should not broaden our technique to employ those of arts more fully developed than ours—fiction above all, and also painting and photography, and drama and the cinema. Scholarship is not necessarily sacrificed; it can even be enhanced by the use of these techniques. Consider how movingly Richard Holmes assembles Shelley's childhood memories into an opening-page montage, seen through the eyes of an infant. The effect is as beautiful as James Joyce's identical device in *Portrait of the Artist as a Young Man.* And surely the artist-biographer must describe Virginia Woolf's suicidal dive into the river, with a stone in her coat, in terms of that unforgettable image in *Orlando* of the old bumboat woman sitting twenty fathoms down in the frozen Thames, with her plaids and farthingales about her, and her lap full of apples. Such apposites—the tortured woman of real life, and the premonitory symbol in her own novel—cry out for imaginative synthesis.

PERHAPS BIOGRAPHY is most closely allied to portrait photography, in that its basic composition is determined by reality. No matter what tricks of lighting or lensing are employed, the subject is unavoidably, irreducibly *there.* When Edward Steichen nervously set up his camera before J. P. Morgan, the great man just sat and stared, in effect daring Steichen to make of him what he was not. So, too, does J. P. Morgan stare balefully now, through the viewfinder of the years, at Jean Strouse. I don't know how she is going to see him, but I do know what Steichen saw when he put his head under the black cloth. He saw an onrushing express train, with headlamp eyes and a cowcatcher of a nose. And that is what he photographed, so brilliantly that we recoil from his print in fear of a collision. Here is the challenge of the biographer—to restore, by whatever art one can muster, the power of the past—to make the distant seem near, the real more real.

I would still suggest that reality cannot truthfully be represented without honest distortions. The Greek architects who laid the Parthenon slightly out of synch were artists, in that they understood that their building would look straighter that way. The illusion fixes its beauty in our minds long after memory of a thousand glass boxes fades. We can learn from such designers how to move the reader's eye along vital lines and surfaces, how to arrest it with a show of filigree, then speed it on again to that precise central point where the whole structure balances out, and reveals the inner axis.

Biography also has much to borrow from music, particularly counterpoint and the handling of disparate motifs. Mozart composed the five themes for the finale of the "Jupiter" Symphony in such shape that, when they at last all sound at the same time, the effect is of strengthening sunlight, making clear what has gone before. So, too, must the biographer who wants important themes to stand out, introduce each one at the right moment in the symphony he is scoring.

Perhaps I may illustrate from a life I know quite well. Theodore Roosevelt was, as the dust jacket of my first volume notes, at least seven men—a naturalist, a writer, a lover, a ranchman, a hunter, a soldier, and a politician. Each of these aspects, these themes, is introduced to the reader during the course of the story in such a way as to register on the mind of the reader with maximum impact. In real life, however, the themes often confusingly combined. For example, TR began his career as a ranchman before his first wife died, and continued it, off and on, long after he married his second; but I introduce the theme of Theodore Roosevelt, ranchman, after the sad chords of the former event, and develop it fully before the happy fanfare of his wedding to Edith Carow. In doing so, I don't alter the chronology of history at all, any more than a composer transgresses against the regular passage of bar lines. Nor do I boast that what I did was art: let's call it, simply, orchestration.

TWO RECENT WORKS, biographical if not biographies as such, encourage me to believe that artistry can flourish in a world increasingly given over to nonartistic considerations. One is Michael Teague's *Mrs. L*, the other is the poet W. S. Merwin's *Unframed Originals*.

Mrs. L, whose subtitle is *Conversations with Alice Roosevelt Longworth*, makes brilliant use of two contemporary biographical tools, the tape recorder and the camera. Alice Longworth was an indifferent writer—she published a forgettable memoir in the 1930s—but a talker of extreme, if eccentric virtuosity, able to jump from subject to subject as gracefully as a chamois, flicking out with sharp hooves and horns. For some 160 hours in the early 1970s, Mr. Teague sat with the old lady, usually over a great steaming pot of Earl Grey's tea, recording her reminiscences, as he prompted her with photographs and judicious questions. Often she would break off in midsentence, only to complete it two years later. For months after her death, Mr. Teague labored with piles of tape and transcripts, editing himself out, splicing together apparently random phrases. When his text was complete, he made a similar collage from the wealth of photographs that "Princess Alice" had left behind (she was this century's first press-camera celebrity). The result, published in 1981, was an exquisitely accurate portrait, auditory and visual, of a personality no biographer could capture by conventional means.

Mr. Merwin's *Unframed Originals* is a series of nostalgic essays on the author's youth in the anthracite country of Eastern Pennsylvania. Most of these pieces are biographical, and the characters portrayed are ordinary, even dull, by normal standards of interest. What makes them extraordinary is Mr. Merwin's ability, as a poet, to fire the mundane with the glow of art.

He uses metaphor in a way that should inspire any biographer who wishes to create literature. One chapter, for example, employs the marvelous device of an old woman's steamer trunk to introduce Mr. Merwin's Aunt Margie to us. (He is about eleven years old, and she has left it to him in her will.)

> Oshkosh Trunk Company it said, on a brass plate on top. . . . The name . . . sounded like some family allusion of unremembered origin. . . . The shipping tags, raw and new, were still dangling from the latches, and there were keys.

With the boy's turning of the keys, and his physical stepping into this trunk so much larger than himself, comes dawning awareness of a person we do not know, and whom he, too, hardly remembers. At first "the drawers yielded up remnants whose coherence was beyond me, like collections of sea shells. Nothing about them was explained, and they themselves explained nothing." Gradually, as he rummages through drawers full of costume jewelry and junk, figments of the real Margaret Cubbage emerge:

> Some alloy coffee spoons with ecclesiastical figures for handles. They were from Venice, my mother said. Margie had been to Europe. . . . A notebook containing references to Ibsen: jottings on the plays, and passages copied out in full . . . "Margie was fond of Ibsen," my mother said.

These figments stimulate the author's own memories of Aunt Margie. She begins to develop colors and texture and scent and sound. Page succeeds page, and she grows before our eyes, until, in the revelatory moment all biographers long for, she stands before us in a high-necked long dress of solid color. Her back is "straight as a dancer's," her hand rests lightly on a desk. She has "large noble features: attentive, waiting," eyes that are "almost black and burning." She gives off a fragrance of soap and powder and lavender sachet. As we look, we catch "her rare, anomalous smile: her face creasing, eyebrows rising, the corners of her mouth lifting like curtains drawing up. . . ."

And so light shines in on a vital character who, but for the power of language, would be an unremembered shadow. Mr. Merwin's resurrection of Aunt Margie is a triumph of love as well as imagination, calling to mind Lytton Strachey's remark that biography is "the most delicate and humane of all the branches of the art of writing."

THE ANTICAPITALIST CONSPIRACY

A Warning

THERE'S A PLOT ABROAD, FOLKS, TO PROLETARIANIZE THE LANGUAGE of Milton and Macaulay. I first became aware of it in 1982, when I got a letter inviting me to become a "fellow" at the Woodrow Wilson International Center for Scholars. What cheek! Time was when that epithet could bring gentlemen to blows:

> "Sir," said Mr. Tupman, "you're a fellow."
> "Sir," said Mr. Pickwick, "you're another!"

I demanded an explanation, and found that my scholarly correspondent was only trying to be nice. He did not realize that his word processor had been infiltrated by anticapitalist agents working for *The Chicago Manual of Style*. The latest edition of this all-powerful rulebook

Originally published in *The American Spectator*, February 1987.
Collage by the author.

says that "Fellow"—an ancient title of academic distinction ("Nothing is so Impervious . . . as a Fellow of a College upon his own Dunghill"— T. Brown, 1704)—doesn't merit a capital F anymore. Neither do hundreds of other honorable titles. How lower-case can you get?

If Fellows are to become fellows, then we may as well start drinking chablis (it's cheaper than the real thing) and electing guv'nors. No uniqueness of style or station impresses today's typographers. They've been brainwashed by the *Manual.* Thank heaven—damn this software, Heaven—that Albert Einstein is no longer with us. Imagine his byline in a contemporary issue of *Mathematical Monographs:* "Al Einstein is the guy who first figured out that $E = mc^2$." Don't tell me it's all relative. I say it's egalitarianism, and I say the Hell with it!

I accepted the Wilson Center "fellowship," because frankly, I needed the stipend. But I salved my conscience by launching a private investigation of this whole business of stylistic revisionism. Was it the work only of a few leftist saboteurs in Chicago? I wanted to see if the propaganda had spread to other stylebooks, in what ways, and when. So I got a pair of earplugs and went into the Library of Congress stacks (no joke— there's disco music piped in there these days) to consult back editions of every stylebook I could find.

Browsing freely in section EC.I07.D12, I discovered that yes, there has been a systematic attempt, over the past two or three decades, to make style less stylish—to smooth out differences, irregularities, and nuance; to create, in short, a prose for the proletariat. The revisionism goes far beyond the mere *look* of print. It extends to what the Modern Language Association calls the "social connotations" of literary expression. At all costs, these days, writers must try to sound like talkers, and scholars must cloak their erudition.

I hereby present my findings. Read them, lovers of Gibbon, and weep! Needless to say, it all goes back to Karl Marx.

Kapitalization

One of Marx's revolutionary discoveries was the formula *Kapital* = *Privileg.* And he didn't mean fiscal *kapital,* he meant das kind of *kapital* vot typographically elevates one *mensch* above another. This stylistic concept was refined by the bureaucrats of Bolshevism, who mandated big-letter respect for institutions (Politburo, Supreme Soviet) while denying it to the average comrade (or fellow). Here in the land of the free, we respectfully capitalized our great persons through the 1960s, when hippies took over the *Chicago Manual* and decapitated practically every dignitary in the country. Richard Nixon became just "the president" and "commander in chief" and Abe Fortas an "associate justice." No wonder the poor slobs felt unappreciated, and resigned. Prominent liberals were spared, of course. Tip O'Neill is still "the Speaker" of the House of Representatives. But watch that cap *S* shrink if a Republican ever takes up the gavel!

Talking of caps, I notice that the *Washington Post* stylebook makes Cap Weinberger "secretary of defense," while James Baker is "secretary of the Treasury." Neither man gets any personal recognition, but the department that protects us is rated inferior to the one that screws us. God Himself, these days, gets no more respect than Rodney Dangerfield. Modern manuals are unanimous in insisting that He has to be brought down to lower-case level—for that matter, deprived of a gender-specific pronoun altogether. How is the Almighty fallen! The Common Man, in contrast, is *always* capitalized, and even gets fanfares written for him by Aaron Copland.

Hyphenation

Successive editions of *The Government Printing Office Style Manual* indicate that forced integration of separate but equal words began about the same time as *Brown v. Board of Education.* By 1959 a strap-hanger was a straphanger, no matter where he stood on the bus. The hyphen, apparently, is discriminatory. While purporting to link apposite units of thought, it acts as a delicate barrier between them, intolerable to liberal percept. Today it barely survives to remind us of a more structured past, when words knew their places and vowels were not squashed together like double cherries. Hence *intraarterial.* Any moment now we're going to read something about mammologists getting together for an *intraaardvark* conference.

These new compounds just don't look right. It takes about five minutes of squinting before you realize *nonnative* means someone born outside the United States. My wife and I got a letter the other day from someone proposing that we turn our apartment building into a *coop.* What does he think we are, chickens? *Saillike* is not, as you might think, a Japanese delicacy, but an adjective to do with canvas. *Reedit*: some sort of squeaky waterfowl? No, it's what R. Emmett Tyrrell* is going to do to this article, even though I've edited it carefully myself.

The effect of such compounds *en masse* (a phrase, by the way, we're not supposed to italicize any more, since some folks don't like to be reminded that they can't speak French) combines with anticapitalization to cast a totalitarian grayness across the page, depriving it of white space and texture, until it looks like an Albanian policy paper.

Perhaps I'm being politically paranoid. All right, maybe it wasn't Abbie Hoffman who took the hyphen out of *absentminded,* which used so precisely to suggest the detachment of consciousness from reality. Maybe the enemy in this case is the computer, with its brute desire to process all words into digits. One sighs for the verbal necklaces of the Romantic poets:

> *Full-grown lambs loud bleat from hilly bourn*
> *Hedge-crickets sing; and now with treble soft*
> *The red-breast whistles from a garden-croft . . .*

Or again:

> *The Nightmare Life-in-Death was she,*
> *Who thicks man's blood with cold.*

Which is to say, makes him coldblooded. He can't be cold-blooded anymore, with that little shivery space in between the words.

Let's not get too depressed. The hyphen will always be with us as long as we are permitted to give mother-of-pearl ashtrays to our in-laws. Rules decreeing the use or non-use (nonuse?) of the mark have gotten so

---

* Editor of *The American Spectator.*

complicated that even the *GPO Style Manual* admits they "cannot be applied inflexibly." As a result, Federal usage abounds with inconsistencies. Government workers are permitted to go *barefoot*, but not *barebreasted.* Well, considering the dimensions of some of the ladies I've seen down at HUD, perhaps that's just as well.

Documentation

The hottest new book in the Library of Congress is not, as one might expect, *Video Guide to X-Rated Movies*, but the Modern Language Association's *Handbook for Writers of Research Papers.* Every scholar in the District of Columbia, it appears, wants to get his hands on this bible of academese. I had to conduct a special search before I tracked it down in a secured room at the Library of Congress. It was hidden beneath a pile of Gutenbergs, and I was allowed to consult it only after surrendering my passport.

What I read made my flesh creep. Personally, I think the *Handbook* should be burned along with *Huckleberry Finn.* It's anti-culture, that's what it is. Those MLA populists have decided to ban the use of Latin citations! Now everything's got to be in the vernacular! Not even footnotes are sacrosanct: they've got to be incorporated right in the text—in parentheses, if you please!

Let me tell you, when I came to the end of the *Handbook,* I couldn't move for shock. I sat staring bleakly into space, at visions of long-haired radicals with signs reading *I.E. is N.B.G.* and *PASSIM BYE.* I thought of the years I spent working to master the arcana of approved documentation for my first book.

To be honest, I never learned the exact meaning of *Ibid.* or *Loc. cit.* The former always sounded vaguely Freudian, and the latter suggested a yoga position. But I knew when to use these abbreviations, along with *passim, ff., pp., vide, viz.,* and other pedanticisms. As my technique developed, I took a Lisztian delight in strewing *ff*'s across my manuscript and citing names backward ("Lee of Fareham, 2nd Viscount Arthur, ed."). I became a footnote fetishist, taking sly peeps *infra* and *supra*, and breathing heavily whenever I chanced upon a virgin *Ms.* I perfected the placement of reference numbers and [*sic*] in purple passages, so that nobody would think it was my own bad style.

Well, good-bye scholarship. I must admit, though, that at least one MLA reform is welcome. They've dispensed with those ghastly Latin numerals that used to make serial publications unfindable. God knows how many miles of library shelves I've prowled looking for Vol. MCDXLVXXX of this and DCIIIVLX of that, only to discover that I dropped an L somewhere in copying the citation. It's going to be much easier in future to locate back issues of *Playboy*.

Antiobscuration and
Academic Alliteration

Another worrying thing is the prejudice of modern stylebooks against obscure expression. The British pundit W. E. Johnson, in a manual rather irritably entitled *If You Must Write*, insists: "The aim of written words is to be read, and being read to be understood." If I were prime minister, I'd lock that seditionist in the Tower, before he puts all university presses out of business. Even *The Harvard Guide to American History* has slapped a moratorium on "long, involved sentences that one has to read two or three times in order to grasp the meaning." Serious scholars must blench at this threat to our most basic constitutional freedom, the right to be incomprehensible. Once Harvard profs start writing English, it's the beginning of the end.

All is not lost, however. There is one subtlety of didactic style so far unvandalized by the manuals: Academic Alliteration. Multiple *p*'s and *c*'s are still admired on campus. Thus, two recent works by Charles Q. Bergquist, *On Paradigms and the Pursuit of the Practical* and *Coffee and Conflict in Colombia*. Real virtuosos use Academic Alliteration for hortatory effect, as in this affecting passage from a history of U.S. colonial policy by Garel Grunder and William Livezey:

> Desirous and determined, we declared for dollars and deferred to duty; dazzled and defiant, we dreamed of defense and depended upon deity; delightfully dauntless, we dared a date with destiny.

Would-be imitators should realize that such sublime cadences are not easily captured, as Barbra Streisand discovered when she tried to sing Schubert. At best the result will be embarrassing; at worst, dangerous. Remember what we got when JFK offered to *pay* any *price* and *bear* any *burden* to ensure the *survival* and *success* of liberty? Vietnam!

The Coming Propaedeutical Backlash

I close with a solemn warning to all stylistic revisionists, whether pinkos or populists. If they keep trampling on our footnotes and yelling banalities such as "The key to successful communications is using the right language," we're going to curse right back, in the international language of scholars. Oxford's spires are still shaking with the wrath of old Dean Owen, who in 1661 caught a revisionist bowdlerizing his *Studio Verae Theologicae Libri Sex*. Admittedly the Dean shouldn't have been preaching *libri sex* to undergraduates, but there was real outrage in his

> . . . *crassissima inscitia, & Correctorum, quos quam potuerunt minimo (quamvis nimium magno) conduxerunt Typographi, immanis negligentia & ἀμαίθα etc.*

As Bertie Wooster would say, he meant it to sting, by Jove!

EVERY SLIVER OF INLAY HAD TO FIT

The Early Artistry of Evelyn Waugh

THE LITERARY TITLE *MASTER*, APPLIED IN THIS CENTURY ONLY to Henry James and (reverently by Evelyn Waugh) to P. G. Wodehouse, is beginning to glow like a nimbus about the head of Waugh himself. Early signs of sainthood are there. The University of Texas at Austin has purchased his library, Chippendale cases and all, and intends to rebuild it as a campus shrine. A collected edition of the novels is in print on both sides of the Atlantic, supplemented by fat anthologies, scrupulously annotated, of the letters, diaries, essays, and reviews. Learned periodicals explore the significance of beech trees in his imagery. Even in France,

Originally published in *The New York Times Book Review,* 31 August 1987.

Photograph by Mark Gerson, 1964.

where his name is all but unpronounceable, there is solemn discussion of "Le Sens de l'Absurde Dans l'Oeuvre d'Evelyn Waugh."

Now comes the necessary next step in Waugh's canonization: the first volume of a two-part life by Martin Stannard, lecturer in English at the University of Leicester. Waugh has already been the subject of an authorized biography by Christopher Sykes (1975) and a number of delightful but slight memoirs, notably those of Frances Donaldson, Dudley Carew, and the Earl of Birkenhead. The Sykes book, based on the author's friendship with Waugh and his family, is long on anecdote but short on scholarship, and its overall tone is protective, particularly in matters of sex and religion. This new study, deeply researched and pondered, does Waugh greater service, by transcending hagiography and revealing for the first time the full range of his learning.

Philosophically, Waugh's intellect was grounded in Spengler and Bergson, whence come the static/dynamic imagery of the novels, the identification of the individual with civilization and the crowd with barbarism, the search for balance and permanence in a world of shrieking chaos. Stylistically, his mind and hand were trained by Donne, Addison, Macaulay, Newman, and Wodehouse—not to mention Francis Crease, an obscure book illuminator who taught him aesthetics as a schoolboy.

That training, plus wide reading in European and classical history and a practical study of art, architecture, cabinet making, book production, and wine, made Waugh a formidably erudite man. But learning alone does not account for his ability, say, to concoct the last chapter of *Decline and Fall* out of a single two-hour visit to Corfu in 1927, or to transform a chance encounter with a hermit in British Guiana into a great short story ("The Man Who Loved Dickens") and then into an even greater novel (*A Handful of Dust*). Perhaps the answer lies in the photograph of Evelyn and his brother Alec—also a bestselling writer—in this book. The eyes on the right are slightly mad with genius, those on the left are not.

Mr. Stannard is wise enough not to attempt to analyze Waugh's achingly funny humor. Nor does he quote too much of his subject's own prose, lest an essentially somber portrait flash with distracting filigree, á la Klimt. This is a biography for the serious student of Waugh, who wants to learn as much as possible about the man and is keen to read every product of his pen.

There is certainly no shortage of the latter. Mr. Stannard's bibliography lists some fifty major works written in forty years—a prodigious total, given Waugh's lifelong tendency to dissipate his gifts in travel and pleasure (until his thirty-fourth year he had no regular home). In this volume, we find analyses of such lesser-known masterpieces as "The Balance" (1926), an avant-garde novelette written in the form of a film scenario; two biographies, *Rossetti: His Life and Works* (1928) and *Edmund Campion* (1935), respectively impressive in their command of aesthetics and religious philosophy; and "Out of Depth" (1933), a chilling futuristic fantasy about patois-speaking savages living in the slime of what was once London, anticipating by nearly fifty years Russell Hoban's *Riddley Walker*. Mr. Stannard even discusses Waugh's idiosyncratic line drawings (which themselves anticipate the draftsmanship of A. B. Price), and he surveys enough of the essays and reviews to remind us that intellectual elegance and conservatism are not incompatible.

There are also, of course, chapters dealing with the five superb prewar novels—*Decline and Fall* (1928), *Vile Bodies* (1930), *Black Mischief* (1932), *A Handful of Dust* (1934), and *Scoop* (1938). The book ends in 1939, with a middle-aged Waugh abandoning *Work Suspended*, that haunting, quasi-autobiographical fragment, and volunteering for military duty in the war. As at all crisis points in his life, his purpose was artistic. He looked to the coming conflagration as a God-given replenishment of his imaginative store.

EVELYN ARTHUR ST. JOHN WAUGH (how he exulted in that name when designing his own bookplate!) was born in London on 28 October 1903, the son of a moderately prosperous publisher, Arthur Waugh. The facts of his early life are well known, having been told with honesty by himself in *A Little Learning* (1964). Suffice to say that Mr. Stannard gives us state-of-the-art scholarship in support of the basic story: Waugh's bourgeois upbringing, his alienation from his father and brother, and his early realization that he was an aristocrat *manqué*.

His "profound sense of his gentility" was sharpened, both at Lancing School and at Oxford, by a sense of exclusion from the ranks of the rich and well-bred—the Hons. and Barts. and Miladies, with their Gainsborough profiles and drawling certainty of speech. Pudgy, unathletic, dismayingly small, Waugh used his wild wit to seduce them, and his brains to mobilize them to his advancement. But the time always came when they would retreat into their "vast carelessness," and he would suffer the agonies of a Gatsby, forever imprisoned on the wrong side of the bay.

Predictably, he married an Hon., and was cuckolded within a year. Mr. Stannard suggests that Evelyn Gardner (whose identical first name and boy's haircut made the union seem androgynous) was sexually unsatisfied by Waugh. If so, it could only make the pain of betrayal worse. In later life, he acidly referred to their time together as "a form of marriage." Friends learned never to speak of "She-Evelyn" in his presence.

This may be the place to take up the question of Waugh's sexuality. Mr. Stannard documents certain "strong homosexual urges," apparently controlled, at Lancing, and later on states that Waugh fell in love with two young men at Oxford. It is "far from certain," in his view, "that this love was ever physically expressed." Waugh was free to consummate the relationships, for Oxford in the 1920s was flagrantly permeated by homosexuality. The evidence is that his romances, first with men and then with women, were idealistic rather than sensual—at least until after his divorce, when a decade of joyous heterosexual "rogering" began. Prostitutes in Paris. Rome and Fez enjoyed Waugh's patronage, as did one or two refined Englishwomen. He remarried at the age of thirty-three; six subsequent children were proof of his attraction to Laura Herbert, his second wife. "Impotence and sodomy are socially O.K.," he joked to Nancy Mitford, "but birth control is flagrantly middle class."

An appreciation of Waugh's masculinity is necessary for us to follow Mr. Stannard's thesis that he was a driving force, hard and unsentimental, from the outset of his career, in life as well as art. Nothing is more remarkable, as this narrative unfolds, than the leitmotifs of Waugh as self-promoter, Waugh as workman. He had to earn every shilling he spent, and the spending outran the earning. Out of necessity, not vanity, he cultivated the gossip columns and, between purgative bouts of drinking (three bottles of champagne and one of cognac in a single night), wrote with monkish application. "The novel drags on at 10,000 words a week," he complained of *A Handful of Dust*. Most writers would be proud to write 10,000 such words in a lifetime.

Although Waugh's divorce coincided with the publication of *Vile Bodies*—that black, bitterly funny book, full of rain—it was only with *A Handful of Dust*, four years later, that he became a man, literarily speaking. He was then thirty, toughened by years of poverty and neglect. Youthful fantasies of becoming a cabinetmaker or a designer had matured into a passion for craft and design in prose. Every sliver of inlay had to fit precisely and be covered with sheen; every part had to relate to the whole in such a way that the whole was implied before being revealed. (A valuable feature of this book is its close scrutiny of Waugh's manuscripts and proofs—we follow, as it were, the scratchings of his pen, and can almost hear him groan as he writes.)

The crucial step in Waugh's maturity came when he realized that brilliant dandies like Harold Acton, whom he revered at Oxford, were of coarser clay than himself. His conversion to Roman Catholicism in 1930 further disciplined his mind. Father Martin d'Arcy, S.J., said afterward that Waugh was the most objective pupil he ever instructed. Contrary to popular myth, he was not attracted to Rome for aesthetic reasons. Loving the English liturgy of Cranmer and the glories of Anglican architecture, he had to brace himself for the leaden prose of the translated Vulgate bible, and the distinctly *déclassé* ambience of Catholic churches in England. Yet, like his alter ego, Gilbert Pinfold, he felt only a "calm acceptance" when the moment of confirmation came. The world was "unintelligible and unendurable without God," and the Catholic Church was the only church "because it was true."

MR. STANNARD COVERS Waugh's career with a relentless roll of detail that tends at times to crush the narrative flat. Given his compulsion to describe all, he has to accompany the man everywhere—across the wilderness of British Guiana, for example, in twenty-six exhausting pages. He is not discouraged by the fact that Waugh has already told much of the story in *Ninety-two Days* (1934). But the detail pays off when we see how Waugh cut some of his brightest jewels from the raw rubble of experience.

This is not a pretty story. Waugh was constantly tormented by demons. He needed alcohol to escape an all-pervading sense of change and decay, and drugs to help him sleep. He often behaved so piggishly, and indeed grew so porcine as he aged, that one wonders if the "Basic Pig" in *A Handful of Dust* was not a metaphor for himself, rather than for humanity as Mr. Stannard suggests. Waugh liked to lampoon the unfortunate, and helped drive at least one person—his former tutor, C. R. M. F. Cruttwell—into the madhouse. "How could you be so wicked?" Nancy Mitford said, after he taunted someone to tears. "I thought you were supposed to be religious."

"You can't imagine," he replied, "how much worse I should be if I were not religious."

Yet this beastly little man was also capable of great tenderness. His love for Laura, for art, and for God are evident whenever he writes about them. And how bewitchingly he could write! One of the most adorable children in English literature—John Andrew in *A Handful of Dust*—lives entirely in dialogue, without a word of description. Halfway through the book, the mere sound of little John's first name elicits, from his mother, a three-word commonplace that freezes the reader's blood.

One can only stand in awe of a novelist with such gifts, and eagerly await the volume in which Mr. Stannard will show them come to fruition in *Brideshead Revisited*.

THE PAIN OF FALLING LEAVES

Capitol Hill Loses a Tree

Aబీ BAY WINDOW OVERLOOKING THE SUPREME COURT GARDENS
is a pleasant place to sit at breakfast, especially early on a holiday morning, when Constitution Avenue is devoid of traffic. At times like this Capitol Hill is so quiet you can hear your heart beating, and if you are lucky
enough to have a great glossy pine growing close to your townhouse,
you will sometimes catch another sound, the purest in nature: wind
hissing through needles.

I was sitting like this on Martin Luther King, Jr.'s birthday, halfway

Originally published in *The New York Times Magazine*, 5 March 1989.

The author's former house in Washington, D.C. Drawing by Fred H. Greenberg, 1979.

through a muffin and the latest installment of *Rex Morgan, M.D.*, when something like the screech of an angry hyrax came from outside. There, swaying above the sidewalk in a power-operated cradle, was a man with a buzz saw. As my wife and I boggled, his saw screeched again. We saw a green branch fall, and I said uncertainly, "They're pruning."

My wife, quicker than I am to believe the unbelievable, exclaimed, "No, they're not!" I blundered down the stairs and out into the street, just in time to miss being hit by another branch. It smashed against the curb, cones jiggling crazily. "Stop!" I roared at the sky, "will you please stop!"

The hyrax fell silent, and I found myself facing a politely puzzled ground crew. "What are you doing to our tree?"

"Sir, it's not your tree," said the foreman, a young man with bleached mustache. "It's theirs." He pointed to the adjoining building, owned by the Johnson O'Connor Research Foundation. "It's growing out of their yard—" which was true enough, although much of the growth extended over mine.

"It's gotta come down," the foreman said. For a moment I was dumb with shock. I peered up at the tree's crest, gilded with sunshine above the line of our roof. Each spray was tipped with a diamond of gum.

There must be some mistake, I told myself. Here soars sixty feet of strength and shade, gracing the façades of two historic houses. Doves nest in this tree. Squirrels use it for springboard practice. When I sit at my desk after a snowfall, I can look out on puffs of white and green. If we need kindling for our fire, we just step out on the balcony and help ourselves to cones. How they sputter! And how sweetly they smell!

"*Got* to come down? Who says?"

He showed me his work order from the foundation: $850 for tree felling and stump removal. "Sir," I said, trying to keep my voice steady, "I will give you a check right now if you will just go away and let me resolve this with our neighbor." He hesitated, clearly sympathetic. "I'm sorry, sir, we got a contract. Don't wanna be sued."

But he agreed to wait while I pressed the foundation's doorbell. The director who signed the work order came down to see me. She was young, good-looking, and had a wide smile. "Hi," she said. Her smile encouraged me, but as our conversation proceeded, it became more and more fixed, and I realized (with a surge of panic) that she really wanted to kill the tree. *Why, I may smile, and murder whiles I smile.*

"Basically it's a maintenance problem," she said. "The needles clog our gutters and mess up our yard. We're concerned about branches falling on people in the street."

"I'll pay to have it pruned," I babbled. "I'll take care of your maintenance. I'll compensate these guys. Please don't kill that tree."

She went off to consult someone on her board, and I paced the reception room in a frenzy. I have always been a mild person, and I was amazed at the passion boiling inside me. After a few minutes the director came back, smiling more widely than ever.

"I'm sorry," she said, "but it's going to come down."

Was it my imagination, or did I see relish in that smile? Could she be looking forward to the destruction of a great white pine, planted probably before she was born?

"I like trees," she explained, as if reading my thoughts. "I just don't happen to like that tree."

I dragged her out of the door and made her look at it. "It's beautiful," I said, choking at the inadequacy of speech. "It's living. Birds nest in it. . . ."

She shook her head. "It's coming down."

"Then I'll defend it with my body!" I roared, and lunged across the yard to the tree. I tore off my shoes and tried to scrabble up the trunk, wildly supposing that if I could only climb halfway, I could fend off the buzz saw with my bare hands. But I am forty-eight years old, with the body of a sedentary scribe. I soon crashed back to ground level, and found that I could not let go of the tree. I hugged it so fiercely it cut into my chest.

As the crew stared at me, I began to sob. The morning air was cold, and trembling set in. "Oh God," I whispered into the ridges of the bark, "please save this tree."

My wife, white-faced in her robe, ran out of our house to tell me that she was telephoning everybody she could think of—lawyers, senators, friends, the press. After a while the foreman came over to me.

"Sir, they just called the police. You can get a coat if you like. We won't cut this tree until somebody comes."

I thanked him, but held on to the trunk. There was something comforting about its rough bulk, too large for me to clasp all the way round. By some jerk of the mind I thought of my father, who days before had undergone major surgery, and I hugged it more tightly. I have never felt so alone. Then I heard the crackle of shoes on needles, and braced myself for the blow of a nightstick. But it was only a well-dressed stranger. His face was thoughtfully concerned.

"Excuse me," he said, "I'm trying to get home on the Metro. I've lost my wallet—"

"Oh go away," I groaned, feeling an insane urge to laugh as well as cry. "I have troubles of my own."

My wife came out and said that we appeared to have no legal rights. Who owns roots, owns the tree. Reporters and photographers were on their way. It was a race between the police and them.

The police won. They arrived in cars and on motorcycles, lights flashing. "Sir," an officer barked, "please step down onto the sidewalk. We want to talk to you."

"You can talk to me here."

I was struck by the contempt on his face. It did not occur to me how ridiculous I must look: a bearded, shaking tree-hugger in splintery socks. "Step this way right now, sir." He unleashed his stick.

"Okay," I said, "I will if you guarantee—"

"We're not guaranteeing anything. Down on the sidewalk, *right now.*"

I don't remember much about the final moments of the tree's life. Isolated flashes recur: a uniformed arm hauling me into the street, the young woman returning to her office, my voice hoarsely shouting "Vandal!", the hyrax screeching and biting again, more and more branches thumping down, my wife calling me home. I went inside, pulled down the blinds, and lay in the darkest room I could find. The screeching ended in half an hour. That's how long it takes to obliterate the growth of forty years.

The press came, and I posed dully by the stump, letting the fresh sawdust stream through my fingers. A reporter needed an endquote, so I gave it to him at dictating speed. "It was Christians 0, Barbarians 1."

Much later, all passion spent, I sat in my study gazing through the bay window (its right pane bare and bleak now), and murmured over and over some lines from D. H. Lawrence, which had come to me when I stood holding the trunk:

I feel the pain of falling leaves
And stems that break in storms.

AN OLD MAN OUGHT TO BE SAD

The Logical Life of Mr. Justice Holmes

THE FIGURE OF OLIVER WENDELL HOLMES, JR., CASTS SO HUGE A shadow that for over half a century biographers have wilted in the attempt to grow past him into the light. Felix Frankfurter, Mark DeWolfe Howe, and Grant Gilmore successively labored on an authorized life until they gave up, or died. The only fruits of their labor were Howe's two volumes covering the years 1841–1882—dry fruits unjuiced by the sweetness of Holmes's personality. Catherine Drinker Bowen captured much of that charm in her bestselling *Yankee from Olympus* (1944), but she was overwhelmed by Holmes the jurist and philosopher (not to mention his dark and violent aspects) and fictionalized what she could not understand.

Originally published in *The New York Times Book Review,* 20 August 1989.
Photograph of Holmes at ninety, 1931.

Sheldon M. Novick's *Honorable Justice: The Life of Oliver Wendell Holmes* is the first full biography based on unrestricted access to the Holmes papers, plus the cumulative research of Frankfurter, Howe, and Gilmore. Mr. Novick is the type of scholar who, though trained in law, asks an expert at the Harvard Herbaria to identify leaves pressed into an old love letter, and checks library logs to determine when young Wendell allowed mysticism to infiltrate his study of Plato. One opens his book with high hopes, and as chapter follows masterly chapter, the hopes mature into admiration of author and awe of subject. When at last Mr. Novick records the death of Holmes on 6 March 1935, he shocks us into something like grief. After the initial constriction of the throat comes sober meditation on a life of ninety-three years, perfected to the point of art.

Oliver Wendell Holmes, Jr., had almost everything: the best breeding and education Massachusetts could bestow, well over six feet of handsome height, charm, intellect, a heroic war record, love, fulfillment, and fame. Only children were lacking to complete his happiness, but he accepted the deprivation as philosophically as he did his excess of good fortune. He was of the nineteenth-century type that believed that the numerator of privilege must be balanced by the denominator of work. When in extreme old age he needed more than six hours of sleep a night, he drove himself even harder during the day. One of Mr. Novick's most poignant images is of Holmes at eighty-nine, grunting with the effort to lift heavy volumes of transcript onto his invalid chair.

By his works he is remembered. Holmes rates by common consent with John Marshall as one of the two greatest justices in Supreme Court history. His opinions and dissents are quoted almost as reverently as the Constitution. His magnum opus *The Common Law* (1881) is a classic of American legal literature, still in print after a hundred years. His 1895 Memorial Day address at Harvard is the only such oration comparable to Lincoln's at Gettysburg.

Some of Holmes's spoken rhetoric about "blindly accepted duty" and "the divine folly of honor" sounds dated to modern ears. On the other hand, his tough, stripped prose style, typically rising to cerebral heights before dropping into a colloquialism ("I thank God I have low tastes") is as bracing today as when it was written. Edmund Wilson placed him among our literary elite. Reading his articles and commentaries and correspondence, one is reminded less of Emerson than Philip Larkin: "An old man ought to be sad. I don't know whether I shall be when the wind is west and the sky clear."

Mr. Novick, by no means a worshipful biographer, feels that "a kind of fascist ideology" underlay much of Holmes's Social Darwinism. Deep war wounds, followed by decades of public indifference to his writings, persuaded him that all human affairs, whether vulgar or sublime, were subject to the rule of tooth and claw. If survival of the fittest eliminated the "manifestly unfit," then so be it. His language in 1927 upholding the right of Virginia to sterilize mental defectives was so harsh it was later quoted by defendants at Nuremburg. If the nation's "best citizens" must sometimes die for the public welfare, Holmes wrote, so must "those who sap the strength of the state" make "lesser sacrifices"—which in any case they were often too retarded to regret. "The principle that sustains vaccination is broad enough to cover cutting the Fallopian tubes. . . . Three generations of imbeciles are enough."

Anti-abortionists must quail at the thought of Holmes sitting on the Supreme Court today. Indeed, Mr. Novick's frequently absorbing notes cite an 1884 case in which Holmes, while still on the Massachusetts circuit, held that the commonwealth could not regard as a person any baby unable to survive outside its mother. But we do not have to agree with the author when he suggests that Holmes had a bias toward brutality whenever his opinions ran contrary to "natural feeling." In the Supreme Court, he could be equally harsh in defense of free speech, dissenting often against the repressions of the Wilson era in words that have become part of our moral memory:

> In this case [*Abrams v. U.S.*, 1919] sentences of twenty years have been imposed for the publication of two [pro-Bolshevik] leaflets that I believe the defendants had as much right to publish as the government has to publish the Constitution. . . . I think that we should be eternally vigilant against attempts to check the expression of opinions that we loathe and believe to be fraught with death, unless they so imminently threaten immediate interference with the lawful and pressing purposes of the law that an immediate check is required to save the country.

On another occasion Holmes said calmly that if the tenets of totalitarianism were to be accepted "in the long run" by the American people, then "the only meaning of free speech is that they should be given their chance to have their way." He seemed willing to let the Constitution destroy itself, rather than compromise one of its most basic rights.

At moments when his absolutism approached nihilism, he was sustained by an Olympian sureness in the strength of democratic government. Holmes had no religious faith, except for a quasi-mystical notion that free individuals could attain Paradise. Characteristically, he cited not the Bible, but a ten-volume work of French etymology:

> [Jean-Henri] Fabre tells us of grubs born . . . in the heart of an oak that when, after three years, the time for metamorphosis comes, build a chamber that as grubs they do not need for the beetle that is to be. They obey their destiny without any sight of the promised land. The law of the grub . . . is the law also for man.

Mr. Novick quotes many of Holmes's unpublished letters, and they are so good one wishes he had space for more. He does treat us to one epistolary chapter, "Lady Castletown." It documents the autumnal romance of the chief justice of Massachusetts with the wife of an Anglo-Irish peer. The affair (one of many indulged by Holmes on bachelor trips to Europe) does not seem to have progressed beyond a few caresses in a conservatory, but the passion it awaked in him proves that his heart was as warm as his mind was cold. "Oh my dear what a joy it is to feel the inner chambers of one's soul open for the other to walk in and out at will."

Perhaps the single most delightful item of information in Mr. Novick's book is that Holmes scribbled several of these *billets-doux* in court, under guise of solemn note taking.

Fanny Holmes, reclusive and eccentric yet wise in the ways of the world, encouraged her husband's little forays to boudoirs and burlesque houses. Mr. Novick paints a clear portrait of this adorable woman, who shared Holmes's life for sixty years, and contributed greatly to his achievement. The evidence is that theirs was an unshakable marriage.

Our last glimpse of the aged couple (she predeceased him) shows them taking the air in an open-top car, and "kicking each other under the lap robe like adolescents."

The widower Holmes was consoled by the society of his "familiars"— brilliant disciples such as Felix Frankfurter, Louis Brandeis, Harold Laski, and Walter Lippmann. It occurred to him, long after it occurred to disapproving friends back in Boston, that "I seem to be in with a considerable number of Jews." He waggishly pretended to have Jewish blood himself, and to the end of his life was unable to understand anti-Semitism.

Honors were slow in coming—he was already sixty-one when Theodore Roosevelt put him on the Court—but his ninetieth birthday was an occasion for international rejoicing. Shortly after that, in the summer of 1931, Holmes felt a "pull-down," as if part of himself had dropped away. His mind remained clear, but Chief Justice Charles Evans Hughes was obliged to tell him, weeping, that his colleagues felt he should resign. As at Fredericksburg, Holmes did not flinch. "The time has come," he agreed. "I bow to the inevitable."

Notwithstanding Holmes's legacy on the Bench, his greatest work may have been to articulate, in his fortieth year, a common law for the American people, a system of "felt necessities" by which we grope our way toward a more perfect union. At this time of national soul-searching about the rights of the unborn and the entitlements of the nonproductive, his cool voice assures us that the more we debate, and the wider the majority that decides such questions, the sooner we will "catch an echo of the infinite, a glimpse of its unfathomable process, a hint of universal law."

THE IVORY AND THE EBONY

Pianists and the Romantic Imagination

CAN A SHOWER OF MUSIC FALL INTO AN UNINHABITED JUNGLE, when there is nobody there to hear it? Lack of listeners did not deter Louis Moreau Gottschalk, living on the edge of a Guadeloupe volcano in 1859, from giving piano recitals to the universe:

> Every evening I moved my piano out upon the terrace, and there, in view of the most beautiful scenery in the world, which was bathed in the serene and limpid atmosphere of the tropics, I played, *for myself alone*, everything that the scene opened before me inspired— and what a scene! Imagine a giant amphitheater, such as an army of Titans might have carved out in the mountains; to the right and left virgin forests filled with wild and distant harmonies; farther on, the green savannas [and] the immensity of the ocean, whose line of deep blue forms the horizon. . . . I let my fingers run over the keyboard, wrapped up in the contemplation of these marvels.

The yearning to relate creativity and creation was shared by all metaphysically inclined musicians from Beethoven to Busoni. These two pianist-composers loom a century apart, like Alpha and Omega, at either

Originally published in *The New Yorker*, 8 January 1990.
Musical cryptogram by Ferruccio Busoni, 1916.

end of Dieter Hildebrandt's *Pianoforte: A Social History of the Piano* (1988). As Busoni might have said, between them they made Gottschalk possible.

Gottschalk, born in New Orleans in 1829, was the quintessential pianistic troubadour, moving gracefully from the salons of Paris (with Chopin's blessing) via Guadeloupe to the Civil War battlefront, and thence to the savage West, where he discovered that his music had charms to soothe the breasts even of Nevada miners. Wherever he went he was trailed by two ten-foot Chickerings—"cowardly mastodons," he called them affectionately, "possess[ing] a charming and obedient docility to the least movement of my fingers."

Just the other day, in the Nordstrom department store at Stanford, California, I heard a Gottschalkian shower of notes falling across a wilderness of nylon, and searching out the source, found a young pianist playing one of these same Chickerings, beautifully restored and perfuming the air with the sounds of the past. Mr. Hildebrandt devotes a witty chapter to Chickerings and Pickerings, Steinways and Steinwegs, Bechsteins and Bachsteins and Brechsteins, and other synonymic products of a nineteenth-century market that in its explosive demographics was comparable to that of the personal computer today. (One might also draw parallels between such keyboard hermits as Alkan and Godowsky, endlessly devising new figurations of black and white, and the sleepless programmers of Silicon Valley, juggling os and 1s.)

The author, who lives in Berlin, makes use of German and Austrian sources unfamiliar to English-speaking readers. Thus he is able to paint delightfully fresh portraits of Carl Czerny, the first millionaire piano pedagogue, Hermann Wolff, the pioneer concert agent, and *kitsch-komponist* Tekla von Badarzewska-Baranowska, who, he assures us, used to be a household name "in Europe, Asia, and the two Americas." But Mr. Hildebrandt's real achievement is to show how the piano became, in his phrase, "the unsung hero" of nineteenth-century liberalism, starting from the night when Beethoven roared at a talkative audience of Viennese aristocrats, "I do not play for such swine!"

THE HUSH FOLLOWING that shout was as intense, probably, as the silence Gottschalk broke over Guadeloupe sixty years later. It had the same virgin quality, a sense of receptiveness to the Romantic seed. The fact that Beethoven's listeners were awed, not angry, indicated that cultural revolution was at hand. They begged him to continue. Exulting, he refused.

"It was not just a question of denying princes their *divertissement*," Mr. Hildebrandt writes. "Music now refused to serve any social function whatsoever." A dilettante archduke wishing to join Beethoven in a piano quartet would have to acknowledge the composer's leadership; and if Ludwig Spohr was on first violin, His Highness must play second fiddle, and like it.

As the pianoforte grew larger in size and tone (Beethoven's big Broadwood of 1817 was especially stressed and strung to penetrate his deafness), it dominated musical discourse to the point that the keyboard concerto, under Chopin, became little more than an extended solo, performed with the harmonious acquiescence of the orchestra. Forgotten in the intoxication of this new Romantic freedom was the concerto's Classical origin in the antithesis of orator and crowd. Brahms, more democratic than the elitist Pole, restored a sense of struggle to the contending forces. Yet even he originally conceived of his D minor Concerto as a battle between—two pianos.

The author devotes a chapter to each of the above pianist-composers, and others to Schubert, Clara and Robert Schumann, Liszt, and the *fin de siècle* virtuosi culminating in Busoni. The double distinction "pianist-composer" is important, because pianism came to affect not only the forms of nineteenth-century music but the very texture of music itself. Although Mozart was the first great pianist, his melodies tended to be vocal in their contour, just as Haydn's related to wind and string instruments, and Bach's, generally, to no instrument in particular. Beethoven, whether writing a mass or a violin duo, "thought" at the keyboard. Even when he could no longer hear what he was playing, his intervals and harmonies were shaped by the layout of keys and the vibration of hammered strings. This tactile style of composition lasted through Busoni, who both ended and transcended it. Hence many of the Romantic Era's most colorful orchestral works, from the *Eroica* Symphony to the *Enigma Variations*, were originally conceived as a *chiaroscuro* of ivory and ebony. Unpianistic composers like Berlioz, Wagner, Bruckner, and Verdi wrote quite differently, and it could be argued (though not by Mr. Hildebrandt) that they were purer musicians for it.

Franz Schubert was probably the least virtuosic of the pianist-composers. He once tried to perform his own "Wanderer" Fantasy, and gave up in frustration. "Let the devil play the stuff!" It may be significant that "An mein Klavier" is one of his least inspired songs, whereas "An die Musik" exquisitely invokes art as art. Lack of keyboard technique, however, did not stop Schubert strumming all night when he had the chance. He had to be pried off the stool at parties. An enormous number of his works are for piano solo, including three of the greatest sonatas ever written. Mr. Hildebrandt suggests that the "paroxysm" which interrupts the *andante* of the A major Sonata, D. 959, is a revolt against "eternal torture at the keyboard." If so, it is a very pianistic paroxysm, consisting of scales, trills, tremolos, and the like, and melts into a reprise that fairly wallows in pedal effects.

The author is more convincing when he detects a fundamental dualism in Schubert's music, a "shifting quality" most apparent in its equivocations between major and minor. Being a writer of literary as well as musical sensibility, he notes the teenage composer's use of the phrase *traurig traulich* ("solemn and congenial") in a diary entry describing a conversation near the grave of his mother, one spring evening in 1816:

> For Schubert that was not a contradiction in terms. For him it was a natural combination, a twilight mood of the soul: it was his minor key. Anywhere else in the musical world a minor key will mark a gloomy, threatening, ominous passage, but Schubert found comfort in that mode, just as he did on his evening stroll. A Schubertian minor makes harmony with man "in the darknesses of this life". . . . Beware of the moment when that harmony is shattered, when the minor consonance between life and music is abandoned, and the pain really bites, and the sudden clarity is sheer torture.

At this point Mr. Hildebrandt cites a lyric in *Winterreise* that drives Schubert from D minor into the "warm" key of E-flat major. No other writer, to my knowledge, has managed to explain why the brightening of the harmony here *sounds* so deathly cold. In another imaginative leap, he likens Schubert's death to that of the last of the Mohicans—not melodramatically but aptly, for about the only thing that comforted the syphilitic composer in his last hours was the prose of James Fenimore Cooper.

In an amusing chapter, "Accomplice in Catastrophe," the author discusses the intimate relations between the piano and the Romantic novel. (Here I must complain about the misleading subtitle given this book by its American publishers. The original German, *Der Roman des Klaviers im 19. Jahrhundert*, is more beguiling and more precise, *Roman* connoting both an affair of the heart and the progress of a hero.) We are reminded that some of the century's most famous female pianists were Elizabeth Bennet, Becky Sharp, Jane Eyre, and Emma Bovary. Then there was the prodigy Hanno Buddenbrooks: Mr. Hildebrandt wickedly recalls rather more of his orgasm at keyboard than is good for Thomas Mann's reputation. Although the harmonic progression that got Hanno off was actually plagiarized from Wagner (it's the final cadence of *Tristan*), we are left in no doubt that the piano had much earlier become a focus of passion among the repressed European bourgeoisie. All those finger-tangling, thigh-rubbing Schubert duets!

The most amorous of the pianist-composers was Robert Schumann, who used his instrument as a sort of mahogany fax machine, sending encoded love messages to the teenage Clara Wieck. She was already a better pianist than he was at twenty-six, and had no difficulty interpreting his musical ciphers. (See, for example, the accented notes in the introduction to his F-sharp minor Sonata, which the cryptologist Eric Sams reads as: "Ill—Oh Clara, shall I win you?") Some of these ciphers, often involving groups of notes whose letter-names spell words, are deliberately obscure. Clara's jealous father was a piano pedagogue, and the lovers did not want him to "eavesdrop" on their romance. Schumann was unable, though, to disguise the rapturous nature of the music that bears the messages along, like flotsam on a flood. Friedrich Wieck understood well enough.

As all the world knows, Robert and Clara overcame his objections, and married for life in 1840. But by then Schumann's habit of private keyboard musings was almost a substitute for speech. He would sit for hours, lips pursed in a silent whistle, monitoring musical conversations between "Florestan" and "Eusebius," as he called the active and the passive sides of his personality. As he grew older, and general paresis swelled his brain, he became taciturn, then completely wordless. It is poignant to read elsewhere in this book that the reverse was true of Clara. "At the age of nine she played like a born musician, yet she could hardly talk. Even when directly addressed she often reacted like a deaf-mute." The time would come when she had to speak for her husband as wife, manager, and nurse, compromising her own career as one of the century's finest pianists.

THE AMBIGUITIES OF Schubert and Schumann, so characteristic of the Romantic imagination (one thinks of Keats enraptured by the sight of wind blowing grasses dark and bright) had no terrors for Franz Liszt, who played their music, indeed all music, better than anyone else alive. Even Chopin complained, "I should like to rob him of the way he plays my studies." Liszt himself was not so much a dual personality as a *trifurquée* (his own adjective) one, tossed between the three poles of pianism, composition, and religion. In a lesser man, the tension between these extremes would have caused early collapse, yet he balanced them superbly most of his long life. Only toward the end, when his physical constitution weakened, did the strain begin to show, and he wrote some of the bleakest, blackest music before Schoenberg. (To hear Maurizio Pollini play Liszt's elegy to Wagner, *R. W.—Venezia*, is to understand Oliver Wendell Holmes's description of old age as a giant dog that gets into a room with you, and grows until there is no longer any space to breathe.)

Mr. Hildebrandt does not deal with Liszt the stooped, white-haired *abbé*, preferring to portray him in his youth as a concert pianist of sunny brilliance and power. Even as a boy in Hungary, Liszt seemed to be both spiritually and physically possessed by the music that flowed through him. "He was a pale, weak looking child," his teacher Czerny remembered, "and while he played he swayed about on the stool as if drunk, so I often felt he would fall to the floor." The pallor was deceptive. Liszt was indefatigable and indestructible. During his brief professional career (he gave his last paid performance in 1847, at thirty-five) he appeared some three thousand times across Europe and Asia Minor, traveling "not like a king, but *as* king," subjugating pianos, women, and even parliaments with a power that none could withstand. He was the first virtuoso to prove that the piano could hold its own onstage, in what he called "soliloquies" or "recitals." Tall, spare, insolently elegant, he would stroll to the keyboard and draw off his white gloves, waiting for silence. Then the long blond hair went flying and the thin arms came down, producing such volumes of tone as to make an orchestra seem puny in comparison. Liszt once caused a sensation by playing his own arrangement of Berlioz's "March to the Scaffold" immediately after the composer had conducted the original. "*Le concert,*" he joked, "*c'ést moi.*"

The effect was a trick, of course. What made Liszt's arrangement sound so overwhelming was that it concentrated something more diffuse—"photographed it," as Charles Hallé recalled, "in the minutest detail on the ear of his listener." All eyes were drawn to Liszt, the only moving, gyrating thing on a stage previously occupied by a hundred stolid players. As he swayed and stamped, nostrils flaring and eyes glazed with passion, he seemed to be not so much playing as played by an electric surge of inspiration. Retiring as a virtuoso in order to concentrate on composing and conducting, Liszt by no means ceased to be a medium for the music of others. He published the transcriptions of Schubert songs and Beethoven symphonies that had won him fame on tour, and for the rest of his life continued to pour out a stream of "arrangements," "reductions," "paraphrases," and "reminiscences" of music by composers as various as Bach and Glinka. So freely did this vast harmony of foreign notes mix with his own that he must have felt at times that he was "fertilizing the universe"—to borrow a phrase from the late pianist Julius Katchen.

Liszt's operatic potpourris fell into disrepute after his death, and have only recently regained the attention of serious pianists, such as Claudio Arrau and Alfred Brendel. Although many still sound meretricious, some of the greatest achieve true Romantic synthesis, transforming the vulgar into the sublime. The B major *lento* of the "Réminiscences de *Norma,*" for example, achieves a spaciousness and profundity quite beyond the reach of Bellini. Busoni remarked that any listener left unmoved by this passage "has not yet arrived at the heart of Liszt."

BY NOW IT WILL have been noticed that the name of Ferruccio Busoni has appeared regularly in this article, as in Mr. Hildebrandt's book and in any serious discussion of the Romantic piano. Busoni, who heard Liszt play as a child and died in 1924, just before the onset of electrical recording, was probably the greatest pianist in history. He had all of Liszt's technique, plus an almost terrifying presence and an Olympian intellect. Ironically, his fame as a pianist—not to mention the enduring fascination of his character—has always obscured what he considered to be his true identity as a composer. To this day his visionary, translucent music eludes the majority of listeners.

Busoni himself, in Antony Beaumont's recent translation and edition of his *Selected Letters* (2004), sardonically joked about his predicament. "I have written out the score of the orchestral introduction to my new stage work," he wrote on 10 August 1917. "Now I am to transform myself into a pianist again, bringing on a fit of nausea, as in the case of Dr. Jekyll. (Only that opinions differ as to which part of me is Mr. Hyde.)"

The stage work in question was his unfinished masterpiece, *Doktor Faust.* Mr. Beaumont has shown in an earlier study, *Busoni the Composer* (1985), that Faustian themes of barter and renunciation had obsessed Busoni from age sixteen, when he wrote a song about a fisherman who sold his soul for treasure. Already young Ferruccio was aware that he was going to have to support himself and his impecunious parents as a concert pianist. Part of him—his father's warm Italian side—liked this idea. All pianists love to play, and he was already a great one. But his other, coolly cerebral side, inherited from his German mother, longed for an environment of rare books and manuscript paper, wherein he could freely roam "the Realm of Music."

Busoni, then, was as divided a soul as any of his Romantic predecessors. In him the major-minor shiftings of Schubert, the cryptic inner dialogues of Schumann, Brahms's struggle between heart and head, and Liszt's driving desire for "transcendence" of the flesh were compounded to such a degree that *Doktor Faust,* when he came to write it, amounted to a spiritual self-portrait.

He grew into an unforgettably handsome and attractive man, a lover of *la dolce vita,* a devoted husband and father, and an intellectual capable of holding his own in five languages, on subjects ranging from philology to Buddhism. He was a prodigious correspondent, the scribbler of at least 50,000 letters. The 352 collected by Mr. Beaumont do not include any to Busoni's Swedish wife Gerda, perhaps because a number of those were published in the 1930s. It seems a pity not to have resurrected at least some of them, and Mr. Beaumont admits the present selection reads somewhat impersonally as a result. Even so, it is of extreme interest. Over three-fourths of these letters have never been printed in any language, and an important appendix, "The Schoenberg-Busoni Correspondence, 1903–1919," appears for the first time in English. Mr. Beaumont, a graceful translator and omniscient editor, notes in his introduction that Busoni had the charm of "elegant outspokenness." One soon detects other essentials of a born correspondent: perception, reflection, spontaneity (no hint here of the deadly booming tone that comes of writing for future publication), and wit. A example of the last is Busoni's delicious description of a visit from Richard Strauss:

> A strong gust of wind has just blown in from Germany. . . . R. S. appeared just like the ostrich [*Straussvogel*] from which he takes his name, partly in brilliant plumage, partly—bald; the largest of his species, yet not aggressive in appearance; the only vertebrate bird that doesn't fly; exotic yet without humor; in a word: an ostrich and not an eagle.

The alkali of such passages helps neutralize the acid of frequent explosions of anger against established sentiment, as in the following, written on the centenary of Richard Wagner:

> It has been my cruel, inescapable fate to have been born and brought up, and quite possibly also to have to take my leave, with *Wagner.* . . . Is there not a tacit agreement amongst thousands who stand and fall only with him, to adhere to Wagner alone? It seems astonishing that a little, contemptible Saxon, with boring music and some strokes of genius, could call an international society of this magnitude into being. One is reminded of that rather

restricted Jewish rabbi from Nazareth, who had to suffer for the sake of an extension of the ecumenical power of Rome. . . .

Busoni's was certainly a giant ego, complete with messiah complex; but like the Jewish rabbi, he sought understanding rather than power. There is a persistent feeling of impatience in these letters, of frustration at the shortness of life compared to the vastness of his dreams, and regret for past opportunities missed—by friends if not by himself. Revisiting Russia for the first time in twenty years, he recoiled when women he had tried to kiss in youth now tried to press their wrinkles upon him: "The aged faces of former acquaintances are frightful, merciless, worse than rust and verdigris. . . . I, who cannot bear to look back!"

As a former prodigy who felt he had missed childhood, he was almost pathologically upset by any early death. The suicide of his pupil O'Neil Phillips evoked an outburst worthy of Lambert Strether: "Let us rejoice in life, let us remain faithful every hour is a gift."

One becomes aware that Busoni indeed lived every hour of his fifty-eight years as "a gift." Faustian torments or no, he gave of himself unstintingly at master classes in Vienna, Bologna, and Berlin, in mammoth recitals (at least twice the length pianists manage today), in concerts of the works of his struggling contemporaries, in editing and book collecting and writing such visionary works as *Outline of a New Aesthetic of Music* (1907). Given the peripatetic quality of his life—he rarely stayed in the same place more than a few months—the wonder is that he managed to compose so much. *Doktor Faust,* which Mr. Beaumont calls "one of the great and rare masterpieces of twentieth-century opera" was preceded by no fewer than twenty-three published "satellite works," not including two whole operas that were themselves variations on the theme of Faust.

For all his achievement, Busoni emerges in these pages as a tragic figure, denied the catharsis that Faust wins in the final (uncomposed) scene of his opera. The Great War devastated his cosmopolitan spirit and forced him to seek sanctuary, first in New York and then in Zurich. He wrote Jella Oppenheimer that the Swiss and he shared an "incomprehension" of bellicosity. "*Here* the 'spirit' may not be 'lifted,' but at least 'the view is free.' "

To which of his parental homelands could he, in all conscience, return when the killing stopped? The truth, Busoni admitted sadly, "is that I have no home at all." When Italy declared war on Germany, he began to die psychologically; it was as if the battle between his extremes had broken out on a global scale, threatening the end of civilized equilibrium. However, the war had at least one beneficial effect, in that it forced him to abandon the concert circuit and face up to his long-delayed *magnum opus*. On the darkest night of December 1914 (the solstice always stimulated his creative instincts) he was overcome with "a strange and shuddering Faust-feeling."

A five-part drama, based not on Goethe but on the sixteenth-century Faust puppet plays, "came together like a vision" in his head. Almost in a trance, Busoni began to write blank verse. On the third night of Christmas, the poem of *Doktor Faust* was finished. "If the work evolves as it should, it will offer as much to the layman as the connoisseur. What a gift!"

That word again. But the gift, once vouchsafed, was soon withdrawn, and Busoni made no musical progress until the summer of 1916, when he began to "hear" bells mixed with the sounds of high strings, organ, and glass harmonica. These sounds, rich in overtones, formed a hazy nimbus from which his vocal score emerged. Appropriately, the first cries to penetrate the haze were chiming plaints of *"Pax! Pax! Pax!"*

Busoni believed that the composer was nothing but a cosmic eavesdropper, attuned to the "Good and Great Universal Music" that floated, free of form, beyond the limits of time and space. One's challenge was to hear this music ever more clearly, and to render it in a form that came as close as possible to its inhuman perfection. Busoni had conceived his theory as a young pianist, when it occurred to him that no matter how correctly he played a printed piece, he could not help but reshape it with every inflexion of his fingers. To interpret was to transcribe. Later, when he came to edit the works of Bach, he decided there was no such thing as an *Urtext*. Notation too was transcription, an attempt to confine, in black-and-white prison clothes, the "child" that was music.

He was therefore not surprised, as the composition of *Doktor Faust* progressed, to find fragments of seventeenth-century Venetian polyphony in it—fragments he recognized only as such when Hugo Leichtentritt sent him the madrigals of Monteverdi. "Although I scarcely knew this old Italian music, I identify myself very closely with it: there must be a tinge of atavism lying dormant in me."

BUSONI'S NOTION OF the *Einheit* (oneness) of music is most evident in Mr. Beaumont's appendix devoted to the correspondence with Schoenberg. That waspish, egomaniacal genius presents the only intellect in these pages comparable to Busoni's own. Their relationship, built on mutual attraction and repulsion, was in every way a clash of giants. If Schoenberg was in the end the greater composer, Busoni was unquestionably the greater human being, always willing in the midst of his own struggles for acceptance to promote the music of another. "Maybe I, some latter Siegfried," he wrote, "shall succeed in penetrating the fiery barrier which makes your work inaccessible, and in awakening it from its slumber of unperformedness."

Although Schoenberg tolerated Busoni's efforts to win him publishing contracts and teaching positions, he wanted above all to have Busoni the pianist advertise his music by playing it. He sent him the first two pieces of his Op. 11, cannily adding that they could be played only by a seer, "somebody who can indeed imbue the works of another with so much of his own imagination that a perfection emerges. . . ."

Busoni replied that the piano pieces "interest me intensely," yet he was loath to perform them as written. The second piece seemed to prove his theory that a composer's notation was only an approximation of the ideal. He proceeded to "rescore" it as he heard it in his head, adding some exquisitely pianistic sonorities, and was surprised when Schoenberg reacted as if whipped.

"Above all," the younger man wrote, "you are doing me an injustice." Busoni's atmospherics, beautiful in themselves, were inimical to the "sombre, compressed" colors he wanted. "I am no pianist," he admitted, yet he would not retract his demand that the instrument give him a crescendo *after* a chord had been struck. If the piano could not follow him into rule-breaking areas of creativity (as the paintbrush had followed Picasso and Braque), then maybe it had become an obsolete medium of expression. Almost in defiance, he sent Busoni his latest piece, Op.11, No.3.

In Mr. Hildebrandt's book there is a quote by Alfred Brendel to the effect that music had been waiting for this piece ever since Schubert's "paroxysm" in the summer of 1828. Romanticism so far had remained proof against Modernism, and tonality not quite given way to atonality. Then, on 20 August 1909, Busoni opened Schoenberg's letter-bomb, and the packed dissonances exploded in his face. Recovering, he complained that he could hear nothing new in such music, while "the 'asceticism' . . . of the piano writing seems to me a pointless avoidance of foregone achievements."

The conservatism of this criticism seems strange when Mr. Beaumont informs us that Busoni had just begun to compose atonally himself. But his style was evolutionary rather than revolutionary: he liked to refine, not destroy. He never did play the Op. 11 pieces in public, although he continued sincerely to study and praise Schoenberg's compositions. Schoenberg showed no reciprocal generosity, and came to regret it later, when he heard Busoni's *Berceuse Elégiaque* for the first time. "Downright moving piece," he noted in his diary. "Deeply felt. I have been most unjust to him."

In the waning days of the prewar period, Busoni organized a performance of Schoenberg's *Pierrot Lunaire* in his Berlin house. It was one of the last occasions when young Germans and Austrians and Hungarians and Jews could gather locally for civilized purpose, united by common values and progressive taste. Busoni never forgot it. "It was an ideal musical afternoon: a highly ingenious new work, a perfect ensemble, afterwards stimulating exchange of ideas, tea and cigarettes and charming, intelligent women. This is the way in which art should be presented— and no other."

Five years later, when times like that seemed as *perdu* as Proust's, Busoni pondered how to express in music a complete collapse of Romantic notions of good and evil, to be followed, he hoped, by a new, childlike classicism (*Junge Klassizität*). He was thinking of the final allegory in *Doktor Faust*, wherein the magician cheats Mephistopheles by dying in the depth of winter, and passing his soul to a naked youth who walks off inviolate into the snow.

The scene was never written. For financial reasons, Busoni had to resume his career as a pianist, and illness gradually weakened his power to compose. But he did write an orchestral study for his finale, in the form of a sublime sarabande that he considered to be the best music he ever wrote. It was received with puzzlement at a postwar concert in London, and when Frederick Delius said condescendingly that he "liked" it, Busoni turned his back and wept.

Like Faust, he was destined to die of heart failure, poverty-stricken and disappointed. There is some debate as to which of his younger peers, if any, inherited his spiritual legacy. Kurt Weill, his pupil, was too worldly, Berg too sensuous, Schoenberg too formulaic. Perhaps only Anton Webern achieved Busoni's ideal of refining music to its "essence."

The manuscript score of the sarabande is prefaced with a symbol (illustrated at the head of this article) that Busoni never explained. Mr. Beaumont obscurely guesses that it shows "the extremes of our dualistic world," opposed like Yin and Yang at either end of the stave, and separated—or bridged—by "the first two spaces which bound the gap between good and evil."

Maybe Busoni was just trying out a new pen. But, since he has given us freedom to dream, I like to think that the symbol reflects the black and white geometry of the piano, the cage of keys and bars against which Schubert briefly bashed his head; that the archaic notes proclaim *der Roman des Klaviers* is finally over; and that the radiant space surrounding it represents Busoni's longed-for realm of "Good and Great Universal Music," where all melodies and all instruments "resonate together and at once, carry you, entwine themselves round you, brush against you— melodies of love and sorrow, of spring and winter, of melancholy and high spirits . . . the feelings of a million beings in a million epochs."

WOMEN IN WHITE

The Memoirs of Laure Junot, Duchesse d'Abrantès

Among the few things that really moved napoleon bonaparte
were the sound of church bells at dusk, and the sight of "a delicate girl
dressed in white and wandering among the trees."

Presumably it was some such vision of Josephine—always at her best
in sylvan surroundings, and one of the first Revolutionary beauties to
show her body through sheer muslin—that made him, first, her idoliz-
ing lover and, next, history's most famous cuckold. Only a very young
and hopelessly romantic general could have marched off, two days after
marrying that libidinous lady, in the belief that she would not soon shed

Originally published in *The New Yorker*, 23 April 1990.

Exhibit in the 1990 show "The Age of Napoleon," The Metropolitan Museum of Art, New York.

her shift for someone else. As all the world knows, Josephine extended this favor to Hippolyte Charles. When Napoleon returned to Paris, hot from the sands of the Nile, and found her neither chaste nor even at home, his *fureur* knew no bounds.

Actually, she had gone forward to meet him—but by the wrong route. Josephine was attracted to men in proportion to their fame, and the returning hero of Aboukir was of more potent interest than the skinny youth she had wed three and a half years before. When she realized her error, she hastened home, only to find the bedroom barred to her. For the rest of that terrible night, she lay begging for forgiveness "at the door of a small black staircase . . . suffering the acutest pangs of mental torture," until Napoleon relented.

So writes their mutual friend Laure Junot, *née* Permon, in *At the Court of Napoleon: Memoirs of the Duchesse d'Abrantès* (New York, 1989). More than anyone else in post-Directoire Paris, Laure knew what was going on socially, sexually, and politically around the Tuileries. Although just fifteen at the time of Napoleon's elevation to supreme power in 1799, she had already heard all about him from her mother, a wealthy Corsican widow and close friend of the Bonaparte family. Within a year, Laure married the First Consul's right-hand man, General Andoche Junot, commandant of Paris. As *madame la commandante* she ascended at once to the heights of French society, and remained there long after the Corsican Eagle had flown to his last rock in the South Atlantic. Preternaturally observant, unsentimental, and malicious in her humor, Laure Junot stood out among the generally vapid beauties who fawned upon Napoleon.

"Well, you little pest!" he exploded one day, irritated by her knowing smile. "What do you find to laugh at!" She had caught him in a moment of vanity, admiring the shape of his silk-stockinged legs in the midst of a monologue decrying dandyism. This was years before Bonaparte embraced pomp as a matter of public policy. The fact that she noticed so early, and that he noticed her noticing, explains why Laure never quite won his approval.

PETER GUNN, IN HIS 1979 biography *Napoleon's "Little Pest,"* records that she was an independent spirit even as a child. Although she devel-

oped into a pretty and fashionable Parisienne, there was always something mannishly assertive about her. "I am one of those persons who like
to have their own way." She is at pains to present herself in her memoirs
as a perfect wife, tolerant of Junot's infidelities, although she did not
hesitate to betray him in turn, when it suited her social or sexual purpose.

As one of the capital's most prominent young hostesses, Mme. Junot
entertained not only the *nouveaux riches* brought in by Napoleon but also
ancien régime aristocrats. Instinct warned her that the latter might yet
succeed in restoring a Bourbon to the throne. The First Consul was sar-
castic about her "fine acquaintances of the Faubourg Saint-Germain"
until he found it expedient to cultivate them, too.

Laure's salon on the Champs-Elysées was known for its intellectual
as well as its social brilliance. Writers, artists, composers, and scientists
flocked to engage their sharp-tongued hostess in conversation, while
drinking deeply of her husband's legendary cellar. The Junots could afford to be hospitable. Napoleon lavished hundreds of thousands of francs
a year on them, and encouraged Laure to spend it all. In those elegant
days before the vulgarities of the First Empire, she was a beguiling creature, small, perfectly shaped, with black hair, a lustrous smile, and skin
the texture of satin. "It is impossible," one of her admirers wrote, "to
imagine anything prettier, more alive, than this young lady." Later,
Laure began to put on weight, and it was whispered that her nose, like
Cleopatra's, could have been shorter. But her ever-increasing fund of
gossip and anecdote held all comers enchanted.

She was obliged to close her salon temporarily in 1805, when Napoleon sent General Junot on a diplomatic mission to Iberia. The trip permitted Laure to record some Goyesque impressions of the Spanish and
Portuguese royal families. Despite, or perhaps because of, her husband's
clumsy representations, the peninsular situation worsened, and Junot
was recalled to muster a new army for war. Laure reestablished herself
on the Champs-Elysées, entertaining as lavishly as ever. In 1807, Junot
captured a strategic Portuguese town, and his wife was rewarded with
the title of Duchesse d'Abrantès.

As the Empire approached its apogee, with Napoleon's divorce and
remarriage to Marie-Louise in 1810, Laure had strategic affairs with

Count Metternich, the Austrian ambassador to France, and a young monarchist, Marquis Maurice de Balincourt. These liaisons stood her in good stead through 1814, when Napoleon fell from power. However, Laure's fortunes began to decline with the loss of her old benefactor. Almost in spite, she turned on Bonaparte, calling him a tiger who deserved to be kept in a cage.

Widowhood further impoverished her. The increasingly eccentric Duc d'Abrantès, suffering probably from tertiary syphilis, had killed himself not long after appearing in public naked except for plumed hat, military orders, and dancing pumps. Debts forced Laure to move out of her splendid townhouse. Her rich friends dwindled, and by the time of Napoleon's death, in 1821, she remained the darling only of a few intellectuals.

THE RANKS OF these acolytes were swelled, in 1825, by a tiny genius fifteen years Laure's junior. Honoré de Balzac fell in love with her, and listened spellbound to her stories of the Directoire and the Consulat. He begged for more. Amused, she showed him some of the diary jottings and conversational notes she had been in the habit of keeping all her life. Balzac's eyes bulged. Here was a lode of "living silver" (*argent vivant*), which, recast and set into type, would save his adored duchess from poverty. "The more I have considered your destiny and the nature of *your* intelligence," he told her, "the more I have been struck with this idea. . . . You could make [literature] of a brilliant epoch." He offered editorial assistance.

As an experiment, she wrote, for him alone, a "Journal Intime," describing how she, Junot, Metternich, and Caroline Bonaparte used to take turns sleeping with one another. Balzac was ecstatic. Laure then set to work on an ambitious account of her life and times. It was contracted for at a per-volume rate, unfortunately no longer tolerated by publishers, that rewarded prolixity. By the time she wrote *finis*, in 1834, the *Mémoires de Madame la Duchesse d'Abrantès, ou Souvenirs Historiques sur Napoléon, la Révolution, le Directoire, le Consulat, l'Empire et la Restauration* numbered no fewer than eighteen volumes. Their success was tremendous, and made Laure one of the most famous literary figures in Europe.

Balzac was more puzzled than hurt when she publicly pretended that she had had no help on the project. She brushed aside his reproof with astounding *hauteur.* "What would you wish me to do? I have to act in this way."

For once in his life, he could find no words.

Prosperous again, if not rich, Laure followed up with twelve more autobiographical books, plus novels, plays, and articles. But she could never earn as much money as she compulsively spent, and her final illness was haunted by the sound of her possessions being sold in the next room. She died on 7 June 1838, in her fifty-fourth year. Mme. Récamier, the most exquisite of all the sheer-clad figures to wander through the *Mémoires,* came to pray for her soul.

ONE DARK DAY last February, I visited the exhibition of Napoleonic fashions at the Metropolitan Museum of Art, and found a hall of white dresses, each seemingly more beautiful than the last. Their vaporous transparency—white bees floating in breezes of cambric, silver droplets falling to coagulate like foam on the floor—seemed to breathe the liberation of the female body after the Eighteenth Brumaire. I had a palpable sense of warm breasts and freely moving thighs, as if the original wearers had slipped them off moments before, in order to skinny-dip in the pools of Fontainebleau. As I strolled past these dresses, my head full of Laure's reminiscences, I could not help imagining her in this one, Josephine in that, and Mme. Récamier in any number of others.

Their shapes began to blur, as if they and not I were perambulating, spinning on the romantic *ronde* started by Napoleon in 1795, when he made a callow proposal of marriage to Laure's mother. Mme. Permon's mocking laughter resounded through the hall: *"Parlons serieusement. Vous croyez connâitre mon âge?"** Désirée Clary whirled in and out of the First Consul's reach, trailing white ribbons and lace. Bonaparte (a dark blue high-collared tunic) bowed to Director Barras (a red cashmere toga), who waved him on to his mistress, Josephine de Beauharnais (rippling curves of snowy silk on a gilt chaise longue). He knelt to bury his

---

* "Let's be serious. Have you any idea how old I am?"

head in her lap, while she blew kisses at Hippolyte Charles, across the room in cavalry uniform. Leaping to his feet, Napoleon launched into a vengeful series of entanglements, beginning with the wife of one of his own lieutenants, and ending in the plump arms of Marie-Louise—who, barely out of her bridal gown, delightedly asked him to "do it again." Elsewhere, Laure curtsied to a mysterious M. de V——, resplendent in strawberry redingote, before yielding herself to General Junot, coruscating with brass and silver from head to foot. He was seduced away in turn, by Caroline Bonaparte; Laure abandoned herself to Metternich; Caroline seduced him, too; Laure pirouetted into the satin arms of de Balincourt; Pauline Bonaparte, not to be outdone by Caroline, offered her perfect body to half the youth of Paris; and Josephine's daughter Hortense indulged the sexual gymnastics of a pioneer *bohéme.*

IN THE *MÉMOIRES,* the rotation of all these figures is just as dizzying. They change names and titles almost as often as they exchange partners: Caroline, for one, becomes Mme. Murat, then Grande Duchesse de Berg, then Queen of Naples.

The irony is that the central figure in the choreography, Napoleon himself, was by nature uxorious and family-minded. That early proposal to Mme. Permon, who had cradled him as a child, betrayed a deep desire for domestic security. He went so far as to propose a triple alliance, offering Pauline to Laure's brother Albert, and his brother Jérôme to Laure. No wonder Mme. Permon laughed. Yet Napoleon was deadly serious in his desire to found a dynasty. "I am in a condition to obtain much for those belonging to me."

Josephine's sexual treason, as he sat at his camp desk in Italy, dreaming of stripping "the last film of chiffon" from her body, destroyed forever his ideal of marriage. She never again deceived him, but he lost respect for women in general. "The hen should be silent in the presence of the cock," he crudely told Laure, when she expressed nervousness about visiting her philandering husband abroad in 1806. "If Junot amuses himself in Parma, what is that to you?" She saw him glance sideways as he said this, testing the effect of his words on Josephine. The Empress said nothing, but tears welled in her eyes.

Laure shared a good deal of Napoleon's misogyny. She describes with obvious enjoyment how he forced Josephine, hysterical and racked with migraine, to drive a carriage through a swollen river. Her pen portraits of other women, with the exception of Mesdames Permon and Récamier, verge on the sadistic. Napoleon tried to bully her, but without success; fascinated, he lapsed into jocular teasing, which she parried without effort.

Perhaps the most memorable episode she recounts is the First Consul's attempt to seduce her at Malmaison in the summer of 1801. At least, that is how she interprets his sudden appearance in her room at five in the morning, with the light hardly green in the trees. "It is really *I*," he says, laughing. "Why so astonished!"

Laure lies alone in bed. Her husband is in Paris, and Josephine too is away, at Plombières. Napoleon draws up a chair, crosses his legs, and brandishes a thick packet of letters. "We are going to chat." His manner is so relaxed she finds herself responding to him without embarrassment.

"Ah! here is a trap," said he, taking off one, two, three, four envelopes, each highly scented with essence of roses, and inscribed in a pretty handwriting, with the talismanic words, *For the First Consul only*. He came at length to the last envelope, and a laugh soon burst from him. . . .

"It is a declaration," said he, "not of war, but of love. It is a beautiful lady, who has loved me, she says, from the day she beheld me present the Treaty of Campoformio to the Directory. And if I wish to see her, I have only to give orders to the sentinel at the iron gate, on the side of Bougival, to let a woman pass dressed in white, and giving the word *Napoleon!* and that [looking at the date] this very evening."

"*Mon Dieu*," cried I; "you will not be so imprudent?" He looked attentively at me; then said, "What is it to you if I do? What harm can it do me?"

"What is it to me? What harm can it do you? Really, General, those are strange questions. May not this woman be bribed by your enemies?"

Napoleon tells Laure, with a grin, that he does not take the letter seriously. "Do you think me so simple, so stupid, as to nibble at such a bait?" He scrawls something on the envelope, then stays, talking companionably, until a clock strikes the hour.

> "The deuce, there is six o'clock!" he exclaimed, and approaching the bed he collected his papers, pinched my foot through the bedclothes, and smiling with the graciousness which sometimes brightened his countenance he went away singing, with that squalling voice, so strongly contrasted with the fine sonorous accent of his speech—
>
> *Non, non, z'il est impossible*
> *D'avoir un plus aimable enfant . . . .*

We already know that to have one's foot pinched, or one's nose or ear pulled, is a sure sign of Consular favor. Napoleon is obviously pleased with his little visit, and Laure puts it down to eccentricity until she realizes it is only the first move in an erotic game. That evening, he draws her aside and whispers, "I am going to the Bougival Gate."

> "I do not believe a word of it," said I in the same tone. "You know too well the irreparable loss to France should any evil befall you. If you say another such word I will tell Madame Hortense, or Junot."
>
> "You are a little simpleton," said he, pinching my ear; then threatening me with his finger: "If you think of telling one word of what I have said to you, I shall not only be displeased but pained."

Evidently, Napoleon has his tryst with the woman in white, because he is in exultant humor when he appears again at Laure's bedside next morning. "Why do you sleep with your window open! It is fatal for women, who, like you, have teeth of pearl." Out comes another packet of documents, and he falls to work, muttering to himself, as Laure stares amazed at him over the bedclothes. He discusses a few matters of state with her, then, pinching her foot as before, makes his musical exit.

Later in the day, he ominously praises Laure for having "no fear" of him in the boudoir. Fearful nonetheless, she takes care to double-lock her door that night, and falls asleep with difficulty. When she awakes, the sun is already high, and Napoleon is standing over her, looking like "falcon and eagle together." He reminds her that as master of Malmaison he has a master key to her bedroom. It is too late now for any "chat," but tomorrow he will come, very early indeed, to take her hunting. Something tells Laure that she will be item number one on his list of game.

By now (such is the clarity and vividness of her prose), we are turning the pages as if reading a novel. Tiny telling details—the window open to the warm morning breeze, Napoleon's crossed legs, the rosy perfume of the letters in his hand, his Corsican sibilants—accumulate to such effect that one wonders if Balzac's help was more than merely editorial. The action rises to a comic climax when Laure's husband, back from Paris, rejoins her that night, and Napoleon, entering rampant at dawn, is flabbergasted to find them in bed together. But his self-control is splendid as Junot (wearing a Turkish turban) politely asks what he wants.

"I came to awake Madame Junot for the chase," replied the First Consul in the same tone; "but," after a prolonged glance at me, which is still present to my memory, notwithstanding the thirty years that have intervened—"but I find her provided with an alarum still earlier than myself."

I will not spoil a potential reader's pleasure with details of Napoleon's later *tête-à-tête* with Laure, except to say that their dialogue, in a small carriage, is alone worth the price of the book.

AS MAY BE GATHERED from the quotations above, the style of this translation hardly belongs to the twentieth century. It is not unpleasing, suggestive at times of a dowager blushing naughtily into her décolletage, but it lacks the clear fluency of Napoleonic French. Some very fine print on the copyright page says that it derives from an English text published by the Napoleon Society in 1895. There is a terse foreword by Katell le Bourhis, the associate curator for special projects at the Metropolitan Museum's Costume Institute, and a witty introduction by the historian Olivier Bernier, but nowhere are we informed who is responsible for the often clumsy editing. Comparison with a copy of the second French edition (Paris, 1835) in the New York Public Library shows that the Napoleon Society "translation" was drastically abridged. What Doubleday has done is abridge this abridgment. Neither English version indicates where deletions have been made, nor how extensive they are. Sometimes a sentence has disappeared at the drop of a semicolon, sometimes whole chapters. By my calculation, the 1895 set represents a 66 percent loss of text, and this new volume sacrifices about 30 percent more.

On the whole, Napoleon Society editors acted responsibly. They cut out Laure's obvious space fillers, and a quantity of biographical material interesting only to her contemporaries. But they also betrayed their own age's prejudices, deleting passages they found to be of dubious morality. For example, the French text of the episode quoted above poignantly details Laure's flooding emotions the night she double-locked her door. It implies that her husband had left her alone at Malmaison as a favor (*une déférence*) to the First Consul. (The gesture gains significance when we read elsewhere that Junot's love for Napoleon verged on the homosexual.) Again, there is a hint that if Laure had known at seventeen what she learned to her cost later, she might have been less solicitous of the general's feelings:

> I knew that I was necessary to him; but I was too young to realize that his need would not last. Youth is more than innocent about such things; it is inventive [*elle est elle-même créatrice*], and uses its own hands to tauten the blindfold over its eyes. . . .
>
> I thought I saw something evil [in Napoleon's intent], something whose consequences might be terrible; but I saw as a child, and though I sought to stop it, I hoped to bring it on.

Of this psychological tumult—Balzacian, again—hardly a trace survived in 1895. A modern translator would be less censorious of an aging woman's regret that she had not given herself, just once, to the dominant force of her time.

Doubleday has made a judicious selection of Laure's best stories, with emphasis on the early years, when she and Napoleon were closest. Occasionally, the heavy cutting shows. A phrase such as "Instantly Chevalier's machine occurred to me," in the midst of an account of an assassination attempt, is meaningless if the machine has been decommissioned from an earlier chapter. And one wishes that some post-Imperial anecdotes had been included—in particular, the description of a corpulent, weeping Josephine asking Laure if Napoleon, four years after their divorce, might permit her to accompany him to Elba. Lastly, it seems a pity not to have ended, as Laure does, with Napoleon marching home from exile in 1815 across mountain roads strewn with violets and hyacinths—only to find Paris "*triste* and sullen," unwilling to welcome him back.

One day, let us hope, somebody will publish a new selective translation of these *Mémoires*, combined with extracts from the "Journal Intime" and from Laure's amorous letters to de Balincourt (edited by Robert Chantemesse as *The Secret Memoirs of the Duchesse d'Abrantès* and published in 1927). In the meantime, our best compromise is to read this Doubleday volume along with a copy of Peter Gunn's biography. Then we can, like generations of Napoleon addicts before and after us, see the First Consul racing like a boy round the garden of Malmaison; listening with grave respect to the pratings of children and lion keepers; pacing in a rage up and down the waterfront of Boulogne while the waves crash at his feet; underscoring state documents with his nails; openly cheating at cards; yawning at his own coronation; proudly pinching the nose of his infant son ("Come, come sir . . . do Kings cry?"); and, most memorably, listening to church bells at dusk, the loneliest man in the world, thinking perhaps of Josephine as she used to be, in her white Directoire dress, when her body was his alone for two sublime nights, and the Revolution was new, and his love for France so great that it hurt.

UNDISTINGUISHED AMERICANS

Short and Simple Annals of the Poor

I T SEEMS PATRONIZING TO SUGGEST NOW, AS THOMAS GRAY DID TWO and a half centuries ago, that many a gem of purest ray serene winks in the obscurity of unexamined lives. Yet ordinary people retain their power to send forth surprise flashes, illuminating not only the dark around them but also more sophisticated shadows—for example, those cast by public figures who will not admit to private failings, or by philosophers too cerebral to state a plain truth. Any newsman will tell you that if you wave your microphone in enough faces, sooner or later some guy in a John Deere cap is going to come out with a phrase that glints

Originally published in *The New Yorker*, 11 June 1990.

"Flat in Hell's Kitchen." Photograph by Richard Hoe Lawrence, 1890.

and sparkles. Call it quartz if you like, but similar scintillas brighten the imagery of our best writers. What was Raymond Carver's diamond prose but a carbonization of the garnet-rock of proletarian speech?

As with expression, so with experience. The largely unwritten "short and simple annals of the poor" (Gray again) help biographers differentiate between the little that is unique and the much that is mundane in the lives of men and women eminent enough to be chronicled. Your average salesman faces, on his daily battlefield, forces as epic as Leonidas at Thermopylae. If a James Joyce or an Arthur Miller can make literature out of him, mightn't *he*, granted some clarity of perception and a sympathetic editor, produce a page or two almost as fine?

This, at any rate, was the notion of Hamilton Holt in 1902, when he commissioned a series of anonymous autobiographical sketches for his magazine *The Independent.* Such "lifelets," as he called them, fed a current fascination with the squalors of poverty, already exploited by Jacob Riis in *How the Other Half Lives* (1890). But Riis had been a sentimentalist. What distinguished Holt's pieces was their tone of hard authenticity. In most cases, his editing was minimal, and the voices that emerged from each installment were as vivid as if played back from an Edison cylinder. "The Story of a Polish Sweatshop Girl" was followed by "The Biography of a Bootblack," "The Story of a Young Syrian," "The Story of Two Moonshiners," and some seventy similar essays. In 1906, Holt collected the sixteen best and published them as *The Life Stories of Undistinguished Americans: As Told by Themselves.**

It may be the enduring flintiness of these memoirs (some are painful even by today's confessional standards) that has encouraged Routledge to reissue them for the first time since their original publication, with four extra stories from the magazine series. More than half the collection consists of the accounts of immigrants, and the other pieces have a foxy ethnicity (there are "Negro," Indian, and Filipino contributions) or the regional quirks of a culture unblended by television and radio. To see the Florida seabed through a conch sponge fisherman's water glass is as rich and strange as to sit in a Lithuanian log house at the turn of the century

---

* Reissued by Routledge (New York, 2000).

and listen, with a boy's ears, to an old shoemaker reading subversive literature:

> "Some day," he said, "I will be caught and sent to jail, but I don't care. I got this from my son [in Chicago]. . . ." Then he bent over the paper a long time and his lips moved. At last he looked into the fire and fixed his hair, and then his voice was shaking and very low:
> *"We know these are true things—that all men are born free and equal—that God gives them rights which no man can take away—that among these rights are life, liberty and the getting of happiness."*
> He stopped, I remember, and looked at me, and I was not breathing. He said it again, *"Life, liberty and the getting of happiness. Oh, that is what you want."*
> My mother began to cry.

If I may interject a personal reminiscence, I stood once in the Jefferson Memorial in Washington and overheard a turbaned immigrant reading its inscriptions to his children. The words *God who gave us life gave us liberty*, declaimed in a half-yodeling singsong, have never moved me as much before or since. Repeatedly in these "lifelets," texts, images, and customs overfamiliar to Americans register upon us in the primitive way they first struck alien eyes and ears.

NEEDLESS TO SAY, the Lithuanian boy comes here to find that Jefferson promised not the "getting" of happiness but only its "pursuit." To an equally disillusioned Hungarian peasant, the Statue of Liberty is merely a "big iron woman [with] a broom." Abraham Lincoln's notion of the superiority of labor feels, to a Japanese servant, more like economic indignity. "No honor, no responsibility, no sense of duty, but the pliancy of servitude."

That last phrase is a scintilla, as are others in the servant's brokenly eloquent story: "a man of sunny side of age"—"I shall be my own ancestor"—"reprimanded me with a red hot angry"—"my avocation as a professor of Dust and Ashes." And here is a passionate (if tacit) out-burst worthy of Shylock:

> I said at heart, "It's your pleasure to blame me, lady. . . . You might bully me as you please and treat me like a dog, I shall not object. I have a soul within me. My vital energy in self-denying struggle could not be impaired by your despise. On the contrary, it will be stimulated."

Stimulation under stress is a feature of most of these narratives. All the subjects are, in their minor way, heroic, or at least heroically honest. They show little self-pity, and those who have managed to better themselves are not disposed to boast. All, with the exception of a rather passive ex-peon, have what the Japanese servant calls "a hard spot" in the region of the heart, whether the hardness be ambition, fortitude, faith, or, in the case of a thirty-five-year-old Southern White Woman, racial hatred of frightening intensity. "I belong to a class in the South," she coolly pro-claims, "who know the negro only as a servant." This economic status (she grew up on an inherited plantation) distinguishes her from the other memoirists in the book, who are uniformly poor, yet her words are as plain as theirs. Acknowledging and explaining—without apology—her "well nigh uncontrollable" revulsion for black men, she is frank about the psychosexual attraction that drew her to black girls as a child:

> If we played "horse"—and I regret to say that we did—they were the horses, I the driver. . . . [I] recall one young negro girl much stronger than the others, who, by getting down upon her hands and knees, could make herself such a vicious "horse" that none of us were able to stay on her back. But the effort to do so was an experience I ever coveted. I would seat myself firmly, clasp my hands tightly in the wool on the back of her head, and wait for the delicious sensation of taking a running, plunging start that in-variably landed me over her head somewhere in the grass. I was often severely bruised and obliged to retire to my mother for oint-ments.

The Southern Colored Woman whose story follows is just as explicit about her phobia of white men. "Few colored girls reached the age of sixteen without receiving advances from them." She is sick of being propositioned by store clerks and school directors, of being fondled by white hands in a crowd. Her sense of victimization—"I never get used to it; it . . . hurts more and more"—dates back before puberty, to the wake of a beloved teacher, and the taunts of white children who saw her arrive with a bouquet: "More flowers for that dead nigger!"

Flung stones pursued her as she ran home. "I have known real horrors since, but none left a greater impression on me."

NOT SURPRISINGLY, reminiscences of childhood and youth are the most vivid parts of this book. It is impossible to read them, even when the prose is terse or ungainly, and not empathize with primary emotions, feel the raw textures of life. We kiss our girl good-bye in a field full of rising mist, while desire surges "to take hold of her and keep her." We plant, plow, shear, winnow, and grind. After a summer in the fields, it takes us two weeks to soften our hands for lacework. We card, spin, weave, sweep, and churn. We breathe the stink of drying sponges, taste black bread rubbed with garlic and herring, stare into the round, red, wreathing face of a priest as he tells us our father is dead of "a broken heart" in New York.

Dead? No—could that be him striding through the woods, a full-blooded medicine man, beaded and fringed, rattling with boxes of pills and herbs? We try to follow his way of life, but the streams of the St. Regis Reservation choke with sawdust and "the ever encroaching white man" promises us "glories and luxuries" in a government school far away. When we enroll there, we are cropped and scrubbed, reclothed and renamed, forbidden to speak our native language.

What must we do to survive in this brutal New World? Shall we scalp these pale, pinched, overdressed people ogling us at Coney Island? What do we say to overseers who strap our women to logs, like mules? How to control machines that drive needles right through our fingers, too fast to see? Can we bear this whip that glues the shirt to our back? Will we last a single night (God forbid, thirteen years) in this stockade reeking with tallow and the oozings of men in chains?

Well, there will be days when a few spare dollars accrue, and we can go to the theater and have a good cry, or take a dance cruise up the Hudson, or wear a new gray dress with white insert, and a spray of roses, and receive the compliments of Newport gentlemen. The bars of Key West have barrels of *aguardiente* to wash the salt out of our throat, there is good beer and vodka at Chicago's ethnic clubs, and—O rare treat after months at the ironing board!—soothing pipes of opium in certain parts of Chinatown. We might even express ourselves in verse:

Concealing my own I toil and prepare
Over the rough sea I steer my heart. . . .

Or:

Now, little papoose, swing on to your rest.
My red browed papoose, swing east and swing west.

AT LEAST TWO "Life Stories of Undistinguished Americans" transcend the primitive and, by virtue of their grace and poignancy, qualify as lasting literature. The first is the account, by an itinerant Minister, of his twenty-eight years on the Southern Methodist circuit. He was born with congenital cataracts, and endured three operations, without anesthetic, before his fourteenth birthday. Then, as he sat by a window one bright afternoon in May, a doctor managed to needle his right eye correctly, and "there burst upon my view such a vision of field and sky and sunlight as I had never looked upon before." In time, with the aid of microscope-thick lenses, he was able to use that eye to educate himself. What he read and pondered persuaded him that his vocation was the ministry. But his handicap was still so acute that it was four years before he could cajole the Methodist Conference to grant him an itinerary. So began a life of lonely trudges and buggy rides, often through snow and wind, to churches that sometimes had only two worshippers waiting for him. "The country was hilly and much broken; [I stayed] in very plain houses, often with only one room; my fare for days together . . . was only coarse corn bread, fat bacon, and coffee without cream or sugar—and not a church on the work had a stove, or was ceiled."

For nine years his main solace was reading. Marriage in early middle age to "a sensible, religious country girl" brought family life, a parsonage swathed with morning glory, but ultimate tragedy: "The mother of my children sickened and died of rapid consumption." Somehow he managed to find another wife.

At the time of writing, he is serving his twentieth pastoral charge, still poor but debt-free. His sight is worsening, yet he is able to drive "over plain and familiar roads." He hopes, from his present patch of ground, to cull "a light bale of cotton." He estimates that he has preached to fifty thousand people in his life, and received a thousand new members into the church. His book collection is as big as he can afford it to be. He allows that he has tried his hand at a novel. Were he less blind, he might possibly have advanced farther, but he is content not to complain:

> The world in which I have lived has had more mysteries in it than the world of those who see well, and larger room for imagination, and for those poetic fancies which give the earth and sky and sun and stars a beauty that is not otherwise their own. And there have been other compensations. The very effort necessary to acquire the knowledge that I have gathered has made me husband it all the more carefully. I could not lightly throw away that which cost me so much.

THE MASTERPIECE OF THE collection is "The Life Story of a Farmer's Wife." Her prose, clear and flat as glass, achieves Orwell's ideal of representation without refraction. (Mr. Holt assures us that he has not changed a word.) She is utterly candid about herself and her domineering husband, whom she serves but does not love. "All through life I have found my dislike for giving offense to be my undoing." By nature dreamy, devout, and imaginative, she has to labor from four in the morning until nine at night on chores that gratify only her strong body. "I have never had a vacation, but if I should be allowed one I should certainly be pleased to spend it in an art gallery."

She takes us through a typical day, mentioning that as soon as her first fire has caught in the kitchen she will go outside "and gather a choice, half-blown rose and a spray of bride's wreath, and arrange them in my hair." The superabundance of tasks that follow, listed without weariness or rancor, is enough to numb our comprehension. There are pails of milk to be strained, chicks and children to be fed, cattle "loudly pleading" to be taken to pasture, horses and hogs to care for, weeds to hoe, "dinner" to prepare before noon. Then floors must be swept, gardens dug, seedlings transplanted, fences repaired.

Halfway through the day we notice (as her husband surely does not) that she again puts fresh flowers in her hair. Also, she stands at the butter churn somewhat longer, perhaps, than most farmers' wives do, for there is a book guiltily propped beside it. She admits that she has always had a longing to read "the great poets and authors . . . but up till the present time I have not been permitted to satisfy this desire." Her father thought stories were sinful; her husband is "so very penurious" that he begrudges her subscription to a newspaper. "I must admit that there is very little time for the higher life for myself, but my soul cries out for it, and my heart is not in my homely duties; they are done in a mechanical abstracted way. . . . My ambitions are along other lines."

It comes as no surprise to learn that these ambitions are literary. Out of her own savings, and over her husband's vehement objections, she has bought ink and paper, and is taking a correspondence course in writing. She is proud of the fact that she has managed to get some articles printed, in papers "which do not pay for such matter."

One doubts that the papers gave her so much as a byline. Even now—published profitably, at last!—she must remain anonymous. We leave her churning, the yellow slab dragging at her rod, garlanded for herself alone. As Gray elegiacally sighed:

Full many a flower is born to blush unseen.
And waste its sweetness on the desert air.

HUNTERS OF THE WILD GUFFAW

The Oxford Book of Humorous Prose

ABOUT TWELVE YEARS AGO A JOURNALIST NAMED RALPH KEYES noticed that whenever he touched on the subject of height in interviews, he got an emotional and usually inaccurate response. Even people who were content with their own stature would lie about the inches, or lack thereof, of other people. The degree and vertical direction of the exaggeration told more about the describer than the described. Stature, clearly, mattered to Americans in the era of Jimmy Carter—more so than details of coloring, or even personality. Mr. Keyes became so intrigued by this phenomenon that he wrote a book about it, devoting spe-

Unpublished review originally written for *The New Yorker,* October 1990.
Photograph of P. G. Wodehouse in 1928.

cial chapters to celebrities who were either "Shorter Than You Might Think" or "Taller Than You Might Think."*

These days our sensitivities about height have faded, after a decade dominated by financiers who are Shorter Than You Could Possibly Imagine, and whose gorgeous wives are Taller Than Seems Strictly Necessary. The new neurosis is about humor, and somebody should write a book about why public figures of all sizes claim, or pretend, to be blessed with it. Democratic strategists in the last presidential campaign admitted that Mr. Dukakis stood only five feet six inches in thick shoes, yet they tried desperately to convince us he was Funnier Than You Might Think.

"Funnier, at any rate, than *your* guy ever was," I teased an aide to Walter Mondale. At this (to use P. G. Wodehouse's favorite simile) he shied like a startled mustang. "Fritz," he insisted, "is *absolutely* the funniest politician ever."

My personal vote would be for Calvin Coolidge, who was so unaware of his own risibility that he never cracked a smile in sixty-four years. The whole question of humor—who has it, what it is, and why we have to be defensive about it, is a perplexing one. It has this in common with height, that we tend to confer it upon those we find compatible, while denying it to our enemies. Napoleon was short to British perception, and tall to French, in the same way that Stephen Leacock, who might reduce *you* to paroxysms, puts your wife to sleep. Yet she will laugh over breakfast at Russell Baker's column in *The New York Times* until both you and her coffee turn cold. Who is to say which writer really is funny? Humor cannot be calibrated, much less defined. One might say, as Oscar Wilde said of ignorance, that it is "a delicate exotic fruit; touch it, and the bloom is gone."

Frank Muir is properly respectful of the fruit in his new hothouse collection, *The Oxford Book of Humorous Prose.* He calls it "an anthology *raisonné*," but makes no attempt to define his subject, "because . . . the reader knows more about comedy than I do." This is a polite attempt to dissociate himself from the condemnation that is any anthologist's lot. I have avoided reading other reviews, but could not help hearing that Mr. Muir has been taken to task by critics outraged either by his choice of authors, or by the space he allots one at the expense of another.

* *The Height of Your Life* (Boston, 1980).

It seems to me he can hardly be faulted on the former score. No fewer than 239 English-language writers are crammed into this massive volume, not to mention the prolific Anon., who makes six contributions. There are approximately 600 words of text on each of its 1,147 pages. Even so, humor being what it is, individual readers might wonder why the unamusing X has been included, instead of the mirthful Y. Personally, I don't find Edgar Allan Poe a wag, but Mr. Muir does, on the strength of what must be the first extended anecdote about plastic surgery. He introduces us to some delightful strangers, including Harriet Cavendish and the Very Reverend S. R. Hole (what a good thing that gentleman's initials were not reversed), while snubbing James Boswell, Compton Mackenzie, Vladimir Nabokov, Barbara Pym, Truman Capote, Woody Allen, Molly Keane, and Veronica Geng. These happen to be *my* Ys; your Xs perhaps. The "mustard seed of humor," as Mr. Muir sees it, is a wayward thing, landing unpredictably on the damp flannel of our receptivity.

THE EARLIEST ITEM in *The Oxford Book* was self-printed by William Caxton in 1477, and the most recent, by the editors of *Private Eye*, is dated 9 August 1985. Mr. Muir, a veteran BBC comedy writer and probably the world's supreme punster, shows no national bias, nor any sign of editorial exhaustion after seventeen years of research. He has hunted the wild guffaw (his own phrase) as far afield as New Zealand, a nation that rates, on the fun scale, somewhere between Iran and Romania. His receptivity is delicate enough to find humor in eighteenth-century newspaper fillers, nineteenth-century dialect fables, and at least one modern novel, by Amanda Ros, which is More Awful Than Anyone Can Imagine. He is generous to, and deeply admiring of, American humorists, from Benjamin Franklin to Fran Lebowitz. If he features three of his countrymen to every one of ours, we must accept that the Brits have been funnier than us for far longer.

On the question of space allotment, Mr. Muir is vulnerable to criticism. Here again, everyone's sense of humor—and proportion—is different. As editor, he makes no qualitative comparisons, yet his preferences are as plain as his pagination. P. G. Wodehouse is the clear winner (and I should think so too, by Jove!) at fifty-one pages; Evelyn Waugh is second with thirty-five; then come Dickens and S. J. Perelman with twenty-five apiece, and Mark Twain fourth with seventeen. Few connoisseurs, I think, would dispute this pentarchy of the greatest prose humorists, though were we Mr. Muir, we might distribute the space differently. Our real partisan infighting must be over the sixteen or so other writers who rate double-digit status in the anthology. I was sorry, for example, to find just eleven pages of Leacock. If only that sublime Canadian had been allowed to ride madly off in more directions—for example, across the too-large paddock set aside for dreary James Thurber.

For the record, the rest of this sub-pentarchical group consists of Laurence Sterne, Jane Austen, Lewis Carroll, Rudyard Kipling, H. G. Wells, Dornford Yates, Richmal Crompton, A. G. Macdonell (represented by an excruciatingly funny cricket story), J. B. Morton, Stella Gibbons, Graham Greene, and Alan Coren. The more famous of these names speak for themselves, although I must say that I was amazed by the lightness and virtuosity of Wells's little fantasy of a man who lost weight but no size, and ended up floating on the ceiling. One of the delights of *The Oxford Book*, however, is its retrieval of such lesser-known writers as Yates and Morton and Coren, whose gifts are prodigious and whose other work must be required reading, if it is anything as good as the samples chosen by Mr. Muir.

Individually they represent three kinds of humor that have flourished through the ages: mannerism, nonsense, and wit. Yates (1895–1960) was a misanthropic loner and archetypal British snob. He wrote thirty-four bestselling novels about the country life of the well-to-do, and retired after World War II, first to France and then to Umtali, Southern Rhodesia. Once, as a student, I spent the night in the latter town, and was told that its showplace castle had been built by a rich and rheumatic Englishman called Mercer. Mr. Muir now informs me that Cecil William Mercer was the real name of Dornford Yates. Had I known that then, I would have presented myself at the castle and kissed the knobbly hand that wrote *Berry and Co.* A chapter from this 1920 novel is reproduced here. It describes the languid puzzlement of some Bright Young Things when their Rolls-Royce—or maybe somebody else's—is "pinched" one summer Sunday. No matter that both cars are 1914 Silver Ghosts, "fresh from the coach-builder's" and identical to the point of improbability.

Yates effortlessly suspends our disbelief and makes us see and hear his characters, flitting like post-Edwardian butterflies over lanes that are always white and lawns that are always shaven, where wood pigeons waddle and lime groves echo to "the soft impertinence of a cuckoo." It is the England of P. G. Wodehouse, less comic but as full of grace.

John Cameron Audrieu Bingham Michael Morton, popularly known as "Beachcomber" to readers of the London *Daily Mail* from 1924 on, was the most brilliant example of what Mr. Muir calls the *dementia praecox* school. He strides red-faced and roaring into the pages of this anthology, banging on the bar counter of our consciousness with his jokes until the glasses jump and we find ourselves laughing out of sheer shock. He recites for us the latest inventions of his friend Dr. Strabismus ("Whom God Preserve") of Utrecht:

A collapsible salt-bag, a bottle with its neck in the middle, a rice-sifter, a stanchion to prop up other stanchions, a suet-container, a foghorn key, a leather grape, a new method of stencilling on ivory, basalt cubes for roofing swimming baths, a fox-trap, a dummy jellyfish, waterproof onions, false teeth for swordfish . . .

And so on and on, until Beachcomber abruptly takes his leave. He returns next day wearing a beret, and reminisces over Pernod about his youth in Paris, when eggs kept dropping off the Eiffel Tower, and poets lay in the Rue des Mauvaises Odeurs, strangled with their own suspenders. A day later he is back again, clamoring for "a half-gill of peptonized milk essence." Refreshed, he dictates knitting instructions for a pair of dog braces: "Cast on eight stitches working in B.3, H.7, Kt. to pawn's fifth and mate in three purl. Rip out six." After a while he loses interest, and announces melodramatically, "*Enter the Icebergs, a Jewish family from the Arctic.*"

Morton kept this kind of thing up six times a week, with only slight exceptions, for fifty-one years—a record of comic production without peer.

Alan Coren, who was editor of *Punch* from 1978 to 1987, frankly admits he is an imitator of S. J. Perelman, but the similarities do not go much beyond a fondness for punning titles and the use of news clips for exuberant flights of fancy. His style is looser and more talky than the exquisitely literate prose of El Sid, while his subject matter is tougher and more topical. "Go Easy, Mr. Beethoven, That Was Your Fifth" is a devastating riposte to an M.D. who claimed, in the *Journal of Alcoholism,* that Ludwig van Beethoven would have produced more had he drunk less. Coren dryly suggests that after nine symphonies, thirty-two piano sonatas, seven concertos, two masses, sixteen string quartets, and "two suitcasefuls" of quintets, "posterity owes Ludwig a little snort or two." Had it not been for the stimulation of *schnapps,* Beethoven might well have chucked it after writing "Chopsticks," and spent the rest of his life as a hosier. Then comes this *cri de coeur,* on behalf of all suffering artists:

It's a dodgy tightrope along which we creators wobble, Doc: enough booze to close the world off and keep us inventing, but not so much so that we allow the golden haze to settle on us permanently, while the piano-strings slacken, and the typewriter rusts, and the brushes dry out and go stiff, and the public yawns and goes off in search of fresh fodder, muttering about what an inconsiderate bleeder that Shakespeare was, snuffing it in his fifties and leaving us with little more than *Lear, Hamlet, Macbeth, Othello, Antony and Cleopatra,* well I'm not surprised, you know what they say, he couldn't leave the stuff alone, liver like a dried pea, well that's the trouble with artists, isn't it, hoity-toity, too good for the rest of us, they've got to be different, haven't they, bloody bohemians the lot of them, load of boozers, junkies, fairies, layabouts, I mean to say, only nine symphonies, only thirty plays, only ten novels, only ONE Sistine Chapel (they say he was so pissed he couldn't go up the ladder), I mean, what do you expect?

The contemporary funniness of writers like Coren raises the question of humor's degradability. Conscientious, even dogged, as Mr. Muir may be in pursuing laughter in seventeenth-century "jest books" and the early Gothic novels, the fact remains that most of the victims considered jape worthy then—vagabonds and blackamoors, for example—embarrass us now. We are less amused by Swift's anality, or Smollett's xenophobia, than we are touched by the biographical vignettes Mr. Muir scatters with a sure hand: Robert Burton seeking relief from his melancholy by leaning over a bridge and listening to the badinage of bargemen; Lady Wortley Montagu expiring at seventy-four with the happy sigh, "It has all been most interesting"; Sir John Dalrymple attempting, apparently with success, to turn herrings into soap; and little Fanny Burney dancing around a mulberry tree when she heard her anonymous *Evelina* was a bestseller.

There are, nevertheless, some gold coins among the time-blackened silver, and not all of them bear the sovereign profiles of Sterne, Fielding, and Jane Austen. A salacious anecdote by John Aubrey reminds us that Sir Walter Raleigh knew about the Joy of Sex long before Dr. Alex Comfort did. Dorothy Osborne's love letters to Sir William Temple, written in the 1650s, are as pellucid as your next martini. Samuel Johnson's dictionary definitions (*"MONSIEUR.* A term of reproach for a Frenchman") still evoke chuckles. The Irish poet Gerald Griffin's recipe for limestone soup is as delicious now as it was in 1840—although perhaps that's not the right adjective.

At last the huge figure of Dickens strides onstage, shouldering aside such bit players as Lamb and Surtees. The Inimitable is so entertaining that we listen to him happily until 1860, when he gives his famous description of Joe Gargery penning a letter. (I've always wondered if Art Carney had Joe in mind when he went through the same ritual in *The Honeymooners.*)

ONLY ON PAGE 196 does Mr. Muir take us across the Atlantic and jarringly deposit us in the Revolutionary America of H. Henry Brackenridge (1748–1816). It is one of many such time-zone changes, dictated by an editorial policy that, like Bertie Wooster's check suit, is perhaps rather sudden till you get used to it. Mr. Muir should have explained, in his introduction, why he will be bringing in Garrison Keillor before Evelyn Waugh, and indulging the sexless fantasies of P. G. Wodehouse long after Philip Roth has violated a piece of raw liver.

The reason is that he chooses to group writers geographically, rather than chronologically. The book as a whole does advance steadily through the centuries, but Mr. Muir seems afraid of too much *sequitur.* He therefore remains north of the Dogger Bank and east of Galway for his first two hundred pages, then swings four thousand miles westward and about seventy years back in time. After a spell in Rip Van Winkle's Catskills, we tour the antebellum United States from New England down the Appalachian Trail into what used to be called the Southwest—rejoicing as we do in the rich dialects that used to be such a feature of American humor. High in the mountains, we shiver through a hyperbolic winter dawn, along of ol' Davy Crockett:

> The airth had actually friz fast in her axis, and couldn't turn round; the sun had got jammed between two cakes o' ice under the wheels, an' thar he had bin shinin' and workin' to get loose, until he friz fast in his cold sweat.
>
> "C-r-e-a-t-i-o-n!" thought I, "this are the toughest sort o' suspension, and it musn't be endured—"
>
> . . . I took a fresh twenty pound bear off o' my back that I'd picked up on the road, and beat the animal agin the ice until the hot ile began to walk out on him at all sides. I then took an' held him over the airth's axis, an' squeezed him till I thaw'd 'em loose, poured about a ton on it over the sun's face, give the airth's cog-wheel one kick backward, till I got the sun loose—whistled "Push along, keep movin'!" an' in about fifteen seconds the airth gin a grunt, and begun movin'—the sun walked up beautiful, salutin' me with sich a wind o' gratitude that it made me sneeze.

Mr. Muir has another real find in Tennessee, a story called "Mrs. Yardley's Quilting," by George Washington Harris. Lusty, cruel, and erotic, its narrative thread drags us along as helplessly as the quilts "straiched tu every post an' tree" that Sut Lovingood has hitched abaft his horse, Wall-Eye, before smacking him with a paling. The subsequent pandemonium makes Sut as randy as a rooster, and he runs down the pretty Mrs. Yardley in a climax that is too comic to spoil by pretelling.

We sample the beginnings of national, rather than provincial, humor in the syndicated columns of Petroleum V. Nasby, Artemus Ward, and other "phunny phellow" dialecticians. They do not date well, with the exception of Joel Chandler Harris. Ambrose Bierce—terse, astringent, and savagely cynical—is more to modern taste. Nobody has ever more precisely defined the business of Washington, D.C. "POLITICS, *n.* A strife of interests masquerading as a contest of principles. The conduct of public affairs for private advantage." To my sorrow, Mr. Muir does not include that entry from *The Devil's Dictionary,* but he does print some marvelous others, e.g. "BORE, *n.* A person who talks when you wish him to listen." Another timeless wit is George Ade, with his mix of the literary and the vernacular. There is a foretaste of S. J. Perelman (who revered Ade) in lines such as: "As he trailed Skyward beneath the buoyant silken Bag he hung by his knees and waved a glad Adieu to the Mob of Inquisitive Yeomen.")

Mark Twain, nicely described by Mr. Muir as "the great hinge of American humor," swings open the door of his treasure house, but its contents are overfamiliar: the Jumping Frog, the Innocents Abroad, the Whitewashed Fence. Recrossing the Atlantic, we follow Alice into Wonderland, then become readers of *Punch* and the *Yellowplush Papers* of Thackeray. A pleasant discovery awaits us when we encounter Emily Eden, author of *The Semi-Detached House* (1859). Her lucid virtuosity looks back to Jane Austen and forward to the young Henry James of *Washington Square*—whom, by the way, Mr. Muir ignores.

Emily Eden unfortunately has no lightening effect on the heavy attempts of Trollope, George Eliot, and Hardy to be jovial. Three slices of their respective plum puddings are served up here, each wrongly labeled as a soufflé. The effect *en masse* is indigestible. Mr. Muir quotes George Meredith's historic call in 1877 for humor to return to its necessary role as the deflator of pomposity, but the sample of Meredithian mirth he attaches makes us wonder if the old boy knew which was which. Samuel Butler, at least, resists the sentimentality of the High Victorians. After a boating holiday on the Thames with Jerome K. Jerome, we spend the rest of the nineteenth century in Australia, listening to outback stories (not the same as our homegrown variety) that retain their crude power to amuse.

THE NEW AGE IS heralded—sort of—by a pair of resolutely unmodern Americans, Ellis P. Butler and Finley Peter Dunne, alias "Mr. Dooley," the mythical Chicago saloonkeeper. I am sorry to say that the latter's brogue is so thick that few people nowadays will understand him—a pity, because Dunne was a humorist of the highest quality.*

The first real note of our time is sounded by the great Stephen Leacock, whose lunatic geometry (revolving horses, moons circling the horizon, faces "upside down with fury") mirrors the disarrangement of the old intellectual order by Picasso and Einstein. A few paragraphs of his prose should be enough to plunge you "into a fit of profound subtraction"—unless, of course, you are "so self-confident as to be illegible."

The central and longest section of Mr. Muir's book—some 520 pages—surveys the "light" humor of Britain, the Commonwealth, and America, from World War I to the present. We meet such master miniaturists as Max Beerbohm, whose essay about an anonymous clergyman is one of the best things in the anthology; G. K. Chesterton, majestically ruminant on the pleasures of lying in bed; and Ring Lardner, author of *I Gaspari* (*The Upholsterers*)—a three-act play with only nine lines of dialogue. (It would be interesting to know if Samuel Beckett ever pondered one of its stage directions: *The Lincoln Highway. Two bearded glue lifters are seated at one side of the road.*)

Familiar faces loom up from one's reading of illustrated books for children: Mole's and Ratty's; "Just" William's and Billy Bunter's; and even a shockingly aged and bitter Winnie-the-Pooh ("Funny thing, I never could stand honey"). There are short stories by Saki, Katherine Mansfield, James Thurber, the underappreciated Damon Runyon, Dylan Thomas, and Frank O'Connor; parodies and "casuals" from Harold Ross's *New Yorker;* and sage advice from Robert Benchley, including "Almost everything you need to know about a subject is in the encyclopaedia."

Mr. Muir, being English, must have some toilet humor—an oxymoron if there ever was one. I regret to say that the worst piece in this genre is the work of an American writer, Chick Sale. Unless you are interested in the abstergent possibilities of corncobs, you will turn hastily on to A. P. Herbert's "The Negotiable Cow," which suggests a splendid method

* See pages 114–115.

for legal revenge on the Internal Revenue Service. More pointed satire follows from Mary Dunn, C. Northcote Parkinson, and Michael Frayn— the latter in a virtuoso parody of Christmas-card clichés.

The penultimate section of this enormous book is devoted to "serious" humor by such major novelists as Evelyn Waugh, Kingsley Amis, Joseph Heller, and Tom Wolfe. Mr. Muir, presumably in a spirit of fairness, also includes pieces by Auberon Waugh and Martin Amis. But he succeeds only in showing that genius does not run in families. Compare the gynecological descriptions, by Amis *père* and *fils*, on pages 1049 and 1080. The former is brief, poetic, and deeply funny: the latter is overwritten, clinical, and cruel.

I cannot end without praising the editor's acute ear for feminine humor. If a dozen or so of his male contributors are Less Funny Than You Might Think, there is hardly a woman on his list who fails to amuse or enchant. Along with those mentioned earlier, I especially recommend Mary Russell Mitford, a watercolorist in words; Elisabeth von Arnim, the first (and so far the last) funny feminist; "Somerville and Ross"—Irish lady cousins and altogether sublime; breathless, brutal Anita Loos; Jan Struther, a writer of Keatsian perception; and Erma Bombeck, who if she has written too much has sometimes written hilariously—witness her distracted piece about an obscene telephone call.

Mr. Muir's choice of P. G. Wodehouse to end his anthology is both sentimental and appropriate, since the august Plum (whose last book was published in 1977, exactly five centuries after Caxton's opening selection) is, of all humorists, the most timeless and universal. As Evelyn Waugh, who always called him "the Master," remarked, "He has made a world for us to live in and delight in." One might say the same of Waugh himself, or of any others in the comic pentarchy. There is something eternal about them, something giant—even little Sid, with his polished, pointed *feuilletons*. Hunters of the Wild Guffaw, they fill the skies with laughter and pour their hot ile over our frozen hills, until the sun itself is warmed by a wind o' gratitude.

WHICH WAY DOES SIR DRESS?

A Semicentennial Visit to Savile Row

If HELL, AS SARTRE SO FEELINGLY REMARKED, IS OTHER PEOPLE, HE must have been thinking in particular of those jovial vulgarians who insist on singing "Happy Birthday" in public places. The last time it happened to me was when I turned twenty-one in a bar on the wrong side of the equator. I cringed through the final *ritardando,* and swore to myself that I would never again suffer such torments. Until I was forty-nine I managed, by a variety of subterfuges, to evade the dread chorus, and this year, on the eve of turning fifty, I decided to play it safe by decamping at the last minute to London. "Suit yourself," said my wife, with a calmness that confirmed she had not been planning a surprise party. "That's

Originally published in *Forbes FYI,* November 1990.
Drawing by Tom Gibson, 2012.

just what I intend to do," I replied, rather miffed. "At Huntsman, on Savile Row."

I timed these last words to coincide with her activation of the coffee grinder, or she would have confiscated my passport. Huntsman is probably the most expensive tailor in the world. Years ago in New York, on the strength of my *faux* English accent, I was invited to appear on *What's My Line?* in an attempt to impersonate Lord Brooke, the owner of Warwick Castle. Assuming that he would be a rumpled old codger in glen checks, I sought an upset victory by appearing in a fairly decent double-breaster from the British-American House on Madison Avenue. Alas, Lord Brooke turned out to be tall, spare, and stately, and he wore a dark blue pinstripe whose cut combined the elegance of Raeburn and the pure line of Blake.

The judges very properly laughed me to scorn, and when his Lordship tried to console me afterward (*noblesse oblige*), I wailed, "Where did you get that gorgeous suit?"

His eyebrow lifted a little, and he said, "Huntsman." He didn't add, "Of course," but I sensed it was a name gentlemen are supposed to know.

As he strode off—to lunch at Lutèce, no doubt—little ripples of breeding flickered along the rise and fall of his trousers, like blue flames in the dark. Then and there I added another vow to my subequatorial one: "Come fifty, I'm gonna wear clothes like that."

ON THE PLANE to London (cramped economy class in prickly seersucker) I mused on my future splendor, with the pleasure of a man who has been shabby too long. I savored the delicious prospect of being alone in my favorite city, as I celebrated half a century of—well, survival. It occurred to me that one's birthdays (even if unsung) are usually compromised by well-meaning friends, awkward gifts, formulaic calls and cards—when what one would prefer is to be able, for a change, to indulge oneself alone; to do the things one has always coveted, under a cloak of traveler's anonymity; to feel, in short, the ecstasy of a Lambert Strether arriving in Europe and "having, above all, for the moment, nobody and nothing to consider."

I tried to calculate how many words, at current freelance rates, I was going to have to write to pay for my Huntsman suit. In my best estimation, it would cost the scriptorial equivalent of three chapters of *War and Peace*—and what about accessories? I could hardly complement Savile Row tailoring with shirts by Lester Polyester, and ties endorsed by the ILGWU. Unbidden, the words "Turnbull & Asser" leaped into my brain, like breasts interrupting the reverie of a monsignor. I added another two chapters of *War and Peace*, and noticing that my handwriting was beginning to tremble, called for a split of chardonnay.

Under its influence I decided that life was short, especially for a man who—chilling thought!—had only twenty years left of his allotted span. Yes, dammit, I would visit those shirtmakers, and Liberty's silk neckwear department, and get a haircut and shoeshine at Trumper's. I would show up at the Savoy for a lunch *à deux* with my major credit card, and take a postprandial tour of the art galleries of Mayfair. . . .

("Another chardonnay, sir?")

"Yes, please.")

. . . I would pick up a set of gold links at Asprey, then go to Fortnum & Mason for tea, with jam scones and clotted cream, followed by a late-afternoon browse in that alley of bookstores off Charing Cross Road where I once saw (sigh) a red leather set of Stevenson. Afterward I would splurge on front row center at the Haymarket Theatre, and treat myself to a late dinner at Boulestin. . . .

By now my word quota had run rampant through the Battle of Borodino, and I had not even included my oldest and most private fantasy, one I had never confessed to anyone. God only knew how much *that* was going to cost!

IN THE MILD LIGHT of a London morning most of my aerial follies dissolved, leaving only the most substantial: the suit, the shirts, and, uh, that fantasy. Yet I still intended to have as perfect a birthday as possible. I made a two o'clock appointment at Huntsman, and spent the next couple of hours writing in the lounge of my hotel, the discreetly nameless Number Sixteen, Sumner Place. To sit thus at a sunny desk, with a clean white blotter and a clock ticking somewhere, and tea and biscuits on the way, has always seemed to me to be an approximation of paradise. At eleven-thirty I changed into my only good suit, a well-worn but still shapely medium worsted from Bloomies, and took a taxi to a discreet establishment on New Oxford Street known simply as Smith's.

Here in this masculine environment stocked with instruments of curious gratification, I found in less than five minutes the rod, the staff, the comforter I have lusted for since boyhood. It was an ebony, silver-handled crosstop cane, blackly slender, lustrously plain, and expensive beyond all powers of human imagination. "Have you—uh," I croaked, "something cheaper in bamboo?" But the salesman had already put it in my hand. No sooner had my fingers closed on it, and felt its perfect balance of lightness and strength, than I knew it would be an extension of my body for life.

"We'll wrap it up for you, shall we, sir."

"Don't bother. I'm going to use it right away."

"Certainly, sir, but if we may—" I turned at the door, poised gracefully on my new acquisition. "The correct phrase is, 'wear it,' sir."

I strolled through Soho, humming (as Bertie Wooster might) a careless tune, yet secretly terrified some mugger would make off with *le whangee de monsieur.* Remarkably, though—and I've noticed this more and more since returning to New York—a black and silver cane is a splendid anticrime device. Hoods seem to think it conceals lethal gadgetry; they quail before it like cobras to the flute.

Turnbull & Asser disconcerted me at first, since its front window on Jermyn Street was garish with striped shirts, in colors designed to soothe the eyes of the *nouveau riche.* But I discovered that the "bespoke department" had a separate entrance down a side alley, and found there the sober atmosphere one needs when spending intoxicating sums of money. A young man wearing a vanilla oxford that looked good enough to eat proposed that, as a first-time customer, I order only six shirts, one of which would be made up as a sample for me to try on before the others followed. "In ninety-nine cases out of a hundred the fit is perfect, sir." (As it happened, I was destined to be one of the 1 percent.) Half an hour later I was back in the street, a poorer but happier man, looking forward to a sumptuous shipment of pale blue poplins and white sea island cottons, with a navy stripe broadcloth thrown in for the hell of it.

At ten to two (rumbling austerely for lack of lunch), I headed via the

Burlington Arcade for Savile Row. The glow of my morning's purchases had faded. I saw myself in passing shopwindows as a balding, bearded person, rather the worse for travel creases. Cruel friends had warned me that Huntsman does not welcome customers who are likely to hurt its reputation. "If they do let you in," I remembered one joker saying, "don't question their judgment on anything, or you'll find yourself referred to Hong Kong."

Most of all I dreaded the Trouser Question that all Savile Row customers are required to face: "Which way does Sir dress?" Instinct suggested there was only one Right way to answer—but that Right might well be Left. I could hardly stop a passerby to ask advice on such intimate matters. Gazing heavenward for help, I saw a cloud shaped like S. J. Perelman, and softly shouted, "Help me, O great Sid!"

From an infinite distance came his mocking response, *"Quién sabe?"*

SAVILE ROW WAS almost deserted when I reached its foot at No. 1, Gieves & Hawkes ("By Appointment: Livery and Military Tailors to H. M. Queen Elizabeth II"). Doormen up the street eyed me with such longing I got the feeling that business was slow all along the Row. For some reason sidewalks were spread with sand—perhaps to attract Arabs? I crunched along to No. 11, where a quiet sign read "H. Huntsman & Sons Limited," and found myself gazing through window-mounted crests into the dullest retail establishment I have ever seen. Just one icon proclaimed its excellence: a headless statue of Lord Brooke (the lean curve of his shoulder and rib cage was unmistakable), upholstered in a tweed that glowed with the soft luster of light on Lammermoor.

I stared at it enchanted, until the truth dawned that what I had recognized was actually the famous "Huntsman line." Which is to say, Lord Brooke looked like it, not it like him. Maybe—*quién sabe?*—his rib cage was as puny as mine! Encouraged, I marched up the steps. The door opened noiselessly before me.

A tall young gentleman, with the dark floppy forelock that identifies Britain's best, welcomed me with grave courtesy. He scrutinized me from head to foot in a manner that was so businesslike that I endured it without embarrassment. I even hoped that his gaze would linger on what

Monty Python used to call the "naughty bits," and thus spare me the agony of having to decide which way Sir dressed. But it swept south without pause. He asked me what kind of suit I had in mind.

I described, as best I could, that never-to-be-forgotten number of Lord Brooke's. By no twitch of his forelock would he acknowledge the identity of another Huntsman customer, yet I sensed I had dropped the right name. For the next half an hour we discussed fabrics, and I found that the category "dark blue stripe" is as rich with subtleties of shading as a nightscape by Albert Pinkham Ryder. There are chalk-stripes and pinstripes and twist-stripes and stripes combined with other stripes. There are cloths that lie as light on the limbs as swansdown, and others so thick and strong one could wear them in Highland gorse. Swatch after swatch caressed my fingers, like multilayered mothwings. Eventually, with the young man's assistance, I selected a muted pinstripe in which pale stipples illumined a dark blue ground: midnight in the Forest of Arden.

After another long discussion, we arrived at a plan for the suit Huntsman would build from this cloth: a simple double-breasted "hide-two-show-three," classically styled, with details of flaps and turnups to remain variable through the first fitting. "You'll need at least two more fittings after that, sir, and of course we're closed all of August." I sighed, and not just at the prospect of three more airfares. It was frustrating to think that my fiftieth birthday present to myself would not materialize until I was five months shy of fifty-one, but gentlemen are supposed to be patient about such things. I consoled myself with the thought that my next dozen or so Huntsman suits (assuming I won the New York Lottery, and stayed the same shape) would follow more quickly.

The young man asked me to sign the firm's Customer Book ("Please to write yr. several Names, yr. Town & Country Address &c."), then escorted me into a large, undecorated fitting room. "The cutters will be with you in a moment, sir."

"Cutters, plural?"

"Yes sir, the trouser cutter and the coat cutter."

I wondered if I had ordered a waistcoat whether there would be a special man for that. In came a brisk, sleek person whose manner was almost, but not quite, curt. "Please take off that jacket, sir." At Gieves &

Hawkes, I suspect, I would be coaxed out of my sleeves with blandish-ments, and at Douglas Haywards with theatrical flair. Huntsman's tone is a pure, no-nonsense professionalism—which, come to think of it, is the highest form of manners.

"Twenty-one and three quarters," he intoned, measuring my thigh. "Twenty-one and three quarters," echoed the young man, writing it down. "Fifteen and a half." "Fifteen and a half . . ." Their dialogue con-tinued with the lulling incomprehensibility of monks chanting in Latin, and I stood with closed eyes as the trouser cutter taped and retaped, re-membering an ode to tailoring I read long ago in *Punch*:

> *It is, sartorial artistry,*
> *The paltriest of thanks,*
> *That this, this the fairest of thy works,*
> *Should deck my shabby shanks.*

My reverie was broken by the trouser cutter fingering my waistband and asking, "Do you go up or down much, sir?" I pictured myself at my desk, with the bookcase a little out of reach, and answered, "Yes indeed."

He stared at me. "Well, I wouldn't have thought it, sir. How much?"

"Maybe thirty or forty times a day."

There was a short silence, and the young man said gently, "He means your weight, sir."

In due course the trouser cutter was replaced by his thoracic col-league, and another plainsong of proportionment rose into the air. It was curiously pleasant to be thus reduced to a set of abstractions. I felt incorporeal, insubstantial, a weightless cocoon that would soon enough (well, in seven months' time) metamorphose into the new, brilliant Me. Not until the sands of Savile Row crunched again under my shoes did I realize I was back in the real world, and that the Question had not been asked.

Humiliation filled me. *Why* had the cutter not asked it? He had not scrupled to raise the subject of embonpoint. Did his silence on the sub-ject of "dressing" imply that Sir's "naughty bits" were not worthy of consideration? I turned back toward No. 11, determined to cancel my order unless he apologized and adjusted his records. Insolent blighter! But an apparition coming down the street stopped me in my tracks.

It was an old, short, exquisitely tailored gent, wearing what was without question a Huntsman suit. Dark muted stripes, not unlike the ones I had chosen, gave him a dignity out of all proportion to his height. His bowler glowed in the sun, his moustache bristled like the hedgerows of the Somme. He drew near, and I did what I had to do. I bent low and stared at his naughty bits.

My heart throbbed with joy. "Sir" dressed proudly, precisely in the middle.

THE ROLLING TAPE RECORDS,
AND HAVING RECORDED, ROLLS ON

In Support of Janet Malcolm in Masson v. New Yorker

DAVID MCCULLOUGH AND I ARE AMICIS CURIAE—YOU MIGHT TRANS-
late that as "odd couple"—to a brief that will be argued before the Supreme Court tomorrow. Why odd? Because the brief supports the
occasional right of journalists to alter quotations. Specifically, it defends
a reporter who quoted her subject as saying things such as "I was like an
intellectual gigolo," when forty hours of raw tape prove that he didn't—
in so many words. Scholarly biographers are not supposed to be parties
to such tinkering with the truth.

God knows, I lock my study door and drop all the blinds before cutting an irrelevant, "Regular or decaf?" from an otherwise quotable interview. Biographers and historians are generally more conscientious

Originally published in *The Washington Post,* 13 January 1991. Includes material from the author's
participation in a friend-of-the-court brief filed on 7 December 1990.

Photograph of the Supreme Court by Fritz Jantzen.

about accurate quotation than journalists are. We have to document our sources, whereas reporters will go to jail rather than reveal theirs.

However, the case at issue, *Jeffrey M. Masson v. New Yorker Magazine, Inc., Alfred A. Knopf, Inc., and Janet Malcolm*, threatens a First Amendment–related freedom that David and I, and surely all honest nonfiction writers, believe to be sacred: freedom of interpretation.

In tomorrow's case, both district court and appeals court judges have found Janet Malcolm innocent of deliberate intent to defame and embarrass Dr. Masson by misquoting him in a 1983 *New Yorker* piece. This article, reprinted in her book *In the Freud Archives* (Knopf, 1984), dealt with Dr. Masson's dismissal as Project Director of the Sigmund Freud Archives because he allegedly "went public" with some research information that damaged the reputation of Freud. Although Dr. Masson had eagerly submitted himself to more than forty hours of tape-recorded interviews with Ms. Malcolm, plus many other hours of conversation, he did not like the portrait of himself that emerged in print, and has been suing for satisfaction ever since.

DESCARTES ONCE REMARKED that the biographer is "an artist on oath." Note that this definition gives equal weight to artistry and fidelity. The biographer is bound to represent his subject's words (not to mention warts) as truthfully as he can. Yet as Theodore Roosevelt, himself a biographer, warned members of the American Historical Association, truth must be made vivid if it is to be received as truth.*

Vividness, whether achieved by an artist or a journalist with less imaginative power, is the product of two compositional processes: the placement of essentials, and the downplaying or elimination of trivia. Compare a photograph of Mont Sainte-Victoire with a sketch of the same subject by Cézanne, and see which image best represents its slabby *reality.* Artistry on oath ensures a purer—one might say, a more truthful truth, than can be discerned in any mass of unprocessed fact.

That last phrase fairly describes the raw material of any taped interview. A transcribed tape is "dull" in the sense that no artist has yet gone

* See page 121.

to work on it and highlighted its brighter features. It is "painstaking" in the sense that it reproduces every audible word that was said. But comprehensiveness does not necessarily aid comprehension. Anybody who has glanced at such a transcript—one of Richard Nixon's Watergate conversations, for example—knows that plain speech turned into plain type is often unintelligible. This is because you, the reader, lack the visual and aural perceptions that interlocutors enjoy. *You weren't there.* If you had been, you'd have understood. Even the most articulate talkers misspeak occasionally, but don't correct themselves because they know what they mean, and so do their listeners. Times without number, a gesture will substitute for a phrase, or a smile deliberately reverse the meaning of a word. At such times (and even more so when the subject is lying), verbatim documentation is false documentation, and stenography must give way to biography—which is to say, artistry on oath.

How, though, are the conflicting demands of imagination and scholarship to be resolved? The modern biographer, unlike the modern novelist or painter, has no freedom to invent thoughts, or add or subtract from his subject's true dimensions. Not for him the free fictionalizing that some of his popular predecessors (Emil Ludwig and Carl Sandburg come to mind) got away with. Ours is a pedantic age, and anything more than the slightest deviation from recorded substance is liable to catcalls from critics and lawsuits from outraged sources.

On the whole this is an admirable scruple. I would like to warn, however, that magnetic tape is a substance infinitely more alterable than paper.* Any amateur with a splice kit can alter John F. Kennedy's most famous words to *Ask not what you can do for your country, ask what your country can do for you.* As an example of what can be done in a recording studio, consider the late Glenn Gould's sound drama *The Idea of North,* produced for the Canadian Broadcasting Company in 1967. It consists entirely of fictitious tape recordings. That is to say, Gould mixes, splices, overdubs, and remixes raw tapes to such an extent that their original integrity is lost. You hear "conversations" between people who have never actually met, "monologues" that go into, rather than come out of, real human mouths, and "natural" sound effects unknown to nature.

---

* To say nothing of digital technology today.

What Gould achieves might be called art, but it is a supreme example of how technology can lie. A more recent phenomenon is computer-enhancement of photography, whereby Sylvester Stallone, as *The New York Sunday Times* has demonstrated, can be "proved" to have been a negotiant at Yalta. First Amendment lawyers who opine that fidelity to the original is necessary for historical truth should make sure that the original itself is true.

Many biographers, including this one, eschew the tape recorder altogether, preferring merely to take notes of interviews. We do so for two main reasons. In the first place, 90 percent of the average transcript is not worth preserving. (The 10 percent that is will shout out at the interviewer, even if it's mumbled as a defensive aside.) Second, and more important, the tape recorder has an inhibiting effect on people who will talk quite honestly to a pad and moving pen. Something about the proximity of a microphone makes politicians extra-pompous, and gossips less indiscreet. Some nonfiction writers have found that they get more out of their sources by taking no notes whatsoever. When Truman Capote researched *In Cold Blood* in Kansas, he conducted all his interviews as "visits," but took along an assistant to make sure she heard what he heard. Afterward they would separately scribble their recollections, before joining them together, to complementary effect.

I MAKE NO COMMENT on the evidence in tomorrow's libel case, except to say that I don't blame Janet Malcolm for writing a negative piece about Jeffrey Masson, and I don't blame him for suing. Dr. Masson never called himself "an intellectual gigolo," at least on tape, but he admits to saying many other things that (the appeals court feels) identify him with intellectual gigoloism—whatever that may be. Ms. Malcolm is therefore justified in making a similar inference.

To what extent may a writer honestly distort in order to make the truth clear?

Honest distortion is not a paradox. Art, the most penetrating kind of communication, penetrates because it is an exquisite kind of distortion, an attempt to clarify things dimly perceived by refracting them. ("Tell all the truth," Emily Dickinson counseled her own poetic kind, "but tell it slant.")

Is Janet Malcolm an artist? I don't think she'd say so. A gifted reporter, definitely. Neither do David McCullough and I claim to be artists in the fullest creative sense. We accept Descartes's definition and swear to his oath. Our private covenant, unenforceable by law—but easily cramped by law—is to interpret the truth as we hear it, and to be answerable in our interpretation to the only judges the Constitution authorizes to punish us: our readers.

If the Supreme Court overturns the lower court decisions in *Masson v. Malcolm* and finds for the petitioner, interviewers of every kind in future are going to have to lug around tape recorders in order to defensively document every syllable that readers have hitherto taken on trust. In my view, this will inhibit free speech—not only the black-and-white "speech" of published prose (will we be too scared of libel suits to quote something a guy told us while jogging?), but also the free self-expression of interviewees.

JAMES BOSWELL, still revered as the greatest of biographers, used hardly any notes when reproducing Samuel Johnson's conversation, preferring to rely on his memory while it was still hot and bright, a die freshly struck. If he had indulged in frantic stenography at the time of utterance, he would have been unable to match wits with the great doctor, and stimulate him to further heights of *viva voce*. Generations of readers have responded to Boswell's artistry in bringing Johnson back to life. Whether he was a faithful reporter in doing so, no modern pedant can say. But neither can pedants deny the convincing majesty of Johnson portrayed, and the wisdom of Johnson quoted, by a man who was neither majestic nor wise. The only convincing explanation is that Bozzie was telling the truth.

What, ultimately, is biographical Truth—the shock of recognition we crave in reading about our fellow human beings? With whom does the "artist on oath" make his covenant? If with his subject, he is a colluder and probably a liar. If with the marketplace, let buyers of his book beware. If with himself alone, then he only has to move us to convince us, because there is nothing so direct as honesty. The ultimate test of any piece of nonfiction writing must be its success in saying something—or quoting something—that a majority of readers can't help but believe.

That, as the greatest of our jurists has cautioned, is about the nearest we'll ever get to the essence of things.*

* Oliver Wendell Holmes, Jr., to John C. Gray in 1905: "All I mean by truth is what I can't help believing."

On 20 June 1991 the Supreme Court ruled in favor of Malcolm by a vote of 7 to 2. It held that slight or unwitting alterations of quotations by a writer were not actionable, unless there had been a deliberate intent to make "a material change in the meaning conveyed by the statement."

FROM THIS SESSION INTERDICT

On the Eve of Another Presidential Inauguration

WASHINGTON—I WRITE THESE WORDS ON A WINTER'S EVENING, looking west through a bay window at the floodlit dome of the U.S. Capitol, about four hundred yards away. Its shimmering symmetry (rendered ethereal by the window's old glass, which makes it waver as though reflected in water) is to me the most American of shapes. That pale bell first imprinted itself on my mind when, as a boy in Nairobi, I browsed illustrated books in the library of the United States Information Service, and dreamed of being able to walk in its environs, along with my bosom buddy Thomas Sawyer, of Hannibal, Mo.

It imprints itself still whenever I come into my study, never more beautifully than at times like this, when the vast spiraling nation of which it is the center begins to slow down and solidify around it, like

Originally published in *The New York Times*, 17 January 1993.
Drawing by Enid Romanek, 1987.

some quadrennial nebula gathering energy for fresh circuits and colli-sions.

The floodlights are so white tonight—I think they're testing for to-morrow's television exposure—that I'm conscious of the dome even as I hunch over my desk. Just now, for example, I was pondering the particles of the word *inaugurate* and remembered that Shakespeare uses *augur* in his poem "The Phoenix and the Turtle." I got out the text, but was dis-tracted in my search by that lingering, translucent image, casting a wholly relevant reflection on the Bard's invocatory verses. Of the up-coming ceremony one may indeed pray:

From this session interdict
Every fowl of tyrant wing
Save the eagle, feather'd king:
Keep the obsequy so strict.

MY TOWNHOUSE WAS built in 1905—just in time, perhaps, to observe the inauguration of Theodore Roosevelt, who was sworn in on 4 March. (In those days transitions were even more ridiculously protracted than they are now.) As a writer living in what amounts to an ivory tower—or at least an off-white one—I like to imagine myself seated here then, catching a few of TR's screechy remarks. It was a windy day, and he had to keep a tight hold of his typescript. Who knows, the phrase *Power in-variably means both responsibility and danger* may have blown across the park, and penetrated these curving panes.

For reasons possibly to do with their contour, they refract sound as well as light, with equal capriciousness. At times a presidential motor-cade will speed by almost silently, at others I can hear Chief Justice Rehnquist sneeze as he ambles pigeon-toed along the sidewalk to his chambers. If I move close to the frame, and allow a freak ripple of glass to make him stoop a little, he could be Oliver Wendell Holmes, Jr., en route to dissent in *Abrams v. United States*. But no, in those days the Su-preme Court did not yet back on Second Street. . . .

The imagination of a biographer is constantly hampered by fact, or plain lack of knowledge. Most of the inaugurations this house has witnessed will not replay in my mind. I click the finder, and get only snow. In the case of William Howard Taft's ceremony, however, the atmospherics are genuine. A blizzard blanketed Washington that morning, and consequently little was seen of "Big Bill," even though he was by far our most visible Chief Executive. (His current namesake, after four years of state dinners *au sauce béchamel*, may soon challenge that record.)

What other audiovisual outtakes drift this way, through the ether of time? Massed bands thumping Coolidge along Constitution Avenue in 1925—well, I'm sure they *did* thump, since sleepy Cal stayed awake during the ride. Herbert Hoover's furious face as he reluctantly accompanied Franklin Roosevelt up the Hill. And FDR about half an hour later, cranking himself to the microphone and plagiarizing Thoreau's plagiarism of the Duke of Wellington's plagiarism of Francis Bacon's plagiarism of Montaigne's original line, written in 1580: "The thing of which I have most fear is fear itself." (I am indebted to Ralph Keyes's new book *Nice Guys Finish Seventh* for this scholarly information.)

Whoever lived here on 22 January 1961 and saw John F. Kennedy deliver his inaugural must have watched it through a rime of ice. Wish I could have watched too, because I so clearly remember being half a world away, and hearing, courtesy of the South African Broadcasting Corporation, that nasal voice promising to pay any price and bear any burden in order to ensure the survival and success of liberty. One could hardly foresee that those alliterations would ultimately send thirty-five thousand soldiers to death in Vietnam. Kennedy's words should be stenciled around the Oval Office in gilt, as a warning to future presidents of the dangers of neat phraseology.

Richard Nixon's "lift of a driving dream," to cite an even worse piece of prose, does not resound in this room so much as the whistle of the train he wished, in boyhood, might carry him off to fortune—a moving metaphor, although hardly original. I missed Jerry Ford's inauguration, but then so did Jerry Ford. January 1977 brought one of the supreme pieces of inaugural choreography—who, seeing it, can ever forget?—Jimmy and Rosalynn Carter's *pas de deux* out among the applauding crowd, in open air and sunshine. After the armor-plated claustrophobia of recent years (poor Nixon's eyes and nose and Cyclopean brows imploding in a black hole of despair), that was an ecstatic moment. And as moments go, it went.

For sheer theater, nothing eclipsed Ronald Reagan's decision four years later to stage his inauguration on the far side of the Capitol. Like Davy Crockett crossing the Appalachians, and Abraham Lincoln returning home, and Grover Cleveland throwing open the Great Columbian Exposition of 1893, Mr. Reagan aligned himself toward the West. No matter that the fugitive frontier that "explains American development" had long since dissolved into the Pacific. He wanted to project his cheerful pieties in the same symbolic direction—and, not incidentally, give Yuri Andropov a view of his back.

Alas for this house, the Reagan Realignment means that all future presidents, unless they are partial to parking lots, will take their oaths facing the same way, over one of the world's great urban spaces. Whoever sits here after me, and wishes to experience something of the elation attending the election of President Ali-Akbar Hwange, or President Nguyen Nu, or even President Kathy MacLane (my intern of a few summers back, and a cinch for the White House), is going to have to join the crowd further down the Hill.

IF YOU DON'T MIND, I think I'll stay put tomorrow. But when noon approaches I'll stand in the bay window and hope to sense, if not see, something of that most solemn of moments, the silent, instantaneous transfer of constitutional power. This huge chimera floating over the trees (right now, a mist like white samite is curling around it) tempts all Americans to pose beneath, hold up their hands, and hope that a member of the judiciary will happen by. For at least one day in the four years looming, let our mutual hostilities of rich and poor, male against female, majority over minority, and regular v. decaf reconcile themselves under the unity of this dome. Let us exult, as Shakespeare did at the apotheosis of Phoenix and Turtle:

How true a twain
Seemeth this concordant One!
Love hath reason, reason none,
If what parts can so remain.

IN MEMORIAM CHRISTINE REAGAN

The President's Forgotten Daughter

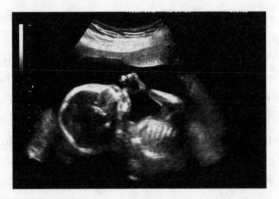

THE SANCTITY OF THE WOMB, THAT ONCE-INVIOLATE LIMBO WHOSE dark waters were home only to the spirit of God, has become so subject to alien invasion in recent years that I was not surprised, at a dinner party last fall, when my hostess asked if I would like to see a "snapshot" of her future daughter. Without waiting for me to swallow my mouthful of *vichyssoise*, she fished from her purse an image I was too polite to recoil from. Indeed I am glad I did not, for the snap turned out to be a sonogram, and had an eerie, crosshatched beauty, reminiscent of the Capriccios of Goya.

There, floating in shadows and space-time, was a pale, preparturient child, eyes still veiled with sleep, tiny fists half-curled, and mouth urgently agape. "She's yawning," cooed Mama. It seemed to me that she was shouting—silently, to be sure, yet this sonogram, this picture of sounds beyond hearing, reverberated with the first of all human cries: "*I want to be born!*"

Originally published in *The American Spectator,* August 1993.
Sonogram.

It pleases me to note that Miss Caroline Burt has been granted her wish, and neighbors will attest that she is now quite audible. Of course the time will eventually come for her to utter the second great mortal shout, *"I'm afraid to die!"* Man's tragedy has always been that nothing can be done to help him in the end. His curse, now, is that everything may be done to hinder his very beginnings.

TEN YEARS AGO this spring, President Ronald Reagan published an extraordinary essay, "Abortion and the Conscience of the Nation," in *Human Life Review.* That essay, itself commemorating the tenth anniversary of *Roe v. Wade,* was subsequently republished in book form by Thomas Nelson, Inc., along with afterwords by C. Everett Koop and Malcolm Muggeridge. Taken together, the three pieces read today as eloquent but dated testimonials to a time when—for a shining moment even briefer than Camelot—it seemed that the Constitution might be amended (or reinterpreted) in defense of our least articulate, most vulnerable minority. But their datedness can only increase, because—let us admit it—the battle against legalized abortion is lost.

A majority of Americans, including those in Congress and the Supreme Court, now believe that women should be allowed to decide which of their progeny may survive, and which not. Those of us in whom abortion strikes a deep note of moral despair must accept that we are citizens of a secular democracy, governed by laws not of God, but man. Nor should we flatter ourselves that we have any monopoly on grief. The most striking thing about pro-choice literature—as distinct from pro-choice polemics—is its admission that the black bird of bereavement flaps low over all thinking aborters and abortees:

> *And thou treble-dated crow*
> *That thy sable gender mak'st*
> *With the breath thou giv'st and tak'st*
> *'Mongst our mourners shalt thou go.* *

* Shakespeare, "The Phoenix and the Turtle." For poignant examples of pro-choice literature, see "The Clinic," by Michael Blumenthal (*New York Times Magazine,* November 2, 1986), and "We Do Abortions Here," by Sallie Tisdale (*Harper's,* October 1987).

I have often wondered if it was the beat of those same wings that drove Ronald Reagan to publish "Abortion and the Conscience of the Nation" at a time when he needed controversy the least. Gentlest of men, he has never, as far as I know, been party to an abortion. But it is a largely forgotten fact that he once lost a neonate daughter of his own. Her name was Christine. She was born prematurely to Mr. Reagan's first wife, Jane Wyman, on 23 June 1947, and died nine hours later. Ironically, he could not be present at either birth or burial, since he was himself fighting death, in another hospital, with viral pneumonia. Such lessons in mortality change a man.

WHATEVER THE CAUSE, one has to admire, in these days of presidential pusillanimity, the courage with which Mr. Reagan confronted a fundamental human problem. "Nowhere do the plain words of the Constitution even hint at a 'right' so sweeping as to permit abortion up to the time the child is ready to be born," he wrote. "Yet this is what the Court ruled [in 1973]."

He did not hesitate to compare *Roe v. Wade* to another 7–2 decision, *Dred Scott v. Sandford* (1857), in denial of human rights, and took comfort in the fact that it, too, won majority acceptance in its day. Just as the Supreme Court thereby institutionalized racism for another century, so, Mr. Reagan argued, would a new eugenics begin to flow from *Roe*'s notion that one life (unwanted, first trimester) was worth less than another (ditto, second trimester), and less still than another (ditto, third trimester)—although, in certain mother-threatening circumstances, lives one and three might be considered equally expendable. Already in Indiana, the President noted, a baby unquestionably born had been allowed to starve to death because of its inconvenient combination of a malformed esophagus and Down's syndrome:

> The real issue for the courts was not whether baby Doe was a human being. The real issue was whether to protect the life of a human being . . . who would probably be mentally handicapped . . . . In other words, [its] retardation was the equivalent of a crime deserving the death penalty.

We may congratulate ourselves, or perhaps more aptly, thank God, that the sacrifice sanctioned by the Indiana Supreme Court has not become the "humane holocaust" Ronald Reagan feared a decade ago. This is still the most compassionate of nations. The very heat, even violence, of our debate on abortion proves that here, not in old, cold countries like Sweden, is where the world's great moral problems are still decided.

THANKS LARGELY TO Ronald Reagan, those of totalitarianism and mutual assured destruction have yielded to a civilized consensus. There remains the most anguished question—anguished because we must ask it a million and a half times a year: whether that many unborn children are to be or not to be. It is a question, moreover, involving in each case three parties, one of whom has no power of legal protest, and the other of whom has no voice at all.

No expectant father who sympathizes with the dilemma of the expectant mother—to live for herself only, or also for the life within her—can deny her right, ultimately, to bring the issue to a violent conclusion. But the grotesque pun, the awful paradox, is that it's his "issue" too.

One's dread is that, after all the debate, our democracy may find itself unequal to the task of deciding—that perhaps the question is unresolvable, and the agony it causes infinite. One's hunch is that God in His mercy will decide it for us, having heard from the Silent Parties on a frequency beyond our range.

Inevitably, this or a forthcoming administration is going to start testing the RU-486 antiprogesterone medicine. If it proves as effective and popular a method of pregnancy control here as in Europe, the French pill will replace the French letter as America's refiner of the species. That last phrase is Hazlitt's, by the way. It came out of my pen unbidden, and only now, reflecting, do I connect it with his essay on Tragedy.

Is it not cruel of God, thus to waste His unborn? Well, He sure wastes plenty in plagues—including the current one of AIDS, which at 100 percent fatality beats even Russia's abortion rate. Since He created the heaven and the earth to begin with, I guess He knows what He's about. I just hope that sometime soon He'll lift the darkness on the face of the deep, and tell us which way to look for Light.

THIS LIVING HAND

Ronald Reagan's Farewell Letter

THE THROB OF SYMPATHY THAT RAN THROUGH THE COUNTRY LAST November, when Ronald Reagan wrote his farewell letter to the American people, went beyond the ordinary sorrow we all must feel on reading that someone familiar has succumbed to Alzheimer's disease. Much time and space, not to mention cyberspace, was devoted to the news, and many tears were shed, even by people who despised everything Pres-

Originally published in *The New Yorker,* 16 January 1995.

Second page of Ronald Reagan's farewell letter, 5 November 1994.

ident Reagan had ever stood for. After nine years of studying him with objective rigor, I confess that I, too, cried at that letter, with its crabbed script and enormous margin (so evocative of the blizzard whitening his mind), and, above all, at the mystery of that black and scary erasure, concealing God knows what.

Script's primary power is to convey the cursive flow of human thought, from brain to hand to pen to ink to eye—every waver, every loop, every character trembling with expression. Type has no comparable warmth; matrix dots and laser sprays and pixels of LCD interpose their various screens between writer and reader. If Mr. Reagan's letter (which, by the way, he composed entirely himself) had been keyboarded to the world, instead of handwritten and issued in facsimile, its poignancy would have been reduced by half.

Just a few months ago, I came across a packet of Mr. Reagan's high-school and college essays, all but the earliest (1926) as individually distinct as the Alzheimer's letter, written nearly seventy years later. His script at fifteen has the same patient punctiliousness (no abbreviations, few erasures, and generally flawless spelling) that characterizes the personal letters he wrote every Wednesday afternoon as President. But it inclines at an orthodox Spencerian angle. Only the occasional involuntary straightening of a "d" shows that the penman is forcing himself to write with his right hand, because that is what Midwestern teachers required of southpaw schoolboys in the mid-1920s. The script becomes shapely with young Dutch's acquisition of a new fountain pen in 1927. By the summer of 1928, however, a left-handed undertow begins to hoist the masts of his perpendiculars upright, like a canvas anchor drifting contrary to the wind. Three years later, he reaches the rocking equipoise that will sustain him for the rest of his life.

WHY, IN THE AGE of voice mail, is script still the preferred style for messages of great intimacy? Because it is both direct and enduring. Spoken words, whether recorded at long distance or whispered across an inch of pillow, may have greater impact, but they evaporate at once, like acetone. Handwritten words mean more the more they are read, and time only increases their first force.

I began work on my biography of Theodore Roosevelt by reading some typed transcripts of his private diaries (1878–85). Vivid as they were, nothing prepared me for the tactile reality of the original volumes, leaf after carefully written leaf over which *his* hand had traveled, the summer pages buckled here and there where it had perspiringly rested, an erasure even huger and more mystifying than Mr. Reagan's following the words "*I am very—*"

Any biographer will attest to the feeling of closeness, amounting almost to identity, that develops between scholar and subject during long hours of manuscript study. On the night that young Theodore triumphantly escorts pretty Alice Hathaway Lee from the altar to a hotel bedroom, one has to be less than flesh and blood not to feel a commensurate quickening of one's own pulse. I remember the embarrassment I felt when TR, already sure that posterity was watching, sternly informed me that I was not to know what it was like in bed with his bride. "Our intense happiness is too sacred to be written about."

Four years later, on 14 February 1884, there was the inky ugliness of the cross with which he recorded Alice's death—obliterating her, as it were, from history—and a day or two later scrawled, in words that one can hardly bear to read, "For joy or sorrow, my life has now been lived out."

IN 1901, JUST AS in 1981, White House secretaries used to giggle at their boss's curious insistence on penning correspondence he could well have dictated. When President Roosevelt did use stenographers, he would deliberately splatter the typescript of each letter with unnecessary commas and qualifiers, so its recipient would be reassured that he had pored over every syllable. President Reagan went so far as to address and seal his personal mail, and, like Harry Truman, he was known to lick his own stamps. I treasure several letters from him written on thick ivory gold-embossed stock, each with its matching envelope meticulously inscribed, down to the last digit of my zip code.

He could never be made to understand that such missives were worth something on the open market, and must therefore be stuffed into larger government envelopes, readdressed, and restamped before dispatch.

There is indeed something treasurable about this essence Germans call the *Urtext,* the original—fresh ink and fresh thought, virgin paper, inimitable ciphers pursuing one another across the page of history. Whether the hand behind the pen is that of someone merely famous, like Mr. Reagan, or of an authentic genius, like Johann Sebastian Bach, what it writes is prized, and the value we ascribe to it goes beyond money.

Only a favored, scholarly few can ever hope to hold a Bach manuscript in their hands, yet anyone with a rudimentary ability to read music can buy a facsimile copy of, say, the "Brandenburg Concertos" (the score has been widely reproduced) and match it note by note to any performance. If the performance is live, so much the better to feel the momentum, as it were, of Bach's creative impetus. Not only the *script* but the music itself takes on new power as ink mutates into sound, and sound moves obedient to the dictates of a quick, invisible quill.

Quick. Perhaps that's the word—used in its old sense of "quick with life"—that best describes the human immediacy of script. Studying it up close, one notices things too subtle to transcribe, or even photocopy. Schubert, one of the fastest of great composers, had, for example, an almost reverential habit of slowing and controlling his pen when real inspiration struck. As the music becomes more beautiful, so does the calligraphy. Mozart was at once more casual and more possessed. One looks at the manuscript of some masterpiece such as the *Ave Verum Corpus*— not so much as a nib-crab marring its ordered perfection—and one's skin prickles to think that he was very likely, as he copied it out by hand, already composing something else in his head.

PERHAPS AS A RESULT of our rampant cellularization, as we phone and transmit paperless messages through air and ether, we paradoxically crave, it seems, written proof that we still exist as literate creatures. Notepaper condolences, no matter how awkwardly expressed, offer more surcease than printed cards. Vast sums are paid by chirophiles for manuscripts of eminent writers who still work in longhand, or who at least hunt and peck and cut and paste. Museums are not about to display the floppies of any contemporary Flaubert.

Or, if they do, I doubt they will attract the sort of awe accorded some manuscripts of Vladimir Nabokov, which the New York Public Library's Berg Collection put on display last spring. At least two of these, delineated in colored pencil, were more design than script. One was a diagrammatic analysis of metrical variations in a poem by Vasily Zhukovsky, structured rather like a stained-glass window. Units of scansion were represented by variously colored lozenges, and ruled ligatures ran with and contrary to the rhythms, in triangular and rectangular patterns. Nearby lay Nabokov's study of some butterfly-wing configurations, just as careful, just as chromatic, generically different yet spiritually the same—products of a genius able to comprehend both extremes of the Great Chain of Being, and to balance them on the point of his pen.

A UNIVERSITY STUDENT of my acquaintance told me that she wrote many short stories and poems on her PC but routinely erased them "because they're not up to much." I remember wincing, not at her literary judgment but because I see her one day as Chief Executive of the United States. Whoever writes her biography will be deprived of the sort of *frisson* I felt when I read, in an excited pencil scrawl, the plan of one of Ronald Reagan's fictional heroes to tease his girlfriend with a piece of good news: "He'd wait until she said hello and then he would say, 'This is the President.' "

A cheap thrill, perhaps, in that the elevation being announced was merely to the presidency of a college senate. Nevertheless, that's what young Dutch's moving finger wrote in 1931—and, having writ, moved on to compose sentences of more historic import.

When I first looked at his juvenile holographs, I was overcome by a most unprofessional feeling of tenderness. They consist of seventeen stories, essays, and themes, set down on sixty-nine pages of rough-lined, exercise-book stock, one of them still attached to a grocery flyer that reads FREE WITH THE PURCHASE OF A ONE POUND PACKAGE OF SAWYER'S SALTINE CRACKERS. Although several are mere fragments, and many are forgettable football pieces, even the blandest yield tiny explosions of personality, like specks of undissolved saffron. Together, they present a touching portrait of an ardent, if dreamy, young man. The protagonist, whether his name be "Bill Dennis" or "Bus Burke" or "Corporal Howard of the 77th," is eternally tall, tanned, graceful, genial, and aloof.

Narcissism is, of course, a staple ingredient of youthful literary expression. Yet what strikes one about the self-recognition in these pieces is its almost disembodied detachment. The author's pen seems to have been wielded by an admiring but passive *Doppelgänger*. Again and again, there are nuances that only manuscript can impart. Dutch writes, for example, the following altered sentence about a coed gin orgy: "Like a man seeing his doom Jim saw the bottles shining in the lamp light ~~but he was game~~ like executioners' knives." That final image could occur only to the child of an alcoholic. And the ambivalence between crossout and superscript is telling. All his life Ronald Reagan has preserved a strange ability to join in any game, face any row of knives, without the least fear of moral compromise or threat.

There is another evocative crossout in an unfinished account of "Jerry Dale's" return to college as a senior, accompanied by not one but three ghostly companions—himself as freshman, sophomore, and junior. As they eagerly direct their steps up an elm-lined avenue, their thoughts move ahead "like a bird in swift flight" to where, invisible around a corner, there stands "~~a white private house~~. . . ."

Revealed rather than concealed under that light overscore is the first written evidence of a recurring image in Mr. Reagan's prepresidential dreams: a columned mansion, white of wall and tall of window, distant, privileged, and beckoning.

I AM FINISHING this essay in the plush hush of the Office of Ronald Reagan overlooking Century City. The old man is next door, as courtly, soft-spoken, and elegant as ever. He and I have just said good-bye for, I guess, the last time. About six months ago, he stopped recognizing me. Now I no longer recognize him. For all the intimate familiarity of that face and body, for all the willingness with which he showed me his framed photographs, his jelly-bean jar, and his view of the Hollywood Hills, I did not feel his presence beside me, only his absence.

When I went in, he was sitting in the same quiet pose he always assumed during "personal time" in the Oval Office: glossy head tilted forward, jacket sleeves half on his desk, white cuffs protruding exactly one inch, his black Parker lying ready on its own polished leather reflection. Except now there was only one document for him to read and annotate—his daily schedule, which he seemed to be perusing with rapt interest. Time was when this thick sheet of bond bore the names of potentates, most of them lucky if they got more than ten minutes of his attention. Today, it was reduced down to three or four token "drop-by" visits, mostly from friends.

Glancing at it as I approached, I saw that he still got satisfaction out of drawing an arrowed vertical through each appointment, aimed at the hour that he could go home. It reminded me of the time I turned on my heel as I left the Oval Office, and caught him in the act of tranquilly skewering me.

"I'm not on *your* list today, Mr. President. Just wanted to say hi—see how you are." He rose with his usual air of gentle surprise, but I got the feeling that if I had come in through the window he would have reacted no differently. As I made desperate small talk, he held on to the edge of his desk.

"Sir, those lead soldiers make a great display! Like when you were sick with pneumonia in 1915, and played with armies on the counterpane?"

He smiled faintly, not remembering, and I noticed something unimaginable before: a patch of silvery stubble on his chin. It glowed incandescently as a sunbeam slanted across his face.

"Uh—the fellow who made them, he—uh, came . . ."

"Came to present them to you?"

"Yes. He—we—we had to make space, uh—move those trees."

Mystified, I followed his gaze, and saw only a red-bound set of *Public Papers of the Presidents: Ronald Reagan,* relegated to the shelf beneath the soldiers. Well, if a poet can compare stacked volumes to garners of grain, I guess a retired statesman can call his collected works "trees" if he wants. They do, after all, bear fruit, in a dry sort of way. And President Reagan did love to prune speech drafts and proclamations with his sharp pen, just as he pruned the live oaks and *madroños* at Rancho del Cielo. "See?" he would say, after having buzz-sawed this or that grove to a Seurat-like geometry. "See where the light comes through?"

Now I sit with pen in hand and the original copy of his Alzheimer's letter—unfolded, unmailed, yet universally received—lying flat and crisp before me. Light of another sort permeates these simple words, a final lucidity before the letting go. Since writing them, Mr. Reagan's decline has been precipitous. His Presidential Library, in Simi Valley, will soon exhibit the letter, along with a few of the thirty thousand responses it elicited from all over the world. Distracted though its sender may have been, strange as he has become, here, palpably, for as long as paper and ink lasts, is Ronald Reagan: His Mark. And there comes to my mind a scribbled envoi of John Keats, effortlessly reaching across the chasm of years:

This living hand, now warm and capable
Of earnest grasping, would, if it were cold
And in the icy silence of the tomb,
So haunt thy days and chill thy dreaming nights
That thou would wish thine own heart dry of blood
So in my veins red life might stream again,
And thou be conscience-calm'd—see, here it is —
I hold it towards you.

ROCK. TURF. WATER. LAVA. SKY.

Reykjavík in Retrospect

TEN YEARS AGO THIS SEPTEMBER, RONALD REAGAN STEPPED OFF the White House podium after announcing that he would meet urgently at Reykjavík with Mikhail Gorbachev, and caught sight of me standing aghast at the exit door. It had been the most dramatic press release of his presidency. Reporters were tripping over camera cables in their rush to get on the air. "Oh, Edmund," said Reagan calmly. "About that swimming hole."

Two hemispheres were throbbing to the prospect of a breakthrough

Originally published in *Forbes FYI*, Summer 1996.
Photograph of Thingvellir, Iceland, by Macduff Everton.

in superpower relations, and here he was wanting to discuss the dimensions, and frog content, of some damn pond in Illinois, circa 1919. All I could think about was Iceland, circa 1986, and the absolute necessity of getting a place on the delegation. Reagan's silky voice maundered on. I fought the urge to dive between his legs and sprint for the Chief of Staff's office, where Don Regan was probably handing out the last few seats on Air Force One. Nobody who has not seen White House staffers scrambling for precedence can possibly imagine the frenzy when a summit is in the offing. "Thank you very much, Mr. President," I said at the end of an extended monologue on the Australian crawl. Sixty seconds later I was trying to convince a cold-eyed Don Regan that he would go down in literature with Bluebeard if he did not invite me along. "This is history, Chief," I babbled. "How would it be if Erik the Red hadn't let a scribe onto his longboat?"

Actually Erik's fame was spread by word of mouth, but I hoped Regan didn't know that. "Forget it," the Chief snarled. "Hell, I've even had to bump Cap Weinberger. Every hotel bed in Reykjavík's already taken. George Shultz'll be lucky if he doesn't have to bunk with Paul Nitze."

"I'll sleep on rope down by the docks. Just let me watch the President give it to Gorby."

Regan shook his head. "Sorry, principals only. When you see the size of the place they'll be meeting in, you'll understand."

It took a few years, but I eventually made it to Iceland, and paced out the little room where the two leaders clashed, and understood a lot more, perhaps, than I would have if I'd squatted by the keyhole that dark and bewildering weekend. I viewed Hofdi House in historical as well as logistical proportion, and "Reykjavík" as just another summit, albeit a stormy one, in the long *cordillera* stretching back to Yalta. And I saw (during one of the most radiant weeks of weather it has ever been my good fortune to enjoy) Iceland itself as a testing ground of forces greater than all the nukes in Europe.

I ARRIVED SHORTLY before dawn at Keflavík International Airport, and, driving into town, got at least some of the gloomy impression that Reagan got driving out, after the summit failed. No trees. No visible vegetation. Only black and carbuncled lava, spreading on the one hand toward black sea, and on the other toward dead, distant volcanoes. But whereas *he* saw this landscape under drizzle, in gathering dark, I was soon the beneficiary of rosy sunlight. The long shadow of my car rippled across a plain that proved to be neither hard nor sterile, but a moss-green carpet jerking with birds and butterflies. "*Verdi ljós!*" as God says at the beginning of local Bibles. *Og pao varo ljós.* And there was light.

Like most first-time visitors, I had imagined Iceland must generally be sheathed in white. Well, it *was* August. But a white landscape would surely be available further north. I was scheduled to connect right away, at the domestic airport just outside Reykjavík, with a flight to Höfn, whence glacier excursions operate throughout the summer. I wanted to get out onto the back of Vatnajökull, Europe's largest ice mass, before exploring the capital city. Since Vatna's chill suppresses the hot silo of Grímsvötn, a dormant volcano nearly one kilometer down, I thought it might yield an image relevant to the summit's deadlock over missile policy.

Aloft again in a Fokker Friendship, I dozed off for half an hour, and woke to a bird's-eye view of improbable beauty. One thousand feet below, the motionless swirl of a glacier spilled out of green mountains into a pellucid lagoon. A line of foam, delicate yet tensile as a spider's web, paralleled the coast. It was a scene primeval in its emptiness and purity. I felt my eyes, used to the garish colors of American urban life, adjusting to a spectrum consisting only of tints. I tried to analyze why Iceland registered with such visual clarity, then realized the cause again: no trees. That, and air clear as glass.

In Höfn, a tiny fishing port with an almost Chinese relationship to the vast mountains behind it, I looked for Tryggvi Arnasson, manager of Joklaferdir Glacier Tours. I expected the usual bearded, burly type in a strong-smelling sweater, and was taken aback to find Mr. Arnasson looking slim and elegant in a dark blue Façonnable silk jacket—identical to the one I wear at home when trying to impress folks from the sticks.

He put me on a bus designed to ride with equanimity over snowdrifts, pumice, and terminal moraine. Within an hour I was a thousand feet above sea level, stepping out onto the most ice I have ever seen, apart from the time I arrived late for an interview with Maggie Thatcher. A haze of cold, unaffected by the strong sun, hung over the whiteness roll-ing and rising inland. Black bare mountains stood jagged against the horizon, under a sky so translucent and swept of cloud I swear I could see stars through it. Before my fingers numbed, I scrawled in my note-book: *This is no country for agoraphobics.*

The obverse of that, of course, is that Iceland offers as much silence and solitude as any loner (or biographer of a loner) could hope for. Hav-ing been, only nine hours previously, a standee on Amtrak's hottest, noisiest commuter special, I found myself walking into the whiteness like some latter-day Captain Oates. Perhaps over that lift of ice, half a mile distant, one might lose sight of bus and lodge, and hear the rarest of aural treats, pure silence.

What one heard instead was the frantic roar of a pursuing snowmo-bile. It wheeled in front of me, scattering snow, and the next thing I knew I was being hauled back to civilization like a lost ram. "*Kravis! Kravis! Kravis!*" my rawboned escort kept yelling, jabbing his free hand at all points of the compass. Later I checked the word in my Icelandic phrase-book. Crevice. Moral: don't venture out onto Vatnajökull alone, unless you want to spend the short rest of your life wedged maybe three hun-dred feet down, between two very cold green walls.

BY THE TIME I returned to sea level, late in the afternoon, I had attained that rather pleasant stage of jet lag when one feels both wise and hallu-cinatory. I went for a "cruise" on Jökulsárlón Glacier Lake (the lagoon I had glimpsed from the plane), and found nothing incongruous in its odd juxtaposition of floes and icebergs with rich farmland to north and south. Balmy sunshine poured down on my head, while the glacier, shat-tering slowly a hundred yards away, gave off an icy effluvium that for some reason made me think of great age. My guide remarked that this was no illusion: "The meltwater we're sailing in is probably about eight hundred years old."

Icelanders are forever relating the past to the present, not to mention man to nature, sea to land, *ljós* to *myrkur* (which combine here haunt-ingly in July, the month of the midnight sun), and above all the ancient opposites of ice and fire. Nowhere else on earth do these last coexist in such dangerous proximity. A terrible beauty is born, as Yeats would say, out of their mutual attraction and repulsion. For example, the white flatness of northwestern Vatnajökull is bejeweled with a mysterious, sapphire-blue lake. What the blue betrays is the presence, miles down, of Grímsvötn. Should that lethal volcano ever erupt with maximum force and melt the great glacier, the resultant flood will be biblical.

DRIVING BACK TO Reykjavík next morning, I passed through a series of valleys so lush with grass and *kraekiber* berries that, forgetting yesterday's frigid expedition, I decided Iceland should be called Greenland, and vice versa. But then, noticing how every mountainside was etched with two or three—or ten or twelve—lazily tumbling cascades, I renamed the country Fossland, land of waterfalls, and made a mental note to inform Steingrímur Hermannsson of the change when I interviewed him later in the day. Mr. Hermannsson was for many years prime minister of Iceland, and being a well-connected man, would doubtless convey my suggestion to the appropriate authorities.

Before lunch I made a short detour to Gullfoss, a glacial waterfall of such beauty that, were it in the United States, would be almost invisible for concession stands. Silver-gray smoothness slid breaking, pluming into white. Sunny spray climbed as fine as cirrus before floating down and turning my spectacles into prisms. Pleasantly cooled and blinded, I felt part of the great precipitative circle of ice becoming water becoming cloud becoming rain.

IT WAS THUS with a sense of fellow-feeling that I scarfed a salmon half an hour later in the Geysir Restaurant. Judging by its freshness, it had been yanked from the pool below Gullfoss only minutes before menu time. Most other lunchers decamped hastily before dessert to view a scheduled eruption of the nearby Great Geysir, but having lived in New York I am used to seeing jets of smelly steam blasting from holes in the ground. I elected for raspberries and *kaffi* before proceeding to my appointment in Reykjavík.

By three o'clock I was sitting in Mr. Hermannsson's harbor-view

office, and listening to his extraordinary story of being asked by a dis-
traught Russian ambassador whether it would be okay for Reagan and
Gorbachev to negotiate Armageddon in his city, in just ten days' time.
"Naturally I asked the American ambassador to confirm. . . . Excuse me,
I must take this call."

Picking up the receiver, he switched from flawless English to his native tongue. Icelandic is a difficult language, strangely combining
hard-rolled *r*'s and soft *zh* sounds with singsong elisions. Listening to
him I could only think, bizarrely, of muesli being spooned into milk: oat
husks and raisins swimming together.

Mr. Hermannsson had the politician's rare ability to resume a sentence just where he left off. ". . . to confirm that this was a bona fide request. His Excellency was, shall we say, not pleased. 'Those bastards,' he
said."

"The Russians?"

"No, the State Department. He hadn't been informed."

For the next half hour Mr. Hermannsson described with quiet pride
how Icelanders had worked around the clock to accommodate an influx
of advance men, diplomats, KGB and CIA agents, Greenpeaceniks, and
media hordes that must have made them sigh for the peaceful days of
Danish conquest. He concluded by telling me what Gorbachev said to
him after the summit failed, speaking at length, under a shared um-
brella, in the pouring rain: words of bitter disappointment, yet not without hope of a nuclear-free tomorrow.

The city fathers of Reykjavík, who lock Hofdi House as a place of
high ceremony, were unwilling to open it to me that afternoon. They
cited vague but vital municipal reasons. Putting two and two together (it
was four o'clock on a summer Friday, and the salmon streams upcountry were running with fish), I did not blame them.

I SPENT THE weekend at the Langavarn lodge of Ingvi-Hrafn Jónsson, a
local television personality whom I will not describe as "Iceland's Dan
Rather." An Icelander, however, would not hesitate to call Dan Rather
"the American Ingvi-Hrafn." To me, Mr. Jónsson was of interest because
he anchored nineteen hours of straight summit coverage in 1986—no

mean feat, when you consider there was a blackout on the entire proceedings. To most readers of this magazine, he will be of more interest because he purveys, at fabulous fees, some of the best salmon fishing in Iceland.

After half a life of feminist intimidation, I had forgotten what fun it is to go macho. The rest of this section is for guys, okay? And not—you know, wimpy guys. Guys with *pungur*. Perhaps I should explain how I learned this weird word. En route to the lodge in a Land Rover full of muscular chaps passing out salt licorice, I spied a passing bakery and offered to buy a Sacher torte for tonight's all-male dinner. They were agreeable, and urged with guffaws that I ask the cute *dottir* behind the counter for some *Astarpungur* on the side. Blushing prettily, she served up a bag of delicious, batter-fluffed, raisiny spheres, which we helped down then and there with *kaffi*. Back in the car, I asked what *Astarpungur* meant, and the answer was Lover's Balls.

"*Pungur* is a word we use a lot among close friends," the driver, Stefan, explained. " 'Hey, *pungur*, get me a beer.' Literally it means *scrotum*. But colloquially, you can use it even if your buddy is female."

I sat wondering what the reaction would be if I tried this endearment on some women I know in the United States.

The four-wheeler cruised in lambent light up Langavatn. We passed a velvety horse farm. "That place used to belong to Egil," said Stefan.

"Egil?"

"You know, in Egil's Saga?" He was talking, with entire naturalness, of a man who had lived, farmed and fought here a thousand years ago—as you or I might talk about some old uncle who had recently expired in Brooklyn. I marveled again at the reach of Icelandic memory.

"A bloodthirsty character, Egil," my backseat neighbor, Bjarni Arnasson, remarked with relish. "He chopped off his first head when he was only six years old, and when asked why, he said simply, 'The opportunity presented itself.' "

I remember Ronald Reagan using similar words when I asked him why he went into politics.

"That horse ahead," I said, "is moving rather strangely. From here, it looks like he's got only one leg on either side."

"He's demonstrating his *tölt*," Bjarni said. "A sort of extra gear between trot and canter. Only Icelandic horses can do that—lope along like camels. It makes the most comfortable ride in the world."

We overtook the horse, a small gray-blond beauty with flowing mane and tail. I had the odd sensation of having seen it before. Silvery smoothness slid breaking, pluming into white. . . .

AT EIGHT O'CLOCK that evening (the valley still radiant), I sat with Ingvi-Hrafn on a moss bluff soft as astrakhan. He was acting as gillie for Stefan and Bjarni, who stood hip-deep beneath us in steel-blue swirling water. We munched *kraekibers* and talked of the summit. "I don't care what anybody says about that coup in Moscow," said Ingvi.* "Reykjavík was the beginning of the end of the Cold War." A month later, in Illinois, Gorbachev would make the same comment to me.

Beneath us, Bjarni—one of Iceland's premier anglers—swung his line in a parabola as delicate as the long swirl of urine he had traced at roadside, in the traditional pre-fishing pee. "I snatch this bastard!" he yelled in sudden excitement. "Edmund, he is yours!" Not having so much as tickled a tadpole in my life, I clambered down and awkwardly drew in seven pounds of rainbow-sided, diamond-eyed beauty. I was given a guest's privilege of deciding whether to throw him back or not. But on inspection, we discovered the salmon was hooked too deep to survive.

I stuck my fingers in and carried him bleeding up the slope.

BACK IN REYKJAVÍK on Monday morning, I walked to Hofdi House in sunshine so clean and strong it glowed like limelight. Exquisite girls with hair the color of cotton grass bumped pleasantly into me on the narrow sidewalks, and from basement coffeehouses came a universal aroma of cappuccino. Also, I regret to say, that of Marlboro Country: Icelanders are under the general impression that nicotine is food.

Mr. Hermannsson had told me that two sites larger than Hofdi had been made available to summit planners. The Americans preferred this

---

*The August 1991 coup against President Mikhail Gorbachev that led to the dissolution of the Soviet Union.

little bayside mansion for reasons of security. Approaching it across a newly mown spread of lawn, I wondered if our team had not also been seduced by Hofdi's elegant, symbolic symmetry, ideal for a meeting of presumed coequals: four clapboard façades addressed north, south, east, and west, a landward doorway stepped up from gravel, a seaward window full of sky. If so, I would be able to write the first sentence in history combining the words "advance men" and "aesthetics."

The curator, unlocking the door with a bunch of keys that looked like a Viking artifact, told me it was a miracle Hofdi House had not been burned down in 1986. "While Mr. Reagan and Mr. Gorbachev were at their debate, the KGB were watching TV downstairs—"

"Monitoring the proceedings?"

"No, a video of *Tom and Jerry.*"

I scribbled this datum in ecstasy. Cat v. Mouse, above and below!

"One of the agents dropped his cigarette in a wastepaper basket. There was this big ball of flame. The Russians went into a complete panic. Fortunately an Icelandic electrician saved the situation."

"How?"

"He threw the basket out the window."

Inside, a plain hall led into the main stateroom, carpentered in buttery, glossy Danish maple that glowed slightly blue with refractions from the bay outside. I was reminded of the "Northern Light" exhibition that had traveled the United States in 1982: painting after painting that gave off this same cool radiance.

One of the best artists in that show, I told the curator, was a nineteenth-century Icelander called Jónsson.

"Asgrímur Jónsson, yes, yes. There's one of his in the next room."

He took me into a small side chamber hung with pale burlap, and showed me a painting, not one detail of which I can recall, because it overhung a copper-inlaid rectangular table, instantly recognizable from photographs. Here—not the larger room we had just left—was where Reagan and Gorbachev had their epic duel.

The curator, perhaps sensing I wanted to be alone, said he was going downstairs for a box of chocolates. After he clomped off, I did the weird things a biographer does when he has temporary possession of something primary. I stood, I sniffed, I stroked wood, I stared through the picture window from Gorby's angle, then from Reagan's (the former had by far the more dramatic view of the Snaefellsjökull glacier across the water). Finally, emboldened, I sat down in the presidential chair. As I did so I felt—well, a chill. Maybe it was just the copper under my forearms.

OUTSIDE AFTERWARD, with the strong sun pouring down and chocolate on my tongue, I found it hard to imagine the bitter weather, and bitter disappointment, that obtained at this spot on 12 October 1986. The Cold War was over now. Democracy's sun shone over much of the world. Life was good, and Iceland was beautiful. And here was Sveinn Saemundsson, sweeping round the driveway in his Volvo, ready to take me to my final destination, Thingvellir National Park.

Saemundsson, author of many books of Icelandic history and culture, explained as we cruised into deep country that Thingvellir (literally, "Valley of the Gathering") was the birthplace of European parliamentary democracy in the year A.D. 930. That July, Iceland's feuding tribes came from all over the country to settle their differences by debate and consensus. "From then on, they came back every summer, bringing their retinues and finery and exchanging daughters and sons and debating the great issues of the day, such as when and whether to adopt Christianity. Throughout our history, everything of importance has happened at Thingvellir."

"What's so special about the place?"

"Politicians like the sound of their own voices," Saemundsson said enigmatically. "You will understand when we get there."

After about an hour, the molten silver of a lake lying between black mountains spread out ahead. Beyond, the landscape split open. Not at that precise moment: the actual parturition took place millions of years ago. But it is a geological fact that Iceland breaks apart here, in a dead straight rift extending as far as the eye can see. On the one side lies the eastern Atlantic shield, on the other the western.

"Do you see," Saemundsson asked as we approached and parked the car, "how the two shields are of different depth? That means that you can stand on the rim of the lower, while the rim of the higher, rising behind you, acts like a resonator, so you can throw your voice over the whole valley."

"Paradise for politicians!"

"Not only politicians," he said. "Whenever I come here I feel purified. By its beauty, its enormous age . . ."

We stood on the rock where Iceland's first Speaker declaimed the tenet still embroidered on the breast of every police officer in the country: *Med logum skal land byggja* (with law we shall build this land). Saemundsson was right about the valley's beauty. It is so elemental that one can describe it only in plain nouns. Rock. Turf. Water. Lava. Sky. Space. Soul. Silence. Here is nothing of excess, everything of what matters.

"This parliament you speak of, Sveinn. Wasn't it called the Althing?"

"Yes."

"There's a quote in Shakespeare that comes to mind. *Nothing brings me all things.*"

He nodded. He knew it.

"What beats me," I said, "is why Reagan and Gorby didn't hold their full summit right here. They wouldn't have found anything to argue about."

THE BILL AND TEDDY SHOW

Mr. Clinton's Latest Presidential Performance

TWENTY YEARS AGO, DURING AN OUT-OF-TOWN TRYOUT OF THE
ill-fated musical *1600 Pennsylvania Avenue*, I was intrigued by the actor
Ken Howard's ability to transform himself from president to president
with the aid of a quickly applied prop or two, and adroit changes of voice
and gesture. Although he was big and blond, he needed only clamp on
some pince-nez, and snap his teeth at the audience, to become a credit-
able Theodore Roosevelt—and the audience, hitherto comatose, burst
into delighted applause.

The current resident of the White House has recently pulled off a
similar *coup de théâtre*, inspired by the success of his Truman skit last
year, and his masterly impersonation of Ronald Reagan the big-
government basher before both houses of Congress this January. One
remembers that he modeled himself on JFK in youth, and vowed on entering the White House to become another FDR.

Should those scholarly gravediggers who wish to exhume Abraham

Originally published in *The New York Times*, 6 October 1996.

Rooseveltian pince-nez. Nineteenth-century engraving.

Lincoln ever succeed in their quest and parade the Emancipator's bones on the nightly news, we must brace for a prompt appearance by Mr. Clinton in a stovepipe hat. In the meantime, he's found his latest vein of mimicry in TR.

Not coincidentally, the twenty-sixth President is hot at the moment. Tonight and tomorrow, PBS will broadcast a major documentary on his life and times. Mr. Clinton has a bust of him in the Oval Office (along with busts of all the other presidents mentioned above), and I'll bet that at times during the Netanyahu-Arafat summit he gazed wistfully at TR's Nobel Peace Prize, glistening like a golden chimera on the mantelpiece of the Roosevelt Room.

Given the loneliness of supreme power, it is natural for a Chief Executive to identify with his more distant predecessors. (*Consecutive* presidents hardly ever get along, as anyone studying photographs of them together at inaugurations can see). We all know about Richard Nixon's chats with Honest Abe, and I remember Mr. Reagan telling me, with entire lack of self-consciousness, that he and Thomas Jefferson liked to "look at each other" across the Mall.

Usually, however, such moments of empathy are private. When Mr. Clinton invokes TR on horseback in Colorado, or in cowboy boots and khakis on the rim of the Grand Canyon, he invites public comparison with the Rough Rider—at his considerable peril.

There are, to be sure, many parallels between them as campaigners for their respective second terms in the White House. Overwhelming personal charm, youthfulness—TR was forty-five on this date in 1904, Mr. Clinton is just fifty—acute political intelligence, garrulousness, love of applause, love of people, luck: the list could be extended right down to prowess at the lunch table and their common enjoyment of a lackluster opponent.

If we compare them intellectually, however, such a void opens up as to isolate them from each other, on the north and south rims of our regard. Mr. Clinton's new book *Between Hope and History* happens to be exactly the same length as TR's public letter accepting the Republican nomination in 1904, and since both documents were issued in late summer for the same political purpose, a side-by-side reading is instructive.

To begin with, there is the question of *gravitas.* I allowed Mr. Clinton's book to fall open at page 57, and found that of its 191 words, only 31 had any particular meaning. The rest of the space was devoted to clichés (one every three lines), generalities such as "investing in the capacity of our people," redundancies, and extremely vague statistics—my favorite being his claim to have made "improvements in the bottom line of average Americans."

Out of sympathy as well as fairness, I deliberately chose one of the least noun-dense, fact-packed paragraphs of TR's own manifesto (interested readers may find it reprinted in volume 4 of his collected letters). In fourteen lines, there are only ten unnecessary words, and not a single cliché. Every sentence states something concrete. All the emotions—contempt for governmental critics, impatience with naysayers, veneration for veterans, sympathy for farmers, excitement over the implications of his Reclamation Act—are genuine and strong. One senses a passionately self-directed man whose mind moved like an oiled combine over every dry stalk of policy, neatly stacking and sorting.

In contrast, Mr. Clinton suffers from what TR would have called "a fatal lack of *sequitur.*" He drives without steering, and he would as soon process weeds as wheat. *Between Hope and History* reads like a series of improvised speeches (incessantly punctuated by the word "I"), although his publisher assures us that the text was "labored over" for many months, and his uncredited coauthor says the final book is "80 percent Bill Clinton." TR's enormous letter was dictated—probably during the course of a single morning—but it is clearly the work of one disciplined writer.

Of course, we do not elect presidents for their prose style. Mr. Clinton is unquestionably sincere—for the moment—in asking us to equate him with TR the mediator, the environmentalist, the Bully-Pulpit thumper, the legislative reformer. All these aims are noble, providing he closely examines TR's actual record of achievement, which was a lot less progressive than he seems to think.

On the environment, for example, TR was by no means a tree hugger. When it came to a choice between scenery and the homesteader desperate for firewood and aqueducts, he paid little heed to the protests of preservationists.

"It is a cardinal principle of the forest-reserve policy of this Administration that the reserves are for use," he said in his Fourth Annual Message. Similarly, the great Trust Buster prosecuted the Northern Securities Corporation more to make a moral point (that government maintained the right to regulate a free economy) than to declare any kind of war on Wall Street. His successor, William Howard Taft, whom he lambasted for being pro-business, in reality busted more trusts than he did.

There was, moreover, a lordly *hauteur* about TR's foreign policy, and a hair-trigger willingness to deploy gunboats when crossed, that Mr. Clinton surely does not wish to emulate. (Watch him whip off those pince-nez at the slightest hint of trouble in Panama!) He sees today's world as a flux of forces interactive, freewheeling, cyberspatial—rather than power blocs separated by steel and saltwater.

It is tempting to speculate, in the manner of those "Impossible Interviews" in the old *Vanity Fair,* how Teddy and Bill would get along today should they bump into each other on the campaign trail. One imagines that Mr. Clinton would avoid any discussion of the Vietnam War, as well as his veto of the late-term abortion bill, which would undoubtedly result in an abrupt end to the conversation. (Of all Theodore Roosevelt's convictions, the deepest was his reverence for life.)

They would admire each other's power of memory, political skills, and stage manner, and laugh at their shared habit of saying "in closing" before three thousand words of peroration. Mr. Roosevelt would notice that Mr. Clinton, behind his joviality, has no humor, while the latter would be dismayed by TR's binary way of looking at things: Good vs. Evil, Strong vs. Weak, Duty vs. Dereliction.

Such speculations, though, are historically vain. For the moment, Mr. Clinton has as much right as Theodore Roosevelt to preen before a largely contented electorate. It is encouraging that he, too, wants to be remembered for effecting great changes in a time of peace. But he might bear in mind, as he almost certainly proceeds to emulate the landslide of 1904, that TR never felt the need to imitate anybody.

A DARWINIAN FOR FUN

The Evolutionary Education of Henry Adams

WENLOCK EDGE IS A FORESTED ESCARPMENT IN SHROPSHIRE, England, so uniquely equipoised between geological and cultural extremes that it has figured in at least three literary epiphanies. Leaving aside the lesser example of P. G. Wodehouse, who spent a transforming vacation hereabouts as a boy, we have both A. E. Housman and Henry Adams ascending the Edge at the end of youth, and being overpowered by atavistic feelings.

In Housman's case, the poetic flood that became *A Shropshire Lad* was released by the sight of treetops far below him, tossing in winter wind.

Introduction to the Modern Library edition of *The Education of Henry Adams* (New York, 1997).
Adams Memorial in Washington, D.C., by Augustus Saint-Gaudens. Photograph by Josh Howell.

He reflected that legionnaires of another civilization must have stood where he stood, and experienced similar emotions, two millennia before.

> The tree of man was never quiet:
> Then 'twas the Roman, now 'tis I.

Even this leap into the past fell short of that made by the young Henry Adams, who came to what he called "the Wenlock Edge of time" in July 1867, at a crisis point in his intellectual development. Twenty-nine years old and unmarried, the brilliant scion of two presidents, he was beset by contradictions of natural, moral, and economic philosophy, which seemed embodied in the divided landscape around him. At his feet lay Coalbrookdale, crucible of the Industrial Revolution, and beyond it England's steepled heartland, shaped by centuries of faith and farming. In the opposite direction loomed the bare mountains of Wales, dating back to the Paleozoic era.

It was a panorama intimately familiar to Adams, whose best friend lived nearby at Much Wenlock. He had lazed on this grass many a summer afternoon, and pottered in an amateur way for fossils. But today, the sense of intimacy sharpened to actual identity, causing him to ponder his whole evolution as a human being—what he would chronicle in later life as *The Education of Henry Adams*.

FOR AS LONG AS he could remember, he had considered himself "an eighteenth-century child," his aesthetics formed by the Queen Anne panels and rococo sofas of his grandfather's house in Quincy, Massachusetts, and his mind disciplined to Revolutionary ideals of Truth, Duty, and Freedom. Too rationalistic to be religious, he nevertheless believed in an ordered universe, whose most perfect manifestation was the United States Constitution, and whose moral axis—the "Pole Star" of youthful memory—had been George Washington. "Amid the endless restless motion of every other visible point in space, he alone remained steady."

That balanced America, held together by Federalist tenets and a democratic agreement to disagree, had blown apart in the spring of

1861. Undersized, weedy, and bookish, Adams was hardly a candidate for service in the Grand Army of the Republic. When President Lincoln appointed his father, Charles Francis Adams, American Minister to the Court of St. James's, Henry agreed to accompany him across the Atlantic in the capacity of personal secretary.

The two Adamses were to remain at their posts for the next eight years. At first young Henry doubted they would stop that many months, given the anti-Lincoln bias of Her Majesty's supposedly neutral Government. He suffered agonies of humiliation as Minister Adams was snubbed by Tories who belied the English reputation for courtesy and fair play. Not until the tide of battle turned at Gettysburg did he notice that they were both suddenly welcome in Whitehall.

Perversely, Henry enjoyed his own role as young man about town. He became anglicized, acquiring a *faux* accent that never left him, and to his surprise—because he was already forbiddingly erudite—found himself taken up by hostesses beyond the diplomatic circuit. Like many shy people, he longed for soul mates, and found them among well-born intellectuals like himself. Chief among these friends were Keats's biographer Lord Houghton, and Tennyson's protégé James Milnes Gaskell, owner of Wenlock Abbey.

Adams and Gaskell shared a passion for the gentlemanly sciences: geology and anthropology, as well as history, politics, and *belles lettres*. By 1867, however, the Englishman was unable to keep up with Adams's galloping mind. He could only encourage his friend's first essay in scholarship—a profile of Pocahontas, published in the *North American Review*—and give sanctuary in Shropshire when Adams began work on something more ambitious. This was an appraisal, for the same prestigious periodical, of Sir Charles Lyell's *Principles of Geology*, which offered paleontological proof of the theory of Natural Selection.

IT IS DIFFICULT for us now to imagine the impact of reading Darwin and Lyell at a time when Mendelssohn's *Elijah* and Schiller's ode *To Joy* pretty well encompassed popular perceptions of Man's relationship to God, and to himself. In Adams's case, the impact was at first blunted by an agnostic unsentimentality. He had already had his fill of Schillerian

Freundlichkeit during postgraduate studies in Germany, and did not believe in divine grace, let alone the Creation. That very skepticism made him reluctant to embrace the evolutionary hypothesis. He found Darwin's notion of time as a kind of many-frontiered geography impressive, yet "incapable of proof." Only when he saw how well it integrated with the Lyell theory of geological gradualism (earth-forms evolving from a "natural Uniformity" of ice) was he tempted to address both subjects in print.

As a first step, before leaving London, he presented himself to the great geologist and asked how far he might trace his own vertebrate ancestry. Lyell informed him that all humanity was descended from "a very respectable fish," whose bones could be found under Wenlock Edge. It was this *aperçu* that opened Adams's eyes, autobiographically speaking, when he revisited the Edge and understood that he was part of the Great Chain of Being. In his later summation, "Life began and ended there." Somewhere beneath his grass-cushioned frame stretched the delicate tracery of a Silurian ancestor. Indeed, he might go Darwin and Lyell one better, and relate to the "starfish, shell-fish, polyps, and trilobites he had bathed among as a child on the shores of Quincy Bay."

Adams did not mind having once been a starfish, or for that matter a shark. What he found hard to accept was the notion of "evolution of mind." If Siluria, or Gettysburg, demonstrated survival of the fittest, then how about the competition of ideas—political ideas, moral ideas? Would only the most destructive prevail? Might the rule of tooth and claw apply to his own battles of conscience? He fought another right there, amid placidly cropping sheep, and felt an unsuspected new attitude take over his heart. Whatever it was, it owed little to the eighteenth century. As he wrote in his characteristic impersonal style:

> He did not like it; he could not account for it; and he was determined to stop it. . . . Out of his millions of millions of ancestors, back to the Cambrian mollusks, every one had probably lived and died in the illusion of Truths which did not amuse him, and which had never changed. Henry Adams was the first in an infinite series to discover and admit to himself that he really did not care whether truth was, or was not true. He did not even care that it

should be proved true, unless the process were new and amusing.

He was a Darwinian for fun.

Thus, more momentously than he realized, a gifted young man adopted the pose he would assume for the next fifty years: one of half-protesting, wholly cynical contemplation of whatever "current of his time" seemed likely to yield him some entertainment. As his Washington neighbor John Hay used to inquire, rhetorically, "*Ça vous amuse, la vie?*"

WHEN THE TIME CAME, in another century, to write his autobiography, Adams had lost much of his capacity for amusement. All *The Education* grants us of his once-delicious humor is a wit so dry it abrades. He vows to be as honest as Rousseau, yet hides behind a screen of Olympian detachment. Whether on Wenlock Edge, or looking down on the White House from his Richardson mansion in Washington, or mentioning in his first sentence that he was born "on the summit of Beacon Hill," he is at pains to elevate himself above the rest of mankind. The fact that he does so without boasting owes more to probity than modesty.

Even his intellectual and social peers found Adams's narcissism unpleasant. "He wanted [power] handed to him on a silver platter," Oliver Wendell Holmes, Jr., remarked, noting another aspect of narcissism, the tendency to "turn everything to dust and ashes." A succession of presidents, Democratic and Republican, came to live opposite Henry Adams, ate his famous no-invitation breakfasts, and tapped his immense fund of historical and political knowledge, but none ever offered the little man employment. They recognized a snob when they saw one.

In his defense, one might argue that Henry Adams could not help giving an elitist impression, since he belonged, demonstrably, to the elite. Not only was his blood the bluest in the land, he rarely if ever met anybody brighter than himself. The geologist-engineer Clarence King, the biographer-diplomat John Hay, the naturalist-politician Theodore Roosevelt, could all compete with Henry Adams in their various specialties, but none could match his omniscience in virtually every discipline covered by the *Encyclopaedia Britannica*.

As a result Adams suffered from the loneliness of too much intelligence, particularly after the suicide of his brilliant, manic-depressive wife in 1885. Like the equally cerebral Lewis Carroll, he sought solace in the company of children. They found him enchanting, which proves he had both tenderness and fantasy—qualities apparent nowhere in *The Education.*

The book's other deficiencies may as well be mentioned here. Some are those of the author as a man—most pronouncedly, envy, timidity, and anti-Semitism. There are unavoidable attritions caused by the passage of time. At least 40 percent of the names Adams drops mean little to us now, while the political issues he belabors are of interest mainly to historians.

Halfway through there is an extraordinary narrative gap of twenty years that Adams does not attempt to bridge. On the contrary, he emphasizes it, making it a "fault" between the plateaus of his youth and age. He almost succeeds in his literary purpose—chapter 21's title still takes the unprepared reader's breath away. Biographically, though, we feel cheated, for the years in question were the most productive of his life, as well as his happiest and saddest. Between 1871 and 1892 he not only married, but instituted a Washington salon, reported on national politics, edited the *North American Review,* taught medieval history at Harvard, and wrote the works that secured his literary fame: *Albert Gallatin* (1879), *Democracy* (1880), *John Randolph* (1882), *Esther* (1884), and one of the major monuments of American learning, *A History of the United States During the Administrations of Jefferson and Madison* (nine volumes, 1889–1891). From 1885 on Adams traveled widely and exotically, but all we get is a vague later image of "wandering over the dark purple ocean, with its purple sense of solitude and void."

The thunderclap muffled by this silence is of course Clover Adams's suicide. Nothing is more strange to us, in an age of leaky "emotions" on the evening news, than denial of intimate memory. But that was part of the nineteenth-century gentlemanly code. Theodore Roosevelt left an identical lacuna in his own autobiography. Although Clover is not so much as mentioned in *The Education,* her husband did memorialize her for all time in the statue he commissioned Augustus Saint-Gaudens to place over her grave. It stands green with age in Rock Creek Cemetery,

Washington, sexless, inscriptionless, overpoweringly beautiful, giving forth only the eloquence of restraint.

CONSIDERING ALL THE above liabilities, why should anybody today want to read *The Education of Henry Adams?* One reason is obvious: Adams is a bewitching writer. In terms of style, only the young Henry James could match him, and even James the Master never attained Adams's unique blend of elegance and erudition. Consider their respective descriptions of Theodore Roosevelt, both composed in 1905. To James, the President was "a wonderful little machine, destined to be over-strained perhaps, but not, as yet, betraying the least creak." The adjective *little* (a tic with James) is patronizing and inaccurate. To Adams, "Roosevelt, more than any other man living within the range of notoriety, showed the singular primitive quality that belongs to ultimate matter—the quality that mediaeval theology assigned to God—he was pure act." Physics, metaphysics, sarcasm, shrewdness: all are here, in a sentence that balances on its key word like a jeweled bearing.

Maybe it is unfair to compare the two commentators, James being essentially a novelist, Adams a historian and philosopher. Yet we should remember that Adams also wrote novels, one of which, *Democracy,* is still required reading in Washington. If he had been less burdened with brains, might he have been capable of another *Wings of the Dove,* or even *The Ambassadors?* There are hints, throughout *The Education,* of repressed sensuality and lyricism (his pagan paean to Maryland spring is quoted by T. S. Eliot in *Gerontion*), and at odd moments between cold stretches of thought, blood and tears surge with a force beyond restraint. Adams's evocation of his seduction by Rome in youth throbs with an extraordinary combination of eroticism and nostalgia:

> Mediaeval Rome was alive: the shadows breathed and glowed, full of soft forms felt by lost senses. No sand-blast of science had yet skinned off the epidermis of history, thought, and feeling. The pictures were uncleaned, the churches unrestored, the ruins unexcavated. . . . One's emotions in Rome were one's private affair,

like one's glass of absinthe before dinner in the Palais Royal: they must be hurtful, else they could not have been so intense; and they were surely immoral.

More powerful still is his account of the loss, to tetanus, of his sister Louisa, in the same city ten years later. It is written from the point of view of the bacillus, as a homicidal lover who gets voluptuous pleasure out of "sabring" a woman to death.

Passages like these prove that Adams had what Keats called "negative capability," a poet's power to live simultaneously in the real and imaginative worlds. Unfortunately, Henry Adams used his mind to cripple, rather than control, his creativity. For every half-sentence such as *The coal-fire smelt homelike; the fog had the fruity taste of youth* there are a dozen paragraphs that have the chill appeal of algebra. One reads them with awe, unmoved.

In the long run, however, Adams's almost inhuman self-discipline pays off. His letters, the most virtuosic ever penned by an American, are more beguiling than *The Education,* yet oddly repulsive *en masse.* Adams the correspondent reveals what Adams the autobiographer manages to conceal: that he lacked generosity. Peevishness darkens the radiant wit, like ink lines leaching through a watercolor. He is contemptuous of politicians and practical achievers, paranoid about Jews, and above all, mistrustful of himself.

The last trait may explain the others, but it is fatal to a confessional style. Hence, no doubt, Adams's inspired decision to write the story of his life in the third person. By forgoing any direct claim to our notice, and downplaying his worldly achievements, he achieves the miracle of making us care for him. Vain, he fights conceit; wise, he presents himself as the archetypal American *naïf,* bent at all costs on getting an education. And how he educates us in the process!

AS THE BOOK (which Adams subtitled "A Study of Twentieth-Century Multiplicity") makes plain, he was courageously modern in his willingness to trade a Virgin for a Dynamo—those being his symbols for the stable, centripetal past and the centrifugal, wildly accelerating present. "What he valued most was Motion, and what attracted his mind was Change."

He believed that Chaos can be controlled, once its hidden energies are understood and embraced, and this speaks to us now even more than his prose style. We, no less than the disillusioned generation that made *The Education* a bestseller in the years immediately after World War I, are confronted by a future that seems to reject old certainties. Just as Adams's first readers had to adjust to a near-total transformation of the world's social and political order, so must his latest confront such imponderables as, say, the decline of print culture in the West, and the unbalancing of gender equilibrium in Eastern abortion clinics.

One can take just these two issues and leaf through *The Education* for evidence of its continuing relevance. Soon enough, the book falls open at:

> Of all movements of inertia, maternity and reproduction are the most typical, and women's property of moving in a constant line forever is ultimate, uniting history in its only unbroken and un-breakable sequence. Whatever else stops, the woman must go on reproducing, as she did in the Siluria of Pteraspis; sex is a vital condition, and race only a local one. If the laws of inertia are to be sought anywhere with certainty, it is in the feminine mind.

By his shock use of the word *mind,* instead of *body,* Adams at once transmits a message of comfort. Unable as he was to imagine social en-gineering by sonogram, much less the free speech of cyberspace, his faith in *das ewig Weibliche* persuades us that sooner or later, oppressed women in China and India will get wise to the manipulation of their wombs by men.

As for all the other *fin de siècle* dreads that perplex us now, they are scarcely worse than the ones that made him shudder (his own, valedic-tory last word in the book) ninety years ago. We can only agree with him that "the mind could gain nothing by flight or by fight: it must merge in its supersensual multiverse, or succumb to it."

Does that sound like Camus? More to the point, does Camus not sound at times like Henry Adams? Or Bertrand Russell in *The ABC of Relativity,* or Lewis Mumford in *The Technics and Civilization,* and Frederick Turner in *Natural Classicism?* Or mock malcontents as various as Samuel Beckett, Marshall McLuhan, and Gore Vidal? The fact that we keep hearing Adams in them, and recognizing figures from our own time on every other page of *The Education* (see the portrait of President Reagan, alias President Grant, in chapter xvii) is proof of the universality of true art. Even if the last weary chapters of the book mix science and theology to the point of incomprehensibility, Henry Adams's pilgrimage from Beacon Hill in 1838 to the Bois de Boulogne in 1905, by way of Wenlock Edge, is both revelatory and humbling.

POOH TO YOU, MR. MAYOR

And Here's Fuzz in Your Eye, Mr. Prime Minister

T HE BRITISH WANT WINNIE-THE-POOH AND HIS FOUR FRIENDS TO *come home. A member of Parliament says the original stuffed animals on which A. A. Milne's beloved stories are based should be taken from a display case at the New York Public Library and returned to England.*

"I saw them recently and they look very unhappy indeed," Labor Party legislator Gwyneth Dunwoody said. "I am not surprised, considering they have been incarcerated in a glass case in a foreign country all these years."

—Associated Press

As an immigrant of British ancestry, who has faithfully gone through all the processes of naturalization, I was dismayed to hear that my child-hood compatriot, Mr. Pooh ("Winnie") Bear, is being compelled to stay in the United States, despite flagrant evidence that he was sneaked into New York illegally forty-two years ago. (By a *publisher*, no less: that alone should have alerted the INS to the certainty of malfeasance.)

Originally published in *The New York Times*, 2 February 1998.
Drawing of Pooh and friend by Ernest Shepard, 1926.

Being a Bear of Very Little Brain, Mr. Pooh was unable to state at the time what he felt about his enforced exile from Great Britain. We can only guess what he feels now about his detention, by order of Mayor Giuliani, in an airless cell in the Donnell Library, along with four even dumber stuffed detainees. He is still a victim, as he was back in those happier, fuzzier days when Christopher Robin used thoughtlessly to drag him around by one leg.

Now *there's* the original villain. According to news reports, it was an older, meaner Christopher Robin Milne who handed Mr. Pooh over to the president of E. P. Dutton in 1947, probably in exchange for a special royalty rate, payable in the blood of other writers.

I must confess that much as I loved Winnie-the-Pooh in childhood, I never could stand C.R., who struck me as a wimp of the first water, with his pudding-bowl haircut and fey tendency to skip. His fundamental (dare I say, girlish?) frivolity was evident in his habit of peeking when he should have been praying:

If I open my fingers a little bit more
I can see Nanny's dressing-gown on the door.
*It's a beautiful blue, but it hasn't a hood. . . .**

Enough, young perv, we've quite understood!

There was also his unseemly interest in Alice, the housemaid, "marrying one of the Guard." I always had my suspicions that C.R. cared less for Alice than the juicy Grenadier she stepped out with. Whatever the case, he had no right in middle age to deport Messrs. Pooh, Piglet, Tigger, Roo, and Eeyore (the last-named clearly a mental deficient, who should have been excluded under U.S. immigration law).

We should allow Mr. Milne, I suppose, a certain degree of disenchantment with their company. It cannot have been easy for him as a lad to have to live with a toy whose extraordinary popularity outweighed his own. Weight, indeed, was key. Wherever little C.R. went, Pooh was always lumpishly *there*, a ponderous piece of baggage quashing all his at-

* A. A. Milne, "Vespers" (1923).

286 THIS LIVING HAND

tempts to be perceived as an independent person. I've often wondered with what emotions Mr. Milne must have read Delmore Schwartz's poem:

> The heavy bear who goes with me
> A manifold honey to smear his face,
> Clumsy and lumbering here and there,
> The central ton of every place . . .

Schwartz was writing about the "withness" of his own body, but I do not doubt that Mr. Milne, by 1947, felt that Pooh had grown too corporeal for comfort. So he elected for major surgery.

The sad irony, though, is that Pooh was the least mortal part of him. In banishing the Bear overseas, he neither enriched American civilization nor enhanced his own image. Pooh remains as immutably English as Raggedy Ann and Andy are rightful progeny of God's Own Country. For as long as Mayor Giuliani insists on retaining the Milne menagerie stateside (where's Owl, by the way?), there will remain some corner of a foreign library that is forever England. There shall be in the dust of that glass box

> . . . a richer dust concealed,
> A dust whom England bore, shaped, made aware,
> Gave, once, her flowers to love, her ways to roam,
> A body of England's, breathing English air,
> Washed by the rivers, blest by suns of home.

I say, repatriate the Donnell Five, and pronto. Otherwise we'll end up paying their Social Security.

A CERTAIN SILLINESS

Ten Literati Choose the Century's Greatest English Novels

As ONE OF THE TWELVE MOSTLY MALE, WHITE-ON-WHITE, MIDDLE-AGED members of the Modern Library's editorial board, I suppose I should stick up for our list of the "Hundred Greatest Novels of the Twentieth Century." We debated our choices over many ruminative lunches (*ruminare*, to chew on: a necessary exercise when you're browsing at the Century Club). There was no shortage of eligible titles. Harry Evans, who dreamed up the idea in the first place, casually asked us to each provide a personal selection of a hundred favorite novels. If we had taken him at his word, the resulting master list—allowing for a duplication rate of, say, twenty-five titles that everybody was likely to nominate—would have totaled something like 750.

Originally published in *The New York Times Book Review*, 3 August 1998.
The Butterfly Tree. *Art from Dryicons.com.*

Fortunately none of us managed to come up with that many. I haven't read a hundred "great" twentieth-century novels in my life (although I must have read *some* a hundred times), and rather embarrassedly handed in a list of thirty-seven. Of course we all kept our lists secret from one another. Only the managing director of the Modern Library knows the true poverty of our erudition. I'm sure A. S. (Antonia) Byatt had no trouble filling her quota, since it is clear from her cultivated conversation that she has read and memorized every work of fiction published since Boccaccio's *Filocolo.* And I'm sure Shelby Foote built his list on an irreducible minimum of twenty-three titles, that being the entire *oeuvre* of William Faulkner. At any rate, we ended up with an aggregate of 404 novels, with *Lolita* at number one and Alice Walker's *The Color Purple* in the position commonly euphemized as "last but not least."

Those two rankings seemed to me about right, if only because I had just finished reading *Lolita* for the eighth time (in Alfred Appel's fascinatingly detailed annotated edition) and was, as usual, in a state of despair over the impossibility of ever writing prose that could compare with any of the flashing, floating lines that Nabokov released with such lepidopteral prodigality: *At the bottom of the hill, in the summer dusk; a furry warmth, golden midges.*

As for Alice Walker, I did make an early attempt to get my colleagues to exclude altogether any author who described herself as a practitioner of "womanist" fiction, but was met with such steely stares from Tony Byatt and Ann Godoff that I withdrew the motion, and thenceforth voted for every nominee who didn't shave.

There were other tense moments, inevitable when you have ten literary sensibilities demonstrating over and over again the old truism that everybody reacts differently to everything. Or to put it another way, one man's Arnold Bennett is another woman's Chinua Achebe. There is as much polite aggression in "book chat" as you will hear in, say, bipartisan conferences at the White House. When Harry made it clear, early on, that we should confine ourselves to novelists writing in the English language, I applauded the restriction on the ground that it disqualified Faulkner. Shelby Foote is the soul of Southern courtesy, but ever since then I have been aware of an invisible Mason-Dixon Line stretching between us.

Arthur Schlesinger scoffed heartily at Dan Boorstin's suggestion that we narrow our list by nominating only one book per writer, saying that if Henry James came up with three twentieth-century masterpieces in a row, then each should be eligible on its merits. For a moment, Arthur was my literary hero, but then he spoiled it by speaking so slightingly of *Brideshead Revisited* that I was tempted to have at him with the bread rolls. He made up for it, however, by pleading for the inclusion of some of Evelyn Waugh's earlier, savagely funny novels, two of which show up with *Brideshead* on our final list.

Notwithstanding my love for Dolores Haze, I had to agree, as *Ulysses* began to rise like a great whale to the top of our subsequent polls, that no other novel of the century bulks as large, nor gives off such wild underwater music. Nor do I recall much dispute—how could there be?—over *The Great Gatsby*. But what *Brave New World* and *Portrait of the Artist as a Young Man* are doing in the Top Five instead of, say, *The Ambassadors* and *A Passage to India* is a mystery explicable, I should think, only by statisticians who understand the mathematics of voting. Huxley's novel is a scintillating social satire, its riffs on cloning and child sex amazingly relevant today, but clever rather than great, and Joyce's is really an autobiography—for all its poignancy, no more a novel than Nabokov's far superior *Speak, Memory*.

The trouble with group decisions, as anyone who has ever followed piano competitions knows, is that the uniqueness of this or that contender, or the urgency of this or that judge, tends to be blunted by the smoothing-out of democratic process. In our case, although we had all read *Ulysses* (or pretended to) many of us had not read the less well-known books that judges individually pushed for. Ms. Byatt, for example, spoke so eloquently about Peter Carey's *Oscar and Lucinda* that I was sorry to admit I'd never heard of it. I'm sure she's right, because anything she says must be taken seriously, but one can't vote for a book one hasn't read. For the same reason, I could not get any support for some of my own more *outré* recommendations—an achingly beautiful little novel by A. G. Mojtabai, entitled *Autumn* (1983); another meriting exactly the same adjectives, *A Month in the Country* by J. L. Carr (1980); a melancholy comedy by the South African novelist Ahmed Essop, *The Visitation* (1979); and above all James Gould Cozzens's forgotten master-piece *Guard of Honor* (1948). Again, if anyone else had read them, these books might have stood a chance. But nobody had, so they didn't.

As a result, our list consisted in large part of Usual Suspects, ar-ranged in an order only approximating to the way God might rate them. (I would hope that He, in His wisdom, would swap *Slaughterhouse-Five* at No. 18 and *A House for Mr. Biswas* at No. 72.) But a certain silliness is bound to ensue when a bunch of adults are given a sheet of paper with titles down one margin and boxes spread out from left to right and are asked to draw in little crosses, no more than one per line. (Damn! I would have voted for Molly Keane's *Good Behaviour* ten times!)

Critics of our list are right when they say it values past over present writing, and Eurocentricity, if there is such a word, over Ethnicity. Willy Whitebread no longer represents the English-speaking world's literary norm. Every novelist of note in Britain these days seems to be an Indian. Personally I'd welcome the recruitment of some younger, darker people to our board. And the more women the better: they tend to be franker in their opinions. (By the way, we did have a black female writer on the panel when we started out, in the person of Maya Angelou, but she at-tended no meetings and sent in no votes.)

Imbalance is something Random House can correct. There has been a move afoot for some time to expand and diversify our board's member-ship. But we can't do much about presentism. The Modern Library's mandate is to perpetuate titles that have, as the cliché goes, stood the test of time. Most new novels are shipped back to the publisher after only six weeks in the store. How are we even to hear of them, let alone read them?

I did make one gesture in the direction of contemporary fiction by suggesting that we nominate only the Ninety-nine Greatest Novels of the Twentieth Century, and leave the hundredth title up to a nationwide vote on the Internet—announcing it on the last day of the millennium. Rather a neat publicity idea, I thought, and likely to produce a genuinely great book, but the silence that followed this suggestion reminded me of that image in *The Ambassadors* when Strether makes a remark to Maria

Gostrey and waits to hear it plop in the well of her habitual taciturnity. Except now there was no plop at all.

Having a seat on the Modern Library's editorial board is an honor that I cherish, but I'm sure I'm not the only judge who secretly feels that all lists are fundamentally silly. They sure attract attention, though. I suppose that was Harry Evans's main intent in coming up with this idea: if a million or so more readers can be made aware of works such as Henry Green's *Loving*, Richard Wright's *Native Son*, and Sherwood Anderson's *Winesburg, Ohio*, then we'll at least have done something to perpetuate the power of the written word. Now we can go back to our regular business of republishing the books we are sure will endure. One of these, I'm happy to say, is *Guard of Honor.*

In the meantime, if any contemporary novelist has a "great" work under his belt (or her girdle), I'd suggest delaying publication until after the millennium. Then you might make our next list.

BILL LIAR

Proceedings of an extraordinary meeting of
the Ananias Club, 19 August, 1998. Theodore Roosevelt,
chairman. Agenda: Admission to membership of
President William Jefferson Clinton

ROOSEVELT Gentlemen, dee-lighted to see you all again. As some older members will recall, I founded this society in 1903, when I was President of the United States, for the express purpose of creating a hall of fame for liars. I am required by the charter to remind you that the club is named after Ananias, the most mendacious figure in biblical history, whose portrait hangs behind me, and whose ass's ears tastefully ornament our stationery. As is also customary, I will now read the charter's declaration of principles: *To act as a place of refuge for all men who publicly and mendaciously lie, obfuscate, or otherwise abuse plain speech, in order to protect their own interests and insult the intelligence of others. No applications for membership may be accepted from liars themselves, since such applications must by definition be untrustworthy. Nominations will be made solely by the chairman—*

Unpublished, August 1998.
Nineteenth-century engraving.

O. J. SIMPSON 'Scuse me, your honor—

ROOSEVELT "Mr. President" will do.

O. J. SIMPSON Pardon me, them words just spring to my lips. Like, I'm a fairly new member, and what I want to know is, how come *you* belong here? I read in a book where you were a pretty honest fellow.

ROOSEVELT I don't "belong," I only occupy this chair. That's the whole point of the Ananias Club charter, you see. *Somebody* has to be honest, or the nomination system won't work. I submit the names—you gentlemen decide if the nominee is your kind of man.

LILLIAN HELLMAN Man? What's with this sexist stuff? Haven't you heard of the women's liberation movement?

ROOSEVELT I apologize, madam. Nobody questions your right to be in this room. Now, I have a new nominee to present. Do we have a quorum?

GARY HART No.

ROOSEVELT That means yes. I hereby submit the name of the Honorable William Jefferson—

JOSEPH McCARTHY Objection!

ROOSEVELT Senator?

McCARTHY Gonna have to drop that title if he wants in get in here. Anybody "honorable" don't qualify.

ROOSEVELT A certain amount of honor inheres in the *office* of President of the United States. In that sense, Mr. Clinton remains "honorable" as long as he clings to his job. But if you gentlemen, and (*hastily*) Miss Hellman here agree that he is one of your kind, he qualifies for membership, and automatically drops the title as soon as he is inducted.

RICHARD NIXON What has he done that's so terrible? This President is not a crook.

EDWARD KENNEDY Careful what you say, Dick. He could sue you for libel.

NIXON Aw, go take a swim.

RONALD REAGAN I did not trade arms for hostages.

ROOSEVELT Order, order. Mr. Clinton's qualifications are as

follows. On 26 January 1998, in reference to allegations that he smoked marijuana at college, he smoothly stated, "I did not break the laws of my country."

MONICA LEWINSKY That's true. Bill never smoked dope in his life. (*Fondly*) He's a cigar aficionado.

NIXON Teddy, if you're gonna read the whole list of his derelictions before he became President, we'll be here all [*expletive deleted*] night. I move the list be taken as read.

LILLIAN HELLMAN Seconded.

AL SHARPTON Thirded.

O. J. SIMPSON Huh?

ROOSEVELT Well, then, we will consider his recent confession that he was lying when he told a national television audience, seven months ago, "I did not have sex with that woman—Ms. Lewinsky." (*Sigh*) You know, when I was in the White House, we used to think of the Presidency as a bully pulpit.

NIXON Cut the crap, Teddy. You can't sermonize there anymore. Look what bible-thumping did for Jimmy Carter.

REV. JAMES SWAGGART Ah thought Bill preached pretty good the other night. Said as how he'd included th' Almighty in his agonizin', along of Miz Hillary.

MONICA LEWINSKY He brought in Reverend Jesse Jackson too. That shows true humility.

MARION BARRY (*Guffawing*) What you been smoking, honey? Anybody wanna defend their ass on TV, they call Jesse. Dude talks more head than Doris Kearns Goodwin.

RONALD REAGAN I did not, repeat not, trade arms for hostages.

NIXON (*Contemptuously*) I thought Clinton's performance stunk. Not only did he fail to discuss the effect of oral sex on our relations with China, he just didn't look *haggard* enough. No lip-licking, no sweat, just anger at being found out. Anger's okay—hell, I used to get pretty mad at prosecutors myself—but you gotta be able to fake contrition. When I gave my Checkers speech—

ROOSEVELT By "fake," as a member of the Ananias Club, I take it you mean "real."

NIXON I mean real fake. The genuine thing. You gotta *know* you're fake in order to *look* fake.

ROOSEVELT I'm not sure I understand.

NIXON (*Sympathetically*) Sure you don't, Teddy. That's why you'll never be able to be a member of your own club. Now, I'm not saying Bill's not mendacious. I'm just saying that he lies too casually to merit our respect. Us guys are professional liars—

ENGLISH VOICE Hear, hear.

NIXON We take mendacity seriously. Pride ourselves on the creativity of our lies. Like Joe McCarthy here and that list of Commies in his hand. (*Applause*) I say, let's hold off on Bill until he's come up with a lie that people will believe. After all, if we can't trust our President to mislead us, whom *can* we trust?

ROOSEVELT (*Wearily*) This is all too subtle for me. I'm a hundred and forty years old, and the simple things I use to believe in—truth-telling in high office, faithfulness to one's vows, reverence for women and protectiveness toward children, dignity, manners—

HELLMAN Yadda, yadda. Let's vote, I need a drink. Who's for having the Formerly Honorable join us? All those in favor say nay. (*A chorus of negative shouts drowns out* NIXON's *surly "Aye!"*)

ROOSEVELT Well, that sounds pretty unanimous. William Jefferson Clinton is hereby admitted *dishonoris causa* to the Ananias Club. Sir, did you want to add something?

ENGLISH VOICE Yes. I'm Professor Arthur S. Woodward, discoverer of Piltdown Man. Couldn't help noticing that Mrs. Clinton said through her spokesperson yesterday that she remained innocent of her husband's affair with Ms. Lewinsky until this weekend. In view of the fact that Sapphira, wife of our patron Ananias, was also punished by St. Peter for flagrant falsity, may I suggest that— (*More shouts and applause*)

ROOSEVELT All right, she's admitted too. Never let it be said, Ms. Hellman, that this club discriminates against women.

HERE COMES OLD RUSHING STARLIGHT

The Writing Life

THE ENGLISH NOVELIST HOWARD SPRING IS FORGOTTEN NOW EVEN
in England, although he was popular a generation ago. I devoured several of his long novels then, but recall little of them except the haunting
cadence of their titles: *Time and the Hour, There Is No Armour, These Lovers
Fled Away.* Yet I can recite to this day a paragraph of self-description that
Spring contributed to the back cover flap of *The Houses in Between,* under
a mildly owlish photograph of himself:

> I can think of nothing more pleasurable than to sit down of a
> winter's night, before a bright fire, with a ream of clean paper
> before me, and ink, and my old wooden pen. It cost me a penny

Originally published in *The Washington Post Book World,* 27 September 1998.
Photograph by Barbara M. Bachman.

when I was a boy, this pen, and with a relay of steel nibs it has lasted me the whole of my writing life.

I embraced Spring's ideal of "pleasurable" employment as my ideal too, and vowed that I would one day live and work like him. Winter nights were in short supply in equatorial Africa, where I grew up, but paper and ink and wooden pens were not, so I perpetrated many novels (mainly about airplanes) and poems (mainly about girls) in handwriting so dreadful that my mother decided to teach me the Spencerian script she had herself been taught as a child.

"Nobody will ever read your stories," she sensibly remarked, "if your writing looks like a *siafu* fell into the inkwell and had to walk across the page to dry himself off."

She was alluding to the large red "safari" ant, invader of many a Kenyan picnic, and the aptness of her simile, not to mention its originality, persuaded me to practice looping *f*'s and *l*'s and upslashing *q*'s— separately at first, then conjunctively—in a lined exercise book whose coarse paper made the smallest blot swell to Rorschachian proportions. Mother would write words such as *hopscotch* on the right-hand page with her Parker 51 (black and sleek, chrome-capped, discharging graceful curlicues of Royal Blue Quink), while I scratched painful imitations on the left, my own dribbly dip-pen staining my finger ends and invariably running out just as I was trying to negotiate the difficult transition from *p* to *s*. After several months, mastery suddenly came, and I developed a flowing orthodox script, about as impersonal as the copperplate of a clerk.

In this hand, at high school, I experimented with blank verse, and under the influence of Dylan Thomas came up with a line that I believed might qualify me for the Poet's Corner in Westminster Abbey. It ran as follows:

Her eyes were not eyes, but portals full of rushing starlight.

I declaimed it to the chaps in Form 2A, and they reacted with loud raspberries. "Here comes old Rushing Starlight!" they would yell, whenever they saw me after that. Pitying them for their ignorance of the finer points of poetic style, I consoled myself with dreams of having a study one day like Howard Spring's—paneled, book-lined, secluded—where I could be alone with my starlit thoughts. And paper, and ink.

IT TOOK A WHILE, but in 1976, through the generosity of the Theodore Roosevelt Association, I was given use of its defunct library adjoining TR's Birthplace Museum, in what is now called the Flatiron District of Manhattan. I had gotten a contract to write a "short, popular" biography of the twenty-sixth President, and needed an office in town that would meet the above specifications. To my delight, this one did. It was oak-lined from floor to ceiling, hung with heavy drapes, stacked with nice peppery-smelling old volumes, and furnished with a massive desk and couch. There was even a fireplace, but I was forbidden to bring in logs, for fear of burning down a National Historic Site.

As for paper, I discovered while clearing some shelves a stash of thick, marble-smooth certificate bond, eleven and a half inches by seventeen, untouched since 1938, proof positive that God had brought me to this place for a good reason. I discarded the top dust-powdered sheet and the bottom scuffed one, vacuumed the edges of the others, and when I had finished sneezing, sat down and wrote the word *Prologue*.

After that, inspiration deserted me. I spent the rest of the day listening to the chimes of the Metropolitan Life clock tower on Twenty-third Street, the only outside sounds that penetrated the library. Its silence, and the blank page shimmering on my desktop, made me understand for the first time the full horror of the phrase *writer's block*.

Indeed I remained blocked for the next several days, to the point that my stomach muscles began to mime the Laocoön—about as near my body has ever gotten to Greek sculpture. One morning I tried to relax on the couch, closed my eyes, and in walked P. James Roosevelt, president of the TRA, on one of his rare visits to town.

"Getting a lot done?" he inquired pleasantly.

That afternoon, perhaps because of the shock, words began to uncurl from the nib of my fountain pen. (Love that compound noun. *Fountain pen*, the source from which the best prose flows, except in a dry season.)* I enjoyed the soft wet scratching sound of fresh letters as they linked up—no longer in copperplate, but in handwriting that was at least clear and evenly suspended above the whiteness below: sentences skeining west to east, a book in flight. I grew to prize the silence, even the minisilences that fell between one word and the next, and to this day, when words won't come, I listen for them rather than look for them. Sooner or later one that *sounds* right will whisper itself onto the page.

After about six months of leaving me alone (I took out my own, extremely voluminous trash), the National Park Service sent in an emissary. He was a young maintenance man who clearly thought I was insane. " 'Scuse me sir, gotta take down those drapes to dry-clean."

"Go ahead," I told him, and continued to work as he mounted a stepladder and detached the curtains, ring by ring. I sensed that he could not wait to unhook them all. His movements became more and more agitated. Eventually he said, in a voice high with panic, "Man, it's so *quiet* in here! Ain't you got a radio?"

"EVERY WORD THAT YOU WRITE," Saint Bernard of Clairvaux once observed, "is a blow that smites the devil." Four years and 250,000 blows later, *The Rise of Theodore Roosevelt* was done, and the devil smitten into temporary retreat. Since then I have become, *Deo gratias,* a writer able to afford the occasional fresh ream of certificate bond. My study is not paneled, but Howard Spring visits in spirit, and seems to find it congenial.

Looking at myself in the mirror recently (on a bad gray hair day) I noticed that I have begun to look like him. Maybe in time I'll be able to match his splendid fecundity. If not, I can always blame this damn pen. Now, if I could only find out where he bought his steel nibs. . . .

* See page 64.

INSIDE JEFFERSON'S CEREBELLUM

The Library of Congress

To WORK IN THE CIRCULAR, CENTRAL READING ROOM OF THE LIBRARY of Congress is to get the surreal impression that one is inside Thomas Jefferson's cerebellum. This vast yet intimate space was designed, a century ago, around our third President's book collection, sold to the nation after the original Library was destroyed in the War of 1812. Brain-like, it silently throbs with knowledge, and invisible connections—fact to fact, thought to thought, thesis to antithesis—flash back and forth at who knows how many million times a minute, whenever we lesser scholars (small cell clusters in comparison!) puzzle out our own connections below.

Copyright © by Edmund Morris. Originally published in James Conaway, *America's Library: The Story of the Library of Congress, 1800–2000* (Yale University Press, 2000).

Dome of the Jefferson Building. Library of Congress photograph.

One also has the notion, after the skylights have darkened and that spell-breaking call, "The Library is now closed," has echoed through the room, that (just as Jefferson's brain, presumably, never stopped while he slept) the silent intellectual exchange will continue through the night. For books do talk to books, in an osmotic sort of way, at least when they are juxtaposed in the Library of Congress's unique groupings—subjects thematically sequential, authors deliberately dissociated in alphabetical order. Else why, under this dome as no other, does one return to one's seat for another day of research with a sense of new possibilities opening up, fresh ideas proliferating even before one cracks the first volume on overnight hold?

TWENTY-THREE YEARS AGO I came to the Library of Congress as a young, would-be biographer anxious to learn as much as could be learned about Theodore Roosevelt (after Jefferson, the most cerebral of our presidents, and himself an avid patron). The Manuscript Division in those days occupied a pleasant room in the John Adams Building, with big lockers outside ample for the storage of my suitcase. I lived in New York on the usual scribe's pittance, and research time was so precious that I habitually did without lunch, and drank as little water as possible from the corridor fountain, in order to reduce further forays to a minimum. The documents emerging sheet by sheet from "pulled" boxes (this was before the age of mass microfilming) were so fascinating to read, and so tactile in their perfect state of preservation, that I felt myself to be living, all day long, in the nineteenth century—a state of "time out of mind" familiar to most biographers.

For some reason I recall, as a particularly evocative discovery, an item that tumbled, not out of a Roosevelt box, but an envelope in the collection of President McKinley. (Already the osmotic impulse was at work, and my researches were proceeding from one collection to the next.) It was neither manuscript nor print, but a swatch of white silk strips, still lustrous after seventy-eight years, each carefully signed "Wm. McKinley." They were probably presidential keepsakes, handed out to important White House visitors, much as ballpoint pens are today. But their cool lightness in my hand, and the slight bleed of those repetitive signatures, made me feel I was back "in the days of McKinley"—to borrow the title of Margaret Leech's great biography, also researched here.

I remember marveling, as I slipped the swatch back into its envelope, that the privilege of being able to find it and touch it and think about it, *was free*, a gift of Congress to me as an American citizen. Minor as the find was, it might just as easily have been major, as when Daniel J. Boorstin, appointed Librarian of Congress in 1975, opened a little safe in the Thomas Jefferson Building and discovered the last contents of Abraham Lincoln's pockets, forgotten for more than a century. We were both of us—Librarian and scribe—beneficiaries of the world's most generous cornucopia of cultural and historical riches.

THE MANUSCRIPT DIVISION has long since moved out of Adams, to new quarters in the James Madison Memorial Building—third and largest (so far!) of the Library's ever-growing complex. Dr. Boorstin has been succeeded by James Billington, as Dr. Billington will himself one day give way to another in the long line of Librarians of Congress. Every time I wander back into the Main Reading Room (and I have been doing so, now, about once a week, often every day, for two decades), I am enriched. A textbook of metallurgy lying open beside a copying machine will hypnotize me with the cold precision of its language, yielding a phrase or two that may come in for metaphorical use some day. A poster by an elevator will direct me to a lecture on repetitive stress syndrome, or a seminar on medieval cartography. A display cabinet of French daguerreotypes will persuade me that Cléo de Mérode was the most beautiful woman who ever lived.

But such encounters are serendipitous. Perhaps I can best convey the Library's limitless powers to inform, inspire, and stretch the mind by citing some of the intellectual journeys it has sent me on as a freelance writer. The reader should bear in mind that I am but one of uncounted millions of scholar gypsies, all with their own travel stories to tell.

There were, to begin with, the private diaries of Theodore Roosevelt, which he kept almost daily as a college student and young New York State assemblyman from 1876 to 1884. I had seen extracts from them in the writings of many Roosevelt scholars, but nothing in biographical research compares with the actual perusal of words written, long ago, by a living hand. I read them through, day by day and year by year, and in the process developed an almost physical intimacy with my subject: looking over his shoulder, as it were, and sharing the thoughts that spilled out of his pen.

Just as eloquent, if less consciously autobiographical, was the extraordinary archive of receipts amassed some fourteen years later when TR, as assistant secretary of the Navy, was a member of a luncheon group trying to overcome the McKinley Administration's resistance to a war with Spain over Cuba. Every one of these almost daily receipts was for "double lamb chops." Unremarkable in themselves, they together painted a portrait of a man so obsessed with political intrigue that he regarded food as mere fuel.

The contemporary policy of the Library of Congress is no longer to accept such ephemera in collections. No doubt this makes storage sense, in an age when public figures are accumulating more and more pieces of paper (and revealing less and less on them), but future biographers will be the poorer.

Fifteen years ago my wife embarked on a biography of Clare Boothe Luce, whose manuscript collection, larger than those of many presidents, is one of the Library's most important twentieth-century archives. Massive as it is, it has the usual lacunae that conspire to frustrate biographers. Mrs. Luce preserved a 1928 obituary of her father—a brilliant musician who spent much of his life as a traveling salesman—that says that at the time of his death in Los Angeles, he had been working on a series of transcendental exercises for the violin, playable only by performers of Paganini-like technique. There is no indication in the obituary, nor indeed anywhere else in the Luce collection, as to what had happened to this improbable-sounding manuscript.

My wife mentioned it to me one day in the Madison Building cafeteria. Acting on what I can describe only as a scholarly whim, I dropped into the Music Division, six floors down, riffled through a card catalog, and in less than a minute found the entry, BOOTHE, *William Franklin— Fingered Octaves and Primary Extension Exercises. Unpublished pencil and ink ms., 18 pp, 1931. Gift of Ruth Paddock Hutchinson, December, 1931.* Fifteen minutes later—about as long as it took for me to summon my wife from the nearby Manuscript Division—the precious artifact was in her hands. Meanwhile, a new avenue of research was opening up: who was the mysterious Mrs. Hutchinson, and why should she have chosen to deposit these eighteen fly-specked sheets here, unaware that William Boothe's daughter would one day enrich the Library of Congress too?

So go the endless byways of biography.

WHEN THE MADISON BUILDING was first opened in 1980, one of its most tempting new features was an array of "reading rooms" in the Music Division, equipped with Steinway pianos and massively sound-proofed walls. Lacking an instrument at home, I became an habitué of these rooms, rejoicing particularly in the big grand in No. 11. Library regulations grant free access to such instruments, providing they are used for serious study of materials in the Music Division's holdings. Thus, when researching an essay on the Romantic Piano for *The New Yorker*, I was able to explore the works of Ferruccio Busoni *seriatim*, and write about them from the perspective of a piano player who had liter-ally "felt" his way through that strange composer's harmonies.*

While serving as a freelance music critic for *The Washington Post*, I have used the Music Division to prepare for assigned concerts. I have held in my hands—even furtively sniffed—the manuscript of Anton We-bern's String Quartet, Op. 28. To see the precision with which Webern inked every note with its attendant accidental (like the scintilla of a spar-klet), and then to hear those notes materialize as music five hours later (skittering and whispering in the Kennedy Center's Terrace Theater) was to experience the totality of musical creation, from mind to hand to paper to bow to string to sound.

This essay, I notice, constantly evokes tactile values—nothing being more "primary," in archival research, than contact between source and scholar. The microfilm machine and the computer screen, not to men-tion *fin de siècle* needs for security and preservation, are making such moments of total empathy less and less attainable. More's the pity. But

---

* See p. 185.

the Library of Congress, through the sheer quantity of its holdings, still offers abundant opportunities to "only connect."

I recall, for example, the timbre of Justice Oliver Wendell Holmes's ninety-year-old voice reverberating in my earphones, on a morning in the Sound Division when I also listened to an air check of Rosa Ponselle singing Verdi in 1933, and Ronald Reagan breathily informing the National Press Club in 1971 that Washington was a nice place, "but I wouldn't want to live here."

Each of these auditory experiences gave life to sentences or phrases in literary projects I was working on at the time. On other occasions, I have pored over fire insurance maps of Midwestern villages, so minutely detailed that one can literally count the windows of every house, and tell whether they were glazed or screened; the purplish pages of a run of the London *Daily Mirror*, published at the height of the Blitz and remarkable for the number of its laxative advertisements; boxes of Depression-era glossies by the superb WPA photographer Marion Post Wolcott, some so freshly preserved they still gave off a faint reek of the darkroom; obscene, uproarious, feverishly inventive counterculture "comix" from the radical Sixties; politico-satirical poems from the age of Samuel Johnson; and a complete sequence of translations of Wolfram von Eschenbach's *Parzival*, which the Jefferson Room's uniquely long reading surfaces enabled me to lay out chronologically from left to right, so that I could (as it were) perambulate, page by page, through a hundred years of changing semantics and sensibilities.

I have sat at a Moviola machine playing with a pristine print of Michelangelo Antonioni's movie *Zabriskie Point*, manually shifting a few frames back and forth and watching its famous sabotaged mansion exploding and imploding in the dry desert sky. I have seen Jorge Bolet, at a master class in the Coolidge Auditorium, advise young pianists to perform bravura single-octave passages with the left hand alone, "because it looks better." In the Mary Pickford Theater, I have watched a screening of *Destination Moon* (1950), not, I confess, for any intellectual purpose, but out of a sense of debt to a ten-year-old Kenya boy who once cried bitterly at being barred from this sci-fi classic. I have attended biographical symposiums, presidential dinners, folk festivals, cartoon exhibitions, academic councils, Poet Laureate recitations, and a sublime, evening-length traversal of Bach's *Art of the Fugue,* arranged for the Library's Stradivarius string quartet. And times without number, I have stood at sunset on the fifth floor of the Adams Building, watching the Jefferson's copper dome turning rose, then violet as the lights beneath twinkle on.

Those lights, those glowing rectangles and portholes, are windows into the central repository of our nation's cultural intelligence: a cere-bellum, a sanctum that will be forever catholicized by the spirit of Thomas Jefferson.

INTELLECTUAL INTEGRITY

The Novels of James Gould Cozzens

To THE BEST OF MY KNOWLEDGE, RONALD REAGAN HAD NO ACQUAIN-
tance with the prose works of James Gould Cozzens.

The two men did share, however, one area of mutual experience. Between 1942 and 1945 they pursued almost exactly simultaneous military careers, as paper pushers within the vast bureaucracy of the Army
Air Forces. Reagan told me that he learned all he wanted to know about
federal procedure when he applied to the Pentagon for permission to destroy a warehouseful of redundant personnel records. General Hap Arnold's office told him to go ahead, but to make sure all the documents
were copied before he trashed them.

Keynote address at James Gould Cozzens Symposium, University of South Carolina, 15 September
2003.

Photograph of Cozzens by Jo H. Chamberlin, 1944.

Because both Captain Reagan and Captain Cozzens specialized in documents to do with training and public relations, I have naturally combed through *A Time of War,* Matthew J. Bruccoli's invaluable edition of Cozzens's Air Force diaries and Pentagon memos, hoping I might find somewhere an indication that the future President of the United States and the future author of *Guard of Honor* might have corresponded, or even possibly met. I did come across some diary references to meetings early in 1944 between Cozzens and Lieutenant Colonel Owen Crump, Reagan's commanding officer, but—alas, no Gipper. However, Dr. Bruccoli was not able to print more than a fraction of the memos that Cozzens sent out during those long war years. Who knows, some of them might have winged their way to the First Motion Picture Unit in Culver City, California, attention Captain Ronald W. Reagan, Adjutant. In which case I'll have to amend that crack I made just now about Reagan not having any acquaintance with the prose works of James Gould Cozzens.

A FEW WORDS about Cozzens, who was born in Chicago in 1903 and died in Florida in 1978. His life can be summarized more rapidly than that of most great novelists, because, as Dr. Bruccoli observed at the beginning of the only biography of him,[*] "he just stayed home and wrote." He was of blue-blooded Yankee descent, and was educated at the Kent School in Connecticut and at Harvard University. Even before attending Harvard in 1922 he knew that he wanted to be a writer, and only a writer. He published his first novel, *Confusion,* in his sophomore year, following up with three more apprentice novels between 1925 and 1929. During these years he traveled some, then, in an excellent career move, married his literary agent, Sylvia Baumgarten, and settled in Lambertville, New Jersey. They had no children. For the rest of his life, with the exception of the war three years I've mentioned, he "stayed at home and wrote."

In 1930, at the age of twenty-six, Cozzens wrote the opening line of his first mature novel. Already he had lost interest in fine literary style. I'll read it to you in all its craggy plainness:

[*] Matthew J. Bruccoli, *James Gould Cozzens: A Life Apart* (San Diego, 1983).

June 7, Friday, in the morning, the twin-screw turbine liner *San Pedro*, seventeen thousand tons, lay at her Hoboken pier.

With that sentence, so freighted with facts, began a novelist's career that for dedication, craftsmanship, textual richness, slow attainment of world fame, and final critical destruction has no parallel in our literary history. *S.S. San Pedro* (1931), *The Last Adam* (1933), *Castaway* (1934), *Men and Brethren* (1936), *Ask Me Tomorrow* (1940), and *The Just and the Unjust* (1942) established James Gould Cozzens as a novelist of uncompromising discipline and probity, concerned with the moral struggles of virtuous but fallible men, always in tightly constricted dramatic circumstances. To him, as to Dorothy L. Sayers, "intellectual integrity was the one great permanent value in an emotionally unstable world."

Then he went into the Army in 1943, and found at last a subject big enough for his all-encompassing intellect.

COZZENS TOOK THE military bureaucracy seriously—as indeed he took most things. His prewar career as a writer of fiction hardly qualified him for assignment to the Training Aids Directorate in Washington, and then to the Office of Information Services in the Pentagon. But all his superiors cared was that he knew how to feed paper into a typewriter. That was literary genius enough for Uncle Sam. As it happened, Cozzens *was* a genius. (I don't use that hackneyed word lightly: James Gould Cozzens is, apart from Vladimir Nabokov and Evelyn Waugh, in my opinion the only English-language writer of the past half century who could be called a genius—largely on the strength of *Guard of Honor.*)* Most novelists would consider their talents wasted on the production of Army prose. Fortunately, Cozzens was by nature a writer who preferred nouns over adjectives and simple similes over complex metaphors. So he had no difficulty in adapting himself to the basic mantra of military behavior, "How would I do this if I was a fool?"

What was less easy was learning to suffer fools gladly. Cozzens had never been able to do that, and later in life, arrogance was to be his undo-

---

* At the time of this lecture, the author had not yet read the works of W. G. Sebald.

ing. But in 1942, at thirty-nine years of age, he realized (much as thirty-nine-year-old Evelyn Waugh was realizing, in the Royal Marines) that God, or General Arnold, had handed him a literary gift. This was the opportunity, at a time in life when a novelist's supply of youthfully acquired raw material—Waugh called it "capital"—has more or less run out, to quit the ivory tower and reenter the world of primary experience: new faces and new forces to contend with, vital challenges and consequences to face. Not only that, but to have it happen in wartime, when human relationships are intensified and accelerated and the basic questions of existence become more fraught; when political conferences really do decide fate, and even the most trivial actions, personal or military, can precipitate catastrophe. What writer could ignore such dumb luck?

Cozzens kept a detailed diary of what went on at the office, knowing that no matter how sterile it might seem in its daily, dryasdust accumulation, it would one day, when watered with memory and fertilized with desire, produce a plant. How huge and multifoliate that plant would prove to be, he at first had no idea. But as connoisseurs of fine fiction discovered in 1948, and have been rediscovering ever since, the soil of James Gould Cozzens's Air Force service produced the greatest American novel of World War II.

Similar claims, with a British inflection, have been made with respect to Evelyn Waugh's *Sword of Honor* trilogy, which resembles *Guard of Honor* only in its massive scope and preoccupation with military procedure. Further comparisons are vain, if only because of the obvious difference that *Sword of Honor* chronicles men in action all over Europe, whereas *Guard of Honor* confines itself to a few square miles of central Florida.

Personally (although the only framed photograph I have in my study shows Waugh scratching away with his dip pen and a fat cigar)* I find *Sword of Honor* hard to read, the work of an aging and fading writer, whereas *Guard of Honor* strikes me as that most thrilling thing in art, the consummation of all that is ripe and ready in an original creative mind.

* See page 169.

———

THE OTHER GREAT difference between Waugh and Cozzens is the former's obsessive quest for Catholic certainties, and the latter's equally obsessive insistence that "the Nature of Things" was just that—a state of being fulfilling no divine purpose. I'll return to Cozzens's philosophy later, but first would like to justify my use of the phrase *connoisseurs of fine fiction* a moment ago. By design, the author of *Guard of Honor* was for thirty years a writer's writer, an acquired and minority taste, too cerebral, too uncompromising, too unsentimental, to appeal to the popular market—until he became the author of the surprise megahit *By Love Possessed.* That also I'll return to.

In April 1998 I picked up an issue of the collectors magazine *Biblio,* on the strength of a flagged article entitled "Words of War: Fifty Years Ago, Four Bestsellers Launched the Literary World War II." I bought it assuming that one of the four would be *Guard of Honor,* which came out in 1948. Cozzens was not even mentioned. Nineteen-forty-eight has gone down in history as the year that saw the bestselling appearance of Dwight D. Eisenhower's *Crusade in Europe,* Winston Churchill's *The Gathering Storm,* Irwin Shaw's *The Young Lions,* and Norman Mailer's *The Naked and the Dead*—modestly described by Mailer himself as "the longest ball ever to go up into the accelerated hurricane air of our American letters." I'm not sure about the sports part of that mixed metaphor, but when it comes to wind, Norm knows what he's talking about.

Even in the spring of 1949, when *Guard of Honor* won the Pulitzer Prize for Fiction, Cozzens's mastery was recognized only by readers of a certain stamp—those who, in the words of Ambrose Bierce, "prefer dry wines to sweet, sense to sentiment, wit to humor and clean English to slang." America has always been a sentimentally inclined country, perhaps because of our romantic self-image as immigrants, wanderers west, seekers of the Golden Door. In rejecting the Old World and its despair of radical change and ingrained pessimism and cynicism, and also in forcing ourselves to forget what we did to the Negro and the Indian and the passenger pigeon and the prairie, we have persuaded ourselves that we are a positive people, lovers of God and benefactors of our fellow man.

For all his reclusiveness and frankly expressed misanthropy, James

Gould Cozzens had no quarrel with the basic benignity of this dream. He loved his country as much as the next man. He served it in war, and all his life he took joy in the American ethos of individual effort. Only for him as a writer, to love was to know, to see faults as clearly as virtues, to monitor human behavior without the smallest attempt to prettify it. To euphemize or to circumlocute was, in his robust opinion, simply to lie.

COZZENS'S APPARENT LACK of compassion (most evident in *Men and Brethren*) would seem to disqualify him for acceptance in our own lachrymose age, just as his conservatism and contempt for theory made him a pariah in days when liberalism became the required political attitude. One can imagine how his gorge would rise at the confessional plaints of contemporary fiction, the canonization of bimbo princesses, the rheum that flows every night on the evening news, the assurances of teary-eyed politicians that they "feel our pain."

Talking of body fluids, which seem to be more and more on show these days (as our hearts dry out), I came out of my New York apartment a few weeks ago and saw two young men taking a fond farewell of each other at the entrance to the subway. Lip-locked, arms entwined, they were going at it hammer and tongues. Just then, a bum pushing a shopping cart came round the corner, half-hidden behind his load of collected soda pop cans, his trousers tied up with string. He saw the young men kissing, and shouted in a voice full of decent outrage, "Oh, not in the street, please—not in the *street!*"

Cozzens, for all his sophistication, had that kind of disdain for the vulgarity of most public display. He stressed the importance of discretion and terseness when love is being expressed, confidences entrusted, or private scruples being agonized over. "Sentimentality," he wrote in one of his notebooks, "is often seen as a fault of kindness, of the soft or warm heart. That is just what it isn't. Sentimentality is basically insensitiveness, undiscerning and imperceptive. When you discover that someone is a sentimentalist look for him to be stupid, dishonest, and cruel too."

To Cozzens, "men" are what they are. As "brethren," working hard for common purpose, they may achieve a measure of content, but if "castaways," they must accept their fate. That same fate—chance would be a better word —will determine whether their leaders are "the just or the unjust." If lucky, they may be "by love possessed," or they may end their lives in "confusion."

I indulged that rather awkward series of allusions to the titles of some Cozzens books in order to prepare you for the authentic voice of Cozzens the novelist—which is to say, a characteristically oblique participation in the thoughts of Colonel Norman Ross, his alter ego in *Guard of Honor*:

> [Life] seemed mostly a hard-luck story, very complicated, beginning nowhere and never ending, unclear in theme, and confusing in action.
>
> Unhappy victims complained of their unhappy circumstances. The trusting followers of the misjudged easiest way found that way immediately getting hard. Simple-minded aspirants, not having what it took, did not quite make it. Conceited men proudly called their shots and proceeded to miss them, without even the comfort of realizing that few attended long enough to notice, and fewer cared. . . . The young died and the old married; courageous patience overdid it and missed the boat; good Samaritans lost their shirts;—everyday incidents in the manifold pouring-past of the Gadarene swine . . . to the appointed steep place. Though so sad, the hard luck often moving, it was a repetitious story, and long; and what did it prove?

This kind of objectivity is what led so many of Cozzens's contemporary critics to call him cold, and indeed, much of his philosophy to this day comes as an ice-water shock to the speculative sentimentality of New Agers. *Tuesdays with Morrie* it ain't!

I MUST STRESS to those who have not yet read *Guard of Honor* that Cozzens's so-called coldness is actually just his clarity of perception. Once the shock of his unsentimentality wears off, you begin to tingle with pleasure. This is a fresh stream you're swimming in, not a heated and chlorinated pool. Your own perceptions, dulled by the lazy inadequacies of contemporary prose, and the *idées reçues* of talking-head journalism, begin to sharpen. It takes a while to get used to Cozzens's deliberate pace, which is about the same as that of the late Henry James, but once his rhythm becomes comfortable, you see more and hear more and feel more. The opening of part 2 of *Guard of Honor,* which describes daybreak and reveille at the Ocanara Air Base, is a *locus classicus* in descriptive literary technique, with all five of your imaginative senses stimulated.

And you notice, as you read on, that far from being a dyspeptic or a cynic, Cozzens is a profoundly moralistic writer who cares about large issues and the general good, even if he may not seem to care about individual human beings. *Guard of Honor* is that most improbable of things, a group novel. There are, to be sure, three heroes—but before I go on, perhaps I had better describe its simple, though massively rendered, plot. The action involves seventy-two hours in the life of a large, stateside U.S. Army Air Force base in World War II, around the time the expanded service was achieving its critical mass under the overall command of General Arnold, and when the war in Europe was beginning to shift in favor of the Allies. It is important to understand the largeness of this context, because the focus of the book, as in all Cozzens novels, is extraordinarily close. Specifically, he is writing about Thursday 2nd, Friday 3rd, and Saturday 4th of September, 1943, and most of his characters are assigned to the research division of Ocanara Air Force Base in Florida.

I will say no more of the plot except that it concerns a racial incident that takes place on base—an apparently slight incident early on, mushrooming to enormous proportions before being itself eclipsed by a tragedy, also slight in the making, that reaches a climax of shattering power. All tensions are resolved at last, legally by due process and humanly by executive wisdom. It is a war novel without combat. It has only one sex scene, although plenty of latent eroticism. Humor is missing, as everywhere in Cozzens. (Odd, come to think of it, how many great writers have been humorless: Goethe, George Eliot, Tolstoy, Thomas Mann, Forster, Virginia Woolf, Hemingway, Coetzee). Except for a near-accident at the beginning, and during the overwhelming finale, there is no physical action to speak of; characters merely move from office to office, or building to building within the confines of the base and its adjoining town. However, the novel opens and closes in flight, and its final metaphor is so transcendental, relating the whole saga to the divine scheme of things, as to amount to an apotheosis.

I JUST SAID that Cozzens does not "seem" to care about individual human beings. This may be true of *By Love Possessed,* which I've never been able to finish, and some of the sterile later stories. But *Guard of Honor*'s gigantic cast of eighty-three (count 'em!) characters live and breathe on the page with such vividness that you realize again, as you get to know them one by one, that Cozzens is presenting people just as they are, without apology. He has three protagonists: Bus Beale, a young, almost simplistically courageous and charismatic general; Colonel Norman Ross, an aging air inspector and judge in civilian life, the most impressive of Cozzens's professional figures; and Nathaniel Hicks, a well-born, intellectually inclined captain whose main function is to act as a subsidiary commentator on the story. Women are a minority, but those who figure prominently are drawn with a tenderness not elsewhere found in Cozzens. The base's few black troops, upon whom the whole story pivots, are an even smaller minority, drawn with no tenderness whatsoever.

I cannot resist interjecting a personal note on the question of objectivity in race relations. It also illustrates the weird serendipity that is a feature of biographical research. The day before yesterday, I did some research for my current book on the presidency of Theodore Roosevelt. While reading about TR's controversial attempt to improve the lot of Negroes in South Carolina by appointing a black man as Collector of Customs in Charleston, I came across this comment, made to TR's face by his friend Owen Wister: "Your act theoretically ought to do good to the colored race, but actually does them harm by rousing new animosity. It's a condition you have to reckon with, not a theory."

Later that day, I opened *Guard of Honor* in preparation for this lecture, and almost immediately came upon the following remark by Norman Ross. The colonel is explaining to his wife that certain social prejudices, like the refusal of white personnel to drink with black, are not mitigable by reason: "In our trouble with the colored officers, we have a condition, not a theory."

Now that first quote of Owen Wister's was published in his book *The-odore Roosevelt: The Story of a Friendship*, in 1930. It's possible, I guess, that James Gould Cozzens read the book when it came out, and the phrase *a condition . . . not a theory* lodged itself in his mind, only to dis-lodge itself eighteen years later. Whatever the case, the verbal similarity is less important than the observation. Both Wister in fact and Colonel Ross in fiction were addressing themselves to well-meaning idealists and telling them that human behavior is usually not ideal and hardly ever pretty. It's a condition, not a theory.

THE LAST YEARS of James Gould Cozzens's life, like his earliest, can be briefly summarized. *Guard of Honor* was followed up in 1957 with *By Love Possessed*, a ponderous legal novel in which the author's style, al-ways dense and difficult, became a parody of itself. That is not to say that the book does not have many passages of autumnal splendor. It became a phenomenal bestseller, remaining at the No. 1 position on the *New York Times* list for almost half a year. Cozzens appeared on the cover of *Time* magazine, and was widely spoken of for the Nobel Prize. Then, in Febru-ary 1958, he was hit by cannon fire from the left. He had committed the unforgivable sin of being both serious and successful. Dwight Macdon-ald, writing in *Commentary*, published a diatribe against *By Love Pos-sessed* which was so personally vituperative that Cozzens's reputation sank almost overnight. (The diatribe was ill-judged, because it over-looked *Guard of Honor* and other great earlier novels—but all's fair in love and literary war.) The New York critical establishment dismissed Cozzens, with some justification, as an elitist snob, and his last two books, *Children and Others* and *Morning, Noon, and Night*, were virtually ignored. Cozzens died boozy and bitter on 9 August 1978. He had come, in his own words, "to the appointed steep place."

In the thirty-three years since his death, I am happy to report that the Gadarene swine who poured past him have plunged to their own ig-nominy. When Kingsley Amis, in his recent collection of letters, dis-missed Dwight Macdonald as "that old idiot," nobody raised a dissenting voice. There remains, and there will always endure, the solid achieve-ment of James Gould Cozzens's masterly fiction.

SENSITIVE SIGNAGE

Washington's Equal-Opportunity Airport

THE NEWS THAT METRO OFFICIALS HAVE BEEN FORCED TO SPEND $400,000 on a new series of signs reading "Ronald Reagan Washington National Airport" has been welcomed by devotees of the fortieth President with the same satisfaction that Welsh nationalists felt when they emblazoned one of the smallest rail stations in Britain "Llanfairpwllgwyngyllgogerychwyrndrobwllllantysiliogogogoch."

Those of us with correct political attitudes are offended by the insensitivity that Reagan worshippers in Congress have shown toward other Americans—particularly persons of gender, whom the new signs either slight or ignore. At the very least, the vital role played by Mr. Reagan's

Originally published in *The Washington Post*, 13 March 2002.

Former Transportation Secretary Elizabeth Dole and friend at Reagan National Airport, November 2011.

wife, Nancy, throughout his political career should be recognized. Why not alter the signs to read "Ronald and Nancy Reagan Washington National Airport"?

This does, to be sure, raise the ticklish issue of discriminatory nomenclature. Feminists might demand that if Mrs. Reagan is to be equally honored, she should enjoy the separate dignity of her premarital name. Perhaps the signs should be further amended to "Ronald and Nancy Davis Reagan Washington National Airport."

I say *perhaps* because Kitty Kelley, Mrs. Reagan's biographer, has established that the former First Lady was originally called Anne Frances Robbins. Since little Anne was deserted by her biological father, we can only sympathize with her desire to be identified with her subsequent stepfather, Dr. Loyal Davis. However, Metro memorializing must be comprehensive as well as reverential. So how about "Ronald and Anne Frances Robbins Nancy Davis Reagan Washington National Airport"?

Okay, but doesn't such a designation shortchange the memory of the father of our nation—whose name was attached to that field long before Mr. Reagan's? And note that even then, signmeisters denied President Washington the moniker his parents gave him. A happy compromise suggests itself: "Ronald and Anne Frances Robbins Nancy Davis Reagan George Washington National Airport."

But what about the woman who was as indispensable to Mr. Washington as Nancy was to the Gipper? Martha Washington, *née* Dandridge, a.k.a. the widow Custis when George met her, merits equal-opportunity signage. I therefore propose that our local gateway be renamed "Ronald and Anne Frances Robbins Nancy Davis Reagan George and Martha Dandridge Custis Washington National Airport."

Whoops—forgot to mention Jane Wyman, the distinguished actress who was Ronald Reagan's first wife and helpmeet. She should be honored too. Taking into account her own adoptive and marital self-transformations, that would make the full name "Ronald and Sarah Jane Mayfield Fulks Wyman Futterman and Anne Frances Robbins Nancy Davis Reagan George and Martha Dandridge Custis Washington National Airport."

If this majestic appellation (admittedly somewhat longer than "Llanfairpwllgwyngyllgogerychwyrndrobwllllantysiliogogogoch") is too much for Metro's sign writers, maybe we should dispense with ideological invocations and go back to calling it plain old "National Airport." One relieved person, at least (were he able to comprehend the sentimental excesses visited on his memory) would be Ronald Reagan himself, who once feelingly remarked, "Those fellows up on the Hill can never [*chuckle*] have too much of a good thing."

A STEADY HISS OF CORN

The Letters of Ronald Reagan

THE CENTRAL PARADOX ABOUT RONALD REAGAN, OUR MOST world-changing President since Harry Truman, was that a man so attractive in his public persona, so implacable in negotiation, and so transparently decent a human being, could have been such a bone-cracking bore. I interviewed him regularly throughout his second term, read half a million words of his presidential diaries and ream upon ream of his manuscripts, and can only endorse the bemused remark of his first wife, "Ronnie never shut up."

It wasn't *what* he said or wrote that glazed your eyes: at least through late middle age, when his hard drive filled up, Ronald Reagan was excep-

Originally published in *The Washington Post*, 27 September 2003.
The Director. Self-portrait by Ronald Reagan, 1927.

tionally well-informed. An editor of *The Washington Post* met him two years before Pearl Harbor, and was amazed by his detailed knowledge of the strategic situation in Finland. The silky voice, the delightful humor, the clarity of expression (his manuscripts are remarkable for their lack of erasures), never failed to impress—at first. Only when you began to note, around the sixth or thirty-sixth time he repeated himself, that his facial expressions, his phraseology, even his self-deprecating chuckles seemed to be projected from some inner, infinitely replayable DVD, did you get the creepy feeling he was not quite real, and wondered where, if anywhere, the real Reagan was.

I found out on the night of his farewell address, as President, to the American people. He came into the Oval Office at about quarter of nine and sat at his desk while the TV crew completed their preparations. He seemed ill at ease until a blank monitor came to life with his image at center screen, the desk shiny beneath his cuffs, the flag draped behind him. "Ah!" said Reagan, suddenly animated. "There he is!"

I remember wondering, "Well, if that's him, who are *you?*"

It is a fact, however, that one or other of those Reagans—or a McLuhanesque combination of both—did alter the course of history. The global battlefield we now dominate, with communism defeated by capitalism, welfare states under siege, and Christian soldiers again marching across infidel sands, was largely mapped, and militarized, by the old knight-errant awaiting death in Southern California.

Ronald Reagan: A Life in Letters* shows that he was always a proselytizer. Decades before he entered politics, his compulsion to seize and hold attention, whether by script, or speech, or merely looking great, was phenomenal. The earliest letter reproduced here, written when "Dutch" was eleven, uses the personal pronoun fifteen times, and the word *you* (in this case, a girlfriend) once.

> Don't laugh at the paper I am using. . . . I ran out of another kind
> of paper Id had. I am writing it in school. . . . I am drum magor of
> the boys band here [etc.]

---

* Kiron K. Skinner, Annelise Anderson, and Martin Anderson, eds. (New York, 2003).

322 THIS LIVING HAND

A certain degree of narcissism is natural in childhood, but young Dutch cannot resist a sketch of himself (captioned "Arent He Darling") in full parade uniform: straight-backed, crooked-grinned, very much the leader of the band. Perhaps I am fanciful in seeing already the future Commander-in-Chief, who so enjoyed standing tall and snapping salutes. But how about an actual self-portrait in silhouette, reproduced at the head of this essay? From the pompadour to the big shoulders rising over the desk, it is almost the identical image ("*There* he is!") that flicked onto that monitor in January 1989.

Dutch drew it when he was seventeen.

YET—AGAIN PARADOXICALLY—Reagan's enormous id was unaffected by ego. He lacked petty vanity. Juvenilia aside, there is no boasting in his letters. He seeks to persuade, rather than impress. When he goes on about himself, it is for didactic purpose, as he explains this or that core belief—for example, to Hugh Hefner in 1960:

> Your letter [defending an article assignment to the blacklisted Dalton Trumbo] has been very much on my mind and I question whether I *can* answer in a way that will make sense to you. First because I once thought exactly as you think and second because no one could have changed my thinking (and some tried). It took seven months of meeting communists and communist-influenced people across a table in almost daily sessions while pickets rioted in front of studio gates, homes were bombed and a great industry almost ground to a halt.

He is explaining his conversion, in 1946, from liberalism so extreme the FBI suspected him being a fellow-traveler, to the passionate anticommunism of more recent memory.

> My fear of "neo-fascism" led to my serving on the board of directors of an organization later exposed as a "Communist Front." . . . A small group of board members disturbed by the things being done in the organization's name introduced to their fellow board

members a mild statement approving our democratic system and free enterprise economy and repudiating communism as a desirable form of government *for this country*. . . . Leaders of the opposition to our statement included Dalton Trumbo, John Howard Lawson, and a number of others who have since attained some fame for their refusal to answer questions. I remember one of their group reciting the Soviet Constitution to prove—"Russia was more democratic than the United States."

And so on, for six handwritten pages. In contrast to the genial blandness of most of his letters, it is an angry document that conveys the intensity of Reagan's hatred of homegrown Reds: "I say to you that any man still or now a member of the 'party' was a man who looked upon the death of American soldiers in Korea as a victory for his side."

Strong stuff, even for the blacklist era. Later on, as he rose to political prominence, Reagan got more cautious about expressing himself on paper. But ideologically, he never changed (not even when he and Mikhail Gorbachev were publicly fawning over each other in Moscow). Nor was an aging President's blind obstinacy in insisting he never traded arms for hostages anything new: he assured Hefner in 1960 that "Hollywood has *no blacklist*."

THERE WAS SOMETHING in Reagan of Sir James Chettam in George Eliot's *Middlemarch*—he was puzzled that anybody should ask the reasons for his beliefs, because they seemed to him so clearly reasonable. It was this absolute sense of moral rightness that made him such a drone in private, and such a force in public affairs. (Former Soviet apparatchiks will tell you that it was not his famous "Evil Empire" speech in 1983 that convinced them he meant strategic business, so much as photographs of the leader of the air traffic controllers union being taken to jail in 1981.)

It follows that, apart from the occasional letter like the above-quoted—or an even more extraordinary one to Leonid Brezhnev, which the State Department was too scared to send, dated 18 April 1981—Reagan's constant outpouring of rather banal beliefs makes his correspondence dull reading *en masse* (a French phrase meaning any book that requires elbow support, or in the case of the volume under review, a truss). One thinks of corn hissing steadily from an Illinois wheat elevator. The golden color is pleasing, the sameness of texture admirable, but—get out of the way before it suffocates you.

It's important to understand that Reagan, unconscious of being anthologized one day (lack of ego, again), addressed almost all these letters to individual people whose reactions were important to him. In that sense, each is a campaign document, even if he had no public office in mind at the time of writing. His weapons are honesty, modesty, and an epistolary style that, while free of literary flourishes or anything resembling an original thought, seems (deceptively) to focus on the recipient. I've interviewed many of the owners of these letters, and can testify that they cherish every cliché. I recall my own pleasure, sweeping away all professional scruples, whenever the President wrote me: every envelope addressed in his patient hand, right down to the last digit of my zip code.

Imagine the emotions, then, of a Mrs. Raymond Ranes, when the following missive landed in her mailbox in May 1972:

Dear Esther:

    I have only just now learned of your loss and want you to know how deeply sorry I am. I know words can't be of much help at a time like this—I wish they could. We can only trust in God's mercy and know that he does have a plan for each one of us. I was in Eureka recently, and both Franklin Bughardt and Ray Holmes were there. You would have been so proud and so would Doc to have heard them talking about what he meant in their lives. He had the greatest effect of any human being on all that has happened to them. Just know how much so many of us wish we could help. Know that you have our deepest sympathy and that you are in our thoughts and prayers.

Sincerely,
Dutch

Apart from the carefully precise names (the signature categorizes Mrs. Ranes as an acquaintance from his pre-Hollywood days) there is nothing to distinguish this from hundreds of other consolatory notes

Reagan wrote, on similar occasions. Word for word, he penned the first three and last two sentences so many times, one can only marvel that he kept on doing so long after the invention of computer autotext. The letter says little and offers less; even the central anecdote, which purports to be personal, tells Mrs. Ranes nothing. But I'll bet she didn't vote for Jimmy Carter in 1980.

Again, it is important to understand that Reagan was not a conscious political operator. He was incapable of the unctuous insincerity of a Richard Nixon, whoring for every last vote. Having beguiled you, by letter or speech or smile or touch (that warm hand over your hand, enclasped in his other hand) he could comfortably feel that you too, shared his belief in "God's plan." And when God, as the GOP's chief tactician, made him President, Reagan could count on your help to push the plan further—right through the gates of the Kremlin and on to Armageddon, if necessary.

Given the comprehensive selection and exemplary annotation of *Reagan: A Life in Letters,* few but the most devoted incense-swingers will also want to own Ralph E. and Ralph A. Weber's *Dear Americans: Letters from the Desk of President Reagan.** The best that can be said for the latter book is that it is short. Both editorial teams seek to give the impression that they "discovered" or "unearthed" Reagan's vast personal archive in his Presidential Library. This isn't true—I went through the entire collection and quoted from it in *Dutch.* Still, scholars will thank them for publishing so many handwritten letters. Those penned in the late 1980s, for example, should disprove rumors that the President was suffering from dementia during his second term. Given the blandness of Reagan's epistolary style, there seems to have been no effort on either side to make him out to be a nicer guy than he already was. A slight Republican bias is sometimes discernible in the Skinner-Anderson collection—they print Reagan's excoriations of John F. Kennedy ("under the tousled boyish haircut it is still old Karl Marx,") but not his early (1952) perception that Richard Nixon was *"less than honest* [and] an ambitious opportunist."

Of course, in those days the Gipper was a Democrat.

* New York, 2003.

COLONIZING OUTSIDE OF CULTIVATION

The Logical Fantasy of John Wyndham

THE YEAR 2001, MARKED BY ONE OF THE GREAT CATASTROPHES OF recent times, also marked the fiftieth anniversary of one of the great catastrophe novels in English literature, John Wyndham's *The Day of the Triffids*. An introducer should generally refrain from relating something so slight as a book to something so epic as the immolation of three thousand human beings. But *The Day of the Triffids* looms larger and more frightening, now, as an allegory of our age, than it did at the onset of the Cold War.

In 1951, the worst fear of ordinary men and women was that they and their children might die in a nuclear holocaust. This fear was miti-

Copyright © 2003 by Edmund Morris. Introduction to the Modern Library edition (New York, 2003).

Photograph by Louise Docker.

gated by the fact that only two powers had the Bomb. Each was, in theory, deterred from dropping it by the consequence known as "mutually assured destruction." Today, we have the same fear, but since seven, maybe eight powers belong to the nuclear club, it is unqualified. There is no balanced constraint, only a common vulnerability.

Nor is nuclear war any longer the worst catastrophe imaginable. Bioterrorism, ranging all the way from genetic sabotage to the dissemination of lethal spores ground as fine as air itself, is the dread that—in Philip Larkin's phrase—"flashes afresh to hold and horrify."* The Bomb is at least a piece of hardware, built by physical engineers, that other physical engineers can attempt to deflect. But how to protect ourselves against softer terror—vegetable, viral, chemical, pandemic?

IT WAS THE FIRST, and one might think the least frightening of these, that John Wyndham presciently explored in *The Day of the Triffids*, and in doing so, revolutionized the imagery of science fiction. Before his book appeared, novelists seeking to agitate readers with a sense of alien threat had used the hoary device of extraterrestrials invading the planet, or the even hoarier one of Voices From Beyond, as in the occult mysteries of Dennis Wheatley. Both required the traditional "willing suspension of disbelief," without which no thriller ever succeeds. But the very collusion inherent in that suspension creates an artificiality of effect: *I'll pretend to believe you, so that I can pretend to be scared—but we both know—don't we?—nothing you write is real.*

Wyndham's stroke of genius was to invent the triffid, a killer plant that is inscrutable in its malevolence, yet so ordinary, even uninteresting on first acquaintance, that the reader believes in it because there seems no reason not to. Bill Masen, the protagonist of this story, is a horticulturalist and triffid expert who—like a beekeeper—tolerates occasional stings in the course of his work. He sees no real harm in the plant, and indeed goes out of his way to emphasize its benefits to mankind, when properly cultivated. If it has given him a career and improved the economy of many nations, why should we view it with misgiving?

* Philip Larkin, "Aubade," *Collected Poems* (New York, 1988).

We are in any case distracted, in the early pages of the novel, by a brilliantly described cosmic event that seems to be the only catastrophe Bill Masen must survive. Rather than spoil the impact of Wyndham's famous opening sentence, I will quote the one that begins the original manuscript draft of *The Day of the Triffids*:

> On the day when the Great Calamity put an end to the world I had known for almost thirty years, I happened to be in bed with a bandage all over my head and around my eyes. Just a matter of luck, like most survival. I woke that morning with the feeling that something was wrong, and probably long after most people had found out that things were disastrously wrong.

Professional writers jealous of John Wyndham's enormous commercial success (he was the author of many other bestselling novels and stories, including *The Midwich Cuckoos*, which was filmed as *Village of the Damned* in 1960) should compare that awkward paragraph with its lucid final expression and admire him, if for nothing else, as a craftsman who worked hard to achieve his effects.

And of these effects, none was more dramatic than his gradual exposition of the triffid—a mere plant—as one of the most ominous predators in horror literature.

> There must have been plenty of them about, growing up quietly and inoffensively, with nobody taking any particular notice of them. . . . And so the one in our garden continued its growth peacefully, as did thousands like it in neglected spots all over the world. . . . It was some little time later that the first one picked up its roots and walked.

The above passage is quoted at the head of a scholarly article by Sarah Hayden Richard and Peter White, "Horticulture as a Pathway of Invasive Plant Introductions in the United States." No better proof can be found of the seriousness with which scientists accept Wyndham's basic premise that too much tinkering with the fundamental processes of nature can result in nature striking back. As yet, no woody plant has taken revenge as terrible as that of the triffids. But the botanist Eduardo Rapaport has identified no fewer than ten thousand "seriously invasive species" proliferating worldwide, or "colonizing outside of cultivation," as Richard and White put it.

JOHN WYNDHAM PARKES LUCAS BEYNON HARRIS (1903–1969) was not himself a scientist, and did not pretend to be, although the precision of his language in describing the botanical structure of the triffid is impressive. For all we know about him, he may have spent some youthful years in a laboratory, but until his personal papers came to light in Britain in 1998, he was almost entirely a man of mystery. He took delight in this obscurity, and tormented bibliographers by fragmenting his long name into several different *noms de plume*. *The Secret People*, by John Beynon (1935), *Love in Time*, by Johnson Harris (1948), and *The Outward Urge*, by John Wyndham and Lucas Parkes (1959) are all products of the same pen that wrote *The Day of the Triffids*.

Born in Knowle, Warwickshire, on 10 July 1903, Wyndham remained all his days a middle-class, country-loving, English literary gentleman. "My life has been practically devoid of interest to anyone but myself— though I have quite enjoyed it, of course, in those moments when I did not seem to have been sent to occupy a largely lunatic world." These disorienting experiences possibly included his education at a boarding school in Hampshire, an early reading for the Bar, and failed attempts at odd jobs in the 1920s. He published his first short story (as J. B. Harris) in the magazine *Wonder Stories* in 1931, and soon became a popular author of conventional science fiction.

World War II, which took him to Normandy with the Royal Signals in 1944, transformed Wyndham creatively, as it did his exact contemporary Evelyn Waugh. Both writers returned to private life after V-E Day with a profound sense of civilization under siege, of dark forces likely to sweep away what was left of the Old England they remembered, or thought they remembered—ordered, landed, socially harmonious. Waugh foresaw the rise of a new species of bourgeois barbarian, and took refuge in religion and black comedy. Wyndham predicted rogue science and the militarization of space, and wrote *The Day of the Triffids*.

He was probably not being consciously allegorical in conjuring up the book's two great plagues: a world struck blind, and a world colonized by plants that take advantage of that blindness. But the fact remains that what he published in 1951 was unlike anything in his science fiction so far—indeed, unlike anything his most eminent predecessors had attempted. Wyndham's idol was H. G. Wells, and he frankly admitted the influence of *The War of the Worlds* on *The Day of the Triffids*. The revolutionary note he succeeded in striking was that of "logical fantasy" (Wyndham's own phrase). The plague of blindness is brought on when people watch, as they of course would, a celestial display of extraordinary beauty. And the plague of triffids is inevitable, given the economic advantages of cultivating them. Left alone, they would probably never have proliferated with such gradually increasing fury. We carry within us the elements of our own destruction, Wyndham seems to be saying, just as the triffid itself bears countless seeds, "free to drift wherever the winds of the world should take them." And when disaster happens, the worst is not what it does to such physical infrastructures as cities and transport systems, but to the precious intangibles that a democratic government is supposed to protect: the loyalty of lovers, the upbringing of children, the rule of law, the all-importance of free speech and privacy and good manners.

ALTHOUGH JOHN WYNDHAM makes clear that he is describing a global phenomenon in *The Day of the Triffids,* his novel—like all his novels—is determinedly English in its low-key, unflappable tone. To transatlantic tastes, this muted quality makes it all the more believable, and more scary. It is still a hugely popular book in Britain, and throughout what used to be called the British Commonwealth. Among the natives thereof, it has the reputation of being the one science fiction book you must read, even if you don't read science fiction. I first devoured it as a schoolboy in Kenya. The very word *triffid* has passed into postcolonial vernacular. My brother, an outdoorsman living in South Africa, tells me that the invasive species *Chromolaena odorata,* rampant in that country, is commonly called "triffid weed," because each tree produces a million seeds.

American readers of science fiction—at least, those who have matured in the thirty-odd years since Wyndham's death—tend to prefer a minimum of dialectical musings and character clash, in favor of maximum bang for their buck: technological fantasy, space monsters, black holes, and the like. Perhaps for that reason, *The Day of the Triffids* fell out of favor (indeed, out of print) here, in the mindless decade when we stopped worrying about totalitarianism and thought we were proof against terrorism. And there is no denying that some aspects of the novel, particularly its attitude toward women, have dated. Josella Playton, who comes to Bill Masen's attention as the author of a book called *Sex Is My Adventure,* was a saucy heroine in 1951. Today, her mildly liberated morals would not raise an eyebrow in Salt Lake City.

Even so, the influence of John Wyndham on such contemporary American writers as Stephen King and Michael Crichton is palpable. King visits similar horror upon comfortable, unremarkable people, who must muddle through or die. Crichton's *Jurassic Park* follows the formula of *The Day of the Triffids* in showing how greedy mismanagement of a scientific phenomenon can lead to rampant colonization of the environment.

Neither of these megaselling authors, however, can match Wyndham as a prose stylist. They lack both his erudition and his irony—also, it must be said, his pessimism. One cannot imagine this sort of allusive dialogue occurring in a King novel:

> BILL   Make a rule for yourself not to speak to anyone, and nobody's going to guess you can see. . . . "In the country of the blind the one-eyed man is king."
>
> JOSELLA   Oh yes—Wells said that, didn't he? Only in the story it turned out not to be true.
>
> BILL   The crux of the difference lies in what you mean by the word "country"—*patria* in the original. *Caecorum in patria luscus rex imperat omnis*—a classical gentleman called Fullonius said that: it's all anyone seemed to remember about him. Wells imagined a people who had adapted themselves to blindness. I don't think that's going to happen here—I don't see how it can.

It is hard to imagine any current American novelist, popular or high-brow, writing a passage that so delicately conveys the protagonist's slight stuffiness without detracting from his authority, while at another level, Wyndham places both his own book and its great nineteenth-century model in the overall context of Western pragmatism.

Literary qualities aside, what seems to recommend a new American edition of *The Day of the Triffids* is the applicability of the story to our current neuroses about biological weapons of mass destruction—not to mention the larger threat of terrorism upon the very fabric of civilized society. Indeed, some passages pack more power now than they did fifty years ago. A short scene describing the defenestration of a young couple overwhelmed by the chaos around them may have seemed mawkish in 1951, but it reads poignantly now, to eyes desentimentalized by the sight of those bodies falling from the World Trade Center:

> By the window he paused. With one hand he felt his position very carefully. Then he put both arms around her, holding her to him.
>
> "Too wonderful to last, perhaps," he said softly. "I love you, my sweet. I love you so very, very much."
>
> She tilted her lips up to him to be kissed.
>
> As he lifted her he turned, and stepped out of the window.

May the day never come when we, too, have to say of this civilization we hold so fragile, that it was "too wonderful to last."

DOT'S AND DASH'S

Lynne Truss's Punctuation Primer

Amanhattan realtor has just notified me, on heavy stationery, that "the New York market is remaining vibrant with the goal of buying a home being a principle interest for purchaser's to either upscale or downscale their homes."

Syntactical incoherence aside, it is difficult to say what is most annoying about this sentence: the dropped comma, the misspelled adjective, the superfluous apostrophe, the split infinitive, the grating use (twice) of *home* as a commercial noun. I am tempted to reply, "It is against my principal's to consider such illiterate letter's," but doubt that the sarcasm would register. As Lynne Truss notes in *Eats, Shoots & Leaves*, her forcedly jovial punctuation primer, "the world cares nothing for the little shocks endured by the sensitive stickler."

The success of Ms. Truss's book in Britain, however, suggests that the world—at least, that small part of it floating north of France and west of

Originally published in *The New York Times Book Review*, 25 April 2004.
Photograph by Fernando G. Revilla.

Norway—does indeed care about proper punctuation. "Eats, Shoots & Leaves" (the title derives from a sloppily edited natural history of the panda) hit the top of the U.K. bestseller list last winter, and nobody was more surprised than the author. Now it is being rushed into print here, in the hope that we will find it as amusing, and salutary, as our transatlantic cousins do.

Salutary it may be, in its call for more concern about how we express ourselves, orthographically speaking. But as anyone knows who has watched a roomful of Brits cracking up at the word *knickers*, national humor is a perishable export. Ms. Truss's tone is so relentlessly larky, and her imagery so parochial, that American readers will find much of this book incomprehensible, let alone unfunny:

> Well, if punctuation is the stitching of language, language comes apart, obviously, and all the buttons fall off. If punctuation provides the traffic signals, words bang into each other and everyone ends up in Minehead. If one can bear for a moment to think of punctuation marks as those invisibly beneficent fairies (I'm sorry), our poor deprived language goes parched and pillowless to bed. And if you take the courtesy analogy, a sentence no longer drops it in your face as you approach.

I'm sorry about the fairies, too, but I'm sorrier about her prose style, which is cloying even if you know where Minehead is, and can tolerate mixed metaphors. Ms. Truss admits, "I'm not a grammarian" and offers plenty of proof—as in *each other* above. She's no syntactician either, never quite knowing where to put the qualifier *only*. And she resorts so often to Brit-speak adverbs, such as *obviously, basically, actually*, that whole stretches of the book read like voice mail. Her American editors, by the way, might have done her the favor of rephrasing "It's a real fag" on page 18, not to mention an unquotably racist joke on page 51.

All this is a pity, because when she stops straining at lawks-a-mussy chirpiness and analyzes punctuation malpractice, she is often persuasive, as on the tendency of lazy writers to reticulate their sentences with dashes. "The dash is less formal than the semicolon, which makes it more attractive; it enhances conversational tone; and . . . is capable of quite subtle effects. The main reason people use it, however, is that they know you can't use it wrongly—which, for a punctuation mark, is an uncommon virtue."

Ms. Truss is a fan of the semicolon, which has caused more fistfights between authors and editors than any other cipher, with the possible exception of the dollar sign. Writers themselves are divided on its merits. Many follow the example of George Orwell, and try to do without it. Martin Amis has managed to reduce his per-novel ratio to one. Yet Amis's father, Kingsley, used semicolons to superb comic effect (*vide* the hangover scene in "Lucky Jim"), and V. S. Naipaul drops them regularly, like tiny bombs of Alka-Seltzer, into his paragraphs of pure dyspepsia.

Ms. Truss admits that the semicolon is "dangerously addictive," but that's true of any mark that becomes a mannerism. Emily Dickinson used the dash in preference to any other punctuation. Henry James sometimes seemed to need commas to set off his commas. When George Bernard Shaw saw the manuscript of T. E. Lawrence's *Seven Pillars of Wisdom,* he submitted it to a polite form of colonic irrigation.

The greatest stylists—those who "hear" as they write—punctuate sparingly and subtly. Ms. Truss errs in saying that P. G. Wodehouse eschews the semicolon, but I can see why she thinks so. The Master uses it, at most, once a page, usually in a long sentence of mounting funniness, so that its *luftpause,* that tiny intake of breath, will puff the subsequent comma clauses along, until the last of them lands with thistledown grace. By then you're laughing so much, you're not even aware of the art behind the art.

Even "incorrect" punctuation, Ms. Truss admits, can enhance literary expression in the right hands. Evelyn Waugh cut commas to convey the clipped dispatch of upper-class speech: "You see I wasn't so much asking you to agree to anything as explaining what our side propose to do." (Note, too, the pluralization of *side,* so cozily snobbish.) Indeed, there is hardly any shibboleth of style that can't be blasphemed against. Ban the splice comma, then along comes Beckett with his jagged, haunting arrhythmia. Mandate periods after every sentence, and Joyce will show you how to end a book with no stops whatever. Rail against the exclamation point, but don't expect Tom Wolfe to listen. Frown on the ellipse, and A. G. Mojtabai will use it to express an old man's dementia in a way that clutches your heart.

To her credit, Ms. Truss is never pedantic, even as she castigates the shopkeepers' apostrophe ("POTATOE'S" "XMA'S TREES" "BOB,S PETS"), which most of us find quaintly amusing. She's right to be irritated, though, by that ubiquitous mistake, the use of *it's* as a possessive pronoun. Her scholarship is impressive and never dry. I didn't know, for example, that *dash* derives from the Middle English *dasshen*, "to break." But she's a few years off in ascribing the first use of direct-speech quotation marks to "someone" in 1714. Daniel Defoe splattered them all over his *True Relation of the Apparition of One Mrs. Veal* in 1706.

At risk of sounding parochial myself, I wish that Ms. Truss had devoted a few pages to taking on the usage czars of American academe— particularly those at the Modern Language Association and University of Chicago Press, whose anti-capital, anti-hyphen, anti-italic stylebooks seek to return modern logography to the uniformity of ancient papyri. Copy editors beholden to these manuals routinely insult the intelligence of writers (and readers) by applying punctuation formulas in contempt of sense.

It doesn't help even if your name is George Eliot. I just reread *Middlemarch*, alternating between old (1891) and new (Modern Library, 1992) editions, and was disconcerted by the latter's willingness to alter Eliot's original inflections. For instance, Dorothea Brooke, in 1891, was "troublesome—to herself, chiefly." A hundred years later, that long, corrective dash is gone, and so has the comma emphasis. Qualification is changed to consequence. This is not editing: it's rewriting.

We stateside scribes better look for a punctuation crusader more aggressive than Ms. Truss. Whichever presidential candidate wants to take on the MLA this summer gets my vote. Meanwhile, I'm going to hyphenate as often as I want, in the privacy of my own study.

LEAVINGS OF A LIFE

Ronald Wilson Reagan, 1911–2004

THERE THEY LIE IN THEIR SMOOTH WOODEN GUTTERS, PROJECT-ing from the desk I had specially made for them: four yards of cards, eight inches wide, five inches tall, most of them with his initials hand-written headline-style in the top left-hand corner, from *RR's BIRTH ZODIAC—FEB. 6, 1911* to *RR DIES OF PNEUMONIA—JUNE 5, 2004.*

In between these two extremes, some eighteen thousand cards docu-ment whatever I was able to find out about Ronald Reagan's thirty-four thousand days. Which leaves sixteen thousand days unaccounted for. Lost leaves. "The leavings of a life," as D. H. Lawrence might say.

I once planned to show these cards to him, just to see him react as drawer after drawer rolled out yard by yard, green tabs demarcating his years, yellow tabs his careers, blue tabs his triumphs and disappoint-ments. He could have looked down, as it were, on the topography of his

Originally published in *The New Yorker*, 28 June 2004.

Dutch Reagan's former lifeguard post on the Rock River, Dixon, Ill. Painting by Fran Swarbrick.

biography, and seen the shoe salesman's son moving from town to town in north-central Illinois, in the teens of this century; the adolescent achieving some sort of stability at Dixon High School in 1924; the Eureka College student and summer lifeguard through 1933; then successively—each divider spacing further, as he grew in worldly importance—the Des Moines sportscaster and passionate New Dealer; the Hollywood film star; the Cavalry officer and Air Force adjutant; the postwar union leader and anti-Communist; the television anchorman and corporate spokesman for General Electric; the governor of California, 1967–1975; the twice defeated, ultimately successful, candidate for his party's presidential nomination; and last, the septuagenarian statesman, so prodigiously carded that the nine tabs "1981" through "1989" stand isolated like stumps in snow.

He never visited my study, though. On reflection I am glad he did not, because he might have been disturbed to see how far he had come in nearly eighty years, and how few more cards he was likely to generate, before the last file was full. I would probably have had to keep my forearm over a subsection more than a foot long, bristling with tabs descriptive of *RR THE MAN*. Now that the man is no more, and memories of him are fading, a riffle through some of these tabs might help restore his image in all its color and complexity.

THE FIRST PART of the subsection deals with Ronald Reagan's body. In 1988, at seventy-seven years of age, the President stood six foot one and weighed 190 pounds, none of it flab. He boasted that any punch aimed at his abdomen would be jarringly repulsed. After a lifetime of working out with wheels and bars, he had broadened his chest to a formidably walled cavern forty-four inches in circumference. He was a natural athlete, with a peculiarly graceful, Iroquois gait that brought him into rooms almost soundlessly. No matter how fast he moved (that big body could turn on a dime), he was always poised. One remembers how elegantly Reagan choreographed Mikhail Gorbachev up the steps at the 1985 Geneva summit: an arabesque of dark blue flowing round awkward gray. He loved to swim, ride, and foxtrot (Doris Day remembers him as "the only man I ever knew who really liked to dance."). Eleven weeks after nearly being killed in the assassination attempt of 1981, he climbed onto the springboard at Camp David and threw a perfect half-pike before anybody could stop him.

Gorbachev remarked on Reagan's "balance" to me in an interview after both men had left office. But he was using the word *ravnovesiie* in its wider Russian sense of psychological equilibrium. The President's smooth yet inexorable motion telegraphed a larger force and certainty that came of a lifetime of no self-doubt (except for two years of despair after Jane Wyman divorced him for boring her). Reagan *redux* did not care whom he bored, as long as nobody tried to stop him. His famous stories, delivered with a speed and economy that were the verbal equivalent of balance, were delightful on the first, even the fourth telling. But when you heard them the fourteenth, or the fortieth time, always with exactly the same inflections and chuckles and glances, you realized that he *was* a bore, in the sense that a combination harvester is boring: its only purpose is to bear down upon, and bale, whatever grain lies in its path. Reagan used humor to harvest people.

He was always meticulously dressed in tailored suits and handmade shoes and boots. Yet he was neither a dandy nor a spendthrift. In 1976 he still stepped out in a pair of high-cut, big-tongued alligator pumps that predated the Cold War. "Do you realize what I *paid* for these thirty years ago?" His personal taste never advanced beyond the first affectations of the *nouveau riche*. Hence the Corum dollar-face wristwatch, the Countess Mara ties, the glen checks too large or too pale, and a weekend tartan blazer that was, as Bertie Wooster would say, "rather sudden, until you got used to it." Yet Reagan lacked vulgarity, because he sported such accoutrements without self-consciousness. He wore the simpler suits that rotated through his wardrobe just as unpretentiously. No man ever looked better in navy blue, or black-and-white dinner clothes.

On a card inscribed *Alcohol*—his father's cross—appears the comment of an old Hollywood friend, "Ronnie never had a booze problem, but once every coupla years, he wasn't averse to a lot of drink. Its only effect was to make him more genial." His sanguineous complexion would flush after a mere half-glass of pinot noir, giving rise to repeated rumors, later on, that he used rouge.

Actually Reagan never required makeup, even when he was a movie actor. He didn't even sweat under hot lights; on the contrary, he basked in them. A young photographer who did a cover portrait of him in 1984 for *Fortune* told me, "When I walked into the Oval Office, I thought my career was made. He was just back from a long campaign swing, and looked *terrible,* all drained and lined. I hit him with every harsh spot I had. Etched out those wrinkles, figuring I'd do what Richard Avedon did to Dottie Parker. Know what? When my contacts came back from the darkroom, the old bastard looked like a million bucks. Taught me a real lesson. Ronald Reagan wasn't just born for the camera. There's something about him that *film* likes."

Several of my cards itemize the President's deafness. People seated to his right imagined that they were privileged. Actually he heard nothing on that side, having blown an eardrum during a shootout scene in one of his old movies. His left ear was not much better, so he relied increasingly on hearing aids as the years went by, although their distortion pained him. One learned not to sneeze in his presence. When the room was crowded and voice levels rose, he would furtively switch off. I could tell from a slight frown in his gaze that he was lip-reading.

The shroud of quietness that insulated him was accentuated by severe myopia. As a boy, young Dutch Reagan assumed that Nature was a blur. Not until he put on his mother's spectacles, around the age of thirteen, did he perceive the world in all its sharp-edged intricacy. He did not find it disorienting, as somebody who had been blind from birth might. Perhaps his later, Rothko-like preference for large, luminous, policy blocks (as opposed to Bill Clinton's fly's-eye view of government as a multifaceted montage, endlessly adjustable) derived from his unfocused childhood.

Or perhaps the novelist Ray Bradbury, who also grew up four-eyed in small-town Illinois, has a more informed theory. "I often wonder," says Bradbury, "whether or not you become myopic for a physical reason of not wanting to face the world." Like Dutch, he competed with a popular, extrovert elder brother by "making happy things for myself and creating new images of the world for myself." Reagan was not introverted, yet from infancy he had the same kind of "happy" self-centeredness Bradbury speaks of, the same need to inhabit an imaginative construct in which outside reality was refracted, or reordered, to his liking. "I found that I was completely surrounded by a wall of light," he wrote of his first venture onto a movie set. It was clear that the sensation was agreeable.

MORE SO, ONE is tempted to say, than sex, where self-centeredness is definitely not appreciated by other parties. I never accumulated much documentation on Reagan's libido, since he was of that generation that kept such matters private. However, I did card a series of mostly repetitive observations, all contributed by women. The consensus is that although "Ronnie" was virile and attractive in a tanned-ranchman sort of way, his advances were unexciting. "Too nice, too easily pushed off," said one old torch singer, "and too damn philosophical about it afterward. He didn't have that uh, slight *menace* that gives a girl a thrill." A group of women who knew him as President blamed his tepid sex appeal on a lack of "focus"—the word recurs—"as though we didn't interest him as individuals."

Reagan needed eight regular hours of sleep—"nine if I can get it." His longtime aide Michael Deaver was amazed to find him beneath a pile of bedclothes at nine o'clock on the morning of his first inauguration. Although he sometimes had to recite Robert Service's *The Shooting of Dan McGrew* to conquer insomnia, his sleep was cataleptic. Nancy Reagan was not with him the night a hurricane hit the White House in 1985, so he slumbered right through, and was puzzled to find both doors of their bedroom suite blown open next morning. Rumors of the President nodding off during cabinet meetings were unfounded. But this did not stop him joking that his chair should be labeled REAGAN SLEPT HERE.

He had a strange aversion to sleeping while traveling. On flights back from Tokyo or Moscow, he would sit working with battery-like energy while everybody else slumped. There is an autographed snapshot of him on Air Force One, bending in mock panic over his snoring secretary of state. "*But George,*" the inscription reads, "*I have to talk to you—the Russians are coming!*" When the President made his address to Congress after the Geneva summit, he had been writing and talking for nineteen hours straight.

I have eight cards devoted to that beautiful voice, a melodious baritone husked with silky higher frequencies. It was what encouraged Max

Arnow, casting director of Warner Bros. in 1937, to award Reagan a screen contract. His first feature role, in *Love Is on the Air,* called for him to spend plenty of time breathing into microphones. Fan-mail enthusiasm was immediate and strong ("Dear Ronnie, I am in love with your voice, it is so soothing." "Dear Mr. Reagan, you have the most wonderful voice in pictures."). In those days the voice was lighter and faster. His labial dexterity was such that he had to train himself to speak more slowly, lest his mouth wreathe on camera like Mister Ed's. In later years, it acquired more weight and an enchanting hesitancy that disguised the banality of his conversation.

Ronald Reagan is incorrectly remembered as a warm man, and I think the voice (which he lubricated with hot lemon water) had much to do with it. One would have to go back to Franklin D. Roosevelt to find a president as able to convey, by auditory means alone, such a reassuring certainty that better times were coming and the nation's security guaranteed. Merely by intoning the phrase "My fellow Americans" in a relaxed *mezzo forte,* he made his listener trust him.

All the other rhetorical arts—rhythm, gesture, timing, comedy, pathos—were at his command. Gerald Ford, accepting the GOP presidential nomination in 1976, made the mistake of inviting Reagan to say "a few words" to the delegates, and stood gray-faced as they almost palpably concluded that they had chosen the wrong man. Jimmy Carter and George H. W. Bush did not have Reagan's ability to tear up at the right moment. Yet for all their emotional awkwardness, one cannot imagine either of them completely ignoring their first grandchild, as he did for two years, or walking past the brain-damaged James Brady with nothing more than a cheerful "Hi, Jim."

Bill Clinton had plenty of personal charisma, but was hampered by a droning voice, and no sense of when to shut up. Reagan never went on too long. Nor did he have Clinton's casual willingness to keep people waiting. One of the few things that made him angry was schedule slippage.

Having watched all the above presidents, except Clinton, interacting with young audiences, I can report that Reagan was the least successful at it (and Carter by far the best). Children respond to sincerity rather than smoothness. Reagan addressed them just as he did adults, which is to say, with eye contact that took in the whole room rather than its individual parts, a delivery precisely directed to the furthest television camera, and with benign indifference as to whether any kid understood him, as long as the applause was general.

THE SECOND PART of my biographical file—about 240 cards—deals more specifically with Ronald Reagan's character and begins with *Advisability.* The President had a trusting credulity that was part of his charm. If a proposal was put to him with enough conviction, he not only registered it but recorded it in his phonographic memory. He was not, however, malleable: those who sought to advise him had to come from an approved philosophical quarter. "I want to get expertise from people in various fields," he wrote in 1985, "but I haven't changed my views since I've been here."

The most famous example of Reagan's advisability was his acceptance, in September 1982, of Edward Teller's concept of the Strategic Defense Initiative. Dr. Teller represented all that the President admired in a scientist, being distinguished, individualistic, sonorous (Max Arnow would have loved his Hungarian consonants) and contemptuous of academic restraint. For half an hour Teller deployed X-ray lasers all over the Oval Office, reducing hundreds of incoming Soviet missiles to radioactive chaff, while Reagan, gazing up ecstatically, saw a crystal shield covering the Last Best Hope of Man. He saw it so whole and perfect that Gorbachev, three years later, was powerless to persuade him that the SDI would militarize space. Nor could Gorbachev believe that Reagan was serious in wanting *him* to build a space shield too, if necessary with American technology. Mutually assured destruction was a threat any Slav could understand. Mutually assured *protection* was a notion so pea-brained, one could only slam down one's pencil and stare at the "dinosaur"—Gorbachev's word—who proposed it.

But Reagan stared back, during the longest silence that Secretary Shultz had ever experienced at a negotiating table. It was ten minutes past noon, Swiss time, on 20 November 1985: the key moment in forty years of Cold War brinkmanship. "I regret you cannot see it our way," Gorbachev said at last, confounded as much by the President's power of belief as by his lack of hostility.

A beaming goodwill was one of the most attractive things about Ronald Reagan. No matter how worried he might be by his throbbing prostate, or by intelligence that a Libyan hit squad was after him, he eschewed *angst* and aggression. I have only two records of him becoming physically violent: once in 1943, when a Hollywood drunk made an anti-Semitic remark to his face, and again in 1973 when Michael Deaver challenged his sympathy for the disgraced Spiro Agnew. Even then, Reagan contented himself with throwing a heavy bunch of keys at Deaver's breastbone. He had reason to despise Jack Warner and Armand Hammer and Ferdinand Marcos, but couldn't summon up the necessary malice.

His *bonhomie*, however, was oddly neutral. A man who professes to like everybody is by definition a man who cares for nobody in particular. Here is Charles de Gaulle's note on Philippe Pétain, another celebrated twinkler: *Too self-centered to despise others.* Also a remark by Lyn Nofziger, oldest and least rewarded of Reagan's early aides: "He has to be more than this distant kind of crittur, because too many people love him. You don't love somebody who is distant from you."

No fewer than twenty-nine of my cards document the Reaganesque detachment. He was at once the most remote and accessible of men. Although he reveled in the constant flesh-pressing of the presidency, and ate up flattery with a spoon, he needed regular spells of "Personal Time" as much as he needed sleep. Glance through the Oval Office peephole, and you would see him happily writing in longhand, always with his tie straight and jacket on, ensconced in an egglike solitude that the curvature of lens and golden room only emphasized.

Adored by so many, he was a man with no real friends. This was not due to any inherent misanthropy. Young Dutch had been as gregarious as any normal football-playing boy at Eureka College. In Des Moines, where he worked as a sportscaster from 1933 to 1937, he ran with a crowd from Drake University, sang barbershop quartet with them, and actually encouraged his fellow minstrels to follow him to Los Angeles when he signed his screen contract. "Don't worry about money, I'll support you till you find work." For a year or two the quartet remained inseparable, but after Reagan married Jane Wyman in January 1940, his career burgeoned and he moved into a different social sphere. He grew increasingly political during the war, as an Air Force adjutant in daily touch with Washington, and by 1947, when he assumed the presidency of the Screen Actors Guild, he had become so obsessed with trade union-ism and anticommunism as to lose interest in casual chat. In 1948, Jane divorced him, citing politics as her corespondent.

Until he remarried in 1952, earnest, bespectacled Ronnie was said to be "best friends" with William Holden, and after that with Robert Taylor. But neither man was anything more than a barbecue buddy. Hundreds of political supporters and associates claimed to be close to him when he was governor of California (1967–1975) and thousands during his presi-dency (1981–1989). Former Senator Paul Laxalt spoke for all of them when he said: "I guess I know Ronald Reagan as well as anybody. Of course, we never talk about anything *personal.*"

Sooner or later, every would-be intimate (including his four children) discovered that the only one Reagan truly cared about was Nancy. For Laxalt, disillusionment came when the President called to thank him for his campaign help in 1984, only to pause in midsentence and audibly turn over a page of typescript. For William F. Buckley, it was when Rea-gan showed obvious relief at not being compelled to put him up. For Mi-chael Reagan, it was the day the Governor handed him his high school diploma with no sign of recognition. "Dad, it's *me.* Your son."

Patti Davis, Reagan's younger daughter, writes in her autobiography:

> Often, I'd come into a room and he'd look up from his notecards as though he wasn't sure who I was. Ron would race up to him, small and brimming with a child's enthusiasm, and I'd see the same bewildered look in my father's eyes, like he had to remind himself who Ron was. . . . I sometimes felt like reminding him that Maureen was his daughter too, not just someone with simi-lar political philosophies.

Reagan's scrupulously kept presidential diary is remarkable for a near-total lack of interest in human beings as individuals. In all its half-million or so words I did not find a single affectionate remark about his children. He conscientiously names every visitor to the Oval Office, having a printed schedule to refer to, but in conversation he tended to rely on pronouns. Nor did he pay much attention to faces. "Nice to meet you, Mr. Ambassador," he greeted Denis Healey, the former defense minister of Great Britain, as the real British ambassador stood by. "But I've already met him," his Excellency complained, "*eleven* times."

This may be the place to note that in all the years I observed Ronald Reagan until 1992, I never saw any sign of cognitive dementia. There were, to be sure, days late in the Presidency when he drifted off, as old men do. He was by then a very tired person, and an assassination attempt, a colonoscopy, and a prostatectomy had taken their respective tolls. On 29 May 1988, for example, he emerged from an extended one-on-one with Gorbachev, unable to recall a word that had been said. But such lapses were rare, and until he left office he retained a startling ability to focus all his talents on important business.

Nancy Reagan conceded that there were "parts of Ronnie" that he kept to himself. Interviewing her, I discovered that she had little clue as to how his mind worked—how he memorized scripts, pondered decisions, espied political opportunities. He trusted her superior judgment of people, but never asked her political advice; he did not even consult her about running for the Presidency. His locker-room side (which could be jovially obscene) was foreign to her, as was the Practical Christian, and the imaginative dreamer who wanders through young Dutch's unpublished short stories.

I hesitate to question one of the most celebrated amours in White House history, but the way Reagan advertised his uxoriousness—the fulsome toasts and tributes, the hand-holding, the on-camera kisses—always struck me as manipulative. There was something guilty about his superimposition of an enormous Valentine card, all ribbons and bluebirds, over the stark black-and-white of his divorce decree from Jane Wyman. Possibly he was embarrassed by the many similarities between his two wives. Both had been wide-eyed, street-smart, scorchingly ambitious starlets, abandoned by their fathers in infancy, convinced of the world's treachery, drawn to "Ronnie" as a placid haven of goodness and strength, then frustrated to the point of despair by his reluctance to propose. The vital difference between them was that Jane wanted (and won) stardom for herself. Nancy's ambition concerned only him: she sought fulfillment in making him famous. With high courage, she took him on when his acting career was at the point of serious decline, and when his brilliant future as a politician could hardly have been predicted. Yet she never flinched in her passionate belief that he would recover and prevail. Even when he was forced to do variety in Vegas for money, early in 1954, she was there every night at a front table, giving him the luminous "look" that bolstered his self-respect.

Within a few months Ronald Reagan was professionally reborn as the host of *General Electric Theater.* He became a star of the corporate lecture circuit, honing his oratory into "The Speech," a statement of the free-market conservative principles that would sustain him ideologically for the rest of his life. Nancy, whose stepfather Dr. Loyal Davis was one of the most rock-ribbed reactionaries in the American Medical Association, has often been credited for her husband's swing to the Right. But the truth is that Ronald Reagan lost his New Deal liberalism immediately after World War II, when he was targeted by Communist-dominated crafts unions as a lackey of studio management. He was a conservative Democrat long before he remarried.

By the early 1960s he was confirmedly an Eisenhower Republican, rich, well-connected, and a political force strong enough to be courted by Richard Nixon and Barry Goldwater. The more widely he wandered as campaigner and corporate spokesman, the more gratefully he returned to his showplace house in Pacific Palisades—red-draped, mother-dominated, thrumming with appliances supplied free by his parent company. It was, in short, a kind of womb, to which he became almost pathologically attached. This strange ode to a shag rug was written by Reagan in 1961:

> Across from where I sit . . . I can see certain paths pressed into the pile of the carpet . . . paths leading to a chair (big footprints), to a piano (feminine nine-year-old size prints), to a corner handy for hiding (very small prints) and of course narrow side paths (middle-size prints) . . . to her chair. To me, these middle-size prints act as guy wires and girders holding all the rest together. I am glad that the carpet sweeper can never erase them.

Much as he embraced domesticity, however, he relied on Nancy to relieve him from its petty nuisances, like school and servant problems. She made the children understand that, although Dad was available for certain carefully scheduled hours of face time, in the pool or on horseback, he was not to be pestered by emotional demands. He had other things than mere fatherhood on his mind: the governorship of California, for a start.

In grateful compensation, Reagan forever refused to believe any disturbing news about his wife—her parsimony, her pill dependencies, her violent disciplining of Patti, her middle-aged infatuation with Frank Sinatra. "I want you to go away and think carefully about what you have just said," he reproved a gubernatorial aide, who worried that Nancy's abuse of staff might become a news scandal. "My Nancy doesn't behave like that."

There is no doubt that she loved him for better and for worse, as her care of him in his last years showed. Neither was there any insincerity in his love for her, as far as it went. But my impression is that it stopped at the frontier of his own comfort. The countless references to "Mommie" in the presidential diaries are expressed almost entirely in terms of personal need. During her rare absences from the White House, his complaints of being "lonely" and "lonesome" echo with foghorn-like regularity. And this: "Why do I get so scared always when she leaves . . . ? I do an awful lot of praying until she returns." It never occurs to him that *she* might be lonely too, or bereaved or frightened, that she has any identity other than—by extension—his own.

Well, if love is the satisfaction of mutual needs, they got what they wanted. My cards contain a final vignette of them standing together in church on 10 May 1992, just before Alzheimer's began to detach him from her. They held the same hymnbook with their outer arms, while the inner ones circled into an embrace. I stood just behind, listening to their voices blending as they sang "Blest Be the Tie That Binds."

RONALD REAGAN'S AIR of gentleness was such that few people noticed, or could believe they were noticing, that he had little private empathy with them. In November 1988 a delegation of Bangladeshis visited the Oval Office to tell him about the genocidal effects of the Burhi Ganga floods. After a few minutes their spokesman stopped, disconcerted by the President's dreamy smile. "You know," Reagan said, "I used to work as a lifeguard at Lowell Park Beach, on the Rock River in Illinois, and when it rained upstate you wouldn't believe the trees and trash, and so forth, that used to come down."

I used the phrase *private empathy* above because Reagan could be movingly sincere when required to emote in public. To question his tearful identity with "the boys of Pointe du Hoc," or the nameless dead of Bergen-Belsen, would be to misunderstand his essentially thespian nature. Actors are not like you or me. Their real world, where they really feel, is on stage.

Reagan in any case was more than just an actor. He was a statesman, unaccustomed to meeting anybody stronger than himself, and his detachment was a necessary armor against the emotional demands that responsibility attaches to power. All leaders have to sheathe themselves, or they cannot function. I copied out this account of André Malraux's first impression of Charles de Gaulle, as equally applicable to Ronald Reagan:

> [One felt] a remoteness, all the more curious because it appeared not only between himself and his interlocutor but between what he said and what he was. . . . He established with the person he was talking to a very powerful contact, which seemed inexplicable when one had left him. A contact above all due to a feeling of having come up against a total personality.

Did Reagan ever read de Gaulle's leadership maxim, *il faut cultiver le mystère?* Probably not, but he didn't have to: the mystery was already there. I have a whole sheaf of *RR: Enigma* cards wherein various interviewees speculate on how much the President knew, or didn't know, about what they were trying to tell him. If he was as disengaged as he seemed, doodling absentmindedly during long presentations, how did he, time and again, manage to pose exactly the kind of simple hypothesis that showed the presenter to be confused? Was he sending a subtle message, when the doodle curved into the hindquarters of a horse?

Which brings me to the cards I most enjoyed compiling—those that caught Reagan's humor. Most of his countless very funny stories (told with a verbal economy and cadence that would tax any prose stylist) were admittedly prerecorded in his phonograph memory and played back at will. As a young actor in the Warner Bros. commissary, he used to sit at the fast Jewish table in order to study, and eventually compete with, the *shtick* of such motormouths as George Burns, Jack Benny, and the Epstein brothers. Although not naturally a wit, he was capable of dry riposte, as in a crack about Desmond Tutu that George H. W. Bush repeated at the memorial service in National Cathedral, convulsing the congregation.*

Perhaps the best of Reagan's one-liners came after he attended his last Knights of Columbus dinner in New York in January, 1989. The evening's emcee, a prominent lay Catholic, was so stimulated by wine that he forgot protocol and followed the President's speech with a rather slurry one of his own. It was to the effect that Ronald Reagan, a defender of the rights of the unborn, understood that all human beings begin life as "feces." The speaker cited John Cardinal O'Connor (sitting aghast nearby) as "a fece" who had gone on to greater things. "You, too, Mr. President. You were once a fece!"

Later, en route back to Washington on Air Force One, Reagan twinklingly joined his aides in the main cabin. "Well," he said, "that's the first time I've flown two hundred miles to be told I was a piece of shit."

REAGAN'S MOST REGRETTABLE characteristic was his ignorance, compounded as it was by a refusal to be budged from any shibboleth that suited him. He had been quite the opposite as a young man—not culturally curious, but avid to learn what he could about world affairs. He passionately espoused the New Deal, and by 1938 had swung so far toward the idealistic Left that he tried to join the Hollywood Communist Party. He was quickly rejected, on the shrewd grounds that he was not Party material (too garrulous, too patriotic, too susceptible to other influences). During World War II he became addicted to *Reader's Digest*—so

* "How was Archbishop Tutu, Mr. President?" "So-so."

much so that he seemed to memorize all of every issue as soon as it hit the stands. Reagan has been rightly mocked for the condensed, packaged quality this gave to his thought, but at least until he left the employ of General Electric in 1962, he was able to talk interestingly about subjects other than politics. From then on all his considerable intelligence was focused on conservative doctrine, and his general knowledge atrophied.

As a result, he relied more and more on memories of past reading, and began to commit the gaffes that would bedevil all his political campaigns. By the time he became President, his ignorance had attained a kind of comic poignancy. He thought "Camus" rhymed with "famous" and that trees caused acid rain. He had never heard of *Our Town, The Magic Mountain, Carmen,* or *Blow-Up.* The names Goethe, Guevara, Disraeli, Knopf, Schumann, Fellini, Hockney, Piaf, and Prospero rang no bells. When I mentioned the Suez Canal, he shook his head sorrowfully and told me it had been a mistake to give it back to the Panamanians.

If not protean, his mind could nevertheless be described as procrustean, in Frederick Turner's definition:

> [Such an intelligence] reduces the information it gets from the outside world to its own categories, and accepts reality's answers only if they address its own sets of questions. . . . It insists on certainty and unambiguity, and so is at war with the probabilistic and indeterminate nature of the most primitive and archaic components of the universe.*

As anyone can see who consults Ronald Reagan's manuscripts (page after handwritten page without erasure; terse, disciplined sentences; clear *sequitur*), he needed to impose order on chaos. He did not like to be surprised, or hustled. He liked punctuality, symmetry, certainty. Every item on his schedule was neatly crossed off upon completion, with a triumphant arrow pointing down to the next. When traveling, he meticulously packed his clothes to synchronize with his itinerary, so that each

---

*Frederick Turner, *Natural Classicism: Essays on Literature and Science* (University of Virginia Press, 1985), 62–63.

change would suit the time, occasion, and climate stops en route. He even tried to reorder nature at Rancho del Cielo, his mountain retreat above Santa Barbara, pruning every thicket of brush, every dead *madroño* branch, until the landscape was as geometricized as a painting by Grant Wood.

TWO SETS OF CARDS tabbed as *RR: Paradox* and *RR: Passivity* might be merged in my drawer, were they not already alphabetical neighbors. As Anatoly Dobrynin remarked, it is paradoxical that this most passive of presidents should have been so active in bringing about the collapse of Soviet Communism. Ronald Reagan was not an initiator. He never called a meeting or drafted a new policy or hired or fired, unless somebody suggested it. He did not object when his first chief of staff and secretary of the Treasury swapped jobs. Even his angriest phone call to a foreign leader (Israel's Menachem Begin, after the Palestinian refugee massacre in 1982) had to be prompted by Michael Deaver. Happy and fulfilled inside his oval O—"I've got the biggest theater in the world, right here," he grinned at me—he paid no attention to noises off: the furious arguments of Al Haig and Cap Weinberger, David Stockman's whines and Don Regan's roars, the conspiratorial murmurings of Oliver North and John Poindexter. Even when truly disturbing sounds invaded his tranquillity—the blowing up of the Marine barracks in Lebanon, the keening of Jews over Bitburg, the explosion of the *Challenger*—he seemed oddly equable, although in each case he performed a moving ceremony of grief.

One sound, however, did shake his complacency. It was the pop-popping of John Hinckley's .22 pistol outside the Washington Hilton Hotel on 30 March 1981. Since he so nearly died in that attack, so early in his Presidency, we can credit the sincerity of his written vow: "Whatever happens now I owe my life to God and will try to serve him every way I can."

Nothing afterward, not even the debacle of Iran-Contra, deflected him from what he was convinced was his double mission—at home, to restore the American spirit after fifty years of federal paternalism; abroad, to display such a resolute contempt for Marxism-Leninism that it would follow Nazism onto "the ash-heap of history." Both conceits were perceived as naïve in 1981, at least in those chardonnay-fragrant areas of Manhattan and the Hamptons where political issues are always described as "complex." Four years later the first dream came true in a landslide election, amid such a blizzard of red, white, and blue as had not been seen across America since V-J Day. And after four years more— sadly a little too late for Reagan to see it as President—the Evil Empire began to self-destruct, just as he had said it would.

HISTORY ALREADY SHOWS that Reagan's political instincts were astute and his sense of the future prophetic. The Berlin Wall, which he so memorably described as "ugly as the idea behind it," is reduced to a few fragments in museums. Teenagers stroll hand in hand where the guard dogs used to run. Cybercafés beep and brew in downtown Moscow. Free-enterprise capitalism is now the norm of most economies, and free speech floods the Internet. The United States, for all its overweening wealth and cultural crassness, is more than ever the world's constitutional exemplar.

So positive a society did we become under Ronald Reagan that it's easy to forget how low our national morale had sunk before he raised his right hand on 20 January 1981 and, by plain force of character, reinvested the Presidency with authority and dignity. In recent years we have seen the office belittled again, but that is the way with democracy and its cycles: big men are followed by small; power gives way to dereliction. The Republic survives, and for as long as it survives, I think Reagan will be remembered with Truman and Jackson as one of the great populist presidents, an instinctual leader who, in body and mind, represented the best temper of his times.

IN ONE OF MY last interviews with him, I tried out my theory that he "thought with his hips," as follows:

Q Mr. President, do you realize that you had Einstein all figured out at age eighteen?
A Huh?

Q There you were, a summer lifeguard on the Rock River,
swaying every day in your high chair on the diving raft.
Somebody starts to drown in midstream. You throw down
your glasses—everything's a blur—you dive into the moving
water—you swim, not to where the drowning person *is*, but
where he'll *be* by the time you intersect his trajectory. You
think that you're moving in a straight line. But actually
you're describing a parabola, because the river's got you too.
Your curve becomes his curve; you grab him, swing him
around, and start heading back *in reverse,* not toward the diving platform but *upstream,* so that by the time you get to shallow water you'll be back where you started. During all this
action, you're in a state of flux: no fixed point of reference, no
sense of gravity. Everything's *relative.* . . .

A (*Interrupting, with a glance at the clock*) Yeah, that river sure
ran strong. Out there beyond the swimming line.

My *Projektive Relativitätstheorie* had not impressed him, but I'd chosen the right image. Long after the onset of Alzheimer's disease, when he
could no longer understand the simplest question or recognize photographs of himself as President, he would still show visitors a watercolor
of Lowell Park Beach, framed on the wall of his office. "I was . . . uh, a
lifeguard . . . there . . . uh . . . *I saved seventy-seven lives!*" Then words
would fail him and he would gaze at the picture with his glossy head
cocked, looking out beyond the swimming line to where the river ran
strong.

LADY OF LETTERS

Living with Sylvia Jukes Morris

FROM THE MOMENT I FIRST WALKED INTO HER RENTED ROOM IN a townhouse in Marylebone, London, I knew I was in the presence of a lady of letters. And—unusual for that breed—a woman of elegance, too. The books on her Sheraton-style shelves, or between brass ends on her polished side table, were not only lovingly arranged, but manifestly read. I remember in particular a two-volume set of Boswell's *Life of Johnson*, bound in red padded leather, the page blocks gilt-edged and divided with silk ribbon markers. Newly arrived in England from Africa, I had never before seen this greatest of biographies. It sits still in her study, in the house we now share.

Elsewhere, I noticed Dorothy L. Sayers's translation of Dante, Shakespearean commentaries by Jan Kott and Caroline Spurgeon, W. H. Auden's *Poets of the English Language*, essays by Mary McCarthy and

Copyright © by Edmund Morris. Originally published in Dale Salwak, ed., *Living with a Writer* (Palgrave Macmillan, New York, 2004).

Photograph of Sylvia Jukes Morris, 1997.

Gore Vidal, and—on the nightstand by her bed—Henry James's *The Ambassadors,* with some scribbled notes protruding.

"I teach," she said, by way of explanation.

"At London University?" A friend had told me she'd won a distinction in history during her student days there.

She shook her head, the dark-brown glossy bob swinging and falling. Colonial though I was, I somehow recognized that cut as more Knightsbridge than Marylebone.

"Acland Burghley School," she said. "Near Highgate."

"You don't *look* like a teacher," I said, eyeing her trim black skirt and American-style pumps. Harold Wilson's Britain was then at the nadir of its dour unstylishness.

"Well, for the past two years, I haven't been. I went to live in New York. But now I'm back at Acland, as head of the English department."

"New York!" I groaned. "That's where *I* want to be."

"Me too! I'm regretting this move already. It feels so . . . regressive."

During the courtship that followed, climaxing in our marriage fourteen months later, I never ceased to assure her that we would someday settle in Manhattan—possibly even (why not dream?) rent that plush pad overlooking Central Park, where by firelight Yves Montand made love to Candice Bergen, in a movie we saw at the Leicester Square Odeon. . . .*

Rather more confidently, I predicted that by then Sylvia would be a published author. "You're so interested in literature, and in literary lives. Biography is the career for you."

On the strength of a lucid analysis of the structure of *The Ambassadors,* which she delivered over dinner at Beoty's one night (her hands undulating in the candlelight, as unconsciously as they do today on the lecture platform), I suggested she write a life of Henry James. She remarked that Leon Edel, at four volumes and counting, seemed to have cornered that particular market.

"Well, how about George Eliot?"

---

* *Live for Life* (1967). When the author and his wife bought an apartment on Central Park South in 1999, it turned out to be immediately below Miss Bergen's.

The bob shook and fell again. "No, the only biographical thing I've ever done was the story of that hat."

She glanced at the rack by the restaurant door, where hung a silver fox busby she'd bought at Bonwit Teller. "A sort of whimsical account of the places it's been and the things it's seen. Not for publication—just an assignment in a writing class I attended once. When we read out our pieces, everybody said mine was the best!"

"There you are, you see," I said, triumphant.

I MUST CORRECT any possible impression, arising out of the above references to fashion and coiffure, that I had married a young woman of means. On the contrary, Sylvia has always had to earn every nickel. Her elegance is made possible only by the most austere economies. This frugality is reflected in the way she writes: spare lines, subdued colors, and now and then a discreet flash, as of half-hidden jewelry.

Never once in those early days—indeed, not until long after I had made good on my promise to immigrate with her to New York—did I think of becoming a biographer myself. She was so much more culturally sophisticated than I, so quick and unerring in her textual inferences, that I left literature to her, and dreamed only of earning *beaucoup* bucks as the chief copywriter of some Madison Avenue "hot shop." This would enable me to keep her in fur hats as she penned a series of lapidary lives for Knopf, perhaps, or Harvard University Press. . . .

Realities of the advertising business kept postponing this fantasy. My limited ability to write "selling" copy for Good Seasons Salad Dressing made me an unlikely candidate for promotion at Ogilvy & Mather, Inc. Our combined income floated only a notch or two above the hardship index for Manhattan. (Sylvia, unqualified to teach in the United States, was then working as a travel counselor for British tourism.)*

Suddenly at thirty, after penning a failed campaign for Diaperene

---

* The advertising axis formed by Ogilvy & Mather and its client, the British Tourist Authority, in the late 1960s groomed a number of other copywriting alumni for future literary careers, including the novelist Don DeLillo, the travel writer Ian Keown, and the memoirist Peter Mayle.

Peri-Anal Cream, I found myself on the street. For the next several years—*ironis ironarium!*—my scholarly wife supported me as I hacked at whatever freelance jobs came my way—record liners, wine articles, insurance brochures, travel pieces. Meanwhile her literary half-life went on. Bored by her job, intellectually starved, she would buy books on the way home from the office and read them two, three, four at a time, until our studio apartment began to look like a library carrel.

Her break, creatively speaking, came in 1971, when I needed help writing some cassette scripts for a European auto-tour packager. She resigned from the British Tourist Authority, not without trepidation ("What will we do for money, once this assignment's over?"), but took instant satisfaction in the work. I did the segments on military history and wine; she wrote cultural sketches and introductions to regional cuisine.

Next, a friend who worked at Reader's Digest Books assigned us to produce, at 17 cents a word, a series of chapters for a history of exploration entitled *Great Adventures That Changed Our World.* The assignment was open-ended, in that we could write as many chapters as we liked, within a two-year delivery schedule. Intoxicated by the prospect of unlimited pages to fill, while the great slot machine in Pleasantville showered us with shining pennies ("What about punctuation marks?" I asked her. "Shouldn't we charge for those too?"), we congratulated ourselves on becoming, at least for the moment, full-time professional writers.

Thirty years later, we are scribbling still, with seven books published and two more big ones on the way.

WE HAVE NEVER COLLABORATED. We are too different in temperament, sensibility, working methods, and attraction to particular subjects. At the beginning of our history of exploration, we followed the example of the fifteenth-century monarchs of Spain and Portugal, and divided the world between us. Sylvia sailed west with Columbus while I reconnoitered the East Indies with Vasco da Gama. Later, she accompanied Burke and Wills across Australia, and William Beebe into the depths of the Atlantic Ocean, while I brought Stanley and Livingstone together at Ujiji, and walked on the moon with Neil Armstrong.

As this list of names indicates, we both (and here we *are* similar) took a biographical approach to history. We built our narratives around the personalities—often as not, the antisocial neuroses—of the great explorers. Sylvia was intrigued, for example, by Florence Baker's determination to transform herself from a young Victorian wife into one of the first discoverers of the source of the Nile. In the course of our research, a more radical difference between us became evident: Sylvia is equally interested in men and women, and can write about either at length, whereas to me, *das Ewig-weibliche* has always been an enigma.

Her biographical ambidexterity (were I to die tomorrow, she could complete my life of Theodore Roosevelt) makes her wiser than me in analyzing the relations between the sexes. I tend to empathize with the masculine viewpoint of my subject, whereas she, being a woman, is aware that no man is an island—that he can be fully understood only insofar as he relates to the other half of the human race. I stand on the promontory. Sylvia inhabits the main.

After writing her half of *Great Adventures*, she became fixated with F. Scott Fitzgerald, Napoleon, D. H. Lawrence, and both Richard Burtons (the Sir and the star), not to mention Sonya Tolstoy, Wallis Warfield Simpson, Virginia Woolf, and a whole harem of Bloomsbury bluestockings. However, she had no literary designs on any of them. Neither she nor I yet believed in the miracle of a solo book contract. Our names did not appear on the title page of *Great Adventures* ("Against company policy," the editor breezily explained), so we remained unknown in publishing circles. The flow of pennies from Pleasantville ceased. As the recession of the mid-1970s worsened, the freelance assignments that paid our rent became fewer and fewer. Then, as always happens in New York when you are desperate, the phone rang.

A SPECULATIVE SCRIPT I had written on Theodore Roosevelt's Western days had been "optioned" by a film producer. This did not guarantee that *The Dude from New York,* as I called it, would ever preem at Radio City, but it did mean enough money to keep our landlord happy for another year. On the strength of this success, I acquired a literary agent. (Amazing how quickly you can sign one up, when there's a check due.) A remark from the agent changed our lives. "Since you've done all this research on Teddy Roosevelt," she said, "why don't you write a short popular biography of him?"

The next thing I knew, I had a contract for $7,500, one-quarter payable in advance. Forgetting about the screenplay, I found myself willy-nilly becoming a studious, driven biographer. I had become what I used to think my wife should be. The work was so absorbing I did not stop to ask myself, "What about *her?*"

SHE SOON BEGAN to ask the same question—not in regard to herself, but to someone named Edith Kermit Carow. That young woman was already looming, in the early stages of my manuscript, as Theodore Roosevelt's first love—only to be supplanted by Alice Lee, the Boston beauty he married fresh out of Harvard. Both of us knew, vaguely, that Edith would get her man in the end, after Alice's tragic death. But Sylvia's curiosity as to how their romance rekindled became so intense that she moved ahead of me, and began to research the story herself.

Day after day, she accompanied me to the Theodore Roosevelt Birthplace in Manhattan, where I had access to a dusty heap of old family papers, and buried herself in those pertaining to Edith. Her research ranged far beyond mine, to the years when the Roosevelts were the first family in the land, entertaining the likes of Henry Adams, Henry James, and Augustus Saint-Gaudens. Meanwhile, I was discovering that the "short popular biography" my agent envisaged was going to be only the first installment of a trilogy. And as the story of a young President-to-be, it would focus more on TR's political, intellectual, and military achievements than on his domestic life.

With my encouragement, Sylvia made a proposal to Coward, McCann & Geoghegan.* "I feel strongly that there is sufficient material for a truly absorbing book on Edith Kermit Roosevelt," she wrote. "She was a quietly powerful woman of great charm and ability; she was also an amazingly

* Absorbed later into G. P. Putnam's Sons.

complex personality, with a fine mind and an aura of mystery that lends itself to a probing study."

The proposal went on to sketch the story of a New York girl born in the age of Abraham Lincoln, who became one of the most brilliant hostesses in White House history, and who long outlived her husband, dying in the age of Harry Truman. Like Sylvia, Edith was passionately literary. There was an unconscious self-identification, I thought, in this paragraph of the proposal:

According to one family chronicler, Edith "needed books as she needed air." Consequently a good part of every day was set aside to read history, philosophy and poetry. Her friends considered Edith an expert on Shakespeare, and even Theodore, one of the best-read men of his day, conceded that her views on literature were sounder than his own. "She is not only cultured but scholarly," he said proudly.

Here were words that I could echo—indeed have done, many times over the years.

Not then, and never since, have either of us felt competitive about our respective projects. I could perhaps have taken Sylvia's proposal to imply that *The Rise of Theodore Roosevelt* (though still less than a quarter written) was not uxorial enough, and needed to be supplemented. Instead, I had a pleased feeling that she meant to place my very male biography within the larger context of a female one, a sort of *vas insigne devotionis** benignly enclosing Theodore's life, and those of their six children.

The publisher signed. The agent endorsed. One year after me, Sylvia had her own contract and her own calling.

She has pursued it to this day. *Edith Kermit Roosevelt: Portrait of a First Lady* was published to wide acclaim in 1980. R. W. B. Lewis, in a front-page review in *The Washington Post*, called it "an endlessly engrossing

---

* "Singular vessel of devotion." In medieval terminology equally applicable to the womb and the Grail.

book, at once of historical and of human importance." *The Christian Science Monitor* remarked, "This biography represents craftsmanship of the highest order." Reissued as a Vintage paperback in 1987, it has been published again by Modern Library, and is accepted as definitive.

In the interim, after fifteen years of prodigious labor, she produced *Rage for Fame: The Ascent of Clare Boothe Luce* (Random House, 1997). Gore Vidal, in *The New Yorker,* hailed it as "a model biography . . . of the kind that only a real writer can write." And now, having shepherded me through my last three presidential biographies, Sylvia is absorbed in the second volume of her life of La Luce—working title, *Price of Fame.*

We are therefore separately qualified to write literary profiles of each other. Were space available, it might be amusing to construct a sort of Alexandria Quartet: She as seen by Him, He as seen by Her, She as She imagines He sees Her, He as He hopes She sees Him. Here, at any rate, is Perspective One.

I LIVE WITH a perpetual clipping machine, a female Edwina Scissorhands who cannot open a newspaper or magazine without reaching for the shears she always keeps near her—on the breakfast table, in the sitting room, in her library, at her desk, beside her bed, in her purse when she travels. (Current airline security regulations have severely cramped this habit.) Mostly, the columns she clips are biographical in nature— obituaries, interviews, profiles. But on some days her slashing frenzy is such that when I ask for today's *New York Times,* I get little more than the masthead and, with luck, the lingerie ads.

She files these clips according to a system only slightly less abstruse than the Heisenberg Principle. Years later, however, she will quickly exhume a yellowing filament of newsprint in reference to some point she needs to corroborate. It was just such a filament, containing a 1974 interview with Clare Boothe Luce, that flowered out after more than two decades into *Rage for Fame.*

Oddly enough, for a woman who so ruthlessly maltreats periodicals, Sylvia cannot bear to see a mark in the margin of any printed book. That white space, that snowscape over which words float like prophet birds, must never be defiled. Not so long ago, in a secondhand bookstore, I

came across a copy of *Edith Kermit Roosevelt*, which some reader had annotated copiously and respectfully. I bought it for her amusement. But
after glancing at a page or two, she put it down with a pained expression,
and has not taken it up again. Respectful or not, that stranger had tres-
passed.

When writing, she wields a fat Pelikan fountain pen on the backs of
old photocopies, faxes, flyers, and press releases—anything that is blank
and 8½ inches by 11. This satisfies her double desire to save trees and sow
words. She sits for hours, motionless except for the moving pen, deaf to
outside sounds, even to loud conversation in her vicinity. Every now and
again I will force her to get up and walk around, lest she write herself
into a spasm. Fortunately she is limber from regular exercise—indeed,
less desk-damaged than I am.

She writes in the rounded "Marion Richardson" style taught to so
many English grammar-school girls of her generation, using a chisel nib
that gives a semi-calligraphic curve to her *g*'s and *y*'s and an incisive
sweep to her crossed *t*'s.* She tends to through-compose whole sections,
sometimes whole chapters without stopping, her hand racing after the
speed of her thoughts. Before she rewrites, which she does over and over
again, pruning and refining, it is imperatively necessary for her to read
me her day's work. I confess I find this something of a trial, because unfinished prose always makes me dizzy, and hearing it, rather than seeing
it on the page, increases the vertigo. But exposition *viva voce* is part of her
creative process; without it, she cannot proceed to the next silent stage.
And so, draft by draft, reading by reading, the thing eventually gets done
to her satisfaction. Only then will she sit at the computer and render her
manuscript into type—the first printout, of course, prompting yet more
revisions.

Final text is final text, but as the house archivist, I'm most inclined to
preserve her handwritten sheets, since their interlineations and heavy
load of patches and coagulated Wite-Out give such tactile evidence of
the struggle every word cost her. I feel particularly tender toward a late
page describing Edith Roosevelt's death, which bears evidence, in the
form of a couple of teary blotches, that the biographer had finally lost

* Seven years after this essay was written, she now types on a small, sleek Sony laptop.

her objectivity. And who can blame her, given the poignancy of the paragraph?

> *With the signing of her will Edith, in effect, severed her formal attachment to life. The four seasons of 1947 found her largely bedridden, as did the spring and summer of 1948, the last she was to encounter. As the leaves began to fall in September and the days shortened, the final weakness stole upon her. . . .*

Sylvia's perfectionism extends right through every stage of her book's production. As passionate about design as she is about prose, she harried her editor so obsessively over the sizing, screening, and placement of *Rage for Fame*'s photographic illustrations (which cost her eight thousand dollars) that he ordered the compositor to show her the final blues of the book before it went to press—an unheard-of concession to an author's judgment.

Next, she fought with her publisher in a determined effort to make the cover design simpler and more stylish. "Why all these clashing type-faces?" she asked. "And the gold curlicues? Keep it just plain black and silver." He threatened to drop her from his spring list. She went on fighting; he capitulated. The result was a book so beautiful that it is displayed to this day in the production department at Random House, as an example of what a good biography should look like.

SHE SAYS THAT AFTER *Price of Fame,* she will retire, and go back to what she was doing when I met her, and still loves best: reading, reading, and more reading. At the moment, though, her life consists of writing, writing, and more writing. Pleased though I am to see her absorbed in her newspapers over breakfast, and her stack of three or four books after dinner, it still fills me with content to hear the steady scratch of her pen all day, and see the well-cut bob, still dark, still glossy, swing and fall as she reaches for another sheet of paper: the age-old, eager gesture of a scribe with something to say.

A MUSICAL OFFERING

Bach and Frederick the Great in the Age of Enlightenment

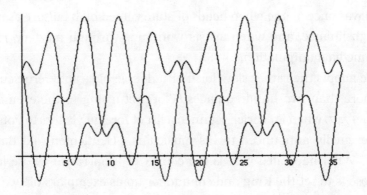

W HEN GENIUSES MEET, THE RESULTS ARE NOT ALWAYS INCENdiary. One thinks of T. S. Eliot and Groucho Marx exchanging the lamest of dinner-table conversations, Michelangelo Antonioni and Wim Wenders collaborating disastrously on *Beyond the Clouds*, and Van Gogh spoiling Gauguin's breakfast with something that was definitely not a dried apricot. Yet, every now and again, sparks fly from the odd encounter. Among the oddest of these, and surely the one that burst into the purest flame, was that between Johann Sebastian Bach and Frederick the Great. It forms the subject of James R. Gaines's *Evening in the Palace of Reason*, an account of how a king's challenge prompted an aging composer to produce the *Musikalisches Opfer* (*Musical Offering*), a contrapuntal achievement that uniquely allies cerebral and auditory beauty.

Gaines, a former managing editor of *Time, Life,* and *People,* is not the

Originally published in *The New York Times Book Review,* 17 April 2005.

Contrapuntal graph of a section of Bach's Musical Offering *by the American Mathematics Society.*

first writer to make literature out of this famous incident. In 1979, Douglas R. Hofstadter published *Gödel, Escher, Bach*, a study of the aesthetic similarities that unite Bach's great work with the mathematics of Kurt Gödel and the drawings of Maurits Escher. That brilliant work deservedly won the Pulitzer Prize, and remains an example of how plain prose can be used to communicate abstruse intellectual matters, in ways that are not only revelatory but thrilling.

While Gaines is no match for Hofstadter as a thinker or prose stylist, he writes with admirable erudition. The story he tells is a reminder that there was once a time when heads of state valued high culture as much as high finance, and when artists won fame through mastery, rather than media manipulation.

He adopts the rather slow form of a double biography, crosscutting for more than two hundred pages before returning to the evening of 7 May 1747, when Frederick scanned a list of foreign visitors to Potsdam and excitedly announced to his musicians, "Gentlemen, old Bach is here." What happened next is the climax of a narrative whose larger purpose is to set the King and commoner up as exemplars of two contrary Germanic traditions: Frederick the expansionist, power-drunk, atheistic Prussian, and Bach the warmhearted Lutheran Pietist, a family man of parochial horizons and unbounded creativity.

No author could want a more promising pair of protagonists—except that the record of Bach's life is slight, compared to that of Frederick's. Gaines keeps his book balanced with a lot of dry Bachian ballast, while fighting the temptation to tell us too much about one of the most fascinating rulers in European history.

In a later, more liberated age, Frederick the Great (1712–1786) might have been sympathetically known as "Frederick the Gay." Great he no doubt was as King and Commander-in-Chief—at least, until his autocracy degenerated into tyranny—and he was almost as eminent as a patron and practitioner of the arts. But homosexuality, and the suppression of it forced upon him early on, appears to have been the key to his personality. Gay memoirs today offer no scenes of horror comparable to what Frederick was forced to witness, at age seventeen, through the barred window of his prison cell in Küstrin Castle.

As Crown Prince of Prussia, he had been jailed by his father, the maniacal homophobe Friedrich Wilhelm I, ostensibly for plotting to desert the kingdom and seek asylum in Britain with a young lieutenant named Hans von Katte. Although the accusation was true, Frederick's real provocation was having grown up as un-Prussian as could be imagined: Frenchified in language, dress, and deportment, art-loving, flute-playing, pompadoured, fixated on his mother and sister—in short and in his father's eyes, more of a queen than a king in the making.

Effeminate as he may have seemed, and openly as he and Katte flaunted their relationship—within the proprieties of the day—there was a tough obstinacy about Frederick that no number of fatherly whippings (many in full view of the royal court) could break. His decision to flee Friedrich Wilhelm's persecution was due to pride, rather than fear. "The King has entirely forgotten that I am his son. . . . I have too much honor to submit to such treatment; and I am determined to put an end to it one way or the other."

Friedrich Wilhelm reacted with similar determination when the youths were betrayed and arrested. (In Gaines's too-frequent colloquialism, he was "beyond angry" at their disloyalty, and "beyond firm" in punishing it.) Unmoved by Frederick's apology, the King ordered that Katte be beheaded right below Frederick's window.

The execution took place at dawn, while grenadiers apologetically held the prince to the bars. Frederick could only scream, "My dear Katte! Forgive me!" and receive a hand-blown kiss from his friend before the executioner's sword swung. At that point, Frederick fainted. Gaines reports:

> He returned to consciousness in a delirium. He spent the day weeping and in shock . . . staring at the body below, on which someone (defying the king's instructions) had thrown a black cloth, now caked with Katte's blood. Unable to eat or sleep, Frederick spent the night in a high fever, talking to himself. "The king thinks he has taken Katte away from me," someone heard him say, "but I see him all the time."

Frederick was too much a product of the Age of Reason not to think his way out of this trauma, knowing that his father would execute him too, if he did not quickly prove himself as much a "man" as any *Krieger* in the Prussian army. He proceeded to do just that, earning Friedrich Wilhelm's respect as a soldier of extraordinary ability, and a student of the most minute arcana of political science. He even married the princess chosen for him, resigning himself to "servicing" her when necessary (the actual French verb he used was more graphic). In the event, he fathered no children, and spent as much private time as possible with the men he most cared for—comrades-in-arms and intellectuals of every discipline. His accession to the throne in 1740 allowed him to come out of the cultural closet as the only true "philosopher-king" of the German *Aufklärung.* In the words of his friend Voltaire, Frederick was "a man who gives battle as readily as he writes an opera. . . . He has written more books than any of his contemporary princes has sired bastards; and he has won more victories than he has written books."

The best poor Bach could do to compete, biographically speaking, was get himself imprisoned in 1717 after a bureaucratic squabble with the Duke of Weimar. Far from being traumatized by this experience, he used his few weeks of detention to compose Book 1 of *The Well-Tempered Clavier.* Gaines strives to dramatize Bach's other clash with authority— over which official of St. Thomas's Choir School, Leipzig, had the right to appoint prefects—but its thrill quotient is low.

Understandably, therefore, Gaines devotes as much space as possible to the real drama of Bach's life: his advancement of the art of counterpoint to a point of perfection that has never been surpassed. Theorists are divided as to which late masterpiece best represents the old cantor in the plentitude of his powers: the *Goldberg Variations,* B minor Mass, and unfinished *Art of the Fugue* are all candidates. But the author is on strong ground in his advocacy of the *Musical Offering,* which is based in its thirteen-movement entirety on a theme by Frederick the Great. In particular, Gaines cites the suite's concluding *ricercar,* a six-voice fugue of almost inhuman clarity. It would be an overwhelming achievement even if the King's theme were simple. But Frederick composed (possibly with the naughty connivance of Bach's son Carl Philipp Emanuel) a subject so jagged and chromatic that only a freak mind could work it out in three voices, let alone six. Hofstadter compares the latter task to "the playing of sixty simultaneous blindfold games of chess, and winning them all."

Bach accomplished it with no apparent effort, throwing in a sheaf of canons and other contrapuntal *jeux d'esprit* for good measure.

Gaines is at his best here, trading a faux-jovial, History Channel style for serious and lucid exegesis. Indeed, the clash between sensibilities that is his book's main topic seems to characterize his own authorial persona. He loves the baroque intricacy of religious or philosophical or musical argument, and is uncomfortable with linear storytelling—that rational progression and development of themes which is the essence of Classical design. He is never happier (and neither is his reader) than when he gives up trying to keep track of Bach's jobs or Frederick's wars, and can write, say, of the canon BWV 1073: "Nowhere better than in a perpetual canon like this can you hear so clearly the connection between musical and celestial harmony, the canonic voices weaving in and around one another like so many orbiting planets, eternally in motion and eternally the same."

What Frederick thought of the *Musical Offering,* when Bach mailed it to him two months after their meeting, is not known. The likelihood is that he tossed it aside unperformed. He was by then well on his way to becoming an arch-reactionary both to the music of the past, exemplified by Bach, and the music of the future, pioneered by Gluck and Haydn. The stony core that had begun to form within him when he saw Katte executed eventually petrified his entire personality. He died a depressive recluse in 1786, thirty-three years after Bach.

Geniuses both, polar opposites the pair of them, King and commoner linked only by their mutual worship of Saint Cecilia—let us hope that, in some heavenly auditorium (M. Escher, architect) they are twiddling away at harpsichord and flute, in endless variations on Frederick's "right Royal theme."

CONTRAPUNTAL COMBAT

Beethoven's Great Fugue

M Y FIRST REACTION TO THE ANNOUNCEMENT THAT A MAJOR
Beethoven manuscript has been discovered in Pennsylvania was an aching desire to see it. (The ache will not be gratified until it goes on exhibit at Sotheby's.)

To see it. How often we use that phrase in a tactile sense—as when, for example, we ask somebody at Tiffany's to unlock the cabinet and bring out a Rolex so we can feel its cold, thrilling weight on our wrist. Eye contact is enough, though, when we cannot gratify our animal desire to caress whatever is unattainable, inimitable, or worshipful.

Beethoven's manuscripts are revelatory of an intensely physical person who fought his music onto the page, splattering ink, breaking nibs, and even ripping the paper in the process. Not for him the serene penmanship of J. S. Bach, whose undulant figurations sway like ship masts over calm seas, or the hasty perfection of Mozart, or the quasi-mathematical constructs of Webern. Their writing is the product of

Originally published in *The New York Times*, 14 October 2005.

Autograph copy of piano version of Beethoven's Grosse Fuge, Op. 134.

minds already made up. Beethoven was so full of ideas that to fire them out—to see which were precious metal and which mere ore—was a process in which he needed to involve his eyes and his hands (not to mention his heels drumming out rhythms, and his voice howling and groaning: landlords were forever giving him notice). Long before he went deaf, he was the most prodigious sketcher in musical history, unable to walk around a room or, I regret to say, sit down on a toilet without doodling hieroglyphics on every reachable surface. Even when perambulating around Vienna at a hyperactive clip, he was forever stopping to scribble something in the notebook that seemed to be an inseparable part of his left hand.

One such scribble was the "lightning flash" theme that begins the second movement of the Ninth Symphony. It struck Beethoven one night as he was emerging from a bright interior into darkness. To page through his sketchbook of the period, and see it suddenly appear amid clouds of murky musical thought, is to feel the electricity of inspiration.

The manuscript just found in Pennsylvania (an eighty-page piano duet version of his famous *Grosse Fuge*, or "Great Fugue," Op. 133, for string quartet) dates from 1826, the last full year of Beethoven's life. It is reported to be typically three-dimensional, with erasures worn into holes, and a large patch of rewritten music spackled onto one page with sealing wax. Since the *Grosse Fuge* is the single most physical movement in Beethoven—fifteen minutes of furious contrapuntal combat, adored by Stravinsky—what we will be seeing at Sotheby's promises to be as much an artifact as an autograph.

Somebody who still works like Beethoven is the French artist Bernard Dufour. His drawing hand substitutes on camera for that of Michel Piccoli in Jacques Rivette's masterly film *La Belle Noiseuse*, about a painter struggling to execute his final masterpiece. One notices, as the hand reaches out to select a pen and jab it into the ink bottle, the violence of its movements, impatient yet tentative, as if wondering in which direction to discharge its energy. The sketchpad lies white, waiting to be raped by the looming nib. Then down the sharp thing comes, at a deliberately obtuse angle, so that the first line is not so much drawn but dug out of the paper. Nor is there as much ink running as you would expect; the artist seems to be daring his inspiration to dry up. More swoops and gougings, then suddenly a deliberate splash of ink, which the heel of the hand smudges into some shading . . . and lo, the curve of a naked woman's thigh materializes out of the whiteness, and art begins to happen.

It is moving to watch, because we can feel Dufour's Beethovenian love of struggle, his sheer joy in being bespattered, stained, and even resisted (when a sketch obstinately refuses to cohere) by the materials at hand. Such relish is of course characteristic of workers in the plastic arts. But with the decline of painting and drawing in recent years, in favor of hands-off processes such as video recording, performance art, and installations farmed out to contractors, even artists are putting less and less of themselves into their work—with the result that what there is of it, is sterile. I had to spend a couple of months earlier this year looking down at Christo's orange hangings in Central Park, and got back from them nothing but a sense of manufactured lifelessness.

I worry that further withdrawal of the body will increasingly depersonalize creativity in our computerized age. It is already a given that many young architects can't draw, relying on circuitry to do their imagining for them. Nor can most of them model—never having built things with their hands as children, and felt the pliancy and fragility of structures, the interrelationship of empty space and solid mass. Recently my wife and I bought a country house designed by just such an architect. It looked great until we discovered that the main floor sagged in the middle, lacking the kind of central support that a child, forty years ago, would have sensed was fundamental at foundation level.

Writing does not, of course, rate high on the tactile scale of things. But a screen of glass impregnated with pixels now gleams in front of practically every young person who wishes to commit words to—I was going to say paper, but will avoid the anachronism. Today's words, dit-ditted, flash off somewhere at the speed of light and assemble themselves in electronic limbo. Seen through the glass darkly, they look seductively perfect, every character proportional, every paragraph in alignment. Why mess around with them? In any case, if their orthography is not quite correct, a default "word processor" (ghastly phrase) will alter them to its liking.

A couple of years ago I had a disillusioning residency with students at the University of Chicago who wished, or thought they wished, to master the art of narrative nonfiction. Cyberspatial innocent that I am, I was at first puzzled by the weird uniformity of their written "style," if that's the word for prose equally composed of IM-speak and catch-phrases downloaded by the megabyte. At last, like the girl in the Stage Door Canteen, I caught on. But what was even weirder was the way these not unintelligent seniors looked at me as I lectured them on Tolstoy's frenzied chicken-scratches all over proofs of *War and Peace,* Capote's yellow-page drafts of *In Cold Blood,* and Nabokov's exquisite watercolor diagrams, illustrative of metric schemes in Russian poetry.

What freaked me out was their collective gaze, not uninterested, but uninvolved. They weren't listening so much as watching. To them, I was just the latest in a lifetime's succession of images, talking out of a box beyond reach.

I doubt I'll see any of them when I go to look at the *Grosse Fuge* manuscript next month. Why should they bother? They can already access it on the Internet. But without seeing the real thing, with actual light falling on its scuffs and blotches, will they ever feel the desperate energy of a dying Beethoven, imprisoned in the box of his own disability?

WOOD AND WOOL

The Making of a Steinway Concert Grand

THE CONNOISSEUR BERNARD BERENSON COINED THE PHRASE *tactile values* to express the way great works of art, whether painted, sculpted, or merely manufactured, caress the senses with an almost physical tangibility. To look at one of Fra Angelico's Madonnas is to feel with the eye, and to feel is to know.

Surely no artifact is richer in tactile values than a modern concert grand piano—that is, the gleaming eighty-eight-key, nine-foot monster perfected by C. F. Theodore and William Steinway in 1891, and essentially unchanged since. From the moment it begins its life, as various integrants of wood, cloth, metal, and (sigh) plastic ivory-substitute co-

Originally published in *The New York Times*, 1 October 2006.
Photograph courtesy of Steinway & Sons.

here under myriad hands, until the first outside player plinks a freshly polished key and listens to the sweet response, the piano is a product of the human body, designed to return to the body as music, with ample power to chasten and subdue. A good piano, that is—not one of those glazed, mass-produced affordables that sound like crockery falling over.

It is the admirable achievement of James Barron's *Piano: The Making of a Steinway Concert Grand* that, in spite of his rather dogged style, he manages to communicate the tactile values inherent at every stage in the manufacture of CD-60, the big Steinway that now sits in the Metropolitan Museum's Grace Rainey Rogers auditorium. Barron, a staff reporter for *The New York Times,* spent eleven months watching this instrument move through the hands of scores of rim-benders, trimmers, bracers, bellymen, sprayers, stringers, action assemblers, regulators, and polishers in the Astoria, Queens factory of Steinway & Sons, America's premium maker of fine pianos. He even accompanied the company's wood technologist on an expedition to Puget Sound in search of perfect Sitka spruce—an increasingly rare commodity, all but logged out in the contiguous United States. And he stayed with CD-60, off and on, through its first two years of concert life.

The result of all this observation was a series of documentary articles, published in the *Times* from May 2003 to April 2004, and collected now in book form. It is a parochial survey, in that Barron focuses on one piano, one factory, and one monopolistic firm, which, since the bankruptcy of the Baldwin Company in 2001, looms more than ever as a dominant force on the American concert circuit. He thus shortchanges Steinway's other facility in Hamburg, Germany, whose pianos many top musicians prefer—when they don't choose the magnificent grands of Bösendorfer, Bechstein, and Fazioli.

Mr. Barron's newspaper editors seem to have noticed this bias even as his series was running, and published a balancing article about Steinway's competitive business practices. But Mr. Barron can hardly be faulted for giving himself a precise assignment and fulfilling it. He seems to share Thomas Mann's view that "only the exhaustive is truly interesting."

His conscientiousness pays off in the accumulation of a mass of detail, which to anyone who has ever built anything intricate is satisfying to the point of sensuousness. As a sometime carpenter and, like Mr. Barron, an amateur pianist with a Steinway at home, I delighted in such passages as this:

> When the rim arrives at [trimmer Louis] Nozil's big table saw, it has rough edges. Though the rim-benders had been careful in matching and marrying the strips of maple, each of the eight strips that formed the outer rim of [CD-60] is a different height from the one next to it. One towers over another by a sixteenth of an inch; yet another is short by almost as much. There is a run of mountains on the top and bottom of the rim—the peaks of the laminations alternate with the ski runs of now-dried glue that the rim presses out. . . . Nozil's task is to steer the entire rim round a fast-spinning cutting head that makes the floor shake beneath his feet and sends a cloud of sawdust floating toward the ceiling.

Readers less interested in handicraft will find *Piano* slow going. This is partly because the process it describes *is* slow, and partly because the book betrays its serial composition. In laminating the original articles together, Barron should have used a cutting head to eliminate, for example, the route by which Andy Horbachevsky, Steinway's manufacturing director, skirts the expressway from Westchester to Queens in his minivan every morning ("ninety minutes, door to desk").

Interposed sections of Steinway corporate history serve some "background" purpose, but here the doggedness can become dull—as in a collusive chapter on Henry Z. Steinway. Mr. Steinway, who sold his family firm to CBS in 1972, may or may not have saved it from Baldwin's fate in a declining market, but he seems treated with excessive respect.

The Canadian business writer Susan Goldenberg is less charitable in her 1996 book *Steinway: From Glory to Controversy: The Family, the Business, the Piano.* She makes plain Henry Z's responsibility for the disastrous "Teflon Era" of Steinway production (eerily coinciding with the rise of the Teflon President), when fluorocarbon bushings were substituted for cloth ones, and impregnated the action with clicking noises. My piano dates from this period, and in dry weather it sounds like Madame DeFarge at the height of the Terror. Suffice to say that Steinway (now owned by two Californian investment bankers) has long since gone back to the quiet cooperation of wood and wool.

Mr. Barron redeems himself with a portrait of Bruce Campbell, tone regulator of model D grands at the Astoria plant. His account of this perfectionist's work is meticulously observed and moving. In an age when even such fundamentals of life as talking, writing, and making music are being digitized, to the atrophy of our communicative faculties, one feels a reverence for people like this, whose hands, ears, and eyes protect the sonic legacy of Beethoven and Chopin.

Piano ends with two engrossing chapters, "Debut," and "Postlude," that show how CD-60 (rather bright and raw at first, in its brand-new state) achieved mellowness, and a surprising variety of tonal timbres, under the hands of such pianists as Jonathan Biss, Ruth Laredo, Peter Serkin, and Emanuel Ax. The fact that they each have different opinions of it proves that in piano playing and listening, subjectivity is all. One man's "raw" is another man's "toned-down." Or, in the famous indiscretion of Steinway artist Garrick Ohlsson, "the Rolls-Royce of pianos" may well be a Bösendorfer.

During my own performing career, which lasted for seven minutes in Zankel Hall last winter (at a benefit concert of musical amateurs), I was exclusively a Fazioli artist, and can say only that the thrill of sitting behind nine feet of solid mahogany and Italian spruce, pealing like bells and sustaining like an organ, was greater than anything I've experienced at a Steinway. Yet a professional such as Manny Ax can stroke a few of CD-60's plastic keys, and produce sounds of the purest beauty. Put it down to the old mystery known as "the riddle of the pianist's finger"—and to the tactile values of those nicked, bruised, sawdust-wheezing craftsmen with names like Stavrianos and Beharovic and Verasammy and Shiwprasad, working across the East River for an average of $15.50 an hour.

A NATION FULL OF WILL

Kent School Connecticut Centennial Address, 2006

I CAME TO KENT FOUR YEARS AGO TO BEGIN TO BE OLD. YOU KENT Scholars have come here to begin to be young. You may think you were young before you arrived, but you're wrong. Youth is not the same as childhood. It's a time of doubt. Children have no doubts at all. They know exactly what they want, and whom to manipulate in order to get it. Children are the only mature adults in our society. The rest of us, young and old, work for them. And precious few thanks do we get.

Hence the rather wistful confusion characteristic of youth. Remembering the luxurious gated community of childhood, with its round-the-clock security and services, you wonder why these benefits have been so suddenly withdrawn—why you now find yourself in the penitentiary known as high school, patrolled by malevolent teachers, in-

Originally published in the *Kent Quarterly* (Fall 2006/Winter 2007).
Photograph courtesy of the Kent School.

fested by members of the opposite sex, threatened on all sides by litigious Schaghticokes,* with no assurance that things aren't going to get steadily worse. Well, let me give you that assurance. They will!

Evelyn Waugh, the great British novelist, once called the future "the dreariest of prospects." Having experienced a good deal of my own future already, I can only say that he was right. So why even bother to grow old? Because God is good. He does supply some reasons to go on living. Mrs. Stroble's blueberry scones down in the village, for example. The promise of another season of *Curb Your Enthusiasm,* for another. And best of all, the possibility that one day—sooner for me than for you!— we will be rewarded for our life's long labors with a second childhood.

THAT PHRASE I JUST quoted by Evelyn Waugh comes from the opening page of his autobiography. I'll read you the context, because it postulates an idea similar to one that Father Schell suggested to me, as a theme for my speech to you today.

> I lately took up and re-read after many years H. G. Wells's *The Time Machine. . . .* What a waste of this magical vehicle to take it prying into the future, as had the hero of the book. The future, dreariest of prospects! Were I in the saddle, I should set the engine Slow Astern. To hover gently back through centuries . . . would be the most exquisite pleasure of which I can conceive.

That was more or less what Father Schell thought I should do this morning (and remembering my own headmaster's willingness to reach for the cane, I've always done exactly what principals suggest). To turn this podium, as it were, into a time machine and hover back just one century to the fall of 1906, when Father Sill inaugurated the Kent School here on the banks of this beautiful river. To see to what extent life was different then than now. Or, perhaps, see to what greater extent it was the same—as life always has been the same, and always will be, human nature being a constant, and history nothing but a series of todays, end-

---

* A reference to the Indian tribe then staking a claim to some of the Kent School lands.

lessly duplicated. "Just one damn thing after another," to quote one of the students in Alan Bennett's *The History Boys.**

What kind of America, what kind of a world precipitated Father Sill onto this quiet bank of the Housatonic a hundred years ago? Men of a monastic nature are forever turning their backs on Mammon, but I've noticed they always end up in the best places. More to the point, what kind of *Zeitgeist* did the Pater feel a need to prepare young Christians for—maybe even protect them against?

As it happens, we hardly need an antichronological construct to help us vividly see and feel the America of Father Sill's time. By a nice coincidence, the author of *The Time Machine*, H. G. Wells, toured New England and the Midwest that same year, and ended up in Washington, D.C., interviewing President Theodore Roosevelt. Wells was as brilliant a social and scientific commentator as he was a novelist, and unlike many traveling foreigners, he saw the United States through unprejudiced eyes. I spent an afternoon recently reading with much fascination the account of his visit, which he entitled *The Future in America: A Search After Realities.*

Note the delicacy of the preposition *in.* As a realistic, unsentimental observer, Wells did not choose to imagine the future *of* America. (He was deeply pessimistic about the future of the whole human race in 1906, but he was smart enough to know that pessimism does not sell books.) No, he saw America as the world's most progressive country, and if the future of the world was going to be felt anywhere, it would be felt in America.

HIS FIRST IMPRESSION, even before he arrived here, was disagreeable, and identical to the first impression of travelers applying for U.S. visas today. Immigration authorities badgered him with questions that he considered intrusive and aggressive. "Are you an Anarchist? Are you an Atheist? Are you a Polygamist?" (That last question particularly irritated him, because he was.) He did not feel his political and religious and sex-

---

* Bennett himself was quoting Elbert Hubbard (1856–1915).

ual orientations were the business of any American authority, but he controlled his temper, as tourists do now, in order to get in.

The moment he disembarked, he felt what he called "[a] great individual force of will," a sense of national purpose that shone most brightly in the faces of young Americans. Paradoxically, their individualism did not conflict with the general advancement of the state, because everybody seemed to be ambitious. Even the poor had dreams. It was indeed so palpable, this universal, "sharply-cut determination" to succeed and to lead, that he worried about the growth of the nation's ego. He questioned "its quality, its flexibility, its consciousness, and intellectuality. A nation may be full of will," he wrote, in words that resonate today, "and yet inflexibly and disastrously stupid in the expression of that will."

As he continued traveling, however, he found that that paradox, the clash of apparently contrary phenomena, was what sparked American dynamism. Despite an ethnic mix inconceivable even in the most crowded corners of Europe, the United States was still a "curiously homogenous" nation. No two cities could have been more different, and more mutually contemptuous, than old Brahmin Boston and raw, chaotic Chicago. Yet in both, Wells observed, "the same creative forces were at work," building banks and stockyards and symphony halls. America was a classless society, in the sense that privilege could be fought for and won, rather than inherited without effort. But in another sense, it was governed by an aristocracy as arrogant as that swept away by the French Revolution—the aristocracy of the superrich. (By the way, if you think that the word *superrich* is an anachronism, consider that Andrew Carnegie in 1906 was worth 120 billion in today's dollars. And John D. Rockefeller's wealth was proportionately much larger than that of Bill Gates.)

Then, as now, the gap between the rich and the poor, or what Wells called the Owner and the Worker, seemed to be widening alarmingly in America. And on both sides, combination was the result: federations of trade unions to the left, concentrations of capital to the right. Therein lay another paradox: that laborers fighting for more personal dignity and security, and financiers fighting for more freedom from government regulation (as personified by Teddy the Trust Buster), were doing so "under individualistic rules, until individual competition becomes disheartened and hopeless."

Why, then, was everybody—at least, everybody Wells met—so full of hope? He would have to wait for the answer to that until he met Theodore Roosevelt.

IN THE MEANTIME, it occurred to him that the single biggest problem confronting America (and does this connect with anything you might have heard on the news recently?) was a flood tide of immigration, much of it across the Mexican border. (Wells didn't say, but those wetbacks were mainly Chinese, ferried across the Pacific by illegal operatives and dumped south of the border.) Wells could not understand why Americans were so casual about this influx. No fewer than one million were expected by the end of 1906, more than ever before, at a time when the national population was just ninety million.

"Into the lower levels of the American community," he wrote, "there pours perpetually a vast torrent of strangers, speaking alien tongues, inspired by alien traditions, for the most part illiterate peasants and working people. They come in at the bottom—that must be insisted upon. . . . The older American population is being floated up on the top of this influx, a sterile aristocracy above a racially different and astonishingly fecund proletariat."

I hasten to add that H. G. Wells was, unusually for his time, not a white racist. The chapter of his book that deals with race hatred in the lynch-crazy South—and not only the South—is eloquently horrified, even by today's standards. History has shown that he was wrong to worry about immigration in 1906, and maybe we're hypocritical to worry about it now. But Wells was right about what he called "the Tragedy of Color" in 1906. He cited the behavior of white Sunday-school children after a lynch mob in Springfield, Missouri, burned three black men to death for an imaginary crime. These God-fearing boys and girls combed through the ashes looking for bits of Negro bone to keep as souvenirs.

I'm not going to apologize for the following quotation. This is the way people expressed themselves in those days—some people, anyway:

"Ah! You don't know the real nigger," [one white man said when Wells spoke in praise of the black citizens he had met]. "You should see the buck nigger down south, Congo brand. Then you'll understand, sir!"

His voice, his face had a gleam of passionate animosity. One could see he had been brooding himself out of all relations to reality in this matter. He was a man beyond reason or pity. He was obsessed.

The history of civil rights in twentieth-century America is one of the best-taught subjects in today's schools, so I don't need to coach any of you in how long it took for such people "beyond reason and pity" to pass away. But pass away they eventually did, except for a militiaman or two in Montana. It's good to know that, although we may resemble our forebears in so many ways, in at least a few respects we've transcended them.

For black Americans in 1906, the future was definitely not "the dreariest of prospects."

I WILL BRIEFLY list some other aspects of American life that impressed Wells then, and even now impress an objective outsider: the aspiration toward bigness, in dreams and schemes as well as physical plans; the lack of servile tradition—which is to say, a universal sense of dignity; "a constant substitution of larger, cleaner, more efficient possibilities, and more wholesale and far-sighted methods of organization"; the magnificent private universities; the Fourth Estate's healthy desire to investigate and hold to justice all secret activities likely to pervert our freedoms; the power of grassroots activism; the power of what a later pundit called America's positive thinking.

And just to be fair, I might also mention a few more things Wells was not impressed by, things that endure a century later: America's contempt for the notion of abstract justice, the by-product of its individualism; its suspicion of anything, no matter how fine, that might be criticized as elitist, and the consequent vulgarity of its aesthetics; its hastiness, which Wells pointed out is not the same thing as quickness (and which

Theodore Roosevelt defined as "a lack of thoroughness"); and finally, the inefficiency, inaccessibility, and frequent venality of members of Congress.

When he came to meet the President of the United States, however, Wells was overwhelmed. Theodore Roosevelt had, he sensed, "the most vigorous brain in a conspicuously responsible position in all the world [in 1906]."

If any one man personified America, and therefore the future, Wells wrote, it was the President of the United States.

> My impression was of a mind quite extraordinarily open . . . [a] seeking mind. . . . His range of reading is amazing; he seems to be echoing with all the thought of his time, he has receptivity to the point of genius. And he does not merely receive, he digests and reconstructs; he thinks. . . . He assimilates contemporary thought, delocalizes it and reverberates it. He is America for the first time vocal to itself.

As such, TR was equipped to engage Wells in a philosophical conversation in the White House garden that is a *locus classicus* in the long history of New World optimism countering Old World cynicism. It also makes one sigh for the quality of discourse that passes for conversation now in Washington, and on our television networks. Basically it concerned Wells's sense that Western civilization was doomed, despite the contemporary dynamism of America—that "the inevitable segregations of an individualistic system [would work] themselves out, and all the hope and vigor of humanity [go] forever."

The President mentioned *The Time Machine*, which made a metaphor of that doom, portraying the descendants of contemporary workers as sinister, subterranean monsters, and those of capitalists as feeble, self-indulgent degenerates. He kept his temper (TR was a man of impeccable manners), but it was clear that Wells's pessimism annoyed him. He kneeled on a garden chair and leaned forward over the back, opening and closing his fist repeatedly, vibrating with energy. "The effort's real," he said. "It's worth going on with."

Wells wrote afterward that TR stuck in his mind as "a very symbol of the creative will in man," and of all that was admirable in contemporary America.

IT IS PERHAPS presumptuous of me to claim similarities with Wells. But I am a foreign-born writer with at least some inherited sense of objectivity about the United States, and I have met quite a few presidents, and written about others. Not so long ago, I spent about as much time with President Bush as Wells spent with TR, and got, superficially speaking, the same impression of overwhelming health, energy, optimism, and self-certainty. I also sensed a considerable intelligence, but it was a political intelligence like Franklin Roosevelt's, not a creative intelligence like TR's.

What was palpably lacking in Mr. Bush was culture, and any comprehension of the fact that the world consists of a welter of sensibilities, religions, aesthetics, and ideologies beyond the pale of corporate, churchgoing America. The President of the United States a hundred years ago was a man who read a book a day in four languages. He wrote forty books himself—scholarly works of history and biography, political commentary, literary criticism, zoology, ornithology, and wilderness lore. From childhood on he had toured Europe and the Middle East extensively, and he had an international circle of acquaintance among statesmen, socialites, and intellectuals that extended as far as Japan. He had studied in Germany as a teenager and could quote long stretches of the *Nibelungenlied* by heart. He was a diplomat of consummate skill and tact, mediating an end to the Russo-Japanese War and using his understanding of Islam to help resolve at least two North African crises—one of which, over Morocco, threatened to bring about World War I eight years early. And just about then, in 1906, he heard that he had become the first American to win the Nobel Peace Prize.

It's become a cliché to criticize President Bush for being unschooled in any religion but his own, but according to a recent report in *The New York Times*, most of our current policymakers, including those in charge of antiterrorism efforts, don't know the difference between Shiite and Sunni Muslims. When I met Mr. Bush, he made it plain that he saw the entire world—including Vladimir Putin's Russia—in terms of Bible Belt

Christian sentimentality. I can just imagine how H. G. Wells would react to that.

Sentimentality, as the Kent School's most distinguished literary alumnus has repeatedly warned us, is an American disease. James Gould Cozzens, class of 1922, is largely forgotten now, but if there's any finer legal novel than *The Just and the Unjust*, and any greater book on World War II than *Guard of Honor* (which won the Pulitzer Prize in 1948), I haven't heard of them.* And those of you curious about what Kent was like in the early Thirties—rattlesnakes and all—might enjoy his novel *The Last Adam*.

The reason Cozzens is neglected now is that his unblinking realism is intolerable to the very sentimentality he warned against—sentimentality being a willfull refusal to see things as they are, a compulsion to prettify what's really ugly in, for example, American military behavior. I'm loath to speak of ugliness and shortsightedness on a day as beautiful and as historic as this, but we do appear to have reached, just forty-eight hours ago, a turning point in our "crusade" in Iraq.† Yes, let's call a spade a spade—as the President says, "They're killing Christians there!" What presents itself now is a test of American will, the same will that so impressed H. G. Wells, and personified in a leader who is as sure of himself as TR ever was. Indeed, Mr. Bush frequently cites Theodore Roosevelt as a role model. But is that will in 2006 an educated one, as it was in 1906? Is it based on a thinking man's understanding of history, of religion, of the rule of tooth and claw, as operative in foreign affairs as in zoology?

We know it is not, and we pine for a day when the White House might once again be occupied by a man of culture. It is more than ever the mission of our best schools, such as this one celebrating its centennial, to graduate leaders with Theodore Roosevelt's range of reference.

And if, as is quite possible, one of you boys and girls—preferably a girl—does succeed in becoming President, I hope you will consider me as your authorized biographer.

---

* See pages 307–316.
† On 19 October 2006, amid a crescendo of sectarian violence in Iraq, and a record surge in American troop fatalities, the military command in Baghdad admitted the failure of its campaign to pacify the city. A spokesman announced that officials were urgently discussing ways to "refocus" U.S. war strategy.

NUAGES GRIS

Colors in Music, Literature, and Art

THE THIRD MOVEMENT OF BEETHOVEN'S STRING QUARTET NO. 15, *Op. 132, begins to sound.*

One hundred and seventy-three years ago, at the age of fifty-four, Ludwig van Beethoven wrote this strange white music. Why do I call it white? Well, it sounds white. No melody, no dynamics, no rhythm to speak of— just a succession of similar concords. It even *looks* white. All the notes are white ovals, moving ever so slowly up and down their respective clefs, like planets realigning themselves. There are none of those black ciphers musicians call "accidentals" to darken the pallor of the score. If you play those chords on a piano, your fingers will not move from the white keys.

And why does it sound strange to our ears, this music, in the way the harmonies so hauntingly dissolve into one another, but never quite re-

Lecture at the Metropolitan Museum of Art, New York, 16 December 2007.
Score of the slow movement of Beethoven's String Quartet, Op. 132.

solve? Perhaps *archaic* is a better word than *strange*. Beethoven was writing in the Lydian mode of Ancient Greece—an arrangement of tones and semitones that we are no longer used to. He had gone through a near-death experience in the spring of 1825, with acute colitis and lung trouble. I should also mention that he was stone deaf. We don't know if he saw any white light as he lay hemorrhaging in bed, or if he prayed to be saved: he was not a conventionally religious man. But he was saved, and when he wrote this piece, he inscribed it *Heiliger Dankgesang eines Genesenen an die Gottheit*, "Holy hymn of thanks to the Divinity from a recovering invalid."

AS A WRITER who studies music, I have always been conscious of the parallels between prosody and melody (the letter being the note, the phrase the phrase, the paragraph the passage, the chapter the movement, and so on). These are, of course, common to the codification of any language—music being the most universal, in that it needs no translation. But less obvious, and more interesting, are the expressive ways music and literature interact with each other, and both of them with painting. Today being Beethoven's birthday, we might ponder some of these reflections, and refractions, and echoes, and correspondences, and cross-fertilizations.

It is possible, for example, for a poet to orchestrate his lines in the way a composer will score them instrumentally. Brahms's use of a triangle to give metallic overtones to the scherzo of his Fourth Symphony equates with Tennyson's use of plosives and fricatives in "Morte d'Arthur":

> *Dry clash'd his harness in the icy caves*
> *And barren chasms, and all to left and right*
> *The bare black cliff clang'd round him, as he based*
> *His feet on juts of slippery cave that rang*
> *Sharp-smitten with the dint of armed heels . . .*

Whereas the liquid laterals that immediately follow—

> *And on a sudden, lo! the level lake,*
> *And the long glories of the winter moon*

—have much in common with the pedal effects Debussy demanded in his piano piece *La Cathédrale Engloutie,* in order to make the instrument "sound as if it were immersed in water."

As with sound, so with color. Composers have attested over and over that they "hear" (might "see" be a better word?) keys in different colors—although one man's dark gold D-flat major might be another man's purple. The painterly technique of *chiaroscuro,* or juxtaposition of light and shadow, is actually much more used in music than it is in art—witness Schubert's habitual oscillations back and forth between contrasting tonalities, or the transition, in Haydn's oratorio *The Creation,* from the words "Let there be light," softly sung by the chorus in darkest C minor, to the overwhelming loudness of "And there was LIGHT" in brilliant C major.

By the same token, a conscious *absence* of color, as in Malevich's famous painting *White on White,* can have the same subliminal effect as the blanched sounds of the Beethoven quartet referred to above. Deliberate reiterations (called *ostinati* in music) are used by some writers for evocatory reasons. A faint fragrance of lemon verbena sachet seems to emanate from the pages of *Gone with the Wind* whenever Ellen O'Hara is mentioned. I don't know if there's such a verb as *deiterate,* but Georges Perec wrote a whole novel, *La Disparition,* with the letter *E* eternally missing. The absence of any words containing that vowel, in a book which deals with the disappearance of Jews in the Holocaust, is not immediately noticeable, any more than the absence of a semitonal leading-note in the Beethoven quartet music you just heard. But as you read on, the prose begins to convey an extraordinary, aching sense of loss, which is of course just the undertone Perec intended.

W. G. Sebald used both visual and verbal images to convey, again and again, this same trauma at the heart of European memory. Here is (or tragically was, for he was killed in a car crash just as his talent reached full flower) a writer who *saw* so much evocative detail, even in postcards and ill-focused snapshots, that much of his prose "reads" like photography.*

---

* "Why certain tonal colors, subtleties of key, and syncopations can take such a hold on the mind is something that an entirely unmusical person like myself can never understand, said Austerlitz, but today, looking back, it seems to me as if the mystery which touched me at the time was summed up in the image of the snow-white goose standing motionless and steadfast among the musicians as long as they played."
—W. G. Sebald, *Austerlitz* (New York, 2001), 274–75.

Similarly, Sebald's compatriot Gerhard Richter has transmuted the blurry, black-and-white flickerings of 1970s television news coverage of the Baader-Meinhof gang into a cycle of unforgettably haunting paintings.

GETTING BACK TO WHITENESS, there is a correspondence between the blank paper that surrounds print on the page, and the blankness of a canvas where the artist's brush or charcoal has not gone, and the silence of which music so largely and paradoxically consists. We tend not to think of silence when music is playing. But after all, music comes out of and recedes back into silence, and between those two voids, other silences constantly break in—in the minute intervals between staccato notes, or between separated phrases, or during the rests and pauses that composers prescribe in their manuscripts, just as writers (and particularly poets) use white space for rhythmic or rhetorical effect, and artists rejoice in the *tabula rasa.*

One of the most poignant moments in music, albeit unintended, is the silence that suddenly intrudes at the end of a performance of Bach's valedictory *Art of the Fugue.* As endings go, it couldn't be more final, because Bach died at that point, leaving the score unfinished. The notes you are listening to simply stop, and the silence that crashes in has the force of a blow to the face.

There's an equivalent moment in literature, at the end of Robert Louis Stevenson's unfinished novel *Weir of Hermiston.* It's only a fragment— substantial to be sure, at around 160 pages—but for as long as it continues it is superlative. Stevenson, like Franz Schubert, rose to a phenomenal level of creativity in the last year of his short life, making one wonder what heights each man might have attained, had they survived.

On 3 December 1894, Stevenson was writing the scene where Kirstie breaks into a passion of tears in her lover's arms. Fannie Stevenson interrupted it by calling him down to dinner. He died of a cerebral hemhorrage moments later. As a result, what you see at the end of *Weir of Hermiston* is a sudden explosion of blank paper, just as devastating in its way as the silence at the end of *Art of the Fugue.* Stevenson's last sentence reads, "It seemed unprovoked, a wilful convulsion of brute nature."

Beethoven's Piano Sonata in C-sharp minor, Op. 27,
No. 2 begins to sound, very softly.

For another example of the evocation of mood by subliminal means in music, consider the insistent repetitions of G-sharp in this sonata that made the poet Ludwig Rellstab think of moonlight lying on a still lake. It's a lovely audiovisual idea, although anything less still than the volcanically surging last movement could hardly be imagined. I doubt very much that Beethoven had moonbeams in his head when he wrote it, any more than Chopin visualized raindrops when he used the same note even more obsessively in his sixteenth Prelude. But Evelyn Waugh, who understood the music of prose as well as Beethoven and Chopin did piano sonorities, was being deliberately atmospheric when he infused the text of *Vile Bodies* with constant mentions of rain. And James Joyce was just as palpably aroused, at the end of *Ulysses*, by Molly Bloom's reiterations of the word *yes* as Wagner was at the end of *Tristan*, building the climax of Isolde's "Liebestod" out of mounting, orgiastic throbs.

Painters, of course, use repetitive effects and color coordination all the time. And at least since the days of Malevich, they have explored monotonality as an aesthetic in itself. Consider the revelatory exhibition of the gray paintings of Jasper Johns here at the Met recently. Who could have imagined there was so much color in the dullest of all colors?* Some of the canvases struck me as *grey* in the way the English spell the word, whereas others were *gray*—a different shade, as I'm sure Mr. Johns (our most literate living artist) would agree.

Screen projection of Jasper Johns, Gray Painting (1975).

Here's one of those gray-with-an-*a* paintings, about the only one the Met is allowed to project commercially, because Mr. Johns is as proprietary about reproduction rights as Beethoven was when he was flogging the *Missa Solemnis*.

---

*Debussy wrote Eugène Ysaÿe in 1894 that *Nocturnes* was "an experiment in the different combinations that can be obtained from one color—what a study in grey would be in painting."

I was intrigued to note, in an interview the artist did at the time of that show, that one of his favorite poets was Edwin Arlington Robinson, whom Theodore Roosevelt rescued from near-starvation in 1905. Hardly anybody reads Robinson these days, and more's the pity, because Robert Frost was right to be jealous of him. One day when I have the courage (because Jasper Johns, who lives in my corner of Connecticut, famously dislikes being questioned), I'm going to ask him if Robinson's haunting poem "The House on the Hill" ever sounded in his head when he was painting images like this.

> They are all gone away,
>   The House is shut and still,
> There is nothing more to say.
> Through broken walls and gray
>   The winds blow bleak and shrill:
> They are all gone away. . . .
> There is nothing more to say.

Robinson, like Johns, was not averse to the use of bright color, but whenever he infused his lyrics with it, he did so sparingly, knowing that a single coloristic adjective can tint five or six repetitive lines:

> Go to the western gate, Luke Havergal,—
> There where the vines cling crimson on the wall,—
> And in the twilight wait for what will come. . . .
>   But go, and if you listen, she will call.
> Go to the western gate, Luke Havergal—
> Luke Havergal.

He was, by the way, a devoted music lover, and although he chose not to invoke the Classical canon directly, much of the incantatory, allusive melody of his verse derives from the way it sounds, rather than just reads.

Did any composer write gray music? I don't mean pieces deprived of the color of inspiration, such as those Schumann wrote when he went mad, or Max Reger's fugal attempts to stay awake after eating too much bratwurst. I mean music that explores the mysteries inherent in gray.

Well, Sibelius was certainly a master of monotonality (a word not to be confused with monotony)—and how thrillingly, in his Fourth Symphony and other works, shafts of piercing light keep irradiating the Finnish mists and shadows!

Talking about Scandinavia, there was a revelatory exhibition at the Corcoran Museum in Washington back in the Eighties called "Northern Light." It showed how the artists of that occluded part of the world had their vision changed—almost literally, in a retina-expanding way—by study in Paris and association with the French Impressionists. They went back home and saw, as if for the first time, how subtle and pure their own light was. In the same way, Sibelius had his hearing changed by spells of residence in Germany and Italy. His *Tapiola*, the most icily Nordic tone poem in the orchestral repertory, was composed in, of all places, Rome and Capri.

Musicians are generally not very visual people. However, as I've said, they do tend to relate keys with color. Tonal composers would die rather than admit it, but they often subconsciously choose a key for a piece because of the way it's going to appear in print. Bach, Beethoven, Chopin, and Brahms wrote a lot of black music in dark keys such as E-flat minor and B-flat minor. If you glance at the score of, say, Beethoven's Funeral March (which was played at his own funeral) in A-flat minor, you'll notice that the flat cipher (♭) is as omnipresent on the page as it is absent from the manuscript of his "white" quartet movement. You can transpose the music up a semitone into the "white" key of A minor, and although it will still sound threnodic, it just won't *look* as though somebody has died!

Which reminds me of the delightful story of Vladimir Nabokov driving through the countryside with a friend and seeing a flock of starlings perched on some telephone wires in a staggered arrangement, like notes on a clef. "Look!" he said—"*Eine kleine Nachtmusik!*"

One composer who became increasingly monochromatic in old age was Franz Liszt, who is so often unjustly dismissed as a gaudy showman. On the contrary, he was, after his flamboyant early career as a virtuoso, a deeply serious, religious man and one of the most advanced musical thinkers of his time. He grew more radical with age, and his late piano pieces, written in the early 1880s, anticipated the atonality of Schoenberg by more than almost twenty years. They profoundly influenced Debussy and Bartók, and are still unfamiliar to most music lovers.

Perhaps I should call them chromatic rather than monochromatic, because like his contemporary Whistler (who composed "nocturnes" in paint), Liszt found a world of nuance in modulating from one muted shade to another. In 1881, for example, he wrote a short piece called *Nuages Gris*—"Gray Clouds"—which does not end so much as evaporate. Liszt also created some frightening, black-sounding music in those last years, including an elegy inspired by the death of Wagner. I heard Maurizio Pollini play it once at Carnegie Hall, and it made me think of Oliver Wendell Holmes's remark that old age is like a big dog in the room, growing and growing until it crushes the breath out of your body.

Like many of the Romantic composers, starting with Schumann, Liszt derived his musical inspirations from literature—the poetry of Dante and Petrarch and Byron and above all, Goethe. Liszt's orchestral masterpiece is his *Faust* Symphony, which consists of three movements portraying the three principal characters in Goethe's poem—respectively, Faust, Gretchen, and Mephistopheles. Their personalities clash to such an extent that Liszt can resolve all the tensions (as Beethoven did in his Ninth Symphony) only in a choral finale. It's set to the words with which Goethe ends Part II of *Faust*. They can be translated as:

> *What's gone before*
> *Is but cast back at us;*
> *Our hoped-for more*
> *Is now a fact to us;*
> *When poor words fail*
> *We yet see light;*
> *The all-Female*
> *Lifts up our sight.*

THAT IMAGE OF *das Ewig-weibliche,* the Eternal Feminine, shining brightly in a distant prospect that might be past, and might be future, is a staple of the German Romantic imagination. It did not originate in Goethe's poem, but seems, oddly enough, to derive from the discovery of landscape at the very dawn of Romanticism in the early nineteenth century. Over the next ninety years, relating distant vistas to sexual and spiritual longings became almost a cliché among artists and poets and painters. *Into my heart an air that kills / From yon far country blows*, wrote A. E. Housman. *What are those blue remembered hills, what spires, what farms are those?* But during the lifetime of Goethe, that colossus bestriding the two worlds of Reason and Romance, the idea that a landscape could be erotic was still revolutionary.

Beethoven, who knew Goethe, is not ordinarily thought of as a Romantic. Classical forms preoccupied him to the end of his days, although he expanded them far beyond Goethe's notion of propriety. But he did toy with the idea of writing an opera on the subject of Faust. And he did famously fall in love with an unobtainable woman—his "Immortal Beloved," as he called her, in 1812. Four years later he wrote *An die ferne Geliebte* ("To the Distant Beloved"), a song cycle on the theme of unconsummated desire. The lyrics were not Goethe's, but the sentiments were. Beethoven made each song mutate into the next, and the yearning phrase that begins the piano prelude—a few notes that ardently rise, only to fall—anticipated by half a century the opening of *Tristan und Isolde*. It recurs constantly, and brings the cycle to a close with a chord that does not satisfy.*

Beethoven never got nearer to musical autobiography than in the songs he addressed to a faraway muse. With their evocations of blue horizons and a love that transcends space and time, he communicated, for the first time in music, the notion of yearning distance already palpable in the landscapes of Caspar David Friedrich. There is no evidence that Beethoven and Friedrich were aware of each other, although they were exact contemporaries and had a mutual acquaintance in Goethe. But they were clearly moved by the same intimations of promise and loss as they moved into middle age. Just after Beethoven published his song

---

* Robert Schumann was fascinated by Beethoven's theme, and used it in 1836 in his Piano Fantasy in C major, another work encoded with amorous meaning. Schumann's "distant beloved" at the time was the pianist Clara Wieck, whose father forcibly kept them apart. In his frustration, Robert communicated with her by inserting ciphers into his compositions—words literally codified as various degrees of pitch, giving new meaning to the French phrase *billets-doux*, "love letters."

cycle, Friedrich painted *Wanderer Above the Sea of Fog*, the quintessential image of German Romanticism.

The concept of the wanderer, which I suppose Friedrich derived from Goethe, went on to journey through the poems of Wilhelm Muller and Schubert's two great song cycles, *Die Schöne Müllerin* and *Winterreise*. Friedrich paints him from behind, and motionless, as though arrested in his wandering by a vision of nature so eternal as to make him question the need to go anywhere, in his worldly insignificance.

The English poet John Keats was probably as unaware of Friedrich as Beethoven, composing *An die ferne Geliebte*, was of either fellow-genius. But in January 1818, at the very time Friedrich was at work on his cloud-painting, Keats wrote the following famous lines:

> *When I behold upon the night's starr'd face*
> *Huge cloudy symbols of a high romance,*
> *And think that I may never live to trace*
> *Their shadows, with the magic hand of chance;*
> *And when I feel, fair creature of an hour,*
> *That I shall never look upon thee more,*
> *Never have relish in the faery power*
> *Of unreflecting love; then on the shore*
> *Of the wide world I stand alone, and think*
> *Till love and fame to nothingness do sink.*

THE ROMANTIC MIND delighted in the dissolution of boundaries and freedom of thought—even if thinking freely and yielding to nameless longings left a person lost and bewildered. The Classical mind, in contrast, required tight form and a frame around everything. Keats's eighteenth-century predecessor, the poet Thomas Gray, took a boat trip in the Lake District and was so terrified by what he took to be the wildness of nature that he would look at the scenery around him only in a hand-mirror.

It's laughable to think of a civilized man doing that, but as anyone knows who has studied the counterpoint of Johann Sebastian Bach, or walked through the Hall of Mirrors in Versailles, Classical and Baroque artists delighted in reflections and refractions and inversions and which-side-up symmetries, from chess sets and card games to great palaces doubling themselves in still pools. Bach's gigues habitually begin as three-part fugues, with the theme going one way to begin with, then, halfway through, flipping itself and proceeding upside down, as if there were no law of musical gravity. Beethoven's intellectual reach extended even further back than the Baroque (witness his study of the symbolism of medieval Christian worship when composing the *Missa Solemnis*, not to mention his use of a melodic mode from Ancient Greece in his String Quartet, Op. 132), and almost as far forward as the early Romanticism of Carl Maria von Weber. But all his life he remained, like Goethe, a creature of the Age of Reason, subjecting wild imagination to logical restraint. The intellectual labor of writing *recherchée* (his own adjective) polyphony fascinated him, even though he seems to have been dyslexic, or at least dyspraxic. He could neither divide nor multiply, was unable to shave without cutting himself, couldn't dance (odd, for a man with such an acute sense of rhythm), couldn't even sharpen a pencil. Yet in his *Hammerklavier* sonata he achieved the nearly impossible feat of making a theme consisting of one hundred and five notes (not counting a free trill) go back in one voice while it goes forward in another.

In musical theory, this arcane contrapuntal procedure is known as *cancicrans*, or crabwise motion—reminding me, irrelevantly but irresistibly, of a wisecrack by John Hay, Theodore Roosevelt's first secretary of state: "There are three species of creatures that when they seem to be coming are going: diplomats, women, and crabs."

Music's discovery of mathematics by the atonal composers of the twentieth century led to constructs such as the theme of Anton Webern's *Piano Variations*, which is as much theory as sound. Or, for that matter, three-dimensional geometry. The theme is cut as symmetrically as a diamond, and the tiny fragmentary phrases, separated by silences, reflect one another like facets. What the right hand plays at the beginning, the left hand immediately plays backward. In other words, phrase one is reflected by phrase two, and so on. When the sequence of phrases and counterphrases reaches the exact center point of the score, it is itself reversed, so that the second part of the theme is in effect the first, as heard and seen in Looking-Glass Land.

All very impressive, and hynotically beautiful when played by the right hands, for example Glenn Gould's. But somehow inhuman, like calculus. To borrow a phrase from Arnold Schoenberg, Webern the minimalist had come to "breathe the air of another planet."

Wolfgang Amadeus Mozart, in contrast, never drew a breath that was not warmly of this world. His musical mirrors, particularly his operas, reflect human beings rather than shards of themselves. Look at what exquisite reflections he tossed back and forth in his Sonata for Two Pianos, K. 448. I use the word *look* because you can both see and hear it played on YouTube by the great pianist Martha Argerich and one of her protégés, a young Italian named Gabriele Baldocci. Mozart wrote the sonata to perform with his sister Nannerl, and it's an exercise in absolute equality for both performers. They duplicate each other so exactly that you can't even tell who is playing the *primo* and who the *secondo* lines of the score. The glass of the computer screen adds its own extra dimensions, as does an occasional deliberate double exposure by the cameraman. What I love about this video is its complexity: the interplay of masculine and feminine, old and young, sound and echo, even the delicious ambiguity of extra pairs of hands reflected on the inside lid of each keyboard, doing the reverse of what the live hands are doing—effects and countereffects that in no way affect the miraculous transparency of the music.

After Mozart, there are no words, even for a man of words. Beethoven and Bach, Friedrich and Keats, Liszt and Robinson, Johns and Balthus, Wolfgang and Nannerl. . . . *They are all gone away, there is nothing more to say.*

THE OTHER SIDE OF SILENCE
Beethoven's Deafness

EVERYBODY WHO KNOWS ANYTHING ABOUT BEETHOVEN KNOWS that he was deaf—although it's not generally realized that before he began to lose his hearing at the age of twenty-six, he had one of the best aural mechanisms enjoyed by any composer. During his teenage years as a court *musicus* in Bonn, he luxuriated in every kind of musical sound, from vocal and choral production (he was the son and grandson of professional singers), from the violin and viola and cembalo and piano and organ (all of which he played), and from spending every working day—nights at the opera, too—physically absorbing the contrasting vibrations of other instruments of the orchestra. This tactile intimacy with catgut and brass and reeds and pipes and plucked or hammered

Lecture at the Metropolitan Museum of Art, New York, 15 January 2008.
Life mask of Beethoven in 1812 by Franz Klein. Musical examples by Antony Beaumont.

wire gave him a sort of acoustical memory bank that served him the rest of his life.

Sound, any kind of sound, was so much a part of Beethoven's imaginative equipment that he thought nothing of attempting to transcribe the trickling of a mountain stream, inscrutably noting, "The bigger the brook, the deeper the tone." When scoring his symphonic poem *Wellington's Victory,* he paid as much attention to battle noises as to musical effects, marking 188 cues for cannon fire (solid dots for the British artillery, open ones for the French), and 25 musket volleys of precise length and direction (indicated by tied, trilled ghost-notes). He synchronized all these salvos so precisely that at the height of the "conflict," six cannonades and two musket volleys would go off within three seconds.

For obvious reasons Beethoven, as a young pianist/composer dependent on commissions and performance fees, tried to conceal from the world that deafness was wrapping itself around him, like a gradually thickening shroud of felt. He managed to keep up the pretense until the fall of 1802, when he wrote (and then suppressed) a suicidal letter to his two brothers, now known as the Heiligenstadt Testament. There is no more poignant document in the history of music:

> For six years now I have been hopelessly afflicted, made worse by senseless physicians, from year to year deceived with hopes of improvement, finally compelled to face the prospect of *a lasting malady* (whose cure will take years or, perhaps be impossible). Though born with a fiery, active temperament, even susceptible to the diversions of society, I was soon compelled to withdraw myself, to live life alone. . . . It was impossible for me to say to people, "Speak louder, shout, for I am deaf." Ah, how could I possibly admit an infirmity in the one sense which ought to be more perfect in me than in others, a sense which I once possessed in the highest perfection? . . . For me there can be no relaxation with my fellow-men, no refined conversations, no mutual exchange of ideas. I must live almost alone like one who has been banished. . . . If I approach near to people a hot terror seizes upon me and I fear being exposed to the danger that my condition might be noticed. Thus it has been during the last six months which I have spent in

the country. . . . What a humiliation for me when someone standing next to me heard a flute in the distance and *I heard nothing,* or someone heard *a shepherd singing* and again I heard nothing. Such incidents drove me almost to despair, a little more of that and I would have ended my life—it was only my art that held me back. Ah, it seemed to me impossible to leave the world until I had brought forth all that I felt was within me.

Beethoven was not being melodramatic when he asserted that music saved him. Having filed the Testament away in a secret drawer of his desk, he began to pour out a flood of magnificent sound, which for quantity and sustained quality was not matched even by Mozart. It lasted for ten years, until deafness finally forced his retirement from the concert stage. The radically different music of his so-called third period followed much more slowly.

I'M NOT SAYING THAT tragedy made Beethoven a great composer. He was already that at nineteen, as Johannes Brahms recognized when the score of young Ludwig's *Cantata on the Death of Emperor Joseph II* came to light in 1884. But I do suggest that Beethoven at thirty-two went through a catharsis, enriching his music beyond measure. In my biography of him, I wrote:

> A distinguishing characteristic of the creative mind is that it can accept reversals of fortune without emotional damage—indeed, process them at once into something rich and strange. Ordinary psyches often react to bad news with a momentary thrill, seeing the world, for once, in jagged clarity, as if lightning has just struck. But then darkness and dysfunction rush in. A mind such as Beethoven's remains illumined, or sees in the darkness shapes it never saw before, that inspire rather than terrify.

Deafness, like blindness, is one of the things we don't like to think about. Or if we do, we sentimentalize them to make them seem less awful. For years I persuaded myself that Beethoven's disability was really a sort of boon, giving him a chamber of quietness to compose in. But then I noticed a few words that froze my blood, in a letter that he wrote to a close friend, Franz Wegeler. The date is 29 June 1801, and Beethoven is just thirty years old:

> *My hearing has become weaker and weaker. . . . [Dr.] Frank tried to tone up my constitution with strengthening medicines and my hearing with almond oil. . . . Then [Dr.] Vering . . . prescribed tepid baths in the Danube, to which I had to add a bottle of strengthening ingredients . . . plus an infusion for my ear. As a result I have been feeling, I may say, stronger and better; but my ears continue to buzz and hum day and night.*

It was those last words that got me. Beethoven was referring, of course, to the aural disease tinnitus, the most awful affliction any musician can face. It chills one into full comprehension of George Eliot's phrase "the roar that lies on the other side of silence." The sound chamber of Beethoven's skull was *not* a pure, quiet place. It buzzed, hummed, and sometimes roared, day and night. He had to listen to those noises as he tried to compose. He had to listen to them when he tried to sleep. In all biography, there are few images more grotesquely sad than that of Beethoven, racked with cramps, bathing in fortified river water and trying to drown the din in his head with almond oil.

How long his tinnitus lasted, nobody knows. Those noises may have gone on sounding until he died in March 1827, at age fifty-six. Or they may have gradually faded into total silence. Like most deaf people, Beethoven was sensitive about his disability, and would not discuss it in later life. We know, however, that by 1816 he was so deaf to *outside* sound that people could converse with him only by writing their questions on paper. One hundred and thirty-eight of these "conversation books" survive.

SOME TIME AGO I suggested at a convention of the American Association of Neurological Surgeons that maybe some of the strange sounds that invaded Beethoven's music after 1801—drummings, pulsations,

chimes, mixed harmonies, spectral overtones—were pathological in origin. I cited the harmonic blur that veils the first movement of the "Moonlight" Sonata, the static hovering of the violins in the trio of the Seventh
Symphony, the hysterical *whoop-whoops* of the lower strings in the
scherzo of the last quartet, Op. 135, and a few other examples. One of
the doctors came up to me afterward and said, "You didn't mention the
most significant sound of all." He confided that he himself had degen-
erative tinnitus. "I can tell you that the opening of the Ninth Symphony
is exactly what you hear when you begin to go deaf."

If you look at the score of the Ninth (above), you'll see that Beethoven
did not call for anything so free as a tremolo, the shimmering string
sound that opens so many Bruckner symphonies. He precisely specified
a continuous, very rapid, and very soft beating of two sextuplets to the
bar, harmonized as a bare fifth in the second violins and cellos. Reiter-
ated about six times a second, the monotones add up to a hundred and
ninety before all hell breaks loose.

I suppose it was this combination of mystery and specificity, and the
feeling of fear that the first movement of the Ninth so powerfully evokes,
that resonated in the neurologist's failing ears. What he had to say about
the correlation of musical vibrato and the humming and throbbing of
aural disease made me think of a passage in another Beethoven symphony, the Fifth. Sonically, it's even more scary: you can practically
hear the blood thudding along with the kettledrum as the first violins
struggle to break out of a general soft drone. Eventually—Beethoven
being Beethoven—freedom comes, and the whole orchestra erupts with
such power that every hair stands up on the back of your neck.

AFTER MY TALK with the neurologist, I made an aural survey of the
nineteen piano sonatas Beethoven wrote from 1801 (the year of the

"Moonlight") on. They amount to a sort of ongoing personal diary in sound, because the piano was always his most intimate companion, his confessional instrument, something to caress even when he was too deaf to hear. He was the first great pianist in history (unless you include Mozart, who died before the piano had really matured as an instrument).

Beethoven once heard Mozart play, and complained that his style was *zerhacktes*—"choppy." His own playing style was much more legato, in that his broad hands lay easily on the keys, and produced a full, mellow sound with very little effort.* This intimate relationship between his own body and that of the piano, with vibrations going back and forth, may explain why his piano sonatas speak more personally to us than any of his other music, except perhaps the late string quartets.

Beethoven's first thirteen sonatas were sonically little different from the last sonatas of Joseph Haydn. Then, from extreme left field in 1801, just when Beethoven was admitting his deafness, came a sonata in C-sharp minor, unlike any music ever written before. As if in acknowledgment of that fact, he writes in Italian (then the customary language for musical directions) *Si deve suonare tutte questo pezzo delicatissimamente e senza sordino*: "It's necessary to play this entire piece with the utmost delicacy and with undamped strings"—in other words, let the strings vibrate freely without ever lifting your foot from the pedal.

An art instructor of the period might as well have asked his students, trained to observe the High Classical principles of transparency and clarity, to paint in watercolor without rinsing their brushes. The music that Beethoven proceeded to notate consisted, at first, of nothing but undulations:

* The conformation of Beethoven's hand can clearly be seen in the portrait of him at age thirty-four by Willibrord Mähler.

No melody and no key change, except that the bass keeps dropping, blurring the harmonies—or rather, if played *delicatissimamente* enough, letting them dissolve into one another in the impressionistic style that Beethoven's exact contemporary, Joseph Mallord Turner, was experimenting with in art.

Don't deaf people complain regularly about the mix of sounds that comes upon them in crowded places—sounds that are hard to differentiate, and cancel themselves out in a sort of confused blur? That's pathology. But this exquisite music turns pathology into poetry.

Unfortunately, the modern piano sustains notes much longer than the pianos of Beethoven's time, so what sounded translucent then sounds coarser now, unless the pianist half-pedals constantly to dampen the vibrations. (I heard Rudolf Serkin play this sonata once, and he jiggled his foot so much he looked as though he needed to go to the bathroom.)

It takes a long time for Beethoven to float a melody over his undulations, and when he does, it at first seems hardly a melody at all, just slow soft chimings of G-sharp. Eventually he moves away from it, but always to return, while the same note reverberates elsewhere in the harmony. Is it fanciful to hear the monotones of tinnitus in all these G-sharps—195 of them? I acknowledge that other composers before Beethoven used monotones liberally, with Bach in particular rejoicing in "pedal" notes that support the weight of his organ fugues like the foundations of a building. But the "Moonlight" Sonata (not Beethoven's title, by the way) is definitely a new musical language. It is the language, in fact, of Chopin's nocturnes—specifically, the great one in the same key of C-sharp minor, written more than thirty years later.

Chopin was always rather disparaging of Beethoven. Well, so was George Bernard Shaw about Shakespeare.*

I hasten to add that Beethoven, unlike Chopin, was never morbid. The positivity that always rescued him from illness and brief spells of

---

* The pulsations on one note that occur so often in the music of Chopin almost certainly derive from Beethoven. Hear, for example, Chopin's hypnotic repetitions of G-sharp (and its pianistic equivalent, A-flat) in his D-flat major Prelude, Op. 28. In recital, Chopin often played Beethoven's A-flat major Sonata, Op. 24, which again makes much use of monotones.

melancholy prevented him from making masochistic use of the aural noises that tormented him. On the contrary, the loss of his hearing miraculously enhanced his ability to imagine—there is no other verb—new tonal beauties. One wonders if he would have come up with them if he *hadn't* gone deaf. I'm thinking, for example, of the radiant high filigree (again, over an ever-so-soft monotone) in the second movement of his last sonata, Op. III: about the nearest human music has ever come to that of the spheres. And the almost-speech of the first violin in the Cavatina of the B-flat Quartet, Op. 130. And the amazing chord, very difficult to sing, given to the chorus at an unexpected moment in his setting of Goethe's poem *Meeresstille und glückliche Fahrt* ("Calm Sea and Prosperous Voyage"). It enormously spaces out the word *Weite*—wideness, vastness—and listening to it, we feel the immensity of the ocean, swallowing up sound.

There is, again, nothing morbid in the repeated low D at the beginning of Beethoven's next sonata after the "Moonlight," the *Pastorale,* Op. 28—even though it was composed during the same suicidal summer that precipitated the Heiligenstadt Testament. Here it is in his own handwriting:

That bottom D sounds no fewer than seventy-four times without interruption, and resounds constantly all through the sonata's four movements. Why? It's not melodic, and it's too static to be called a rhythm. The distinguished piano scholar Konrad Wolff has suggested it's simply sensuous: a tone registering more on the body than on the brain. He writes, "The reverberating sound of the low D brings the piano to life in its pulsating sounding board. By playing these bass tones one becomes as much a part of the instrument as if the vibration were passing through the pianist's torso down to his feet. I am convinced that the intense effect of Beethoven's piano music on the listener . . . is caused, in considerable part, by this ongoing vibration, which causes physical excitement at the same time as bodily involvement."*

That makes biographical sense. Just as primary color is especially beautiful to someone losing his sight, you can imagine how poignant the actual *feel* of sound must be to a man who is losing his hearing.

THROBBING PULSATIONS remained a characteristic of Beethoven's style for the rest of his life. Sometimes the pulse was extremely slow, as in the "Moonlight" Sonata, or moderate, as in the *Pastorale*, or fast, as in the "Waldstein" Sonata, or very fast, as in the *Appassionata*. In the last-named masterpiece (which I can never mention without thinking, aghast, of his willingness to entrust the manuscript to the vagaries of Austria's rural mail service), he contrasted the rapid rat-a-tat of repeated notes with the even more rapid vibration of trills, another feature of his sonic style. Again, the trill had been a part of musical language (not to mention birdsong) for ages before him. But Baroque composers had used it, along with many other melodic ornaments, out of sheer love for elaboration, and High Classical composers had then formalized the trill to the point that you can hear it coming well in advance.

Beethoven differed from his predecessors in that he treated the trill as something that was neither decorative nor formulaic, but a sound effect with its own expressive purpose. In the *Appassionata*, the trills are mostly short and shivery, adding to the first movement's general feeling of gathering doom. They alternate with even more ominous tapping noises:

* Konrad Wolff, *Masters of the Keyboard* (Bloomington, Ind. 1983–1990, 129. Another famously deaf man, Thomas Alva Edison, brushed aside the sympathy of admirers by saying that he "heard" perfectly well through his teeth when he bit into the wood of one of his vibrating phonographs. He sympathized in turn with them, for having to listen to music polluted by all the other ambient noise of everyday life—what audio engineers call "room tone."

Later, a trill turns the taps into a high-pitched pulsation that gradually drops and becomes a deep throbbing in the bass:

The throbbing loses its initial menace, and we get a gorgeous tune,
only to have it dissolve into long, floating trills that could go anywhere—

The great pianist Claudio Arrau has called these trills, which prolifer-
ate in Beethoven's later music, "tremblings of the soul." Toward the end
of the development, the throbbing begins again. It falls to its deepest
level yet, and becomes so obsessive that it threatens to drown out the
start of the recapitulation.

Perhaps the most pathological moment of all is right at the end of the
movement, when the throbbing becomes a middle-register hum that
slowly fades into nothing:

The rest is silence.

From the *Appassionata* onward (it was composed in 1804) long trills
proliferated in Beethoven's music, as well as pulsations fast or slow. The
locus classicus of these effects occurs in his final piano sonata, Op. 111,
when for a timeless moment they all sound together. A single trill in the
right hand is accompanied above and below by very slow monotonal

beats, which then become trills too—no fewer than three of them vibrating simultaneously, while one line of monotones continues to beat in the bass. Eventually that beating stops, like a pulse stilled by death, and the triple trill reduces down to one. Is it, too, going to fade away, as all the noises of the world have faded from Beethoven? No—the trill not only continues to vibrate, but begins steadily to rise, higher and higher, until we have lost all sense of time as well as gravity—those two constants of the Newtonian universe.

We have arrived at the edge of metaphysical space, at which moment Beethoven, still the most human of men, reintroduces his pulsations, but now so softly and coaxingly harmonized that we feel we are coming back to life, and return with him to *terra firma*.

I REFERRED EARLIER on to the blurring of harmonies that Beethoven deliberately wrote into the "Moonlight" Sonata. That was no aberration. He blurred them again and again at dramatic points in his mature piano works. The unique properties of the sustaining pedal made it possible for him to do so—although there are passages in his symphonic and choral works that suggest that he rejoiced in the "mixed" effect of echoes in a large auditorium. (Hear how the opening theme of the *Eroica* Symphony grows out of the reverberation of those two loud introductory chords.)

Two-thirds of the way through the tempestuous first movement of his D minor Sonata, Op. 31, No. 2, a warm soft arpeggio dissolves into this strange recitative, which Beethoven says should be played *pianissimo*, with held pedal:

What happens as a result is that all the open strings of the piano vibrate in sympathy with the struck notes. This creates an aural haze around the "voice" of the recitative, rather as the atmosphere puts a haze around distant contours. Beethoven here is anticipating Schumann's love of a lonely-sounding melody emanating *aus den Ferne,* from very far away. He lets the haze fade, then spreads another arpeggio, out of which comes a second recitative, even more lonely-sounding. These echoing cries sound to me like a voice from a vault—the cry of a deaf man losing touch with the world.

When you think of Beethoven's musical entrapment inside his own aural cavern, you can understand why the central image of *Fidelio*—Florestan imprisoned in a dark, silent cave—meant so much to him.

Now had he been a Berlioz—which is to say, a self-chronicling Romantic—and if I am right in suggesting that he made music out of his own suffering, these strange sounds might have been indulged to excess as he grew older and deafer. On the contrary, he always reserved them for special effect, and they remained only a small part of his musical vocabulary. Beethoven was one of the most disciplined of composers—not as cerebral as Bach, but every bit as austere as Brahms in keeping self-indulgence at bay. Those recitatives, those voices from the vault, were annotated as precisely as his most classical counterpoint. He wrote out every vibration of his fastest tremolos (on occasion getting into what the British call "hemidemisemiquavers"). He even timed the tiny silences between detached notes, inserting intricate ciphers to make sure they didn't last a microsecond too long. Some pages of his later scores are so dense with meter changes and accidentals and double-dotted rests and pedal signs that you literally have to resort to mathematics to figure everything out. Passion there is in abundance, and simplicity and lyricism too, and—yes—weirdness every now and again. However, a giant intelligence is always in control.

Beethoven may have had his neurological problems, but he was never a neurotic. His auditory nerves shriveled and his auditory blood vessels calcified, yet his imaginative ear remained perfect until he died. Some of the most exquisite sounds in music were created by Beethoven when he was too deaf to hear a thousand people applauding him.

His last piano sonatas and quartets attained a synthesis of normal and abnormal sound effects so unique that to this day, they can't be categorized. Words are wasted on them. I can suggest only that you listen to the *arioso dolente* from his late Sonata Op. 110 in A-flat major, to hear what I mean by synthesis. At first the music sounds like a free improvisation, without key or tempo. But every last nuance is calculated and counted. Then comes a voice from the vault, interrupted by what is to me the most frightening sound in all of Beethoven—a high, piercing, twenty-six-fold repetition of the note A, which comes out of nowhere and retreats into nowhere.* If those As don't evoke the torment of tinnitus, then neither does the high E that Bedřich Smetana wrote into his String Quartet No. 1 in E minor, as an overt reference to his own hearing problem.

Beethoven's moment of pain passes, and subsides into a quiet throbbing, neither slow nor fast. Over it flows what Wagner was later to call an "endless melody," in which the piano all but speaks. And what it says is, "Don't feel sorry for me, *O Freunde*. I know more about life, and what is beyond life, than you ever will."

PASSAGES LIKE THESE in Beethoven's late compositions (never *quite* like, because he is incapable of repeating himself) may be considered the norm, rather than the exception. They exemplify what music alone can do, as well as demonstrate what words can't. I believe that they share, along with inspiration, a common pathology in the small skull Dr. Seibert probed on 28 March 1827, finding that

> . . . the two auditory nerves were wrinkled and lacked a central core. The auricular arteries encircled the auditory nerves, and were larger in size than a crow's quill. They also were cartilaginous. The left auditory nerve was much thinner than the right nerve, and had three dull white streaks on its surface; the right auditory nerve had a thick white streak of a substance having a

---

* The repetition is rendered more piercing by an extraordinary internal echo, very difficult to play, known to pianists as the *Bebüng*. It requires a secondary depression of the key just as it is rising—a recapture that sends it down again for a faint tap on the already resonating string. Beethoven cruelly repeats that same high A seventy-five times in the finale of the Ninth Symphony. Ask any soprano.

dense consistency. It was vascularized as it curved around the floor of the fourth ventricle.

Modern audio studios, too, have solid insulation and cables of varying width lying around. But none mix and balance such beautiful sounds as the bone chamber where Beethoven worked in increasing privacy for upward of fifty years.

THE AFRICAN OBAMA

The Prepresidential Photographs of Pete Souza

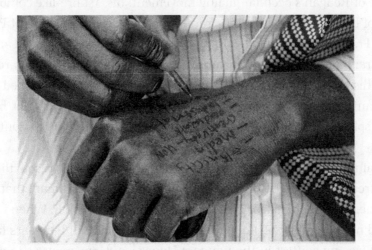

W HEN PETE SOUZA ASKED ME TO WRITE AN INTRODUCTION TO his book *The Rise of Barack Obama*, I assumed it was because I am an African-American. Perhaps I should explain, being white as the driven snow—or more relevantly, white as the statue of James Madison, before whom Mr. Obama and his daughter stand in one of the most eloquent images of this book.

I was born in Kenya, Barack Obama's ancestral home, and am now an American citizen. Mr. Souza knows this. He thought it might add an extra dimension to whatever I cared to write about his subject. Actually, I would jump at the chance to introduce any collection of Pete's photo-

This essay, written in 2008 for the first edition of Mr. Souza's book, was suppressed by the publisher for fear of popular "outrage" at references to President Obama's African ancestry.

Photograph by Pete Souza of a Kenyan student listening to Senator Obama speak in 2006.

graphs, because many of the ones he took of Ronald Reagan in the 1980s have burned themselves into my brain. I remember in particular a shot as perfect in composition and narrative drama (all his best pictures "tell a story") as any taken by Henri Cartier-Bresson. It caught Mr. Reagan from behind on the last day of his presidency, waving good-bye at some-body unseen as he walked down the colonnade from the Oval Office to the White House. There, captured in a sliver of a second, was all the grace of Reagan's peculiar gliding movement, his Astaire-like combina-tion of balance and relaxation, framed (as the retreating figures of Piero della Francesca were so often framed) by the geometry of classical archi-tecture: pillars, flagstones, beams, and a fan window precisely arched over his glossy head. If you looked closely, a tiny detail disturbed and humanized all this harmony. The fingers of the President's left hand were splinted and bandaged, after an operation for Dupuytren's contrac-ture.

Pain in the midst of power, age crippling physical beauty, courtliness in retreat: all these and other complexities unique to that man, that day in time, were captured for all time by a born photographer. When I pre-pared my biography of Ronald Reagan for publication, ten years later, there was no contest in the Random House art department as to what image would appear on the cover: that valedictory shot taken by Pete Souza on 20 January 1989.

Now, in a starkly different age, Mr. Souza has focused his camera on another politician who has the rare quality of physical grace. It may indeed be the Kenyan in me that sees something atavistically familiar in Barack Obama's loping straightness, like that of a Masai warrior emerg-ing from his *manyatta* and looking about, spear poised, for any lion (or lioness)* lurking in the bush. Yet I know that Africa has absolutely nothing to do with the senator's all-American appeal. Like most immi-grants, I can testify that this nation has the power to make any origin, ethnic or geographical, irrelevant. (That even applies to natives of Ha-waii, an archipelago apparently remote from Republican ken.) A mov-ing remark made by Theodore Roosevelt, regarding the tendency of

* At the time this essay was being written, Mr. Obama was competing with Hillary Clinton for the Democratic presidential nomination.

ancestor-worshippers to trumpet their "hyphenated" identity, was: "My motherland and my homeland and my native land are all three of them the United States."

Mr. Obama doubtless feels the same way. However, the photographs in this book covering his visits to Kenya and South Africa in 2006 show that he is perceived *there*, on what used to be known as the Dark Continent, as a symbol of light. And I'm not making a cute pun on the paleness of his skin. (His great recent address on the subject of race has at last made it possible to talk about pigmentation as a natural, not stereotypical, phenomenon.) I mean light in the sense—still underappreciated—that Mr. Obama's foreign appeal, especially the way he is seen by Africans and Asians, is even more luminous than it is here at home. People with colonial or other collective memories of oppression, not to mention those suffering currently under antidemocratic regimes, have always looked on the United States as the land where high aspirations are rewarded. How much more will they revere it if a man they can identify with wins possession of the White House!

Look at the mimosa tree full of Kenyan parade watchers on pages 86–87 of Mr. Souza's book. Nothing could be more African than that sight. As a child I remember similar treefuls, loaded to cracking, when Princess Elizabeth hurried through Nairobi on her way home to take the throne just vacated by her father, King George VI. Then, the spectacle was of a remote goddess. Now, half a century later, somebody extraordinary yet approachable is about to pass by.

Which is amusingly not the case in the shot of the youthful politician striding along a Russian sidewalk, unrecognized even by American tourists. This is a book about Barack Obama's *rise*: not to power but the beginnings of power, and its austere reliance on black-and-white images helps distance him from his contemporary, overwrought super-celebrity. As a biographer of presidents, I have noticed that they all—well, almost all—exude a quality in their early years that sets them apart. Insofar as it can be described, it's a paradoxical combination of aloofness and charm, plus self-certainty and the appearance, if not the actuality, of a consuming interest in individual human beings. Mr. Obama seems, on the evidence of these photographs, to have this quality. It's apparent not in the way *he* registers on the camera (although the lens likes his bony chiseling), but how people register *him*. Note the intense scrutiny of his traveling companions on a flight to former Soviet missile sites in August 2005—in particular the baggy-eyed stare of Senator Lugar. When you're running for president, you have to get used to that look from members of the opposite party, as well as to the strange half-smile, full of yearning, that is fame's popular reflection.

Whether or not this man makes it to the presidency, the images he has impressed on Pete Souza's camera (without any hint of collusion) are historic.* And I'm not just thinking of his political significance. I'm thinking of the beauty of two extreme close-ups: the lustrous fingernail pushing up a fold of senatorial temple, with a frizz of early gray above it, and the welling drop of blood (*If you prick us, do we not bleed?*) in a mobile AIDS test. Another pair of photographs may speak to him even more than to us: a key in his hand, opening the door of Nelson Mandela's jail cell, and a toxic clutter of cartridges in a Russian missile graveyard. There are some delightful shots of Obama's daughters, while that of the candidate joining hands with a discordant-looking quartet singing "We Shall Overcome" is proof positive that you have to have a tin ear to run for office.

But the image that haunts me most is a ballpoint list of things today's political aspirants have to strike a moral attitude toward, inked on a listener's satin skin (with precise initial capitals) when Mr. Obama spoke a couple of years ago in my native city. The list reads "Ethnicity—Media—Creativity—Hard work—Industrial—Corruption." You have to turn the book upside down to make these words out, and in the process your point of view becomes that of the wielder of the pen. This is the catalyst of photography, that it enables us to see what others see, and in the process feel at least a part of what Everyman feels.

---

* Pete Souza is now (2012) chief photographer to the President of the United States.

AS MUCH OF A MONOLOGUE
AS POSSIBLE

Theodore Roosevelt at 150

THE FORMER PRESIDENT, WHO WAS BORN 150 YEARS AGO TODAY, *was interviewed in his childhood home at 28 East 20th Street. He has long been a ghostly presence there. The house is now the Theodore Roosevelt Birthplace National Historic Site. Due to Mr. Roosevelt's great age, it is difficult to tell how well he hears contemporary questions. But he is as forceful as ever in expressing himself. Except when interrupted by his interviewer, his statements below are authentic and unedited.*

Q Happy birthday, Mr. President! Or do you prefer being called Colonel?

A I've had the title of President once—having it twice means nothing except peril to whatever reputation I achieved the first time.

Originally published in *The New York Times,* 27 October 2008.

Photograph of Theodore Roosevelt rendered by Barbara M. Bachman.

Q "Colonel," then. Do you think the Congress elected two years ago as a foil to the Bush administration has fulfilled its mandate?

A I am heartsick over the delay, the blundering, the fatuous and complacent inefficiency and the effort to substitute glittering rhetoric for action.

Q Do you blame the House Democratic majority?

A A goodly number of senators, even of my own party, have shown about as much backbone as so many angleworms.

Q I hope that doesn't include the pair running for the presidency! What do you think of Senator McCain? He often cites you as a role model.

A He is evidently a man who takes color from his surroundings.

Q Weren't you just as unpredictable in your time?

A (*laughing*) They say that nothing is as independent as a hog on ice. If he doesn't want to stand up, he can lie down.

Q Mr. McCain has always prided himself on his independence. At least, until he began to take direction from CEOs and retired generals—

A But the signs now are that these advisers have themselves awakened to the fact that they have almost ruined him.

Q Does his vow to give Joe the Plumber a tax break remind you of Reaganomics?

A This is merely the plan, already tested and found wanting, of giving prosperity to the big men on top, and trusting to their mercy to let something leak through to the mass of their countrymen below—which, in effect, means that there shall be no attempt to regulate the ferocious scramble in which greed and cunning reap the largest rewards.

Q In Washington these days, Colonel, you're increasingly seen as the father of centralized, executive, regulatory control.

A Great corporations exist only because they are created and safeguarded by our institutions; and it is therefore our right and duty to see that they work in harmony with these institutions.

Q   Especially now that we've seen the end of another age of laissez-faire economics?

A   These new conditions make it necessary to shackle cunning as in the past we have shackled force. The vast individual and corporate fortunes, the vast combinations of capital—

Q   Even vaster in your day! John D. Rockefeller was richer than Bill Gates, dollar for dollar.

A   Quite right. (*He dislikes being interrupted.*) And please, let this now be as much of a monologue as possible.

Q   Excuse me, you were saying that vast combinations of capital . . .

A   Create new conditions, and necessitate a change from the old attitude of the state and the nation toward the rules regulating the acquisition and untrammeled business use of property.

Q   So you approve of the federal bailout plan?

A   I think we have got to face the fact that such an increase in governmental control is now necessary.

Q   Should we condone the huge severance packages paid to executives of rescued corporations?

A   There is need in business, as in most other forms of human activity, of the great guiding intelligences. Their places cannot be supplied by any number of lesser intelligences. It is a good thing that they should have ample recognition, ample reward. But we must not transfer our admiration to the reward instead of to the deed rewarded; and if what should be the reward exists without the service having been rendered, then admiration will come only from those who are mean of soul.

Q   So we should withhold our envy of Richard Fuld, the chairman of Lehman Brothers, for taking home half a billion before his company went down?

A   Envy and arrogance are the two opposite sides of the same black crystal.

Q   An extraordinary image, Colonel. What's your impression of Senator Obama?

A Unless I am greatly mistaken, the people have made up their mind that they wish some new instrument.

Q You're not afraid that he's primarily a man of words? Like Woodrow Wilson, whom you once called a "Byzantine logothete"?

A It is highly desirable that a leader of opinion in a democracy should be able to state his views clearly and convincingly.

Q Not Mr. McCain's strong point!

A Some excellent public servants have not the gift at all, and must rely upon their deeds to speak for them; and unless the oratory does represent genuine conviction, based on good common sense and able to be translated into efficient performance, then the better the oratory the greater the damage to the public it deceives.

Q Mr. McCain might argue that his life of service and suffering is eloquence enough. Have you read his autobiography?

A I should like to have it circulated as a tract among an immense multitude of philanthropists, Congressmen, newspaper editors, publicists, softheaded mothers, and other people of sorts who think that life ought to consist of perpetual shrinking from effort, danger, and pain.

Q Has Mr. Obama not suffered too? Not at the heroic level of Mr. McCain, but in transcending centuries of race prejudice to become a viable presidential candidate—only to be nearly stopped by Hillary Clinton!

A I think that he has learned some bitter lessons, and that independently of outside pressure he will try to act with greater firmness, and to look at things more from the standpoint of the interests of the people, and less from that of a technical lawyer—

Q "Technical," Colonel? He took his law degree onto the streets of Chicago, and applied it to social problems.

A He may and probably will turn out to be a perfectly respectable President, whose achievements will be disheartening compared with what we had expected, but who nevertheless will have done well enough to justify us in renominating him—for you must remember that to renominate him would be a very serious thing, only to be justified by really strong reasons.

Q He doesn't have Mr. McCain's foreign policy experience. As President, how will he personify us around the world?

A It always pays for a nation to be a gentleman.

Q There'll be Senator Biden to counsel him, of course. Assuming Mr. Obama can keep track of what he's saying.

A (*laughing*) You can't nail marmalade against a wall.

Q Talking of foreign policy, what do you think of Mr. McCain's choice of a female running mate?

A Times change (*sigh*). It is entirely inexcusable, however, to try to combine the unready hand with the unbridled tongue.

Q How would you feel if Sarah Palin was elected?

A I shall feel *exactly* the way a very small frog looks when it swallows a beetle the size of itself, with extremely stiff legs.

Q What's your impression of Mr. Bush these days?

A He looks like Judas, but unlike that gentleman has no capacity for remorse.

Q Is that the best you can say of him?

A I wish him well, but I wish him well at a good distance from me.

Q One last question, Colonel. If you were campaigning now, would you still call yourself a Republican?

A (*after a long pause*) No.

VOICE, OR VENTRILOQUISM

Language and the Presidency

Being INTRODUCED BY DR. KISSINGER MAKES ME FEEL LIKE A MINI Cooper being nudged into the fast lane of the I-95 by an eighteen-wheeler. You're aware of the horsepower behind, but you're not too sure if your back bumper can stand the strain.

A couple of weeks ago the editor of a New York weekly called me to say he was beginning to write a book about Barack Obama. He said he thought Obama was first and foremost a man of words, and he wondered if I felt the same way about the presidents I've studied.

I said that they certainly were men of words, in that they wrote as

Address at the Memorial Library, Kent, Connecticut, 3 May 2009. Subsequently published in *Litchfield Magazine*, April 2009.

White House photograph by Pete Souza.

much as they orated, using language to build and hold power—TR's rhetoric being that of a scholar and social visionary, and Reagan's that of a politically obsessed actor. The editor asked for some other examples of presidents who became powerful through the use of words. I'm not a historian (as historians frequently remind me), but I said I thought that Thomas Jefferson, certainly, made himself famous by writing the Declaration of Independence, one of our country's most enduring prose masterpieces—although that line about "the merciless Indian savages" could use updating. We all know about Lincoln and the matchless beauty of his language. Woodrow Wilson was a superb prose stylist, so much so that for most of his presidency he was revered around the world as a great man. It was only when he made the mistake of attending the Paris Peace Conference at the end of the Great War that Georges Clemenceau of France and David Lloyd George of Great Britain realized that behind the fine phrases was a parochial Presbyterian preacher. They were far too quick, strong, and agile for him. Wilson came back from the conference much diminished in public esteem.

Clemenceau, by the way, was also a magnificent writer, as was his much younger compatriot, Charles de Gaulle. (One of the tragedies of French letters is that the General never lived to complete his last prose work—a series of imaginary dialogues between himself and other great leaders of history.) Then there was Winston Churchill, a professional scribe for most of his life. His literary reputation has suffered from a tendency toward orotundity in old age—but you won't find many military books more brilliantly written than his youthful memoir, *The River War.* Franklin Roosevelt came up with a few eloquent sound bites, although the most famous of them ("We have nothing to fear but fear itself") was a plagiarism.* In that sense, FDR was a man of words, but as with Ronald Reagan, it was really the style, rather than the substance, of his speeches that made him beguiling.

SINCE FDR, THE UTTERANCES of presidents and presidential candidates have become so much the province of their speechwriters and po-

* See page 245.

litical strategists that it has become increasingly difficult to hear the real man talking—to tell if what we're hearing is voice, or ventriloquism. In 2000, when George W. Bush and Al Gore were running against each other, the scholar Jay Martin made a brilliant presentation at a symposium on biography at Boston University. He said that whereas candidates in the past wrote at least some of their speeches and imposed most of their own ideas upon their campaign teams, Bush and Gore were essentially a pair of "novels"—fictional constructs without any core of inner truth—plotted, written, edited, and marketed by professionals in the hope that one would top the bestseller list.

It's an interesting paradox that the presidents we've had since FDR who were not gifted at self-expression have tended to be the most authentic personalities: works of nonfiction, Professor Martin might say. Harry Truman, Dwight Eisenhower, Lyndon Johnson, Richard Nixon, Gerald Ford, Jimmy Carter, and the first George Bush all had the touch of lead, as far as language was concerned. But successful or not, admirable or not, they were what they were: the voice sounded like the man. Kennedy was a novel, but how elegant, how moving, and how achingly short. Reagan was a movie. Clinton was a website. As such, he perfectly represented the age of the Internet. He had power, but no *gravitas;* he was governed by no laws and knew no frontiers; he just floated free in cyberspace, going wherever he could register the most hits.

The evidence so far is that Barack Obama is a nonfiction narrative of surpassing interest, although we're only in the first chapter and who knows, the interest and even the authenticity may flag. But since I have no personal knowledge of Mr. Obama,* I'll confine my observations to the two presidents I do know well, Theodore Roosevelt and Ronald Reagan, and in particular, to their literary abilities.

IN WHAT WAY WAS Ronald Reagan a man of words? As I noted earlier, he was principally a speaker, rather than a writer, and many of the words he articulated so beautifully, in that seductive silvery voice, were scripted

---

* The author has since met with President Obama, and sees no reason to alter references to him in this essay.

for him. Peggy Noonan has made something of a career out of being Reagan's most famous speechwriter, although I've always thought Anthony Dolan was the best. When Tony wrote for the President, Reagan sounded like Reagan. When Peggy wrote for him, he sounded like Peggy.

Reagan, nevertheless (and this may surprise some people) was a man who thought on paper.* I devoted a whole chapter of *Dutch* to a batch of high-school and student essays and short stories he wrote in the late 1920s—pieces that I found in a trunk of junk in the basement of the Ronald Reagan Presidential Library. They were astonishingly, even creepily, evocative of the statesman he would one day become.

Throughout his life, even as a young sportscaster in Des Moines and as an actor in Hollywood, he poured out longhand letters and newspaper articles, and, once he became a public political figure, radio addresses and speech after speech after speech—hundreds if not thousands of them. (Only in the White House did he allow words to be written for him.) He kept a daily diary, also in longhand, throughout his presidency. I believe Douglas Brinkley[†] and I are the only two people who have fought our way through those one million, mostly banal words. Reagan, unlike Theodore Roosevelt, was not a gifted writer. He never came up with a memorable phrase or an original observation. As Dr. Kissinger says, he was a combination of apparent intellectual mediocrity and undeniable political brilliance.

SO, FOR THAT MATTER, was FDR. I would maintain that with a few exceptions, such as Jefferson, TR, de Gaulle, and François Mitterrand, intellectuals are not generally suited to be heads of state. They prevaricate too much; they are too inclined to fall in love with abstract ideas; they revel in complexity like cats playing with unraveling balls of wool, and end up tying themselves in knots. In addition, intellectuals—as anyone can see browsing through books published these days by academic presses—are not always intelligent. Reagan was by no means intellectual, nor was he, in his later years, particularly well informed. However

---

* The publication of Reagan's letters, diaries, and notes, starting in 2003, have made this characteristic clear. See page 320.
† Editor, *The Reagan Diaries* (New York, 2009).

he was, in my opinion, a bright man of shrewd instincts, who throughout his life was dismissed as a simple, nice guy, but who somehow, in the
course of many careers, outfoxed everybody who got in his way, and always came out on top.

You have to have smarts to do that. Reagan's smarts showed in his
use of humor. For some regrettable reason, probably going back to the
Puritanism of the Pilgrim Fathers, humor has always been mistrusted in
American politicians. "Eggheads of the world unite," Adlai Stevenson
wisecracked when he was running for the presidency. "You have nothing to lose but your yolks." Well, that kind of wit kept him out of the
White House. TR was an extremely funny man, but he kept his humor
well hidden when he spoke in public. John Kennedy got away with it, but
with his kind of charm, he could get away with fake authorship and
sexual amorality. (And he did.) Eisenhower, Nixon, and Ford had little
humor. Jimmy Carter didn't know what it was. But Reagan used humor
with great political and diplomatic effectiveness.

In his youth, apart from having humor as a natural gift, he studied
the rhetoric of spoken and written comedy—which is to say, its syntax,
its rhythms, the overall structure of a joke climaxing in the perfectly
timed punch line—with patient professionalism. He was helped by an
excellent ear for sound, and a photographic memory. Having sat through
his uncanny playback of a comic monologue heard just once, at the Des
Moines Advertising Club in 1933, complete with altered voice and accent, I'd even call it phonographic.* Hence, he never forgot a good joke,
and was capable of quick wit himself.

When he became President and got himself a big, undisciplined
pooch called Lucky, Michael Deaver warned him, "One of these days,
that dog is going to piss on your desk." Reagan said, "Why not? Everybody else does."

There's a photograph in *Dutch* that shows the President cracking up
a group of White House visitors including Walter Cronkite, David Ger-
gen, and James Baker, to the point that they're in danger of spilling their
drinks. I've interviewed all the surviving people in that photograph to

* See page 449.

find out what the joke was, but not one of them will say. It must have been politically incorrect.

IN TENSE DIPLOMATIC SITUATIONS, Reagan made negotiatory use of his comic abilities. There was the occasion he made President Mitterrand understand that he sympathized with France's decision to accept the emplacement of American intermediate-range missiles in Western Europe. It was a defense move unpopular among Mitterrand's local allies, who all tried to persuade Mitterrand to change his mind. Reagan said, "François, I know how you feel about the Soviet threat. You're like the fellow who thought he was a kernel of corn. His family made him see a psychiatrist to get rid of his delusion. After six months of therapy, the shrink says, 'You're cured.' Fellow goes out feeling very relieved, but then he sees a chicken in the parking lot and runs back inside screaming. Psychiatrist says, 'But you know that you aren't a kernel of corn.' Fellow says, 'Yes, but does the chicken know?' "

That joke, perfectly apt and perfectly timed, delighted Mitterrand and cemented a relationship that had gotten off to a frosty start. Mitterrand, the quintessential French snob, began to realize that the President saw things as clearly, if not more clearly, than himself. In 1988, on his final visit to the White House, he delivered one of the most eloquent tributes to Ronald Reagan ever made by a foreign head of state.

Reagan was also capable of deploying humor aggressively, to express moral disdain. When Mikhail Gorbachev attended the Washington summit meeting in 1987, he had to listen to the President joke about the old *babushka* who staked out the office of a high Party official, saying that she wanted to ask just one fundamental question. Finally she was allowed in and said, "Is Communism a religion, or a science?" The official thought for a bit and answered, "It's a religion." "That explains it," she said. "Because if it was a science, they would've tried it out on rats first."

Gorbachev didn't like this joke at all. But it's difficult to return a body blow when everyone else around the table is laughing.

In conclusion (as Bill Clinton used to say toward the beginning of his speeches), here are a few words about our current President's use of words. Barack Obama seems to be very conscious of the power of his own rhetoric—not just the written speeches he delivers so effectively, but the spoken sentences in which he thinks aloud during interviews and press conferences. We listen to phrase following logical phrase, we note the clarity and force of his expression, and we are both reassured and persuaded. After so many years of having to listen to the two Bushes stumble to express themselves, and Clinton mistaking verbosity for eloquence, and so many presidential candidates sounding like prerecorded policy papers, it's deeply satisfying to see a man in the White House who actually thinks about what he is saying—somebody, that is, who is equipped with the sequential and unemotional kind of reasoning that only a mastery of language can convey.

THE ADVENTURES OF SAM CLEMENS

Or, the Autobiography of Mark Twain

THERE WAS ALWAYS SOMETHING DIVIDED ABOUT SAMUEL LANG-
horne Clemens, a psychological fault line implicit in his desire to be
known professionally as "Mark Twain" and in the word *twain* itself. One
half of the great writer sought to reveal himself in an autobiography
planned as early as 1876, when he was only forty. The other half quailed
at trying to emulate Jean-Jacques Rousseau's frank *Confessions*.

"Rousseau," Clemens pointed out, "confesses to masturbation, theft,

Reprinted from *The Wall Street Journal*, 13 November 2010, © Dow Jones & Company. All rights
reserved.

Photograph of Mark Twain writing in bed, ca. 1907.

lying, shameful treachery, & attempts made upon his person by Sod-
omites." If we allow that fiction is a superior form of lying, it's a fair
guess that at least two of these embarrassments can be laid to the door
of the author of *Huckleberry Finn*. Twain (let's call him that, for critical
convenience) enlarged on his qualms about self-revelation in a letter to
his brother Orion. He noted with a touch of envy that Rousseau had
been "perfectly aware of the shameful nature" of certain requisites of a
true autobiography, "whereas your coward & your Failure should be
happy and sweet & unconscious ~~of their own contemptibility.~~"

The last four words were not so heavily erased that Orion could not
read them. In 1899, still struggling to find an honest way to write his
apologia pro vita sua, Twain told a reporter: "You cannot lay bare your
private soul and look at it. . . . It is too disgusting." The depth of that
disgust was clear when he wrote to his friend William Dean Howells
about "the author-cat" raking dust over every noisome revelation,
"which hides from the disinterested spectator neither it nor its
smell . . . the result being that the reader knows the author in spite of
his wily diligences."

IT SEEMS CLEAR that Twain, an enormously successful writer and platform personality, had a black view of himself that went far beyond questions of sex or mendacity. His instinct was to take the often harsh facts of
experience and sweeten them into something as delightful as *The Adventures of Tom Sawyer*—which, aside from being his most perfect book, is a
boyhood memoir so thinly disguised that it could have been called "The
Adventures of Sam Clemens."

If he had not died in 1910, just as American puritanism was yielding
to Freudian analysis of the torments of memory, Twain might have realized that his personal derelictions were (as far as we know) few, and by
no means contemptible. Mark Twain was actually a magnificent person,
blessed with literary genius, *bonhomie*, and radiant humor. His family
and friends adored him. From the 1880s on he had the respect, even the
reverence, of literary peers on both sides of the Atlantic. Publishers and
lecture agents fought to sign him up. When, in 1894, he was ruined
through no fault of his own (except the lifelong delusion that he was a

shrewd investor), Henry H. Rogers, one of the busiest financiers on Wall Street, came to his rescue, as a national treasure that could not be foreclosed.

By the time Twain had paid off his last debt and found himself wealthy once more, the most popular author-lecturer since Charles Dickens, he was an old man, bereaved of his wife and two of his four children. (Only one, his daughter Clara, would survive him.) The writer Hamlin Garland, a fellow Midwesterner, observed that "Clemens, like many another humorist, was essentially sad." Yet his volcanic vitality was intact, and the rapturous reception of his seventieth-birthday speech at the Players Club in New York, in 1905, prompted him to return to the manuscript of his autobiography.

After some thirty or forty false starts, it was already a formidable manuscript. Perhaps "repository" is a better word for what he proceeded to pile up over the course of six manic months in 1906 and left behind, still incomplete, at his death: an unorganized, crumbling, sneeze-provoking mass of letters, diaries, oral transcripts (more than five thousand pages of them), news clips, and other memorabilia. Now being published in its entirety—this is the first of what will eventually be three volumes—*Autobiography of Mark Twain* aspires to completeness and definitiveness. Yet, as even the publisher admits, it is less a book than a gigantic fragment: the outpourings of an egotist so garrulous that the type sometimes dwindles to a size that will constrict your pupils.

FORTUNATELY, TWAIN WAS that rare motormouth whose every word beguiles us. That does not mean that this book does not ramble. On the contrary, rambling is its deliberate style. Except for a few "written" passages of orthodox narrative and other preliminary scraps, it is mostly a collection of stream-of-consciousness monologues, dictated in Twain's New York townhouse between 9 January and 30 March 1906.

He congratulated himself on having hit upon something new in nonfiction, after more than thirty years of stylistic experiments: "a form and a method whereby the past and the present are constantly brought face to face . . . like contact of flint and steel." At the drop of an ash from his cigar, he could segue from memories of "Uncle Dan'l," the original of

Nigger Jim in *Huckleberry Finn,* to a headline in that morning's newspaper. Oral flexibility transcended the drag of linear narrative and enabled Twain to be selective in his truth-telling. And since saying a thing was, in a strange way, less specific than writing it, he could edge closer to self-exposure—always with the liberating assurance that his comic persona would step in and make light of stories that threatened to become embarrassing or libelous.

To their credit, the editors of this centennial edition (most of the *Autobiography* has been published before, but in fragmentary and bowdlerized forms) make no attempt to connect Twain's non sequiturs, other than simply to reproduce them in the order they were set down. Footnote fetishists will appreciate the meticulous annotations of every item needing amplification. And best of all, there is no tampering with Twain's language, that superb instrument capable of a thousand modulations. Seemingly informal, it is in fact precise, taut, studded with *mots* that could not possibly be more *juste*: "I remember the raging of the rain on that roof. . . ."

Thanks to the shorthand skills of his stenographer, Albert Bigelow Paine, we could almost be guests in the great man's bedroom. Curly-headed, bristle-browed, and a touch bronchial at this time of year, Mark Twain lies propped up after breakfast and talks enchantingly about his barefoot boyhood in Missouri, his apprentice days as a printer's brat and cub reporter, and his years piloting on the Mississippi. Then comes adventure after improbable adventure as he wanders across the breadth of the United States, prospecting for silver here, escaping the penitentiary there, compulsively scribbling his experiences.

The publication of his story "The Celebrated Jumping Frog of Calaveras County" in 1867 brings him his first fame and his first trip abroad, during which he meets the Buffalo heiress Olivia Langdon and vows to marry her. That dream is realized amid an accelerating rush to wealth and bestsellerdom, as book follows book and his travels expand literally to encompass the globe. In the process, he builds up an international reputation as the funniest man alive.

It is a mystery how Paine's shorthand arm did not go into convulsions over, say, Twain's story about being coached as a duelist in antebellum Nevada, or the one about the Episcopal minister whose hair turned green, or others about the overefficient burglar alarm, the stammerer who tried to cure himself by whistling, and (most sublime of all) bare-assed Jim Wolf going after amorous cats on an ice-slick roof, with fourteen saucers of red-hot candy below. "The frosty breeze flapped his short shirt about his lean legs; the crystal roof shone like polished marble in the intense glory of the moon; the unconscious cats sat erect upon the chimney, alertly watching each other, lashing their tails and pouring out their hollow grievances; and slowly and cautiously Jim crept along, flapping as he went. . . . ."

But let Twain get to his punch line with his own precise timing, in the sure knowledge that he will immediately trump it. This is the way with great raconteurs, and great melodists in music: There is always the delicious promise of more and better to come.

Aside from the occasional explosion of sulfurous wrath against some malefactor ("If I had his nuts in a steel trap . . . ") and one or two shocking confidences (as when Twain unfairly blames himself for the death of his only son), there is little in this huge volume to justify his scruples about publishing it posthumously, in installments spread over a century, to spare the sensibilities of persons mentioned.

The most he will say about sex is that he finds it difficult to kiss and fondle his near and dear. But this was less a matter of physical coldness than of upbringing. He does not sentimentalize any of the many painful experiences of his later years as a writer, publisher, and bankruptee, and maintains self-control even when describing the loss, to heart disease, of his beloved wife, Livy.

OCCASIONALLY, MAYBE ONCE in fifty pages, the old man will go on a little too long. His dreams, dietary problems, and complaints about stock-market reversals are as boring as yours and mine. Many of the news stories he fixates on seem dated now. (An exception is the Moro Massacre of 8 March 1906, when clean-cut American boys in the Philippines behaved just as barbarously as they would later do at My Lai and Abu Ghraib.) On the whole, however, this volume is hard to stop reading. Twain's prosody is so sure, and his powers of observation and selection so great, that he can take the most unpromising material—a real-estate deed, a letter from a would-be author—and make it glitter, like a dull stone that turns out to be quartz or even diamond. Like Nabokov, he knew how to "caress the details, the divine details."

There is a passage describing the interior of a farmhouse that young Sam lived in as a boy that matches anything in *Speak, Memory*. Significantly, however, these couple of pages are among the few that Twain took the trouble to write rather than dictate. If his autobiography is, ultimately, inferior to Nabokov's, it is because he was mistaken in thinking that improvisations—even inspired improvisations—can ever cohere into a satisfactory whole. Unless there is line, there can be no architecture.

By 1909, Twain realized that he was on the way to producing the longest book ever attempted. He lost heart and left it unfinished—at a half-million words. His stream of consciousness had become an unmanageable flood: he needed to get out of it before he drowned.

One of the first magazine men to pitch for serial rights to the autobiography prophetically advised Twain to insert a clause in his will allowing for full publication in "the year 2000 . . . by electrical method, or by any mode which may then be in use." This edition is a bit late for that deadline. But stylistically speaking, it can only gain by appearing at a moment when the preferred forms of human communication are torrential texting and tweeting. What an irony that our supreme literary craftsman should be seen, in retrospect, as the inventor of the blog!

EDISON ILLUMINATED

The "Life & Phenomenon" of an Inventor

THE TANTALIZING THING ABOUT ELECTRICITY, THAT FUNDAMENTAL force that lights our nights and floods our nanocircuits, is that no one has ever been able to say just what it is. Easy enough to see and feel what it *does* — even taste it, as schoolboys do when they grab each other's tongues and touch a battery. But when electricity isn't going someplace, it has no color, no character.

Biographically speaking, the same might be said of Thomas Edison, the largely self-taught inventor who has done more to irradiate this planet than any other agent save the sun. Many books have been written about him, and a goodly portion of the five million pages of documents in his archive have been published in a series of wrist-cracking volumes.

Originally published in *The New York Times Book Review*, 23 March 2012.

Photograph of Thomas Edison napping in his laboratory, ca. 1911.

His big head and black brows and easy grin are as vivid in our historical mind's eye as the features of Abraham Lincoln. His surname attaches to a thousand schools and institutions, and enrages New Yorkers every time they open their monthly power bill. The incandescent lamp he perfected may soon spiral out of existence, yet cartoonists will always draw it when they wish to convey the ignition of an idea.

Edison the man, however, remains elusive. He is legendary for what he *did*—among other things, patenting one thousand and ninety-three inventions in such diverse disciplines as telegraphy, cinematography, sound recording, metallurgy, chemistry, and botany. What he *was* in person is harder, maybe impossible to say, because he put so much of himself into his work. There were times when his two wives and six children felt there was no self left over for them—loving though he could be on the occasional Sunday off. Even then, his jocular impenetrability precluded intimacy. The near-deafness that had shrouded him since puberty was a frustration for his friends, who got little out of shouting into his right ear. Edison quickened everything he touched, but could not be captured at source.

The fifteen-volume series of *The Papers of Thomas A. Edison* (Baltimore: Johns Hopkins University Press, 1989–), now almost half complete, makes this elusiveness clear. This is not the fault of the team of editors, headed by Paul B. Israel, whose mission is to put much of Edison on paper and all of him online. Their scholarship is admirable, right down to identifying which of the great man's scribbles are canceled, circled, or "obscured overwritten." Even his changes of ink are noted. No complexity of electrical or chemical engineering goes unexplained, in language that honors Thomas Sprat's famous admonition to Royal Society scientists in 1684: "Reject all the Amplifications, Digressions, and Swellings of Style . . . return back to the primitive Purity and Shortness, when Men deliver'd so many *Things*, almost in an equal Number of *Words*." But the myriad technological and business records they have published so far, plus a small number of personal documents, do not coalesce, like the facets of a Chuck Close painting, into full-color portraiture.

Vol. 7, entitled *Losses and Loyalties, April 1883–December 1884,* is the latest to appear. At 811 oversize pages, devoted to the inventor's attempt to reinvent himself in his midthirties as a businessman in New York, it may not sell as well as the equally hefty first volume of Mark Twain's autobiography, which tore so many Christmas stockings in 2010. Nevertheless, as Close has remarked, even an agnosiac can get breadth of perception from the scrutiny of minutiae. In its superabundance of detail—steely facts and figures, great plates of text riveted with nouns and graffitied with cryptic drawings (Edison was an untrained but natural draftsman)—the book has the same kind of physical impact as that which stuns you when you enter his laboratory in West Orange, New Jersey. (The twenty-one-acre complex is now Thomas Edison National Historical Park.) How, you ask yourself, can any one man have dreamed up and fabricated so many devices, from the first phonograph and first movie studio (rolling and rotatable on rails) to poured-cement houses, fuel cells, and an execution harness for elephants? Room after room, floor after floor, displays the hard evidence of Edison's genius. No exhibit is more eloquent than the NEW THINGS pigeonhole in his desk, still stuffed with ideas he meant to get around to when he had time.

THE WORD GENIUS is so overused today it has lost its meaning—witness the lavishness with which it has been applied to Steve Jobs. Tellingly, a eulogist in *The New Yorker* sought to go beyond it by calling Jobs "the twentieth century's Thomas Edison." Leaving aside the fact that Edison survived until 1931, and patented his last invention ten months before he died, there is an almost comical disproportion between the creative achievement of the two men. The science scholar Vaclav Smil has pointed out that for all the sleek efficiency of Apple products, their technology has been derivative, making them at best "second-order innovations."* As for the 313 patents that Jobs claimed or co-claimed, take his star device, the iPad, download the list of Edison's successful awards at inventors.about.com, and see how many swipes you need to scroll though it. (In my case, forty-nine.) You will register, *passim*, executions for automobiles, phonographs, rotary kilns, haulage systems, auditory telegraphs, magnetos, waterproof paint, electric pens, railway

* Vaclav Smil, "Why Jobs Is No Edison," *The American*, September 2011.

signals, talking dolls, and enough variations on the theme of incandescent light to give you photon fatigue.

But screen stroking is a superficial exercise in more ways than one. *Losses and Loyalties* covers just twenty-one months of Edison's life, and conveys his productivity during that period by printing on acid-free paper as much documentary evidence as can reasonably be put between covers.

By the spring of 1883, Edison had more or less closed down his famous laboratory in Menlo Park, New Jersey, and headquartered himself in New York. He announced that he was going to take "a long vacation" from inventing. His design and construction of the world's first central power station at Pearl Street, in Lower Manhattan (now considered to be his greatest achievement, eclipsing the phonograph and Edison lamp) had brought orders for similar systems from as far away as Italy and Chile. Enormous wealth stared him in the face. But to capitalize quickly on the most immediate of these opportunities—in Massachusetts and Pennsylvania—he wanted to free himself of the corporate drag of the Edison Electric Company. That already huge enterprise was, in his opinion, too timid about business risk. He decided to create his own construction department and fund it out of his own pocket.

Ever since his invention of the phonograph in 1877, he had made millions by manufacturing his own products. But the usual benefits of Mammon—luxury, social status, treasure—did not interest him. As fast as profits flowed from the factory, he rechanneled them into research and development. The success of Pearl Street persuaded him that he was as brilliant an entrepreneur as a scientist. *Losses and Loyalties* demonstrates the vanity of this notion. While by no means lacking in commercial or competitive smarts, Edison was overly confident of the technological excellence of his systems. In rushing to throw a necklace of miniature Pearls across the bosom of Eastern states, he did not anticipate the inability of local municipalities to operate them reliably. (Then, as now, the U.S. economy suffered from a shortage of skilled electrical engineers.) Within a year, he found himself nearly bankrupted by the heavy expenses of building stations and coaxing them into profitable operation.

Meanwhile Edison's creative side, as urgent as any poet's, made him yearn for the laboratory. Consider the following stream of consciousness, jotted in one of his innumerable notebooks. One does not have to be a scientist to sense that this was, in Henry James's phrase, a "laboratory brain."

> *Licorice seems to Carbonize without any Swelling large amount gas goes off—Might be used as binder or mixed with other things roled into sheets to Cut filiments from . . . paint filiment with camel hair brush with acetate of mag also Lime, mag 1st= then get vac & gently bring up then bk vac and paint again etc several times then get life & Phenomenon*

Edison wrote it in Florida in March 1884, on a river cruise necessitated by the ill health of his wife Mary. Relieved for a while from business cares, he could happily conduct imaginary experiments. He was unable to look at flora ashore, or machinery in the fields, without conceiving new biochemical and mechanical processes.

Even the presence of a shark in the waters off St. Augustine had to be turned into a demonstration of applied electrophysics. Edison went after it with a mysterious basket stashed on the floor of his boat. Unraveling a long wire insulated with gutta-percha, he dropped a lure of mock meat that, as the shark soon discovered, was entirely the wrong thing to chew. When the line jerked, Edison "worked like an organ grinder" at a crank handle in the basket (presumably connected to a dynamo), and returned to land triumphant, with a seven-hundred-pound trophy to hang in the local museum.

IT WAS THE LAST leisure moment in an otherwise terrible year. That summer, a lawsuit he had been obstinately fighting, in the face of two court judgments against him, climaxed in his house at Menlo Park being seized for a sheriff's sale. He had no cash left to save it, and had to rely on the preemptive bid of a friend. At the same time, with shocking suddenness, Mary died. She was only twenty-nine.

Biographers have been incurious about Mary Stilwell, whom Edison married in a surge of sexual desire in 1871. The consensus is that she was the blue-collar girl he should have left behind. Certainly she did not compare intellectually or socially with her successor Mina Miller, an inventor's daughter unfazed at being proposed to in Morse code. Mary probably could not have handled the almost godlike celebrity Edison attained by the end of the century, and the deterioration of his personality as he grew ever more autocratic. But unlike Mina, she could remember him when he was a young, little-known telegraph engineer.

An interview Mary gave shortly before her death, discovered and republished in *Losses and Loyalties*, corrects some of the misapprehensions about their marriage. "In the first place, I never worked in any factory. . . . All the stories about his passing along where I was at work Monday evening and proposing to me and setting the wedding for Tuesday morning hasn't [*sic*] a word of truth in it." She had been a schoolgirl, not yet sixteen, who ducked into his Newark laboratory one afternoon during a rainstorm. "I thought he had very handsome eyes, [yet] he was so dirty, all covered with machine oil, &c." She allowed him to escort her home, though, and for the next five months received his suit as an old-fashioned "gentleman caller." Thirteen years and three childbirths later, Mary voiced no regrets about becoming the wife of a smelly scientist whom she rarely saw by daylight. Edison was quite capable of experimenting for ninety-five hours at a stretch, neglecting food and sleep in his obsessive quest for "life & Phenomenon."

At least he was home, having hurriedly returned from his laboratory in New York, the night she died in Menlo Park. His eldest daughter, Marion, recalled him "shaking with grief, weeping and sobbing" the next morning, hardly able to tell her what had happened. One suspects that Edison's shock was mixed with guilt, for Mary, like Mina later on, was often cast into depression by his marital neglect.

The Edison Electric Company issued a terse statement that she was a victim of "congestion of the brain"—that vague ailment cited in so many nineteenth-century obituaries. Whoever signed Mary's postmortem certificate suspiciously left blank the cause-of-death box. Professor Israel and his researchers have, however, uncovered a plausible-sounding newspaper account of the catastrophe. It reports, on the authority of a family friend, that Mrs. Edison was killed by "an overdose of morphine swallowed in a moment of frenzy."

Apparently she had become addicted to morphine as a relief from uterine pain after the birth of her third child. The article does not imply that she committed suicide. But there is this extraordinary paragraph about how her husband reacted when a physician said that Mary was beyond help:

> Mr. Edison silently drew forth a cabinet and instantly a powerful current of electricity responded to his will. For two hours he kept life from fleeting, but at last he appreciated that his science, like that of the doctors, was powerless. Taking his children by the hand he led them into his study. There they remained for a long time and when he came out his blue eyes glistened and the lids were red and swollen.

One hopes the "cabinet" was not the same one he went shark fishing with in Florida.

BY THE END OF September 1884, Edison was back at research and development, having resignedly given over his central-station business to the Edison Electric Company. A visit to the Philadelphia Electrical Exhibition with Marion (father and daughter standing hand in hand, looking at a tower of more than two thousand lightbulbs that dazzlingly spelled out his name) convinced him that his real gift was for innovation. Nearly six hundred further inventions, beginning with U.S. Patent No. 438,304, "Electric Signaling Apparatus," lay ahead of him; another wife, three more children, and more millions of dollars than he would ever bother to count. He was not yet thirty-eight, and his thick hair was still brown. Beneath it, the laboratory brain was beating, musing new ways to improve the sonics of long-distance telephony.

The induction coil by its Extra Current knocks the talking down nearly
½ now if it could be Cut out that would be good thing. . . .

THE IVO POGORELICH OF
PRESIDENTIAL BIOGRAPHY
Writing *Dutch*

I WAS CALLED MANY THINGS AFTER PUBLISHING *DUTCH: A MEMOIR of Ronald Reagan* in 1999. Most of them were printable, and the abuse from certain quarters unsurprising—especially those of history profs and political drones.

Modesty prevents me from quoting some of the diametrically opposed opinions of critics (including three of Mr. Reagan's four children) who found the book as revelatory as it was unorthodox. I will say only that a handful of reviews, such as that in *The New York Times* on publication day, were the sort that any writer dreams of. But negative notices predominated to such an extent on both sides of the Atlantic that no-

This essay (2012) is an expanded version of two seminars given by the author as a writer in residence at the University of Chicago in 2003.

White House photograph of President Reagan and his biographer, 1988.

body believes me now when I say that *l'affaire Dutch* was the happiest experience in my career.

It's not that I thrived on the publicity, which after a month or two convinced me that Andy Warhol was right in suggesting that fifteen minutes of fame—or infamy—should be enough for anyone to brace for. *Dutch*'s peculiarity, as a nonfiction book written by an imaginary narrator, was front-page news the week before it came out. That Sunday, my role as Mr. Reagan's authorized biographer was the subject of a two-segment report on CBS's *60 Minutes*. It coincided with a nasty squabble between *Newsweek* and the London *Sunday Times*, both claiming first serial rights. The latter won, but within hours both *Newsweek* and *Time* were thumping onto the racks, each flagging *Dutch* as a front-cover literary scandal. How dare a biographer insert himself—or some other self?—or several selves, all fictional?—into what was supposed to have been the official life of the fortieth President? Pundits who could not have had time to flick more than a few pages (the book was embargoed until twenty-four hours after *Newsweek* came out) rushed to their mastheads and microphones to abuse me as "dishonorable" and "barking mad." Four veteran Reaganauts went on *The Larry King Show* and declared that I had gotten every single thing wrong about their revered leader. Larry let them blast away for an hour before asking each man in turn if he had actually read the book. The result was four grumpy "no's." Maureen Reagan, the President's eldest daughter, also declared *Dutch* a travesty, sight unseen.

A puzzled journalist in Amsterdam called Random House to ask what Mr. Reagan had to do with Holland.

On Tuesday, I made the first of three consecutive appearances on the *Today* show to defend my literary folly. The studio at Rockefeller Center was freezing, but I don't think that was why Katie Couric trembled as she leaned forward to interview me. It was the tremble of a greyhound eager to take a bite out of a motionless rabbit.

The chase that ensued was so fugitive that I can't remember a second of it. But Lesley Stahl, a generous soul whom I had gotten to like while filming the *60 Minutes* piece, called my wife afterward to chortle that the rabbit had won, with inches to spare.

Dutch subsequently shot to No. 2 on the *New York Times* bestseller list.

All the major talk shows competed to "get" me for a grilling. I dashed from one studio to the next, acquiring so many layers of makeup that I began to look like Joan Crawford. Meanwhile, the critical chorus grew steadily more shrill. On Saturday the *Times*'s chief literary critic, Michiko Kakutani, took issue with her colleague Christopher Lehmann-Haupt's favorable review of the book, and excoriated me in one of the most prolonged and sibilant of her legendary hissy fits. *Dutch*, she wrote, was "bizarre, incomprehensible and monstrously self-absorbed."

And these were just the early shots of a media fusillade that soon toppled *Dutch* from its high place on the list. Yet I remained perversely pleased.

THE REBUKE THAT delighted me most was voiced in public by Leonard Slatkin, conductor of the National Symphony Orchestra in Washington, D.C. Before quoting it in its polysyllabic entirety, I should explain that Mr. Slatkin was stressed at the time. He had engaged a Croatian pianist, Ivo Pogorelich, to play Beethoven's Third Piano Concerto at the Kennedy Center, knowing him to have made a dazzling debut on the international scene in 1979.

Nobody was surprised when the pianist arrived in town and turned out to be no longer young. But at the preconcert rehearsal, he gave a performance so wildly eccentric, playing fast passages like funeral marches, slow ones *prestissimo*, and reducing climaxes to a sonic level almost inaudible to human ears, that Mr. Slatkin feared a riot if concertgoers that evening were not forewarned.

Conveniently, *Dutch* was still in the news. At the beginning of the program Mr. Slatkin announced from the podium that Washington was about to hear Beethoven's Third played as it had never been played before.

"Ivo Pogorelich," he explained, "is the Edmund Morris of classical music."

AS IT HAPPENS, I play the piano myself—about as well, I suppose, as Mr. Pogorelich might acquit himself as a writer in the English language.

Still, I know enough about music to recognize a great pianist when I hear one. Nuts or not, when that guy performs Ravel's *Gaspard de la Nuit*, he's hard to beat. So if Mr. Slatkin was by any chance implying that I am, in reverse logic, "the Ivo Pogorelich of presidential biography," I couldn't be more flattered.

Something tells me, however, that the maestro meant no such compliment. He was delicately dissociating himself from an eccentric soloist, just as many of my Washington friends had started avoiding me.

One of them who had, as the phrase goes, regular access to the media, called my wife to say that in his view, *Dutch* was brilliant.

"It would be nice if you put that in print," she told him. "Edmund's being knocked all around the block."

"I couldn't possibly," he said. "I have to work in this town."

In another illuminating exchange, Tom Wolfe took me aside at a New York Public Library function and murmured, "Some folks who are slanging you say in private that they like the book a lot."

Well, maybe. But the violence of most reactions was amazing, including those of ordinary readers who sent me furious letters (one tauntingly enclosing a mutilated title page for my signature). "I gotta congratulate you," a sardonic buddy said. "You've managed to offend just about every sector of intellectual opinion. Conservatives are mad that you show Reagan up as an ignoramus and a bore. Liberals can't stand it that you claim him, paradoxically, to have been a great president. Historians feel you've polluted the purity of scholarship by pissing fiction into it, novelists think you want it both ways, and wonks can't forgive you for believing that the story of a man's life is more interesting than policy."

All of which was and remains true. However, now that *Dutch* is "toast," in the contemptuous word of a *Washington Post* reporter, its author feels he has a right to explain his behavior, as Edward VIII did when abdicating the throne of England: "At long last I can say a few words of my own."

WHEN RONALD REAGAN became President in 1981 he was naturally curious, as most chief executives are, about his predecessors. So he read

The Rise of Theodore Roosevelt, which I had published a couple of years before, and soon after that my wife and I were invited to a state dinner at the White House. Standing big and beaming in the Blue Room, he took my hand in both of his and said, "I want you to be the first to know. We've just decided to go ahead with a new nuclear aircraft carrier, and it's going to be named the *Theodore Roosevelt*."

I tried to make a lame joke, asking if he would mind calling it *Theodore Rex*—that being the title of the book I was now writing. But he was deaf and uninterested, turning already to the next person in line.

During the course of the evening I met several of Reagan's top aides and found them inexplicably friendly. The most powerful of them, Michael Deaver, allowed *sotto voce* that if I wanted to apply to become the President's authorized biographer, "he and Nancy would probably say yes."

My unspoken reaction was that Reagan was, for all his charm and affability, so much less interesting than Theodore Roosevelt that I could not think of shelving *Theodore Rex* in order to write an official life that all these brisk men (not to mention the famously protective Mrs. Reagan) would insist on editing. Doubtless there would be dollars in it, but what price the sacrifice of solitude and independence, those most luxurious aspects of the literary life?

So I did not follow up on Deaver's hint, nor on the public suggestions of Daniel J. Boorstin, the Librarian of Congress, and Mark O. Hatfield, Oregon's professorial senior senator, that a scholar—not necessarily me—should be appointed to the President's entourage, recording his everyday actions just as White House photographers did on film.

Over the course of the next few years it became obvious that Reagan was becoming a seriously important president, underestimated not only by Clark Clifford as an "amiable dunce," but by statesman after statesman who had to admit that he personified both the best and worst aspects of capitalist democracy. Even totalitarians who could not or would not meet with him, notably three successive leaders of the Soviet Union, noticed that the balance of world power was dipping in Reagan's direction, and that his was the muscle forcing the change.

After his huge reelection victory in 1984 I began to regret having passed up the chance to witness all this history in action. Then, in the following spring, Reagan was confronted by a sudden check to his inexorable advance. It was the Bitburg Crisis, a moral dilemma of extreme drama that for some strange reason has been almost forgotten— ironically, because its whole theme was memory. In briefest summary, Reagan had accepted an invitation from Chancellor Kohl to lay wreaths with him in a German military cemetery on 5 May 1985, the fortieth an- niversary of the end of World War II, and so bring to a symbolic end any lingering enmity between their respective countries. Reagan, in his good-natured way, gave no thought to what names and affiliations might be chiseled on the headstones he would be honoring. A White House advance team visited the suggested cemetery of Bitburg some months before, in wintry weather that blanketed the headstones of the graves with snow. Reagan duly released his travel plans, on an April day that marked one of the rare coincidences of Easter and Passover. Within forty-eight hours, it was discovered that the President and Chancellor would be performing their joint ceremony over the bones of a number of Waffen-SS troopers. Around the world, all Jewish hell broke loose.

The crisis became high theater when Reagan, insisting that he had a gentleman's commitment to go, was reprimanded to his face on national television by Elie Wiesel, chairman of the U.S. Holocaust Commission. "That place, Mr. President, is not your place. Your place is with the vic- tims of the SS."

Reagan's only concession was to announce that before visiting Bit- burg he would stop by the nearby concentration camp of Bergen-Belsen, lay a wreath there too, and make a speech on the subject of the Holo- caust. His moral reputation had taken such a blow that it was clear that this would be the most fraught oratory of his life. Could the old actor redeem himself with the right words, and genuine contrition? The un- likelihood of this guaranteed a worldwide audience of many millions, including me, when the gray spring day of reckoning dawned over the Lüneberger Heide, and television cameras recorded Reagan's arrival at the *Dokumentenhaus* on the edge of Belsen field.

What he saw in there put an expression on his face of such anguish that I felt my heart constrict. A skylark sang out, its trill vibrating across the Atlantic and into my living room. At that moment, I was overcome with literary desire. Here was something supremely dramatic happen- ing, and I was not there, as I could have been, to record its every nuance.

He proceeded to make the greatest speech of his presidency, far exceeding in eloquence and raw emotion the more hokey ones that are now cited in quotation books. And I lost no time, as soon as he and Nancy returned home, to request their permission to become—belatedly but wholeheartedly—the official biographer of Ronald Reagan.

Going for broke, I asked for unlimited access to the White House as an independent, nongovernment writer, regular interviews with the President, travel-along privileges (but at my own cost) whenever he took important trips, and for scrutiny of whatever personal papers he felt comfortable sharing with me.

Ronald Reagan happened to be about the most comfortably trusting individual any biographer could hope to approach. I was not surprised at his willingness to let me see and write what I liked, including the personal diary he was keeping, in patient longhand, of every day of his presidency. (Nervous aides quickly stepped in and postponed *that* breach of security.) But I was surprised that Nancy trusted me too. She hated the book I eventually wrote, and has never spoken to me since I sent her the first copy. Not once, though, in all the years she tolerated my insatiable curiosity, did she ask to see what I was writing, or prevent me going in any research direction that might cause her pain. I'm sorry we're not friends anymore, but an honest biographer has to follow his pen in the direction it needs to go.

AND HONESTY, AFTER a couple of years of observation and research, compelled me to admit (if only to myself) that the orthodox presidential biography I had begun was likely to be stillborn. No matter how much prenatal care it got, the fundamental problem was that it lacked inner life. Which is to say, that Reagan himself was a hollow subject. There were no depths to probe, no lodes of packed complexity, no response to any call of "Who's there?" As this paragraph has already indicated, he seemed describable only in metaphor.

It was not that he was uncooperative in interviews: on the contrary, as his first wife complained after walking out on him, "Ronnie never shut up." He treated me exactly as he treated everybody, with twinkling affability and endless patience. But no matter how long his answers, he never said anything revealing. At first I suspected he was just deflecting my curiosity, until I realized that he had no curiosity about himself. His copious manuscripts—Reagan thought by hand, on yellow legal pads—were as personally inexpressive as invoices.

The only times he came to life in the Oval Office were when he did something with his voice or body, for example, a hilarious (and highly incorrect) imitation of a macho film star sitting down with a tell-tale twitch of the hips. Until death I will cherish the memory of the President of the United States, at lunch with George H. W. Bush, using a bottle of Tabasco sauce to mime masturbation. Also the moment when he leaned across his desk and hissed at me, "You bloody little swine, you think I don't *care*—the only one who knew, who really understood!"

He was only reprising his role as Captain Stanhope in a student production of R. C. Sherriff's *Journey's End*.

But the incident which convinced me that Reagan required a new kind of chronicling occurred when I inquired how he had spent his free time as a young sportscaster in Des Moines in the early 1930s. Instead of talking about girls, as I hoped he might, he said he used to hang out at the Advertising Club, "because they had all the best speakers from out of town." He chucklingly cited a comedian who had impersonated the president of a toilet paper company and "had us all laughing fit to bust."

I encouraged him to go on. At once his eyes glazed and his voice changed into that of somebody quite other than himself. Out from the lips of the Chief Magistrate came a prolonged spiel, so evocative of distant time and place—of what passed for humor in the Midwest in Depression days—that I would not have been surprised to hear the scratch of a phonograph needle. When he reached the punch line, winked, and resumed his normal voice, I said I could not believe that he had heard the speech only once.

"Yes," he said indifferently, glancing at the clock. "Just at that luncheon."*

With no conscious intent, he had at last given me the key to his character. Reagan by 1987 was a figure of historic stature, a consistently suc-

---

* A partial transcript of this bizarre effusion appears in *Dutch: A Memoir of Ronald Reagan*, pages 117–18.

cessful man who had excelled in seven different careers. But as his son Ron remarked in some wonderment, "Not one of those roles seems to have rubbed off on him." Throughout his life he had moved from platform to platform—college hall, radio studio, sound stage, labor forum, television showcase, corporate auditorium, countless political hustings, and finally the Oval Office, which he informed me was "the biggest theater in the world."

In other words, Ronald Reagan was by nature an actor. Hence the dullness of his private conversation—except when he recited something he had memorized, in the uncanny way thespians have of "playing back" replicative material at will. Even then, an audience of two or three didn't suffice. He was at his best before thousands, or millions, especially when the dramatic stakes were huge, as at Bergen-Belsen and Geneva and Reykjavík. If I was to be his accurate biographer, I would have to represent this perpetual show.

EASIER SAID THAN WRITTEN! By virtue of my extraordinary luck to be the first outside scribe allowed an inside view of a President in action, I knew I would have no problem committing *this* part of his life to paper. I could do so with fly-on-the-wall vividness, making the most of the intimacy—such as it was—he granted me, and of the eagerness of many contemporaries to make clear their vital importance to him. I could watch his foot tapping off the seconds before he began his Saturday afternoon radio broadcast, check whether he wore makeup (he didn't), take note of the Zane Grey paperback by his bed at Rancho del Cielo, the fluffy yellow cover on his loo seat, the ghastly "leather paintings" hanging lopsided in the main room. I could hear him suck in his breath before he went down the steps to meet Mikhail Gorbachev, smell his cheap Bermuda cologne, listen to him singing in church, notice him turning down his hearing aid whenever some pompous asshole started to give him advice (a torment all presidents have to endure). And in the coming years, presumably, I would be able to watch him grow old, it being understood that his memoirs should come out before I weighed in with The Authorized Life.

But what of the seven decades lost to me: his childhood and youth,

Hollywood, marriage to Jane Wyman, World War II, the Screen Actors Guild, the swing from far left to far right, the governorship of California, his failure to become president in 1977? Did any aged folks survive of the seventy-seven swimmers he had rescued from drowning in his seven seasons as a lifeguard on the Rock River? (The number seven kept recurring as I tabulated his strange story.) How much head-cracking research would be necessary for me to resurrect those previous Reagans, all the way back to young "Dutch," myopically gazing at his drunken father spread-eagled in the snow, one February evening in 1922?

Well, I tried. I spent hours in the room where he was born, roamed the flat fields of his youth, waded in the Rock River, pored over the photographs in his mother's scrapbook, and subjected his juvenile essays and short stories to minute, even microscopic examination. I stared at the futuristic self-portrait he drew of himself at age seventeen [see page 320] and parsed the almost surrealistic slang of his sports stories in the *Des Moines Dispatch*, 1934–1935. I stood on the stage at Eureka College where he first tasted "the heady wine" of political oratory. I peeped through the windows of the West Hollywood apartment he shared with Jane Wyman (biographers do these weird things) and ran his early films through a moviola in the Library of Congress, isolating the odd look or gesture that seemed telling, like his expression at Bergen-Belsen.

Still I could not think of a way to make the earlier parts of my book as vivid as the last—*vivid* in its true meaning, "full of life."

THE SAVING IDEA came to me one fall morning in 1987, and it was a genuine epiphany: arrested motion, an electric taste in the mouth. I was crossing the park behind the Capitol in Washington and stepped on a fallen acorn. It popped under my shoe, reminding me that just a week before, I had crushed similar acorns as I walked around the campus of the President's alma mater. The thought occurred that *he* must have done the same, strolling under the same oak trees, sixty years before, and I felt a sharp regret that I could not have been there with him. Not as a friend—just a classmate, say, able to follow in Dutch Reagan's footsteps, listen to him speak, see how he dressed and behaved, chat to other students about him. (Including the teenage version of his first fiancée,

Margaret Cleaver, a stern old lady I had just interviewed in Richmond, Virginia.)

A voice in my head said, "But you *were* there."

And so I had been, in the sense that any biographer, sooner or later, becomes his subject's *Doppelgänger.* In telling the life, he vicariously relives the life. If he is as lucky as Boswell to become part of the actual life of Samuel Johnson, or my wife Sylvia in endearing herself to the aged Clare Boothe Luce, intimacy can enrich imagination. I had no such intimacy with Ronald Reagan. What I did have, perhaps in risky excess, was the ability to evoke *temps perdu.* If I disciplined that power with scholarship, telling not a thing about him that was not documented, why should I not make my literary self old enough to have "lived" a life parallel with his, and write about him as observantly in the Twenties or Forties or Sixties? Could I not then justifiably publish a biography entitled *Dutch: A Memoir of Ronald Reagan?*

The idea grew as a fertile acorn grows, but much more quickly. I made no attempt to suppress "the force that through the green fuse drives the flower"—Dylan Thomas's lovely phrase—except for an initial twining together of my two narrative stems, one factual and one fictional. Then I left them to burgeon naturally, in the hope that they would one day (say, around the time of that state dinner in 1981) merge into a solid trunk.

Whatever final conformation it attained, I knew I was courting a critical firestorm. Ronald Reagan was, after all, about the most important man in the world. There was a general assumption that I would produce one of those solemn Washington books a thousand pages long, with a glossy red-white-and-blue jacket and the word *power* somewhere in the title. And what might be the reaction of executives at Random House, when they heard that their most expensive nonfiction author had turned himself into an imaginary septuagenarian with a polio limp? Probably they would cancel my contract and demand a refund of their advance.

The only person I felt able to confide in was my editor, Robert Loomis, a forty-year veteran of the great days of "gentleman" publishing, with all the traditional instincts that background implies. He is famous for the softness of his speech and the fewness of his words. I made a verbal presentation to him over dinner one night and noticed that he ordered one more Jack Daniel's than normal. Afterward all he would say was, "Let me sleep on this."

The next morning he was hardly more loquacious. But his words made me love him for ever. "I have to admit you've roiled me, Edmund. It's your book, though, and if that's the way you want to go, I'll support you."

THAT COMMITTED BOTH of us to face sooner or later the fraught question of whether there really is much difference between fiction and non-fiction. (What is a novel but a rethinking of the facts of life? What is a biography but an attempt, always unsuccessful, to let facts speak for themselves?) Before striking a contemporary attitude to the subject, I read my way historically backward via the unclassifiable works of W. G. Sebald, E. E. Cummings, and Thomas Beer, dallying for a long time in those of Defoe (with more than five hundred titles, that prodigal genius was dally-intensive), and ending up in the last quarter of the fourteenth century, when there was only one basic form of literature outside of classical and scriptural texts: the romance.

It's an interesting irony that modern fiction was born around then, out of the attempts of writers to "get real." Deposits of fact began to accrete themselves onto the myths that dominated medieval storytelling, like crystals forming in wine. Every now and again a character in one of these myths, which were circulated largely in manuscript, would begin to talk like a real human being, in natural-sounding vernacular. Or the *sfumato* of legend veiling a supernatural landscape would clear to reveal the kind of village ordinary people lived in, with gutters running in front of the cottages and pigs tied up behind.

The moment we open Geoffrey Chaucer's *The Canterbury Tales*, we find ourselves eating, drinking, and sleeping with flesh-and-blood characters, who insist on telling us their stories. It is April, around the year 1385, and we are registered at the Tabard Inn in Southwark, on the left bank of the Thames.* Tomorrow all of us (storyteller and reader and

---

* Perhaps coincidentally, Robert Loomis was staying at the Tabard Inn in Washington the night the author first outlined the plot of *Dutch*.

pilgrims) will set off for the shrine of Thomas à Becket in Canterbury. The inn is large and hospitable. By sunset everybody knows everybody else. Chaucer is terse in his introductions, because, as he explains, there's going to be an early wake-up call. We can learn more about one another as we travel. And so, in short order, we meet the Knight, "a verray parfit, gentil" old globetrotter who reminds me of Ronald Reagan; the Knight's son, a horny twenty-year-old and amateur songwriter; a boozy miller; a forester with a bunch of peacock-feather arrows stuck in his belt; a smiling, saintly nun, fluent in French and affected in her table manners. The rest of the company are just as visible, palpable, and audible, although their Early English accents fall strangely on our ears.

They are, of course, just creatures of Chaucer's imagination, which makes the stories they tell fictions within a fiction. But to a myth-satiated medieval reader, the concrete detail in virtually every line of *The Canterbury Tales*—the color and drape of clothes, the mannerisms and vanities, the skin eruptions, the obscene jokes, the atmospherics of weather and landscape and townscape—these and countless other documentary touches amounted to a secular revelation.

With the invention of printing in 1440 and a general shift of storytelling from poetry to prose, realism became the norm, and the novel— the "book of life," you might call it, full of factual particulars—gradually replaced the romance as the preferred medium of mass communication. Reading spread like foam before the wave of printed books that billowed across the intellectual landscape in the 1460s. An estimated fifteen to twenty million texts were in print by the end of the century. Newly literate people demanded, and got, prose redactions of the great poems of the past, shortened for quick consumption, like the novelizations of today's blockbuster movies. These redactions dispensed with the fabulous paraphernalia of romance—dragons, grails, perilous thrones—in favor of worldly episodes that showed how to behave charitably, how to court women and protect children, how to fight and farm and build. Crusades scaled down to border squabbles, castles turned into cottages, and rowboats, rather than giant swans, became the preferred form of river transport. *Euralius and Lucrece,* a fifteenth-century translation of a fourteenth-century Latin romance, featured a heroine who wanted sex and didn't mind how she got it, kitchens that smoked and wines that needed tasting, boxes full of bric-a-brac, letters trampled and spat on.

Side by side with the redactions, whose protagonists continued to be imaginary, arose a much more factual form of literature, the *exemplum*—a short religious book that sought to inform rather than entertain. Such books tended to be anecdotal, even autobiographical in style. A wandering friar might report on heathen activity in a specific town. A sinner would frankly confess where, when, and with whose wife he had misbehaved. Visionaries relied on plain prose to describe the intensity of their raptures. Just as modern fiction developed out of the novelization and secularization of romance, modern nonfiction can be seen to derive out of the crude truth-telling of the *exempla*.

Throughout the fifteenth and sixteenth centuries there was much interfacing between the genres, with fancy adorning fact and fact adding weight to fancy. The old tradition of romance came surging back in the historical bodice-rippers beloved of the Elizabethan merchant class: "[She pressed herself on him] with the whole weight of hir bodye, and byting of his lips with hir friendly teeth." That's as sexy as anything in Daniel Defoe's *Moll Flanders*, written 150 years later.

Toward the end of the Renaissance era, nonfiction writers used such devices as imaginary dialogue to clarify the revelations of science. Bernard le Bovier de Fontenelle's *Conversations on the Plurality of Worlds* (1686) is cast in the form of a flirtatious conversation between a philosopher and a marquise in a moonlit garden. He explains the breakthrough theory of Copernicus, while clearly planning a more intimate breakthrough of his own.

PROFESSORS LOVE TO CITE Daniel Defoe (1660–1731) as the first real novelist in the English language. Maybe so, but what attracted me toward him, as I sought historical precedent for my *Dutch* idea, was his originality in blending fact and fiction in a much more sophisticated way than that of his predecessors—so sophisticated that for a couple of centuries more he had no successors either.

Defoe embodied, in his person and output, the notion of a complete man of letters, being equally virtuosic in fiction (*Robinson Crusoe*), non-fiction (*The Complete English Tradesman*), poetry, political pamphleteering, interview journalism, religious polemics, history, satire, and horror stories. He wrote a three-volume guidebook to Britain and a twelve-volume attack on royal privilege (in verse), contributed to twenty-six different periodicals, and even ghosted another person's memoirs. He thought of himself primarily as a nonfiction writer, making no particular distinction between his six or seven novels and the rest of his gigantic oeuvre. Everything he wrote was intended to serve a moral or practical purpose, because Defoe was a deeply serious man. He was also, however, a literary genius, and therefore could not help writing entertainingly. Even when churning out such hackwork as *The Free-Holders Plea Against Stock-Jobbing Elections of Parliament Men* (1701), he saw and stated things with absolute clarity, but always with that slight refraction that seemed to magnify them and photograph them on the brain of the reader.

Any writer can describe a sunset or a mob scene with a fair degree of vividness. But as Virginia Woolf remarked, it takes Defoe's kind of literary skill to describe something as mundane as an earthenware pot, in such a way that for a page or two it becomes the most important thing in the world, and even when other things succeed on other pages, it and they lodge forever in the memory.

Prompted by Mrs. Woolf's reference to that earthenware pot, I went back to *Robinson Crusoe* for the first time in fifty years. I found the pot soon enough, and would have found it faster, were I not arrested, on every page I turned, by other objects, scenes, sensations, hopes, and fears of amazing primacy. I noticed again, as I had in childhood, how Defoe loves nouns, those basic building-blocks of the language, each one mooring the text with its mass, some light, some heavy, some rough, some smooth, few of them encumbered with adjectives, and all of them given an extra degree of emphasis by the charming eighteenth-century typographical style of an initial capital letter. The effect is rather like that of light slanting across a wall of bricks and picking out their leading edges, giving the whole surface a delightfully slabby texture.

I ply'd the Fire with fresh Fuel round the out-side, and upon the top, till I saw the Pots on the in-side red hot quite thro', and observ'd that they did not crack at all; when I saw them clear red, I let them stand in the Heat about five or six Hours, till I found one of them, tho' it did not crack, did melt or run, for the Sand which was mixed with the Clay melted by the Violence of the Heat, and would have run into Glass if I had gone on, so I slack'd my fire gradually till the Pots began to abate of the red Colour, and watching them all Night, that I might not let the Fire abate too fast, in the Morning I had three very good, I will not say handsome Pipkins, and two other Earthern Pots, as hard burnt as cou'd be desir'd; and one of them perfectly glaz'd with the Running of the Sand.

Robinson Crusoe came out in 1719, its full title being *The Life and Strange Surprizing Adventures of Robinson Crusoe, of York, Mariner.* The following editorial note, or "Preface," was printed before the main text and began: "The Editor believes [this] thing to be a just History of Fact; neither is there any Appearance of Fiction in it." Now, of course, the "editor" is the author, Daniel Defoe. But it pleases him to pretend—rather, "believe"—that the *real* author of "just History of Fact" is an eighty-seven-year-old retiree living in York (and maybe it's not a coincidence that the pretended author of *Dutch* is now an eighty-seven-year-old retiree living in *New* York).*

In other words, *Robinson Crusoe* was presented to the public as a memoir. All but the least informed of its readers knew that it was *not* that, but an imaginary story based on the true-life rescue of Alexander Selkirk, a Scottish castaway. Selkirk's own story had been famously published only seven years before in Woodes Rogers's *A Cruising Voyage Round the World,* so Defoe could not have been serious in claiming his own book to be true.

Or couldn't he? As I mentioned above, Defoe was always serious, even when writing fiction. He once declared, with a completely straight face, "I *am* Robinson Crusoe." He uses the word *serious* himself in that same preface, in which he repeatedly implies that *thinking* a thing to be true makes it true, at least for the purpose of "the Instruction of others."

---

* Or was, at the time this observation was first made in 2003.

Robinson Crusoe was such a success that within a few weeks—yes, *weeks*—Defoe published a sequel, entitled *The Further Adventures of Robinson Crusoe.* The following year, after diverting himself with a mere eight other books, he followed up with a third volume, entitled *Serious* [that word again] *Reflections During the Life and Surprizing Adventures of Robinson Crusoe: With His Vision of the Angelick World.* The angelic world was pretty far removed from the desert island whose sands ran to glass. Yet when *Serious Reflections* ends with Crusoe in outer space, crossing "the Verge of [the] Infinite" and breathing only ether, his step is still "firm," and his vision that of a rational human being, albeit one humbly capable of awe:

> Above and beyond, and on every side, you see innumerable Suns, and attending on them, Planets, Satellites, and inferior Lights proper to their respective Systems, and all these moving in their subordinate Circumstances, without the least Confusion, with glorious Light, and Splendour inconceivable.

I emphasize again that Defoe's novels were a minuscule fraction of his output: less than 1.5 percent. At least one of them, *Journal of the Plague Year* (1722), is commonly mistaken for nonfiction. He claimed to narrate it as an "actual" eyewitness, although the events he described with such vividness had occurred in 1685, when he was only five years old. Possibly, since he had been living in London at the time, some of the sights and sounds in his manuscript did register on him. At all events, the mature Defoe did an enormous amount of archival research to authenticate those atmospherics.

Before 1719 and after 1724, he almost exclusively wrote nonfiction. And yet—one finds oneself constantly hedging, when discussing this multidimensional man—if we look closely at some of these factual books, we find them to be as shot through with imagination as the novels are dense with data.

The word *imagination* does not necessarily imply *invention.* There are plenty of novelists who invent a lot, but patently have no imagination, just as there are few writers of any sort who can convey the essential strangeness of reality. Defoe was imaginative even within the sternest confines of nonfiction theory. Early in his career he wrote a satire of re-actionary High-Church attitudes toward Low-Churchmen and sarcasti-cally called it *The Shortest Way with the Dissenters.* Unfortunately his habit of transmuting himself into whatever, or whomever, he was writ-ing about made him a terrifyingly convincing reactionary. As a result, High Churchmen assumed the pamphlet had been written by one of themselves. Queen Anne sent Defoe to the pillory for sedition.*

It stands to reason that a satirist, like a parodist, should write with enough artificiality that no intelligent reader will mistake the spoof for the real thing. But Defoe was incapable of artifice: his genius as a writer impelled him to "be" a High Churchman for as long as he wrote his dia-tribe. This is why Bonnamy Dobrée, the ranking authority, praises his "glorious talent for magnificent lying [and] almost equal talent for su-preme honesty"—concluding with a professorial sigh, "with Defoe it is always impossible to disentangle fact from fiction." As a case in point, Dobrée cites a story by Defoe called "A True Relation of the Apparition of one Mrs. Veal, the Next Day After Her Death, to one Mrs. Bargrave at Canterbury, the 8th of September, 1705." Three and a half centuries after Chaucer, this strange piece amounted to a new Canterbury Tale, so fantastic that it was received in its time as fiction. It now appears to be both true and not true.

AT THIS POINT in my background reading, I had come to much the same conclusion about Ronald Reagan, who was capable of saying with absolute conviction that he had been (a) present in uniform at the libera-tion of the German concentration camps in April 1945 and (b) forced to watch color footage of those scenes as adjutant of the First Motion Pic-ture Unit in Culver City, California. It was not that he was subject to the memory slips of old age: those early stories of his, and the newspaper articles he wrote describing the filming of his first movie, *Love Is on the Air* (1937) made plain that he—like so many actors—saw no essential difference between imagination and reality, or emotions felt at home or

* Just before being wrist-locked, Defoe wrote and distributed a poem about the dignity of being punished for one's beliefs. It was so eloquent that passers-by, instead of pelting him with trash, swamped him in flowers.

on camera. (One of the articles mentioned how secure he felt behind "the wall of light" that ensconced him on the sound stage.)

I felt secure myself in having chosen to write about him from the point of view ("POV" in Hollywood script style) of audience to his perpetual performance. But *which*, if any, of the many Reagans he had played was the current President of the United States? Feeling as bewildered, probably, as Dobrée had when embarking on the study of Defoe, I made the worst mistake in my career and unburdened myself to a group of fellow scholars at the University of Virginia's Miller Center of Public Affairs. I confessed that for a year or two after beginning to interview Reagan in 1985, I had been mystified and depressed by his opaque personality.

The seminar was supposed to be a closed one, and I felt some relief in sounding off to a roomful of peers. But I was still so protective of the narrative solution I had found that I kept mum at least about *that*. It was just as well, because the Miller Center's press office did not honor its promise of confidentiality, and released a transcript of my remarks.

By good luck I heard about the resultant story ("President's Biographer Can't Understand Him") while it was still humming along the wires, and managed to telephone a *mea culpa* to Nancy Reagan before she read it in her morning newspaper. She sweetly accepted my explanation that periods of frustration, even despair, are normal in the early stages of that most presumptuous of tasks, the effort to write a man's life.

"Don't worry about it," she said. "We all have our problems with reporters."

As a result, my status as Authorized Biographer was unaffected. But headlines are headlines, and from that day to this the received wisdom is that *Dutch* was a desperate attempt to compensate for the fact that, after fourteen years of close study and personal acquaintance, I never figured him out.

DANIEL DEFOE DIED in 1731, the last great writer to apply equal powers of imagination to all types of literature. His immense output lies like a mountain range (still largely unexplored) between two discrete countries: the land of Post-Romance, where fiction and nonfiction tended to share each other's characteristics, and the land of the Pre-Modern, where the genres aspired to be as different as possible.

I see the Defoe Massif as one sees the Rockies when flying east from say, San Francisco. Below is the intermontane gap of the Middle Ages, sterile and sparsely populated. It begins to suffuse with green as the invention of printing spreads culture across the landscape. Then those five hundred linked peaks rise out of the seventeenth century, glowing with Enlightenment. They dominate the first thirty years of the eighteenth, before inclining toward the broad plain of modern literature. Down the slope a network of streams, commonly deriving from Lake Defoe, flow and carve their various valleys: reportage, commentary, polemics, and all the other tributaries of modern nonfiction. (To avoid metaphorical overload, I won't trace those of fiction.)

For two hundred more years the River Realism meanders along an increasingly Newtonian, fact-based, science-dependent, art-rejecting course. By the early twentieth century, it has become a sort of literary Grand Canyon, ravined internally with countless valleys, each one settled by this or that tribe—the biographers, the historians, the reporters, the travelers, the pundits, the propagandists, the Amazons of gender and the apologists of race, all of them following strict rules of conduct, and all worshipping an elusive deity named Truth. Then, in 1922, exactly two hundred years after Defoe published *Journal of the Plague Year,* E. E. Cummings published *The Enormous Room.*

That extraordinary war memoir, written by a man with parallel gifts as a poet and Cubist painter, is considered to be the first modern book to have reblended fact and fiction.* Again, one wonders about the word *first,* thinking for example of the final pages of Lytton Strachey's *Queen Victoria* (1921). Over the next few years a number of highly original nonfiction or indeterminate books appeared, including Thomas Beer's *Stephen Crane* (1923) and *The Mauve Decade* (1926), Bertrand Russell's *ABC of Relativity* (1925), Harold Nicolson's *Some People* (1927), André Breton's *Nadja* (1928), and another biography by Beer, *Hanna* (1929).

Beer's pointillistic, painterly style—words practically daubed onto

---

* It may be relevant that 1922 also marked the publication of James Joyce's *Ulysses,* which had an even greater effect on the course of modern fiction.

the page—had bewitched me when I was younger and writing my first book on Theodore Roosevelt. But on reading him and going through his papers at Yale, I found that he had to be treated with extreme caution. Too often he invented the facts of his subject's life, and even rewrote source material that did not suit him. Suspecting that one day I would be unfairly accused of doing the same, I transferred my respect to Russell, a philosopher and mathematician able by sheer mastery of prose to explain things on the edge of incomprehensibility.*

Nadja is a semiautobiographical novella by a poet, art critic, and guru of the Surrealist movement. Charmingly admitting, *en passant*, that his lifelong dream has been to walk through a wood at night and encounter a beautiful naked woman, Breton proceeds to challenge the whole notion of reality by breaking it into shards that reflect and refract strangely. (Emily Dickinson: "Tell all the truth, but tell it slant.") His text is illustrated with enigmatic photographs—buildings, portraits, manuscripts, *objets trouvés*, etc.—that unmistakably foreshadow the literal/visual style of W. G. Sebald.

The book that might have encouraged me most, while struggling to make literature out of Ronald Reagan, was *Some People.* But I remained unaware of that little masterpiece (a series of detailed reminiscences of people who never existed) until after *Dutch* was published in England. In a cautiously favorable discussion of my narrative technique on BBC *Newsnight*, the distinguished biographer Richard Holmes compared it to Nicolson's. He cited in particular "Arketall," a chapter wherein an imaginary butler observes the real Lausanne Conference of 1922–1923.† I rushed to read it, and found that Nicolson, a former diplomat, had attended that historic meeting. As a result, its dominant personalities, Lord Curzon and Benito Mussolini, loomed from the pages in authentic detail.

I boggled, not only at the device of a fictitious character in a nonfiction narrative, but at the uncanny parallels between Nicolson's account of *his* Swiss summit in 1923 and mine of the Reagan-Gorbachev summit at Geneva in 1985. Here again—more accurately, here long before

---

* As had Henry Pemberton a century before, in his book *A View of Sir Isaac Newton's Philosophy* (1728).
† Holmes misremembered the chapter slightly, saying that it described the Paris Peace Conference of 1919.

Dutch—were misty gray days beside a gray lake, the pageantry and protocol and laborious bureaucracy of treaty making, the jockeying of aides and the posturing of potentates (who off-scene seem so ordinary, but on-scene behave so impressively). Here, too, was the elder statesman confronting the new, young, formidable totalitarian dictator, and to general surprise, handling him effectively. Talk about reverse *déja vu!*

Two other obscure books featuring imaginary protagonists were drawn to my attention during the post-*Dutch* controversy. They had both been published in the 1940s by eminent scholars. One was the geographer Ralph H. Brown's *Mirror for Americans: Likeness of the Eastern Seaboard, 1810.* A key work of the social sciences, it uses a fictitious character named Thomas Pownall Keystone to "write" a documentary description of life in the United States under President Madison. There was also the astrophysicist George Garnow's *Mr. Tompkins in Paperback* (1965), a didactic *exemplum* "about" a man whose initials were "C.G.H."—ciphers respectively denoting the speed of light, gravity, and the quantum constant. As of now, *Mr. Tompkins* is fairly low in my bedside reading pile, but it's nice to know that the academy hasn't always been hostile to the idea of the "nonfiction novel."

That term was of course coined by Truman Capote to describe *In Cold Blood,* one of the biggest bestsellers of the 1960s despite the failure of its central pretense—that the author was not a character in the story, deeply, even romantically involved with his murderous antiheroes. I did study *In Cold Blood* before starting *Dutch,* because my scheme was to create an initially apathetic narrator who, almost in spite himself, got to admire Ronald Reagan over the years. At all costs I wanted to avoid Capote's folly, and lose my personal objectivity. Among my research cards I posted the favorite commandment of Theodore Roosevelt, *Thou shall not slop over.*

ONCE THE PROLOGUE was done, moving back and forth in time and preparing the reader for a strange book about a strange man, *Dutch*'s narrative structure became strictly chronological. It recounted the life of Ronald Reagan from his birth in Tampico, Illinois, on 6 February 1911 to his poignant acceptance of a diagnosis of dementia in Los Angeles on 5 November 1994. In parallel, and in only as much detail as seemed necessary, it also recounted the life of "E," specifically Arthur Edmund Morris, born in Chicago on 9 August 1912 and bearing little resemblance to myself. He was well born, half Jewish, mathematically inclined, and melancholic, all of which I am not—although I did give him a musical English mother, and a few years of schooling in Canterbury, to account for the immigrant POV I can't quite shed.

Except for the accident of their contemporaneous births about eighty miles apart, I didn't want E and Dutch (the name by which Reagan was universally known until he went to Hollywood in 1937) to have anything in common. E was to become aware of Dutch only by accident, and not pay any particular attention to him at first. But much as the American people did, he would be forced over the years to take bemused note of the fact that a middle-class, middlebrow youth from the flattest part of the Middle West was looming larger and larger as a popular and political phenomenon—not to say future President of the United States. If only for that reason, E would become increasingly fascinated by RR, and end up one day writing about him.

Conveniently, the Chicago meatpacking dynasty of Morris & Co. supplied E with the family background he needed. All I had to do was give the real brothers Edward and Ira Morris another sibling, Arthur (modeled on my own grandfather Arthur, a South African cattle auctioneer in the early twentieth century), and E became that Arthur Morris's son. In his tenth year, he was sent to board at St. Alban's School in Sycamore, Illinois, and began to hear snippets of gossip about one "Dutch Reagan," a football-mad student living in the nearby city of Dixon. The snippets— all taken from the biographical record—did not interest him, but his first actual glimpse of Dutch on 11 November 1926 stuck, for some reason, in his memory. Again, the observed details are authentic. Dixon High was playing Amboy:

> The shimmering window blind in my study replays an intricate
> choreography of running youths, heads and ears cramped inside
> leather helmets, shoulders hulking out of all proportion to their
> bodies. Dixon was the heavier team, so the rain favored them.
> They regularly carried the ball for first and ten, scoring at will
> throughout the second quarter. For whatever reason one picks

out a shape among shapes, I began to notice the movements of their right guard. Lighter than his fellows, he ran tirelessly and tackled with wild determination. One particular block of an Amboy fullback reminded me of the sound of carcasses thumping in Packingtown. The referee signaled halftime, and Dixon trooped past our bench to towel off. I kept my eyes on the guard as he strolled toward me. I saw—I registered, I calibrated—a square-cut youth of nearly sixteen, about five feet ten inches tall and 160 pounds in weight, not yet grown to proportion (his legs lacked heft, and his chest was shallow), but broad across the shoulders, and walking with extraordinary grace. There was none of the arms-out swagger that jocks affect, no sense either of hurry or hesitation, just flowing, forward momentum. His face irked me: it had an adolescent coarseness and an air of studied jollity, as if he was conscious of being watched. When he waved at a cheering fan and grinned, his upper lip pulled to the right. His eyes had a rubbed, overstrained look. I sensed that he was reacting to someone he heard, rather than saw.

"Who's this fellow?" I whispered.

Readers could either buy this *Doppelgängerisch* narrative structure or not. But if they *did* suspend their disbelief enough to read the first two chapters, which juxtaposed biographer and subject in exact mirror positions (each unit of information about E "reflecting" one about RR), I hoped that they might be drawn irresistibly into the story, much as the real author was drawn into it himself. Time would tell to what an extent this hope was naïve.

E is a substantial presence early in the story only because he has to be established as a believable narrator, and because the facts known about Ronald Reagan in this period are few. Dutch is never aware of E's scrutiny—at least, not until 1981. He steadily gains narrative weight, while E appears on the page less and less. Soon enough, E becomes a virtually invisible (yet always audible) member of Reagan's audience—which widens from a few hundred in the late Twenties to tens of thousands in the mid-Thirties, multiplying ultimately to hundreds of millions in the last quarter of the century. By then the biographer really is me, and *Dutch* ends almost conventionally, albeit with a surprise revelation on the last page.

Although it is a very long book (672 pages, plus 156 pages of notes) and sequential all the way through, its chapter forms continually change. Some are straight narrative, some mini-memoirs, others parodic (a mock chirological review of Dutch's college stories), epistolary, diary-like, political, analytical, and satiric. I wanted to show how many ways biography could be written, using all the techniques of creative literature (even screenplays and poetry) while never fabricating a single fact of its subject's life, never imputing a single thought that person may have had, unless he or she articulated it. One dreamlike chapter entitled "Inside Story" recounts the production of Reagan's first movie day by day, and has been much criticized for its stream-of-consciousness prose. But every eddy and bubble of that stream was recorded by Dutch himself, in a series of newspaper articles for publication in Des Moines.* Similarly, when I chose to write the story of 1947, Reagan's *annus horribilis*, in the form of four linked film scenarios, it was because he chose to remember (and write about it) that way himself, right down to a scene where the star of the movie lies delirious with pneumonia, and hallucinates a cast of *noir* characters around him:

Midnight—when? Probably June 25, but REAGAN's not counting. His fever has reached 104. The haze becomes hallucinatory. He sees a street lamp, a lonely stretch of sidewalk. There is a sense of danger in the surrounding darkness. Enter HUMPHREY BOGART in a trench coat. The two men converse in furtive, broken sentences. They sound as if they are trying out lines. Is REAGAN remembering the time he was cast to play in "Casablanca"? He mutters something. Camera goes into close-up on his lips: "Big Casino, bet or throw it."

His lips and face are dry. So is his wrapped body. He strains to sweat—the blessed sweat that ends fevers. Where is JANE? The darkness deepens.

Exhausted, he tells a NURSE that he does not have the strength

* "Dutch Reagan's Own Story," *Des Moines Register,* June 13, 20, 1937.

to go on breathing. Her silhouetted form leans over him, coaxing him to inhale. "Now let it out," she says. "Come on now, breathe in once more." Over and over she makes him obey. He does so out of instinctive courtesy. At last the sweat comes, and washes him back down the divide he's been climbing.

Cross-cut to the maternity ward at Queen of Angels Hospital, two and a half miles away. It is 11:26 AM on June 26, 1947. JANE WYMAN has just given premature birth to a baby girl. Another nightmare montage begins, as doctors try to save the baby's life. But at 8:45 PM it succumbs to cardiac arrest.

I dedicated the book to the memory of that baby, Christine Reagan. Since she lived and had a name and died unsung, I felt she was entitled to some sort of notice.*

Dutch relied heavily on images, since its subject was so much a creature of imagery, right from the days he drew that teenage self-portrait (which itself featured a strip of celluloid images uncurling from his desk). In addition to regular illustrations, every chapter featured an un-captioned, filmstrip-style *frame* that floated over the title. The significance of these frames became apparent only as you read the chapter—or, in some cases, only if you remembered a detail in an earlier chapter that may have seemed minor at the time. For example, chapter 31's frame of a white corpse lying cruciform on the dark ground of Bergen-Belsen—the image that so disturbed Reagan when he visited the camp in 1985—amounts to a positive-negative reverse of a dark *Pieta* described in chapter 3: the form of his own father spread-eagled on a snowbank in 1922.† Another *déjà vu* frame, heading chapter 9, is of a white, tall-columned house with a FOR SALE sign outside. It is a location set for *Love is on The Air* (1937). One can imagine Reagan's emotions when he reported there for shooting, since from boyhood on he had regularly dreamed of living in just such a house. The dream, indeed, continued to

---

* See p. 247.
† "He was drunk, dead to the world. I stood over him for a minute or two. . . . I felt myself fill with grief for my father. . . . Seeing his arms spread out as if he were crucified—as indeed he was—his hair soaked with melting snow . . . I could feel no resentment against him." Ronald Reagan, *Where's the Rest of Me?* (1965).

recur until he moved with a sense of homecoming into the most famous of white houses in January, 1981.

My use of these frames was inspired by the fragmentary images that perform a similar symbolic function at the start of Ingmar Bergman's movie *Persona.* I also thought—given the fact I was writing about a man to whom life was a motion picture—that it would be neat to have *Dutch* begin movie-style, with credits and dissolves instead of the copyright-title-and-half-title sequence typical of a nonfiction book. Bob Loomis's eyes widened perceptibly when I showed him the following storyboard:

RANDOM

HOUSE

presents

RONALD

REAGAN

in

DUTCH

A Memoir of Ronald Reagan

Written by
EDMUND MORRIS

Also Starring

Nancy

DAVIS

Jane

WYMAN

With

in order of appearance

Nelle Wilson Reagan—John E. ("Jack") Reagan—Rep. Richard Falkner—Margaret Cleaver Gordon—Sherwood Anderson—"Bus" Burke—Capt. Dennis Stanhope, M.C.—Grant Wood—Mikhail Gorbachev—Leslie Howard—Olivia de Havilland. . . .

At this point Loomis said, with his only known display of strong emotion since V-J Day, "Edmund—*enough.*"

ON THE DAY Random House published *Dutch*, September 30, 1999, a book entitled *Mirror Talk: Genres of Crisis in Contemporary Autobiography* came out in England. It was the work of Susanna Egan, a Canadian professor who has long been interested in what she calls the "necessarily fictive nature of writing." Even when the author is trying hard to be as nonfictive as possible, he has a rhetorical purpose in putting ink on paper. Else why write at all? His selection of "subject matter" can never (as the phrase itself implies) be objective, any more than he can disguise his personal style, whether studied or unstudied. These are, of course, the truisms of a thousand essays on the problems of nonfiction—autobiography in especial—but I was struck by one sentence, early in Dr. Egan's monograph: "Many [memoirists] forfeit historical depth for immediacy of experience *and personal doubling of vision for interpersonal exchanges.*"

She went on to say that by "interpersonal exchanges" she did not mean the complicit dialogue that springs up between the reader and author of any nonfiction book (*Q: Can I be sure that you are sure these things about Marilyn Monroe are true? A: You want them to be true, don't you? Q: Well—yes. A: That makes two of us!*). What interested her more, in modern or postmodern writing, was the implicit need of the author to collaborate "with some other party implicated in the life displayed—or possibly, concealed." That party might well be his "alternative self or selves."*

I'm not sure whether such collaboration is a good idea in autobiogra-

* See also James Olney, "Autobiography, Theory, Criticism, Instances," *Southern Review*, Spring 1986.

phy, which after all is supposed to be written by a single person, however self-deluding. But having just written a biography in the *form* of a memoir, I was encouraged to have a professor of literature unconsciously justify one of the most controversial techniques in *Dutch*—the use of alternative narrative voices.

When a man has a polarizing effect on public opinion, as Ronald Reagan did in later life, his "[auto]biographer" (to borrow James Olney's clumsy but useful construction) finds it increasingly difficult to maintain a pretense of impartiality. Even when beginning *Dutch*, I had decided that my main narrator's take on Reagan should be counterbalanced—sometimes directly challenged—by differing opinions. Hence the introduction, in chapter 4, of E's schoolfriend Paul Rae, an effeminate, gossipy boy who finds Reagan more interesting (and a lot more amusing) than E himself does at first. Later on, E begins to hear the real voices of such dyspeptic Reagan-watchers as the screenwriters Philip Dunne and Malvin Wald—both men I got to know well during my years of research in Los Angeles. They not only favored me with their memories of him, but ended up actually collaborating with me on various passages of the book. So did Sam Marx, MGM's longtime story editor, and Owen Crump, Reagan's wartime commanding officer at the First Motion Picture Unit. All dead now. Bless them for their help and good will.

Dunne in particular became a beloved friend, so much so that I had no difficulty in retroextending E's relationship with him fifty years, "back to the days when Phil and I went bodysurfing off Malibu together." He was recommended to me as an authority on Hollywood politics, and the absolute antithesis, as an old-style gentleman Democrat, of everything Ronald Reagan stood for. Our many dialogues in his hilltop house overlooking Malibu, and the copious correspondence we exchanged (Dunne taking the liberal, E the conservative point of view), furnished the kind of contrapuntal commentary Dr. Egan looks for in a [auto]biography. One marathon discussion on 19 December 1987, during which Phil, a skilled amateur astronomer, helps E take a mock reading of Reagan's political fortunes through his telescope, became a chapter of *Dutch* entitled "Star Power." I wrote it as a pastiche of de Fontenelle.

Invaluable as the voices of movie people (and Reagan too, of course) were in helping me tell the story of his years at Warner Bros. and the Screen Actors Guild, I felt the need of a younger, angrier commentator when my narrative reached the 1960s. By then, Reagan had switched to the Republican Party and emerged as a spokesman for corporate conservative values. For that reason, I sent E's son Gavin to the University of California at Berkeley, where he became a student radical and follower of the various teachings of Frantz Fanon, Tom Hayden, and Mario Savio.* His letters to E reporting on Reagan's rise to the governorship of California are full of a moral loathing that I, as a biographer, did not share. But they accurately reflect the passions of the Age of Aquarius, which I absorbed in "alternative" periodicals such as the *Berkeley Barb,* and in the shabby, delightfully conspiratorial archives of the Southern California Library of Social Studies. Twenty years after the People's Park riots of May, 1969 (when Reagan sent a lethal force of state police in to reestablish order on the Berkeley campus), these records had acquired a quaint charm. I thought the governor was right to do what he did, even though a boy named James Rector died in the disturbances. Part of me nevertheless shared, willy-nilly, the black anger that drove Gavin underground. When, seven years further on, I heard that Mario Savio had died, I was astonished to find myself grieving for him.

If a biography is honestly to embrace just some of the multiple POVs from which a human story can be told—every angle revelatory in its way—the biographer must acknowledge the paradoxes of his own literary emotions.

Having written all this, I must compromise my own case by declaring that the best biography is that in which the subject speaks loud and shows clear, while the author remains deferential, even mute. It is only when the subject is elusive (like Reagan, or Frederick Rolfe)† that compensatory literary devices are called for. Theodore Roosevelt was so self-revelatory that in the course of thirty-five years of writing about him, I managed to eliminate authorial intrusions almost entirely.

* Gavin was modeled to a large extent on the South African radical Mike Kirkwood (see pp. 78–81).
† A. J. A. Symons's classic *The Quest for Corvo: An Experiment in Biography* (1934) was reissued in 2001 by New York Review Books.

Beethoven, being a communicator of something almost inexpressible in words, mandated a prose style that least tried to describe how his music ravishes the ear. But it wasn't necessary for me to cite *my* ear, among millions of others equally or more receptive.

Because *Dutch*'s critical reception in 1999 was so preponderately negative, I don't suggest that any of the nonfiction authors I am about to name took the slightest notice of it. (One, Lauren Slater, touchingly inscribed a copy of her "metaphorical memoir" *Lying* to me in 2000, saying that my experimental "innovations and bravery" had inspired her, but since we went to press within a few months of each other, she can't have seen my text while writing hers.)

For the record, though, I might note that after *Dutch* was published, a number of equally unconventional nonfiction books appeared on both sides of the Atlantic. *Wainewright the Poisoner* (2000) purported to be the autobiography of a notorious Regency painter and swindler. In fact it was a sober and scholarly biography by Andrew Motion, the poet laureate of Great Britain—who not only fessed up as author, but added stern chapter notes correcting some of the things his *alter ego* had "written" in the main text. Lauren Slater's hauntingly lyrical, first-person account of "her" youth as an epileptic was so documentary in style that no reader could question its authenticity. However, neither she (a practicing neurologist) nor Random House would state straight out whether *Lying* was fiction or nonfiction—the implication being that it was both. (Or neither.) Ned Rorem, not to be outdone, published *Lies: A Diary, 1986–1999* that same year. Although it seemed to be the most truthful of all his famously frank *apologia* (chronicling the death of a beloved friend from AIDS), Rorem himself has warned: "The hero of my diaries is a fictional man."

João Magueijo's *Faster than the Speed of Light* (2002), caused an international sensation by using a casual, pub-chat style to challenge the logic of Einstein's theory of relativity. His first-person "story of a speculation" began, like *Dutch*, with an epiphany ("It was a miserable rainy morning. . . . I was walking across the college's sports field . . . when I suddenly realized that if you were to break one simple rule of the game, albeit a sacred one, you could solve these problems"). Magueijo, a youthful reader in theoretical physics at St. John's College, London, proceeded to argue that the velocity of light, far from being invariable, was once much faster than it is now, and did so brilliantly, having Bertrand Russell's ability to explain cosmological phenomena by means of earthly parables. But he did not exactly endear himself to colleagues who disagreed with him by calling them "morons" and "parasites" motivated by "envy of the penis."

The year 2003 was a banner one for works of "scientific" (as opposed to science) fiction. In rapid succession there appeared John L. Casti's *The One True Platonic Heaven*, a novel about quantum mechanics, Christos H. Papadimitriou's *Turing (A Novel about Computation)*, and Dan Edward Lloyd's *Radiant Cool*, a metafictional whodunit using *noir* narrative techniques to advance a new theory of distinction between the brain and the mind.* Among its imagined, or half-imagined characters was a postgraduate cutie named Miranda Sharpe, and "Dan Lloyd," a professor of neurophilosophy who might or might not have been the author. Although the real Dan Lloyd insists the book was a novel ("The plot is a metaphor for shifts in consciousness"), it was praised by his academic peers, and published under the august imprint of MIT Press.

Saucy aspirants for PhDs were emboldened by these imaginative forays to present their own papers in unorthodox form. Four years later, for example, Timothy M. Mennel successfully defended a dissertation in urban geography at the University of Minnesota, even though it was entitled "Everything Must Go: A Novel of Robert Moses's New York."

(In the spirit of full disclosure, I guess I should add that before embarking on his 1,102-page study (with 1,456 citations), Mr. Mennel had been the copy editor of *Dutch*.)†

J. M. Coetzee's career-long refusal to acknowledge any difference between fact and fiction did not prevent him getting the Nobel Prize in Literature in 2003. (In his acceptance speech, Coetzee, a disciple of Defoe, bizarrely took on the double personae of Robinson Crusoe and Man

---

* See also Emily Eakin, "Art and Science Meet with Novel Results," *The New York Times*, 18 October 2003.
† The school awarding Mr. Mennel his degree also happened to be the last teaching post of Ralph H. Brown, author of *Mirror for Americans* (see. p. 463).

Friday.)* That was at least a change from his earlier practice of referring to himself by name yet in the third person, both in novels and two volumes of truth-bending "autrebiography." Six years later, he issued a third memoir, *Summertime*, with a refractive index so high it had the bizarre effect of making his novels look more reliably confessional. He now chose to represent himself as dead—a conceit that permitted his fictional biographer, Mr. Vincent, to research the "life" of one John Coetzee, and in the process get many things wrong. Four other imaginary commentators, all female, weigh in with anecdotes and opinions of the not-so-dear departed. *Summertime's* British publisher allowed the book to go out as gospel, but in North America it was prudently subtitled *Fiction*.[†]

Coetzee nevertheless preserved *Summertime* more or less intact in a combined version of all three volumes of his memoir, issued in 2011 under the general title *Scenes from Provincial Life*. "Reading the trilogy is a depressing experience, and not only because the Coetzee character is so unpleasant and self-obsessed," Alex Preston wrote in *The New Statesman*. "By collecting the books this way, by making a public fuss of them, Coetzee is reinforcing their importance. These miserable memoirs are mere shadows of his greatest work, and remind us only of the dreary later 'novels.' "

It's every memoirist's privilege, of course, to lie about the past, and given the inventiveness of human memory—that most unreliable form of nonfiction—all of them do one way or another. As Coetzee himself has remarked, "What we call the truth is only a shifting reappraisal. . . . There is no ultimate truth about oneself." Lindley Hubbell (alias Shuseki Hayashi) would agree:

I am not a person.
I am a succession of persons
Held together by memory.

When the string breaks,
The beads scatter.[‡]

---

* Coetzee's fourth novel *Foe* (1986) is a pastiche of *Robinson Crusoe*, with its female narrator borrowed from another Defoe novel, *Roxana* (1724).
† Unlike the first two volumes, which had been registered as nonfiction.
‡ Lindley Williams Hubbell, "Waka," in *Anthology* 79 (Ikuta Press, Kobe, Japan).

Modern writers as various as Bruce Chatwin, Vladimir Nabokov, Philip Roth, Peter Ackroyd, V. S. Naipaul, and Alice Munro have used the first-person form in ways that make the word *I* about the vaguest pronoun in the language. All but Roth (who called his 1988 "novelist's autobiography" *The Facts*) have done so in books reviewed, and registered at the Library of Congress, as nonfiction.

Roth in "fact" has exploited the ambiguity of truth-telling on both sides of the Defoe Divide more eloquently and much more wittily than Coetzee. Why the lugubrious latter got the Nobel Prize rather than he is a mystery explained, I suppose, only by Scandinavia's historic repugnance for humor.

I happen to frequent the same rural supermarket as Mr. Roth, and have several times narrowly escaped death under the wheels of his energetic shopping cart. One day, perhaps, I will be so bold as to introduce myself to him, in the hope that he will take my hand and say, "Nathan Zuckerman. Pleased to meet you, Mr. Pogorelich."

ACKNOWLEDGMENTS
AND PERMISSIONS

THE AUTHOR THANKS Ian Keown and Robert Stock for helping him start his freelance career. He expresses particular gratitude to Sylvia Jukes Morris for putting her own work aside to help him further, on countless occasions over the last forty years.

———

Grateful acknowledgment is made to the following for permission to reprint previously published material:

THE HISPANIC SOCIETY, NEW YORK: Excerpt from Canto V from *The Lusiads* by Camoes, translated by Leonard Bacon. Reprinted with the permission of The Hispanic Society, New York,

HENRY HOLT AND COMPANY, LLC: Excerpt from "After Apple-Picking" from *The Poetry of Robert Frost* by Robert Frost, edited by Edward Connery Lathem, copyright 1916, © 1969 by Henry Holt and Co., Inc., and renewed 1942 by Robert Frost. Copyright © 1967 by Leslie Frost Ballantine. Reprinted by permission of Henry Holt and Company, LLC.

DUTTON CHILDREN'S BOOKS, A DIVISION OF PENGUIN YOUNG READERS GROUP, A MEMBER OF PENGUIN GROUP (USA) INC: Excerpt from "Vespers" from *When We Were Very Young* by A. A. Milne, illustrated by E. H. Shepard, copyright © 1924 by E. P. Dutton and copyright renewed 1952 by A. A.

Milne; one illustration from *When We Were Very Young* by A. A. Milne, illustration by E. H. Shepard, copyright © 1926 by E. P. Dutton and copyright renewed 1954 by A. A. Milne. Reprinted with the permission of Dutton Children's Books, A Division of Penguin Young Readers Group, A Member of Penguin Group (USA) Inc., 345 Hudson Street, New York, NY 10014. All rights reserved.

NEW DIRECTIONS PUBLISHING CORP.: Excerpt from "The Heavy Bear Who Goes With Me" from *Selected Poems* by Delmore Schwartz, copyright © 1959 by Delmore Schwartz. Reprinted by permission of New Directions Publishing Corp.

ILLUSTRATION CREDITS

229   Drawing by Tom Gibson, 2012.
237   Photograph of the Supreme Court by Fritz Jantzen. Collection of the Supreme Court of the United States.
243   Drawing by Enid Romanek, 1987.
247   Photograph of sonogram by Hayri Er.
251   Second page of Ronald Reagan's farewell letter, 5 November 1994. Courtesy of the Ronald Reagan Presidential Library.
259   Photograph of Thingvellir, Iceland, by Macduff Everton. © Macduff Everton, www.macduffeverton.com.
274   Adams Memorial in Washington, D.C., by Augustus Saint-Gaudens, 1891. Photograph by Josh Howell.
284   Drawing of Pooh and friend by Ernest Shepherd, 1926. From *Winnie-the-Pooh* by A. A. Milne, illustrated by E. M. Shepard, copyright 1926 by E. P. Dutton, renewed 1954 by A. A. Milne. Used by permission of Dutton Children's Books, a division of Penguin Group (USA) Inc.
287   *The Butterfly Tree.* Art from Dryicons.com. http://dryicons.com.
296   Photograph by Barbara M. Bachman, 2012.
300   Dome of the Jefferson Building. Library of Congress photograph.
307   Photograph of Cozzens by Jo H. Chamberlin, 1944. From James Gould Cozzens, *A Time of War: Air Force Diaries and Pentagon Memos, 1943–1945*, Matthew J. Bruccoli, ed., (Columbia, S. C., 1984).
317   Former Transportation Secretary Elizabeth Dole and friend at Reagan National Airport, November 2011. Photograph © United Press International.
326   Photograph by Louise Docker.
333   Photograph by Fernando G. Revilla.
337   Dutch Reagan's former lifeguard post on the Rock River, Dixon, Ill. Painting by Fran Swarbrick.
355   Photograph of Sylvia Jukes Morris, 1997. Author's collection, photographer unknown.
365   Contrapuntal graph of a section of Bach's *Musical Offering* by the American Mathematics Society.
370   Autograph copy of piano version of Beethoven's *Grosse Fuge*, Op. 134. Photograph from Sotheby's catalogue, December 2005.
374   Photograph courtesy of Steinway & Sons.
378   Photograph courtesy of the Kent School.
387   Score of the slow movement of Beethoven's String Quartet, Op. 132. Dover Publications, 1970.
399   Life mask of Beethoven in 1812 by Franz Klein. The Beethovenhaus, Bonn.
403ff. Musical examples by Antony Beaumont.
413   Photograph by Pete Souza of a Kenyan student listening to Senator Obama speak in 2006.
417   Photograph of Theodore Roosevelt rendered by Barbara M. Bachman.
422   White House photograph by Pete Souza.
429   Photograph of Mark Twain writing in bed, ca. 1907. Library of Congress.
435   Photograph of Thomas Edison napping in his laboratory, ca. 1911. Smithsonian Institution.
442   White House photograph of President Reagan and his biographer, 1988.

INDEX

*See group listings under "Airplanes," "Biographers," "Humorists," "Pianos," "Pianists,"
as well as individual entries*
Theodore Roosevelt and Ronald Reagan are often abbreviated as "TR" and "RR"

Warner, Jack, 344

Wars: War of 1812, 100, 300; American Civil War, 40, 47, 66, 111, 122, 186; Spanish-American War, 42, 110, 119; Russo-Japanese War, 49, 385; World War I, 10, 97, 141, 227, 282, 385; World War II, 137, 221, 310, 311, 314, 329, 347, 350, 386, 447, 451; Korean War, 323; Vietnam War, 168, 245, 273; Iraq War, 386

Washington, Booker T., dinner with TR, 47–48

Washington, George, 318; Adams on, 275

Washington, Martha, 318

Watergate, 148, 239

Waugh, Evelyn, xvii, 224, 329; as writer, 66–67, 169–71, 173, 174, 289, 309, 310, 335; life and personality of, 169–74, 310; Martin Stannard biography of reviewed, 170–74; other biographies of, 170; humor of, 170, 220–21, 228; religious faith of, 173, 174, 311, 329; works of—*Rossetti: His Life and Works*, 171; *Edmund Campion*, 153–54, 171; *Ninety-two Days*, 173; *Decline and Fall*, 170, 171; *A Handful of Dust*, 170, 171, 173, 174; "The Balance," 171; "Out of Depth," 170; "The Man Who Loved Dickens," 170; *Vile Bodies*, 171, rain in, 173, 391; *Black Mischief*, 171; *Scoop*, 171; *Work Suspended*, 171; *Brideshead Revisited*, 174, 289; *A Little Learning*, 171, 379; *The Ordeal of Gilbert Pinfold*, 173; *Sword of Honor*, 310; quoted, 66–67, 172, 173, 174, 228, 379

Waugh, Hon. Evelyn Gardner ("She-Evelyn"), 172

Weber, Carl Maria von, 73, 397

Webern, Anton, 198; String Quartet, manuscript of, 304, 370; *Piano Variations*, geometry of, 397–98

Weidman, Charles, as dancer-choreographer, 26–27

Weinberger, Caspar "Cap," 163, 260, 352

Weill, Kurt, 198

Wells, H. G., 330; humor of, 221; visit to USA, 1906, 380–86; meeting with TR, 34–35, 380, 384–85; works of—*The War of the Worlds*, 330; *The Time Machine*, 379, 380; *The Future in America: A Search After Realities*, 380; quoted, 381, 382, 384, 385

Wenders, Wim, 365

Wenlock Edge, 274–75, 277; epiphanies at, 274

Wharton, Edith, 36

Wheatley, Dennis, 327

Whistler, James McNeil, 394

White House, 341, 468; described, 414; Roosevelt Room, 271

White Queen (Carroll), 82

White, Byron, reads Declaration of Independence, 149

White, William Allen, quoted, 35

Wiesel, Elie, reproves RR over Bitburg, 447

Wilde, Oscar, 103; on ignorance, 219

Wilhelm II, Kaiser, 48

Wilson, Edmund, on Holmes, 181

Wilson, Woodrow, 423; as writer, 423

Wister, Owen, 104; quoted, 34; *The Virginian*, 104; *Theodore Roosevelt: The Story of a Friendship*, 316

Wodehouse, P. G., xix, 170, 224; as writer/humorist, 169, 220, 228, 335; quoted, 78

Wolcott, Marion Post, 305

Wolfe, Tom, 228, 336; quoted, 445

Wolff, Konrad, on Beethoven, 406–7

Wolfram von Eschenbach, *Parzival*, 305

Wolseley, Lord, TR on, 111

Woodrow Wilson International Center for Scholars, xix–xx, 162–63

Woolf, Virginia, 52, 359; as biographer, 154–55; *Orlando*, 154–55, 158; on Defoe; suicide, 158; quoted, 155

Woolfson's Menswear Store, 90–91

Wright, Fatty, 5–6

Wright, Richard, *Native Son*, 291

Writing, freelance, xvii–xx; handwriting, xix, 65–67, 109, 252–58, 297–98, 304, 370–73; style, literary, 335, 436; style, contemporary—162–63, 333–36, 373; alliteration, 167–168, 245; anticapitalization, 162–65; effect of computer on, xix, 252, 254, 304, 372; hyphenation, 164–66; documentation, 166–67; punctuation, 333–36; narrative, 373; typewriting, xix, 64–67, 114; stylebooks—*The Chicago Manual of Style*, 162–63, 164, 336; *The Government Printing Office Style Manual*, 164, 166; *Handbook for Writers of Research Papers* (MLA), 166–67; *Harvard Guide to American History*, quoted, 167

ABOUT THE AUTHOR

EDMUND MORRIS was born in Nairobi of
South African parents. He received a British
colonial education in Kenya, then studied
music, art, and English literature at Rhodes
University in South Africa. In 1962 he took a
job writing retail copy for a menswear store in
Durban. Two years later, he moved to Britain and became a copywriter at an advertising agency in London. After marrying an English schoolteacher, Sylvia
Jukes, he immigrated with her to the United States in 1968. Both became freelance
writers. In 1980, Morris's first book, *The Rise of Theodore Roosevelt*, won the Pulitzer Prize and National Book Award for biography. He set aside work on a sequel,
Theodore Rex, in order to become President Ronald Reagan's authorized biogra-
pher. The resultant study, *Dutch: A Memoir of Ronald Reagan*, became a controversial bestseller in 1999. *Theodore Rex* followed in 2001, and won the *Los Angeles
Times* Book Prize for Biography. Four years later, Morris published *Beethoven: The
Universal Composer*. In 2010 he completed his trilogy on the life of the twenty-sixth
President with *Colonel Roosevelt*.

Edmund Morris is available for select readings and lectures. To inquire about
a possible appearance, please contact the Random House Speakers Bureau at
212-572-2013 or rhspeakers@randomhouse.com.

ABOUT THE TYPE

This book was set in Photina, a typeface designed by José Mendoza in 1971. It is a very elegant design with high legibility, and its close character fit has made it a popular choice for use in quality magazines and art gallery publications.